D1594427

OSCAR WILDE

Art and Egotism

Rodney Shewan

First published 1977 by
THE MACMILLAN PRESS LTD
London and Basingstoke
Associated companies in New York
Dublin Melbourne Johannesburg and Madras

ISBN 0 333 18038 0

Printed in Great Britain by
BILLING AND SONS LTD
Guildford, Worcester and London

To
D. S. and S. S.
and to
A. S. H.

Contents

List of Plates

Acknowledgements

Plate 1 appears by courtesy of © William Andrews Clark Memorial Library, University of California, Los Angeles; Plates 2, 3, 14 by courtesy of *Punch*; Plate 4 by permission of the British Library Board; Plate 5 by permission of the Philadelphia Museum of Art: the W. P. Wilstach Collection; Plate 8 by permission of the Tate Gallery; Plate 9 by courtesy of Le Cabinet des Dessins, Musée du Louvre; Plate 10 by courtesy of the artist's executors, Sir John Rothenstein and Mr Michael Rothenstein; Plate 12 by courtesy of Princeton University Library; Plate 15 by permission of the Radio Times Hulton Picture Library.

Preface

I began the work which led to this book under the supervision of the late Mr John Bryson, Fellow Emeritus of Balliol College, with the guidance of Mr Michael Gearin-Tosh, Fellow of St Catherine's College, Oxford, to both of whom I am indebted. Miss Elizabeth Sweeting, then Administrator of the Oxford Playhouse, was also a great source of encouragement, and I am grateful to Mr. H. Montgomery Hyde for his friendly assistance. As it is now several years since Professors Peter Stansky and Bliss Carnochan read an early draft of one chapter, they may well have forgotten that extra-curricular chore. I have not forgotten their kindness in undertaking it, and I trust that the section in question is now unrecognisable. More recently, Dr Ian Fletcher placed at my disposal both his wide knowledge of the period and the proofs of the new Wilde bibliography by himself and John Stokes. If the book fails to reflect these good offices, the fault is mine. In addition to those Wilde scholars whose work I mention in the text, I owe a particular debt to the published work of Professors M. H. Abrams and Carolyn Heilbrun.

I am grateful to Mrs Mary Hyde for opening her unique collection to me at a very busy time, also for various other kindnesses, including permission to quote from MSS in her possession. I wish to thank the staffs of the British Library; the Bodleian Library; the English Faculty Library, Oxford; the Pierpont Morgan Library, New York; the New York Public Library; the Princeton University Library; the Beinecke Rare Book Library, Yale University; the Humanities Research Centre, University of Texas at Austin; and the Stanford University Libraries. Especial thanks are due to the Librarian and staff of the William Andrews Clark Memorial Library, University of California at Los Angeles, for their willing co-operation at all times, their unfailing efficiency and courtesy.

Mr Merlin Holland allowed me generous quotation from his grandfather's unpublished MSS. Extracts from Wilde's letters are repro-duced by permission of Mr Holland and Sir Rupert Hart-Davis.

Much of my research was carried out in the United States, and this would have been impossible without the generous help and unstinting hospitality of many friends and colleagues. I should like to thank especially Professor Virgil K. Whitaker, Professor and Mrs Charles N. Fifer, Mr Howard Tarter, Ms Linda Lohn, Mr James I. Warren, Mr Craig F. Thompson, Ms Constance Anne Howell, and Mr S. Corbin Smith. I must also thank Stanford University for a study leave, and Mrs Monica Bowen and Mrs Bryony Welsh for their fortitude in typing successive versions of the text.

My most longstanding debts are expressed by the Dedication: to my mother and father, without whose remarkable patience the project would never have left the ground; and to the late Allen Sainsbury Hicks, teacher and friend, but for whose constant impatience, fed by a love for other and greater authors, it might never have come down again. It is a grief to me that he did not live to see the book complete.

A Note on the Title

Wilde used 'egoism' and 'egotism' without clear distinction. The latter occurs more often, however, and this preference reflects a recognised, if not invariable, contemporary usage. An anonymous reviewer of Meredith's *The Egoist* (*Saturday Review*, 15 November 1879) regarded the two words as wholly interchangeable, 'egoist' being merely 'current slang'. The O. E. D. defines the non-technical meaning of 'egoism' as 'the habit of looking upon all questions chiefly in relation to oneself'. This is clearly the sense in which Wilde commonly used 'egotism'. However, the opening of "The Decay of Lying" shows him using 'egotism' in the O. E. D. sense of that word—'the too frequent use of the word *I*; hence, the practice of talking about oneself and one's doings'—while in other contexts Wilde's sense lies between the two definitions or comprehends both. In June 1897, for example, writing to Douglas about Gide's *Les Nourritures Terrestres*, Wilde essentially summed up his own literary career (already concluded) in terms which touch a literary as well as an autobiographical truth: 'The egoistic note is, of course, and always has been to me, the primal and ultimate note in modern art, *but to be an Egoist one must have an Ego*. It is not everyone who says "I, I" who can enter the Kingdom of Art.' The irony of Wilde's reputation lies here: few would consider that he succeeded in balancing self-absorption by self-awareness. In attempting to argue the contrary, I have chosen the form 'egotism' for the title (and, generally in the commentary) in spite of modern connotations, following Wilde's preference.

A Note on References

As yet, there is no authoritative edition of Wilde's literary works. I have therefore arranged references with a view to maximum convenience for most readers. The collected editions of 1908 and 1909 are not widely available and lack certain important items. I have used *The Works of Oscar Wilde* (Collins, London, 1970) which, for all its typographical and other errors, assembles practically everything necessary in a single volume that seems likely to remain in print. Wilde's major critical works and his novel are available in critical editions (listed in the Bibliography), but here, as elsewhere, I have cited *Works*. In the case of the comedies, I have given title, page and Act to facilitate cross-reference.

R. S.

Cliveden House
Buckinghamshire

Chronological Table

This table provides an outline of Wilde's literary career, together with the most important biographical details so far as they are known. I have drawn on Sir Rupert Hart-Davis' indispensable edition of *The Letters of Oscar Wilde*, also on the handy but not entirely reliable Table in *The Works of Oscar Wilde* (Collins, 1970, with an Introduction by Vyvyan Holland). All the datings used in my study are included below, whether established or conjectural. I have not considered it necessary to give comprehensive listings of the first publication of all of Wilde's poems: these, together with the fullest detail on a variety of related matters, can be found in Stuart Mason's *A Bibliography of Oscar Wilde*.

1854	16 October	Oscar Wilde born at 21 Westland Row, Dublin
1855		Family moves to 1 Merrion Square North, Dublin
1864		*Poems by Speranza, Lady Wilde* published, Dublin and London
1864–71		Attends Portora Royal School, Enniskillen
1871–4		Attends Trinity College, Dublin, where he wins the Berkeley Gold Medal for Greek
1873		Pater's *Studies in the History of the Renaissance* published
1874	October	Goes up to Magdalen College, Oxford, as Demy
1875	June	Travels in Italy with J. P. Mahaffy, his Trinity College tutor
1876	19 April	Wilde's father, Sir William, dies
	5 July	First Class in Classical Moderations
		Poems published in the *Dublin University Magazine* and the *Month and Catholic Review*
1877	March–April	All set for a pilgrimage to Rome, contemplating conversion to Catholicism, when he goes instead to Greece with Mahaffy, returning via Rome and Ravenna
	July	Review article, "The Grosvenor Gallery", published in the *Dublin University Magazine*
		Poems published in the *Irish Monthly*, the *Illustrated Monitor* and *Kottabos*

1878	10 June	Wins the Newdigate Prize for English poetry with *Ravenna*
	19 July	First Class in Greats (Literae Humaniores)
	25 November	Ruskin–Whistler trial
	28 November	Takes B.A. degree
		Poems published in the *Irish Monthly*
1879		"The Rise of Historical Criticism" entered, unsuccessfully, for the Chancellor's English Essay Prize at Oxford
		Magdalen Demyship extended for a fifth year
	Autumn	Takes rooms with Frank Miles, an artist, at 13 Salisbury Street, London
		Poems published in *Time, The World, Waifs and Strays, Kottabos*
1880	August	Moves with Frank Miles to Keats House, Tite Street, Chelsea, thereby becoming a neighbour of Whistler
		Poems published in *The World, Waifs and Strays*
1881	?30 June	*Poems* published
		Poems in *Pan, The World*
	24 December	Embarks for American lecture tour, which continued throughout 1882 in U.S.A. and Canada
1882	9 January	"The English Renaissance of Art" delivered at the Chickering Hall, New York
	Summer	Rennell Rodd's volume of verse, *Rose Leaf and Apple Leaf*, designed by Wilde and with his Prefatory essay, "L'Envoi", published in Philadelphia
1883	Spring	At the Hôtel Voltaire, Paris. Works on *The Sphinx*, and, possibly, on *The Cardinal of Avignon, alias Beatrice and Astone Manfredi* (see note 55, p. 132). Mary Anderson rejects *The Duchess of Padua*
	?July	Moves into rooms at 9 Charles Street, Grosvenor Square, London
	August	*The Duchess of Padua* published
	August–September	Briefly visits U.S.A. to see *Vera* produced, unsuccessfully, by Marie Prescott
	24 September	Begins British lecture tour, which continues sporadically for a year
	26 November	Engaged to Constance Lloyd
1884	29 May	Married to Constance Lloyd. Honeymoons in Paris and Dieppe
	July	Lady Archibald Campbell's pastoral production

		of the woodland scenes in *As You Like It* at Coombe House, Richmond-upon-Thames, under the artistic direction of E. W. Godwin
1885	1 January	Moves into 16 Tite Street. Godwin (architect of Whistler's The White House) had been superintending its refurbishment since the preceding summer
	14 March	"Shakespeare on Scenery" published (*Dramatic Review*)
	April	"The Harlot's House" published (*Dramatic Review*)
	May	"Shakespeare and Stage Costume" published (*Nineteenth Century*; republished in 1891 as "The Truth of Masks")
	Early June	*As You Like It* revived
	5 June	Cyril Wilde born
	6 June	"As You Like It at Coombe House" published (*Dramatic Review*)
1886		Meets Robert Ross
	?Autumn	Writes essay (lecture) on Chatterton
	24 November	Lectures on Chatterton at Birkbeck College, London
1887		Accepts editorship of the *Woman's World*
	3 February and 2 March	"The Canterville Ghost" published (*Court and Society Review*)
	11, 18, 25 May	"Lord Arthur Savile's Crime" published (*Court and Society Review*)
	25 May	"Lady Alroy" published (*The World*)
	22 June	"The Model Millionaire" published (*The World*)
		Poems published (Christmas Number of the *Lady's Journal*)
1888	May	*The Happy Prince and Other Tales* published, illustrated by Walter Crane.
		"The Young King" published (Christmas Number of the *Lady's Pictorial*)
1889	January	"Pen, Pencil and Poison" published (*Fortnightly Review*), and "The Decay of Lying" (*Nineteenth Century*)
	February	"Symphony in Yellow" published (*Centennial Magazine*)
	March	"The Birthday of the Infanta" published (*Paris Illustré*)
	July	"The Portrait of Mr W. H." published (*Blackwood's Edinburgh Magazine*). Gives up

		editorship of the *Woman's World*. "In the Forest" published (Christmas Number of the *Lady's Pictorial*)
1890	20 June	"The Picture of Dorian Gray" published (*Lippincott's Monthly*)
	November	Revival of Boucicault's comedy *London Assurance*, which is still running in February of the following year
	July, September	"The True Function and Value of Criticism" published (*Nineteenth Century*)
	?November – December	Writing "The Fisherman and his Soul"
1891	? January	Meets Lord Alfred Douglas
	January	*The Duchess of Padua* produced, at first anonymously, in New York, under the title *Guido Ferranti*
	February	"The Soul of Man under Socialism" published (*Fortnightly*); busy with early draft of *Lady Windermere's Fan*
	March	Preface to *The Picture of Dorian Gray* published (*Fortnightly*)
	April	*The Picture of Dorian Gray*, enlarged and revised, published in book form
	2 May	*Intentions* published, containing "Pen, Pencil and Poison", "The Decay of Lying" (revised), "The Critic as Artist" (revised, formerly "The True Function and Value of Criticism"), and "The Truth of Masks" (minimally revised, formerly "Shakespeare and Stage Costume")
	July	*Lord Arthur Savile's Crime and Other Stories* published, containing the four stories which appeared in 1887 ("Lady Alroy" being retitled "The Sphinx without a Secret")
	November	*A House of Pomegranates* published, designed by Ricketts and Shannon and containing "The Young King", "The Birthday of the Infanta", "The Fisherman and his Soul", and "The Star Child", the two latter previously unpublished
	November– December	Writes *Salomé* in Paris
1892	20 February	*Lady Windermere's Fan* produced at the St James's Theatre
	26 May	Limited edition of *Poems* published
	June	*Salomé*, in rehearsal at the Palace Theatre for

Sarah Bernhardt's London season, refused a licence by the Lord Chamberlain on the grounds that it contains Biblical characters

August– September — Writes *A Woman of No Importance* in Norfolk

November — Rents Babbacombe Cliff, near Torquay, from Lady Mount-Temple, a cousin of his wife. Retains it until following 1 March. (Douglas visits in February)

1893 February — "The House of Judgement", prose-poem, published (*The Spirit Lamp*)

22 February — *Salomé* published in French

19 April — *A Woman of No Importance* produced at the Haymarket Theatre

June — "The Disciple", prose-poem, published (*The Spirit Lamp*)

June– October — At The Cottage, Goring-on-Thames

September — Quarrel over Douglas' 'attempted translation' of *Salomé*

October — Takes rooms at 10 and 11 St James's Place

9 November — *Lady Windermere's Fan* published
Douglas leaves for Egypt

December — *A Florentine Tragedy* and *La Sainte Courtisane* 'conceived' and, by the following March, 'almost finished'. *An Ideal Husband*, begun in September and interrupted by Douglas, completed

1894 9 February — English translation of *Salomé* (drawings by Beardsley) published in the absence of its dedicatee, Douglas

April — Writes out scenario for *The Cardinal of Avignon*

May — In Florence with Douglas

11 June — *The Sphinx*, designed by Ricketts, published

July — *Poems in Prose*, comprising "The Artist", "The Doer of Good", "The Disciple", "The Master", "The House of Judgment", published (*Fortnightly*)

August — Sends George Alexander the scenario later written up by Frank Harris as *Mr and Mrs Daventry* and produced successfully on 25 October, 1900 at the Royalty Theatre

August– September — Writes *The Importance of Being Earnest* at Worthing

September — Lengthened version of "The Portrait of Mr W.

		H.", first proposed in 1889 to Blackwood, refused by Elkin Mathews and John Lane
	October	At Brighton with Douglas
	9 October	*A Woman of No Importance* published
	December	"Phrases and Philosophies for the Use of the Young" published (*The Chameleon*)
1895	3 January	*An Ideal Husband* produced
	January–February	Visits Algiers with Douglas
	14 February	*The Importance of Being Earnest* produced
	18 February	Finds Queensberry's card at the Albemarle Club
	1 March	Obtains warrant for Queensberry's arrest
	9 March	Queensberry remanded at Bow Street for trial at Old Bailey
	March	Visits Monte Carlo with Douglas
	3 April	Queensberry trial opens
	5 April	Queensberry acquitted. Wilde arrested
	6–26 April	Imprisoned at Holloway
	26 April	First trial opens
	1 May	Jury disagree. New trial ordered
	7 May	Released on bail
	20 May	Second trial opens
	25 May	Sentenced to two years' hard labour
	24 September	First examination in bankruptcy
	12 November	Second examination in bankruptcy
	20 November	Transferred from Wandsworth gaol to Reading
1896	3 February	Lady Wilde dies
	11 February	*Salomé* produced in Paris at the Théâtre de L'Oeuvre
1897	January–March	Writes *De Profundis*
	19 May	Released. Crosses to Dieppe by night boat
	26 May	Moves from Dieppe to Berneval-sur-Mer, where he writes *The Ballad of Reading Gaol*
	late August	Meets Douglas at Rouen
	4–11 September	At Rouen
	15 September	Leaves Dieppe for Paris
	September – December	Southern Italy and Sicily, including Capri with Douglas
1898	January	Moves to Naples
	February	Moves to Paris
	13 February	*The Ballad of Reading Gaol* published
	March	Moves to the Hôtel d'Alsace
	7 April	Constance Wilde dies

	June – July	At Nogent-sur-Marne
	August	At Chennevières-sur-Marne
	15 December	Leaves for Napoule, near Cannes
1899	February	*The Importance of Being Earnest* published
		Leaves Napoule for Nice
	25 February	Leaves Nice for Gland, Switzerland
	April – May	Returns to Paris
	23 – 26 June	At Trouville and Le Havre
	July	*An Ideal Husband* published
	July	At Chennevières-sur-Marne
	August	Back to Paris
1900	2 – 10 April	At Palermo
	May	Rome
		Ten days at Gland
	May – June	Paris
	10 October	Operated on
	November	Dies in Paris, Hôtel d'Alsace

1 Introduction

Although it touches on what have come to be regarded as the 'usual' Wildean issues, this book is principally about Wilde's relationship with literature. Wilde criticism has sometimes risked turning its subject into a simple case of psycho-sexual determinism, nor has it always been the scandalmongers who have hunted down the scandalous (to misquote Vivian in "The Decay of Lying") with the enthusiasm of the short-sighted detective. There is doubtless some truth in the clichés of the misused great man and the reckless deviationist turned magdalen, and a good deal more in the idea of the artist-criminal, first developed by Richard Ellmann and then elaborated by Christopher Nassaar: readers familiar with the subject will recognise my indebtedness to their work. Much of the interest of Wilde's writing and career lies elsewhere, however, and my account of his response to social pressures and expectations is determined largely by my conclusions about his choice and treatment of literary forms.

Wilde is proverbially elusive – 'the fish's tail flicks, flashes, and disappears'[1] – and, with the rejection of the psycho-sexual approach, the critic may find himself casting in vain from no solid standpoint. One solution is to take Wilde's own objective stance, and to begin with his most characteristic definitions of art. Art is 'really a form of exaggeration'[2] which springs from and appeals to 'personality' above all other qualities.[3] It is 'the intensest mood of Individualism that the world has known';[4] and, even more personally (addressing Alfred Douglas), 'You knew what my Art was to me, the great primal note by which I revealed, first myself to myself, then myself to the world'.[5] Admittedly, these statements return us at once to the subjective, but their importance lies in their deliberate formality. Rather than impulses to be concealed, they are principles to be realised with full self-consciousness – 'for out of ourselves we can never pass'.[6] Wilde devoted his career to investigating that most elusive of subject matter, the self, and creating an expressive medium for his findings.

So specialised an artistic procedure offers more problems than most: in particular, the danger that the artist will confuse his interest in formal means of expression with his curiosity about the findings to be expressed. In aesthetic criticism, Wilde pinioned the danger: 'It is exactly because Hecuba is nothing to us that her sorrows are such an admirable motive for a tragedy'.[7] Elsewhere, notably in fiction, the danger runs free. While the artist as critic preaches 'objective form' and insists on self-concealment in the interests of uninterrupted research as well as of literary perfection, the individualist as hero cross-questions in private the 'Muse-Sphinx' of personality,[8] bent on self-revelation. It is surely no accident that all of Wilde's modern dress fiction contains elements of the detective story. If the artist is sometimes the criminal, he is no less often the sleuth.

Lady Wilde, shrewder than her literary-bohemian image would suggest, seems to have cut through the precautionary theory. 'Caro Oscuro,' one of her letters begins, ' – or – Chiaro Oscuro'.[9] True to his mother's pun, Wilde's personality and career assumed their familiar form not by virtue of their brilliant or shady stretches alone, but from the balance or contrast between the two. Hardly visible in *Poems*, the contrast first emerged in "Lord Arthur Savile's Crime", a dapper parody of detective fiction, and was developed in "The Fisherman and his Soul" and *The Picture of Dorian Gray*. In each of them, what might be called Wilde's moral *chiaroscuro* hints at the force of the unconscious and its unpredictable influence over motive and behaviour. This seems to raise promising psychological matter; but Wilde leaves such territory, for the most part, unexplored. His imagery may sometimes beckon towards the interior, but, being by nature atmospheric or decorative rather than dialectical, most often leads up blind alleys, inviting and rebuffing specific diagnoses. It is largely a question of literary procedure. Whenever Wilde wishes to clinch a point, we are given the intellectual hyperbole of paradox, or some comparison with a scientific principle. Imagery, a form of emotional hyperbole, is generally reserved for fixing a mood, and consequently offers a very shaky basis for diagnostic techniques. Indeed, with the exception of *Salomé* and, perhaps, "The Birthday of the Infanta", none of his works possesses a fully coherent and self-consistent pattern of imagery. This is especially true of the highly pictorial prose fiction, where Symbolist, Naturalist, Impressionist, Parnassian, and other stylistic devices and usages may share no common ground beyond their dramatic effectiveness in context, or some 'Aesthetic' value which contributes to tone but hardly to plot or character. In the second version of *Dorian Gray*, Wilde had begun to develop that blend of Aesthetic and Symbolist imagery which dominates *Salomé*; but even in this revision, and certainly in "Lord Arthur Savile's Crime", the secrets which seem to lurk in the shadows dwindle in the light of analysis. Their real size is their uncertainty. Meanwhile, both of these works are formally consistent within their generic and narrative assumptions, and are, at that level, self-sufficient as they stand. While conceding in criticism that 'self-consciousness is not yet adequate to explain the contents of the Ego',[10] Wilde still felt that ideally it would be, and considered it the artist's proper goal. It is true that he reached it only intermittently. In some of the fairy tales, for instance, confused images encroach upon the narrative structure with unsettling didactic intent. Subjective blurs objective. A too carefully stylised surface seems to betray the author's interior monologue. Here, some kind of reference to the circumstances of Wilde's personal life, as distinct from the details of his formalised imaginative life, may prove fruitful. In the best pieces, of course, there is no such ambiguity. The inner monologue is ventriloquised as a one-man show with audience: *The Importance of Being Earnest* is the obvious example. The author's voice proceeds from no one character but from the whole play. Nothing, perhaps, so fully confirms his objectivity in such cases as the widely various interpretations, not necessarily psychoanalytical or psychological, which have been provoked. 'When critics disagree,' Wilde hazarded, 'the artist is in accord with himself.'[11]

The charismatic qualities of the 1890s have obscured several simple but important points: that Wilde was by training a classicist,[12] that he was educated during the 'seventies and had produced the greater part of his best work by the end of 1890. Capably exploiting the Decadent movement's publicity, he remained firmly rooted in the earlier humanist tradition. His favourite poets were Keats and Shakespeare; his favourite critics, Pater (as much a humanist as a proto-Decadent) and Goethe. Optimistically, he celebrated the Aesthetic movement, or his peculiar vision of it, as 'The English Renaissance' – a forlorn gesture towards the second coming of humanism. And, of course, he was also an eminent, though reluctant, Victorian. If the prose writer whom he plagiarised most shamelessly was Flaubert, the poet whom he plagiarised most imaginatively was Tennyson.

The proper balance of these various influences first becomes apparent in the 'English Renaissance' lecture. The Aesthetic movement, Wilde told America, united classical and Romantic by treating the momentary and exceptional under the conditions of serene and dispassionate form. Whatever one thinks of this judgement, it provided the working principle of his career. Soon bored by the 'Romantic pantomime' of his first period, Wilde remained a Romantic, according to his own definition, throughout his life, devoted to the moment and convinced that he was exceptional. Circumstances eventually forced a reassessment of the nature of that exceptional status, but the conviction never wavered. This, rather than specific anxieties about latent or actual homosexual behaviour, was, I suggest, the basis for his numerous and varied anti-social manifestations.

At the same time, he never convinced himself that the Romantic attitude, or any single attitude, was the right one. As early as 1886 the doubts proliferated. 'There is no such thing as a romantic experience; there are romantic memories and there is the desire for romance – that is all.'[13] Though far more extrovert than his philosophic mentor, Pater, Wilde was still too timid, too irresolute (and, perhaps, too traditional) to undertake anything as systematic as Rimbaud's disordering of the senses, for example, or to adopt any course of conduct which guaranteed rebel status, with the resulting confiscation of the privileges of civilised society. 'I would go to the stake for a sensation and be a sceptic to the last.'[14] The boast sounds now like a mortgage on the future; but Wilde preferred meanwhile, as Richard Ellmann has persuasively argued, 'to drift with every' or almost every 'passion'.[15] A quotation recorded in his holograph Commonplace Book (which probably dates from 1880 or thereabouts) shows apt foresight in glossing the poetic débutant's own metaphor: 'Dans la vie morale il est beau de quelquefois faire [sic] naufrage.'[16]

The practical effect of this in literary terms was that 'the two supreme and highest arts – Life and Literature – life and the perfect expression of life'[17] became unusually closely fused. Certainly, Wilde's most celebrated pronouncement, that he had put all his genius into his life and his talent, merely, into his art,[18] remains his most misleading. Nothing in his career was that simple. 'Work,' he ruefully admitted, 'never seems to me a reality, but a way of getting rid of reality.'[19] Inconsistency grew into a virtue: 'We are never so true to ourselves as when we are inconsistent.'[20] Thus, continually veering between life and art, passionate commitment and dispassionate contemplation, the ecstasy of Romantic moments and the timeless spectating of the all-knowing critic, Wilde, like a pendulum, rests in one extreme only to return to the other. It is the law of his imaginative mechanism. The inert state is the state of pastoral – unconsciousness of the world and of self; and one of those progressions which are visible both in literary and in personal terms is the progression towards completer self-knowledge. In the fairy tales, Wilde's protagonists are sometimes reluctant to leave their pastoral; but by the time of *Dorian Gray*, contemporary with the Romantic theories of all-inclusive criticism, they are eager to do so, while in the comedies people are pushed into some form of self-knowledge, for the most part, whether they like it or not.

Such obsessive solipsism has caused bewilderment and sometimes disgust, expressed generally in the charge of insincerity: among so many Wildes some must surely be fakes. Whatever sincerity may be taken to mean in the context of art, Wilde's view of it can be summed up by saying that the artist, or Individualist, is never more sincere than when doing as he wishes, never less sincere than when doing as other people wish. If the tension between these two states provoked the stridency of "The Soul of Man under Socialism", it produced also the poise of *The Importance of Being Earnest*.

Given that such tensions formed the basis of all Wilde's responses, it is not surprising that paradox should have become his most characteristic form of utterance. Fruitful opposition shapes the smallest units as well as the largest: the numerous alliterative epigrams – 'The only difference between a saint and a sinner is that every saint has a past and every sinner has a future'[21] – no less than the career as a whole. Of these tensions, three are especially prominent: between intellect and emotion, or critical and romantic attitudes; between individualistic self-expression and socially imposed roles (including sex roles); and between the artist and the norm, or the artist and the ideal. The first seems to have been the strongest. Often subsuming the others, it spanned Wilde's career. Already present in *Poems*, it passes unresolved into the early dramas, *Vera* and *The Duchess of Padua*. In *The Happy Prince and Other Tales*, specific issues become clearer; so does Wilde's irresolution. Thereafter, the separate impulses find their distinctive voices in mythopoeic fiction (*A House of Pomegranates*) and critical dialogues and essays (*Intentions*). "The Portrait of Mr W. H." and *The Picture of Dorian Gray* confirm Wilde's longstanding distrust of Romantic impulse, also its unabated fascination for him. *Salomé* refutes Romantic impulse categorically, and the comedies which followed show the idealistic critic compromising with social probabilities. While the suspicious neatness of this summary may be challenged by reference to several fragmentary works,[22] they mostly read like false starts, and Wilde never returned to them.

An unfinished book review of 1886 or 1887 happens, however, to provide a fascinating glimpse into Wilde's progressive attempts to confront this central conflict. The review has two subjects: Disraeli's correspondence and Amiel's *journal intime*. Wilde dramatises the two personalities – the books, he observes, might be called 'the letters of Osric' and 'the diary of Hamlet' – and uses the pretext of their 'simultaneous publication'[23] as the occasion for rehearsing afresh his own extremes. His clear preference for the persona projected by Lord Beaconsfield confirms his gradual change from Romantic posturing in verse and tragedy to social sparring in prose, eventually in stage comedy dominated by the dandy. Amiel may be 'spoken of on Parnassus' but 'Lord Beaconsfield is quoted in Piccadilly'. There can be little doubt about who is the more modern or clubbable man. (We may infer a similar conclusion about a similar contrast in "Lord Arthur Savile's Crime", written about this time.[24]) Yet, Wilde continues, there is a point of resemblance:

> Each of them was an actor, and each of them, like most actors, was interested only in himself. . . . Lord Beaconsfield played a brilliant comedy to a 'pit full of kings', and was immensely pleased at his own performance, Amiel played a tragedy to an empty house and was deeply affected by his own pathos. Lord Beaconsfield let off fireworks to gratify the groundlings, Amiel kept a rain-gauge of his tears for the use of posterity. Lord Beaconsfield had one distinct advantage, besides, over the Genovese Professor. He did not take himself seriously.[25]

The two characters were recast in "The Remarkable Rocket", published in 1888, but their personal significance extended into the author's darkest years. Reduced in Reading gaol to playing the role of Amiel, Wilde was finally obliged to concede that 'the most tedious of tragedies' was not merely 'a tragedy without a hero' but also one which outlasted its audience.[26]

Wilde's *débâcle* is usually cited as proof that one extreme inevitably implies or brings about its opposite. Wilde himself was first with a full statement of the proposition as it affected his especial case; and *De Profundis*, its argument based on direct personal experience, is also, aptly enough, his last mythopoeic structure. Denied any life worthy the name, the critic as dramatist returns to his Romantic assumptions, detecting in Christ the archetypal Romantic artist and individualist: he who created himself 'out of his own imagination' and thus proved not only imagination's superiority over any 'factual' status quo but also life's superiority over art as a mode of complete self-expression.

Without prison and disgrace, however, the conflicts would still have had to reach some resolution, and the likeliest form for this would surely have been stage comedy. For there Wilde had already reconciled to a large extent the ruling preoccupations of his career, not merely accommodating them all within one literary form, but expressing their fusion in a new stage character – the dandy – unlikely voice of the author's dramatic and social criticism. It is he, or she, in whom intellect and emotion, 'male' and 'female' attitudes, ideal and real standards, individual and society are seen somehow, sometimes, to converge. The best of these agile spirits, who by 'normal' standards are heartless, socially irresponsible, and self-centred, are by the terms of Wilde's comic characterisation amused and enlightened sceptics, self-sufficient and healthily androgynous personalities. There is just a hint here, briefly expanded in *Earnest*, that 'the real life' need not always be 'the life we do not lead'.[27]

In tracing these patterns of self-projection and self-objectification through Wilde's career, I have been more concerned with trying to elucidate technique and intention than with making absolute value judgements. The most important value judgement remains implicit: that Wilde's serious artistic aims and ideas still provide the truest light in which to consider him.

2 Art and Pastoral

I. *Poems*: 'The Last Endymion'

Although Wilde had published his first play, *Vera, or The Nihilists*, the previous year, the production had been cancelled at the last minute.[1] Public curiosity was consequently focused on *Poems*; and *Punch*, sensing the comic potential of a probable anti-climax – 'The poet is Wilde but his poetry's tame'[2] – brought the book far more attention than its unaided literary merit could have guaranteed it, and sped Wilde on his career as 'Professor of Aesthetics'. Other, more pretentious, criticism followed in England and the United States, and the brouhaha of the trans-American lecture tour ensured a *succès de scandale* for the author, if not for his work. Wilde tended to stand on his dignity in the face of frequent abusive sallies, but he also encouraged them: "Charmides", which relates how a Greek sailor-boy sexually assaults a sacred statue of Athene, and which enraged Boston puritans, was, in his view, 'the most perfect' piece in the volume.[3]

Some critics, confident that 'Swinburne and Water'[4] was harmless enough, took Wilde to task for being shamelessly derivative. 'He is conscious of the charm of graceful echoes,' wrote Arthur Symons, ten years later 'and is always original in his quotations.'[5] The remark refers to *Intentions* (1891) with which *Poems* has close links (see below, pp. 95–6), but could as easily have been applied to the earlier volume. Indeed, for certain critics the truth about Wilde's entire career is encapsulated in the celebrated exchange with Whistler: 'I wish I'd said that, Jimmy' – 'You will, Oscar, you will'. More recently, attention has been turned to stylistic analysis of the poems. Both Roditi[6] and San Juan,[7] for instance, see the early verse as a form of 'art-history'. This approach is clearly an advance. Even so, by reducing the volume to its technique, it implies, no less than the plagiarism theory, that the aesthete by definition has nothing to say. Indeed, Wilde's latest commentator dismisses all of the pre-1886 work as 'an exercise in imitation', the 'clearly second-rate' productions of that 'boyish, carefree plagiariser' who had not yet developed into 'the sin-conscious homosexual' worthy of serious literary investigation.[8] Juvenilia, however, often fascinate or signify independently of their deficiencies. If *Poems* is often bad, it has a closer bearing on Wilde's development than is generally supposed. Far from being devoid of ideas, it prefigures much of his mature work. Even the plagiarism serves an implicit subjective purpose.

Poems initiates a series of works which stamp Wilde one of 'the last

Romantics', not merely in posterity's eyes but also, quite clearly, in his own. It is a heterogeneous clutch of studies, tribute to the aesthete's eclectic taste – Parnassian or neo-Gongorist pastorals, Pre-Raphaelite ditties, declamatory sonnets after Milton and Wordsworth, Shelleyesque lamentations and Keatsian invocations – and at first, in spite of a series of poetically titled sub-sections ("Eleutheria", "Rosa Mystica", "Wind Flowers", "Flowers of Gold", "Impressions de Théâtre", "The Fourth Movement"[9]), seems to have little internal organisation and no governing artistic or intellectual purpose. These sections, however, which consist mostly of short lyrics, are divided by five longer poems ("The Garden of Eros", "The Burden of Itys", "Charmides", "Panthea", and "Humanitad") in which the 'plagiarisms' are most extensive, and which the poet himself plagiarised for later prose works. They also contain the basic themes of the volume, which duly pass into fiction and criticism: the superior charms of 'paganism' over Christianity, the seductive perils of Romantic impulse, the secure but forbidding 'sunlit heights' of philosophic endeavour, the baseness of modern life and its indifference to the poetic temper. In spite of the poetic 'we', Wilde already identifies himself in all but name with Schiller's disaffected *sentimentalisch* artist, cut off from the rest of society and divided against himself.

In his particular case, however, there was an added burden. The young poet (Wilde was twenty-six) is not merely eclectic but, in addition, passionately valetudinarian. To protest against 'an age of prose' in various conventional metres is in itself anachronistic; but, as the reviewer to the *Athenaeum* observed, there was an additional anachronism involved: 'Mr Wilde's volume of poems may be regarded as the evangel of a new creed. From other gospels it differs in coming after, instead of before, the cult it seeks to establish.'[10] The stance was conscious and deliberate. Thinking of the Aesthetic lectures, Max Beerbohm quipped, 'Beauty had existed long before 1880. It was Mr Oscar Wilde who managed her *début*';[11] and one of the remarkable features of those lectures had been their combination of the prophet's voice, the impresario's manner and the tones of the indulgent parent. But before undertaking America's 'aesthetic education', Wilde had already set about conducting his own in *Poems*, often with a self-conscious heroic flair which derives less from Aesthetic adventures or doctrines than from earlier Romantic stimuli.

The common factor linking lectures and poems is Keats. In "The English Renaissance of Art" (1882), Wilde formally recognised Keats as the inspirer of the Pre-Raphaelites and subsequently, since he combined 'personality' with 'perfection', of the Aesthetic movement itself. A year earlier, in *Poems*, where Keats (supported by Shelley and Wordsworth) played an equally vital role, readers could have found many passages which might have been written by a latter-day Lycius. 'For, sweet, to feel is better than to know, / And wisdom is a childless heritage', cries the poet, striving against all the odds to deflect 'the Gorgon eyes of Truth' with the shield of poetic fancy. Furthermore, the moonstruck lover of beauty, the cultural rebel, and the idealistic sensationalist are all comprehended in a specific neo-Keatsian projection:

> . . . what if we
> Have analysed the rainbow, robbed the moon
>   Of her most ancient, chastest mystery,
> Shall I, the last Endymion, lose all hope
> Because rude eyes peer at my mistress through a telescope![12]

This whimsical outburst shows the main technical weakness of Wilde's early verse. The poet is restricted, as Roditi observed, by the vocabulary and metaphoric patterns of his classical training, which can accommodate neither his Romantic attitudes nor adequate reference to the contemporary world. However, if the effect created by the last Endymion is comic – a lame absurdity which has neither the wit of later prose work nor the ironic poise of Laforgue's moon-gazing in *L'Imitation de Notre-Dame la Lune* (1885) – his basic assumption is serious enough. Humanistic values have disintegrated under commercial and industrial pressure; the 'Spirit of Beauty' has fled from art; poetry has rigidified into the corpus of accepted classics, most of them built on mythologies or metaphysics superseded by modern social, scientific or intellectual developments. In *Adonais*, laid heavily under contribution by Wilde, Shelley had spoken rhetorically of the body-blow given to poetry by Keats's death. The aesthete seems inclined to take the image literally. With one exception – a short lyric apparently written on a trans-Atlantic liner – Wilde never explored the poetic possibilities of machinery.[13] Instead, he turned to painting for new effects, or, as in the greater part of *Poems*, became not so much the bare-faced imitator as the egocentric and flamboyant editor of "other men's flowers". Considered in this light, the volume reads like a personal anthology through which the poet, as nostalgic critic of some five centuries of verse, attempts to define his relationship to a tradition which has disintegrated before he has had the chance to contribute to it.

Had this been his only personal stake in the volume, *Poems* would have been a singularly futile book. However, Wilde recognised his weaknesses, and in *Poems* seems to have tried to capitalise on them. In 1880, Clement Scott published Wilde's 'translation', under the title "The Artist's Dream", of a Polish poem by the actress Helena Modjeska. Writing to Scott to thank him for his encouragement, he admitted, 'You dare to do what I hardly dare, to sing of the passion and joy and sorrow of the lives of the men and women among whom we live, and of the world which is the world of all of us. . . . For my own part, I fear I too often "trundle back my soul five hundred years", as Aurora Leigh says, and find myself more at home in the woods of Colonus or the glades of Arcady than I do in this little fiery-coloured world of ours. I envy you your strength. I have not got it.'[14] The reference to *Aurora Leigh* (1856) is significant. Wilde had discovered Mrs Browning's fictional verse-biography while still at Oxford, and had been deeply impressed by it.[15] Book I is particularly suggestive. It gives a witty account of the inept flutterings of a callow poet, and compares the true poet's flight with the giddy sensations of Ganymede – an interesting choice of image for a crusading female author – while, in her discussion of the 'woman problem', Aurora echoes Shelley (and anticipates the claim of Wilde's utopian criticism) by insisting that real improvement of the human lot can be reached only through the improvement of the individual, ideally by contact with the poet's vision. Among various pictures that Wilde did not forget, the most striking is an anticipation of Pater's piece on La Gioconda.[16]

Wilde's enthusiasm for Mrs Browning may have been associated with Speranza's (Lady Wilde's) accomplishments,[17] but his admiration of Aurora Leigh seems to have been spontaneous. It is the more interesting in the light of his subsequent development of the 'woman hero' in drama,[18] and for certain remarks about poetry in his Commonplace Book: 'The feminine nature ascribed to the Muses – though there may be considerations of primitive manners to account for it – [is] at any rate symbolic for us [of] the close connection of poetry with feeling and sentiment – and even when Apollo took the place of the Goddesses of song his status always preserved some of that effeminacy and languor and voluptuousness which are the character-istics of that "passionate humanity" which is the background of true poetry.'[19] In "the Garden of Eros" he goes further, assuring the 'spirit of Beauty' that, although 'there are few / Who for thy sake would give their manlihood / And consecrate their being, I at least / Have done so'. The confession is ambiguous, but the less flattering sense was rapidly endorsed by Punch, and by such 'manly' reviewers as T. W. Higginson.[20] That Wilde thought (or knew that others thought) the poetic and emotional responses to be characteristically and properly feminine and the intellectual and critical responses to be proportionally masculine is, then, evident even at this early stage, although the knowledge was not put to creative use until the comedies of ten years later. Whereas poetry, or those Romantic attitudes which speak through it, seems to imply some sort of personal risk, almost some sort of wound, an unmanning of oneself in full public view, ratiocination offers difficult but sequestered security.

The idea is connected with Wilde's considerable ambition and with a puritanism as yet unexorcised. "Taedium Vitae" combines all three suggestions, but the tenor of the poet's relationship with his work and his aspirations is best expressed by the overall arrangement of Poems, in particular by its opening and concluding items. Preceding the first section, "Eleutheria", and acting as epigraph to the volume, is a piece of 'Romantic pantomime'[21] entitled "Hélas!". Its precise meaning is obscure, but the poet's dereliction, whatever it is, has sprung from impulsive self-indulgence for which "Hélas!" (the title a further self-indulgence) is public penance. The last poem, "Flower of Love", seems out of place after the rhetorical full-close of "Humanitad", but the anti-climax is intentional since the lyric contains the poet's apologia (the earliest expression of that attitude later to take the epigrammatic form reported by Gide): 'I have made my choice, have lived my poems, and, though youth is gone in wasted days, / I have found the lover's crown of myrtle better than the poet's crown of bays.'

Romantic impulse, then, provides both epigraph and epitaph for the last Endymion. An alternative first appears in "Theoretikos". After seven, often ambiguous, songs of political liberty, most of them elegies to frenzied action, this sonnet concerns itself specifically with individual freedom.[22] It was mercilessly parodied by *Punch*, to whose satirical eye Wilde's ideal of contemplation and 'maudlin Culchaw' proved irresistible,[23] but it looks forward to the later critical absolutes, with their rejection of 'the world' and 'the mart', their neo-Epicurean indifference to public life, and their Platonic ideal of self-culture. Neither "Hélas!" nor "Theoretikos" is a good poem; but between them they give us in little the ruling dichotomy of Wilde's life. The longer poems follow this pattern, offering conflicting solutions to the last Endymion's problematical desires – fame, passion, self-fulfilment through action, conquering time – all of which deny the secure contemplative ideal and demand some form of practical commitment.

"The New Helen", "The Artist's Dream", "The Burden of Itys", "Charmides", "Humanitad", "Panthea".
Of those poems which touch on the enduring concerns of Wilde's career, two treat of the modern poet's predicament; one attempts a post-Christian Greek pastoral; two variously interpret the relation between pastoral or prentice youth and the formidable goddess of knowledge, Athene; while a sixth not only proposes an optimistic corollary to Wordsworth's "Immortality" ode, but also posits for the poet and his lover an egotistical sublime of galactic proportions.

Both "The New Helen" and "The Artist's Dream"[24] are set in a somewhat Pre-Raphaelite 'garden close', and speak in their different ways of the restriction of self and of cultural claustrophobia. In "The Artist's Dream", the artist is 'Ambition's slave', and finds nature 'but a pageant, and an unreal show / That mocked my heart'. At sunset, he sees a figure reminiscent of the Soul which appeared to Rossetti's Chiaro dell'Erma.[25] She wears a laurel crown, and the artist, recognising her as 'Glory', begs to hear 'the trump of loud ambition sound my name / And for the rest I care not.' Unlike Chiaro's lady, the 'angel' treats him as a child, one 'made for light and love and laughter, not to waste / Thy youth in shooting arrows at the sun', and counsels him to take the easier course, contenting himself with nature. But the artist rejects nature's pleasures, which are fleeting by comparison with 'thy crown of deathless laurel'. He then finds that the laurel conceals a thorn-crown which makes 'the garden' of his brain 'a bare desert'. Tempted later to regard the whole episode as a dream, he is convinced of its truth by feeling 'this restless pain that gnaws my heart' and seeing 'the red wounds of thorns upon my brow'. The symbolism of this poem was developed in "The Young King".

"The New Helen" uses the same basic images for a different purpose. Reworking the stanza form of "Ode on a Grecian Urn", it celebrates Lily Langtry as the embodiment of a new Hellenic ideal which, the poet fears, will all too quickly vanish:

> Nor shall I ever see thy face again,
>   But in this poisonous garden close must stay,
> Crowning my brows with the thorn-crown of pain,
>   Till all my loveless life shall pass away.

The New Helen, even so, is less woman than symbol. Nothing was so apt among the events of Wilde's Oxford years as his involuntary substitution of a trip to Greece for a trip to Rome in 1877. (He took in Rome on the way back.) After much soul-searching about whether to follow Newman and 'go over' to Rome, he allowed himself to be whisked away to the Peloponnesus. 'I hope,' he wrote just before leaving, 'to see the golden dome of St Peter's and the Eternal City by Tuesday night. This is an era in my life, a crisis. I wish I could look into the seeds of time and see what is coming.' A few days later, he had to confess, 'I never went to Rome at all! What a changeable fellow you must think me, but Mahaffy my old tutor carried me off to Greece with him to see Mykenae and Athens. I am awfully ashamed of myself, but I could not help it.'[26] The 'poisonous garden close' in which the poet here languishes is evidently some form of artists' Gethsemane, though whether he is condemned by Catholicism, Nonconformity, or some less specific pressure remains unclear. However, the placing of the poem within "Rosa Mystica" implies some connection with the bewildering choice between Catholicism and Hellenism. "Rosa Mystica" mainly consists of sonnets on Italian Catholic subjects, but Wilde concludes it inconclusively, by three poems of a different character: "Vita Nuova", which glimpses not a Dantesque but a regenerative pagan vision; "Madonna Mia", a Rossettian revision of a sonnet (originally describing a young boy painted in watercolours) which regretted the 'wasted days' of self-unconscious youth; and, finally, "The New Helen" – illuminator of our present-day 'house of gloom', life-bringing last resort for 'wasted lives' and 'lingering wretchedness', co-outlaw with the medieval Venus ('that discrowned Queen men call the Ericyne'), rival and eclipser of Mariolatry.

The next long poem, "The Burden of Itys", pushes the Christian-pagan conflict further. It is modelled on "Ode to a Nightingale", and, instead of alluding systematically to the legend of the ravished Philomela and her murdered son, Itys, Wilde turns the nightingale into a symbol for the modern or Romantic artist (he extended the idea in "The Nightingale and the Rose") and therefore a specific reference point for the last Endymion's poetic plight:

And like a blossom blown before the breeze
A white moon drifts across a shimmering sky,
Mute arbitress of all thy sad, thy rapturous threnody.

She does not heed thee, wherefore should she heed,
    She knows Endymion is not far away;
'Tis I, 'tis I whose soul is as the reed
    Which has no message of its own to play,
So pipes another's bidding. . . .

Using the bird's song as a kind of incantation, the poet conjures up a series of
classical figures intended to justify his opening line: 'This English Thames is
holier far than Rome'. The daffodil, its poetic associations all but fixed for
the Romantic, here marks the poet's personal change of allegiance:

Men say it bloomed upon the sepulchre
    Of one I sometime worshipped, but to me
It seems to bring diviner memories
    Of faun-loved Heliconian glades and blue nymph-haunted seas,

Of an untrodden vale at Tempe where
    On the clear river's marge Narcissus lies,
The tangle of the forest in his hair,
    The silence of the woodland in his eyes....

Upon the heels of Narcissus comes Salmacis, 'Fed by two fires and
unsatisfied / Through their excess'. It is clearly an idiosyncratic pantheon
where Narcissus and Salmacis replace Christ. (In fact, the lines on Narcissus,
the best in the poem, were reworked in "The Young King", a story which
traces the growth of its hero from pastoral self-unawareness, through
narcissism, to Christian love.) Even so, the nightingale's song cannot blot out
unwelcome memories for ever: 'memory, / That foster-brother of remorse
and pain, / Drops poison in my ear, – O to be free, / To burn one's old ships!'
As Elizabeth Barrett Browning had put it, 'The memory mixes with the
vision, spoils, / And works it turbid'.[27] Mrs Browning had projected as the
poet's true precinct a 'melancholy desert' barren of memory and association,
extending 'behind you as before', but from whose emptiness one might
conjure the elusive 'Muse-Sphinx'.[28] Wilde is for the moment less
ambitious. His career soon developed into a search for his own Muse-
Sphinx; but his immediate aim is to induce a state of poetical
oblivion to the modern world, and the last Endymion swigs metaphors as if
they were opiates:

Sing on! Sing on! I would be drunk with life,
    Drunk with the trampled vintage of my youth,
I would forget the wearying wasted strife,
    The riven veil, the Gorgon eyes of Truth,

The prayerless vigil and the cry for prayer,
The barren gifts, the lifted arms, the dull insensate air!

All to no avail, however. Like the Baptist's aureoled head in Gustave Moreau's "L'Apparition" (see Plate 10), Christ's image arrests the intoxicated pagan:

Sing louder yet, why must I still behold
    The wan white face of that deserted Christ
Whose bleeding hands my hands did once enfold,
    Whose smitten lips my lips so oft have kissed,
And now in mute and marble misery
Sits in his lone dishonoured House and weeps, perchance for me?

Keats's 'immortal bird' flew the enchanted path from fevered life into the healing calm of poetic contemplation. Wilde's faces a stiffer task: raising the ghosts of dead creeds to replace the spiritual heritage of Christianity. This forlorn hope suggests a further mythical allusion which permeates Wilde's thinking – the equation of 'the cry of Marsyas' with the peculiar voice of modern art. Realising that his enchantments have faltered, the poet cries, 'No more thou wingèd Marsyas complain, / Apollo loveth not to hear such troubled songs of pain!' Marsyas, like Christ, fulfilled himself through pain, even though the one did so willingly, the other unwillingly; and the contrast here between Apollonian perfection and the too-human cry of Marsyas anticipates the passage in "The Soul of Man under Socialism" where Christ appears as a perfect yet superseded type – since, with the advent of 'the new Hellenism', self-realisation through pain will give way to self-realisation through joy.

The ending hangs somewhat limply from these lofty allusions. The 'curfew' from Tom Tower 'warns' the rebel pagan 'to return', and, catching sight of Magdalen's Gothic tower 'tipped with tremulous gold', he hastens so as not to be locked out of college. Are these grey cloistered quadrangles the equivalent of the poisonous or splenetic garden close from which the poet longs to escape? Not entirely, perhaps; yet, once Wilde left Oxford, he soon abandoned all idea of going over to Rome, or allowed such ideas to become submerged in the more pressing quest for 'Glory' and for the 'Muse-Sphinx' of personality, as well as in the development of the new Hellenism in prose criticism.

As Roditi noted, the new Hellenism is implicit in several of the poems. Implicit, too, is the dependence on Pater's Conclusion to The Renaissance (1873, 1878) which Wilde revamped in the Aesthetic lectures and reinterpreted in later fiction. In Poems, however, Pater's discriminating search for sensations and moments tends to give way to the last Endymion's fatalistic forays into passion:

> O we are born too late!
> What balm for us in bruisèd poppy seed
> Who crowd into one finite pulse of time
> The joy of infinite love and the fierce pain of infinite crime?[29]

The most extravagant of these forays occurs in "Charmides", a poem probably based on Lucian,[30] but owing much to the narratives of Morris's *Earthly Paradise*. The simple plot is covered in description far in excess of what Morris would have used, and often closer in atmosphere to that of "Venus and Adonis", *Hero and Leander*, or to the pastoral audacities of Richard Barnfield. This tends to obscure its connection with two of Wilde's favourite themes: the protagonist 'affronting his [or her] destiny',[31] and the fall into knowledge. The sailor-hero, ironically bearing the same name as Socrates' philosophic acolyte, literally affronts the statue of Athene, goddess of knowledge. As punishment, she appears to him on board ship, and he plunges in ecstasy to his death. Venus, deploring his unfulfilled passion and that of the nymph who had pined for him, arranges their brief rendezvous in 'melancholy moonless Acheron': 'enough that once their lips could meet / In that wild throb when all existences / Seemed narrowed to one single ecstasy'; 'Enough that he whose life had been / A fiery pulse of sin, a splendid shame, / could in the loveless land of Hades glean / One scorching harvest.'

Charmides' crime is so generalised by these lines – it is not even specifically hubris – that the inference that he was consciously violating the shrine of knowledge can be supported only by "Humanitad", which is something of a companion piece. Here the poet rejects Venus in favour of Athene: 'The chariot wheels of passion sweep too near, / Hence! hence! I pass unto a life more barren, more austere. . . . For I am hers who loves not any man, / Whose white and stainless bosom bears the sign Gorgonian.'[32] At the same time, he realises that her discipline is beyond him; he cannot live without 'desire, fear, and pain', nor 'nurture' the Socratic calm, 'self-poised, self-centred, and self-comforted'. Faced with a failing world, he turns to a Whitmanesque vision of 'the harmony / Of living in the healthful air, the swift / Clean beauty of strong limbs when men are free / And women chaste'.[33] Such things are more uplifting even than Renaissance master-works, for 'somehow life is bigger after all / Than any painted Angel, could we see / The God that is within us!' Although truth and knowledge may turn us to stone, then, the risk is justified. Indeed, 'that old Greek serenity' is significantly compared to ideal forms in stone: the 'level line / Of marble youths, who with untroubled eyes / And chastened limbs ride round Athena's shrine / And mirror her divine economies'. If we could ever reach this state, says the poet, apparently without having noticed its incongruity, 'Temptation would grow hoarse, and pallid sin / Would walk ashamed of his adulteries, / And Passion creep from out the House of Lust with startled eyes.' This would be 'to find the last, the perfect creed'.

Wilde elaborated the creed in *The Picture of Dorian Gray* and "The Critic as Artist", each in its way a utopian construct; but the climax of "Humanitad" is less utopian than merely rhetorical. We learn that the creed would 'make the Body and the Spirit one / With all right things'; keep 'the soul in flawless essence high enthroned'; allow us to mark 'with serene impartiality / The strife of things', because philosophic contemplation assures us that 'All separate existences are wed / Into one supreme whole, whose utterance / Is joy, or holier praise!'; ensure that 'the rational intellect would find / In passion its expression, and mere sense, / Ignoble else, lend fire to the mind'. From this union, 'we' would strike a new music of the spheres.

Just as one might have remarked that this Hellenist is 'terribly at ease in Zion', Wilde interrupts himself with a Decadent view of that 'consciousness of sin' which, Arnold said, invalidated the Socratic ideal for modern man.[34]'From our sad lips another song is wrung'; 'Somehow the grace, the bloom of things has flown'. But there is a characteristic paradox. We have strayed from self-development not through our own sins but through those of others. The false altruism of the age has killed the higher sense of self-responsibility: 'of all men we are most wretched who / Must live each other's lives and not our own / For very pity's sake, and then undo / All that we lived for—it was otherwise / When soul and body seemed to blend in mystic symphonies.' This is the gist of "The Soul of Man under Socialism", and Wilde concludes the poem by anticipating the essay's argument. We have exchanged the healthy egotism and harmony of the Greek ideal for a delusory ideal of self-torture. We ourselves are Christ: we plod to 'the new Calvary, / Where we behold, as one who in a glass / Sees his own face, self-slain Humanity'. We are 'the spear that pierces and the side that bleeds'. We did not know that when we stabbed Christ's side 'it was our own real hearts we slew'.[35] 'Lords of the natural world' and 'yet our own dread enemy', we are, however, 'but crucified'. We shall descend and 'be whole again' once we realise that 'That which is purely human, that is Godlike, that is God.' While the poem's argument is not of the clearest, a definite progression is visible—from pained awareness of modern man's fragmented consciousness, through invocation of various poetic and political liberationists, to an iconoclastic assertion of man's intrinsic supremacy which aptly reverses a Christian image to proclaim the 'perfect creed' of Hellenism.

"Panthea" traces a similar pattern. The title suggests philosophic exposition, but the poem is concerned wholly with 'passion' – the force which not merely justifies man's ways to man, but, further, unites him with the vital forces of the universe. On the one hand, the poem is relentlessly *fin-de-siècle*: 'For man is weak; God sleeps; and heaven is high; / One fiery coloured moment: one great love, and lo! we die.' On the other, it interprets Shelleyan pantheism with supreme optimism:

> The yellow buttercups that shake for mirth
> At daybreak know a pleasure not less real

Than we do, when in some fresh-blossoming wood,
We draw the spring into our hearts, and feel that life is good.

It also repeats Wilde's concern with the avoidance of pain: 'without life's conscious torturing pain / In some sweet flower we will feel the sun'; and implies with a certain relish the necessary disintegration of Christian terminology in the progression back to nature:

> How my heart leaps up
> To think of that grand living after death
> In beast and bird and flower, when this cup,
>   Being filled too full of spirit, bursts for breath,
> And with the pale leaves of some autumn day
> The soul, earth's earliest conqueror, becomes earth's last great prey.

To partake of nature's anonymity is also to share in nature's dynamism. Transfigured poets and lovers are the unacknowledged inseminators of the world spirit: 'Methinks no leaf would ever bud in spring, / But for the lovers' lips that kiss, the poets' lips that sing.' Wilde's paganism and his pantheism are analagous. Both turn the tables on the modern world – and especially on Wordsworth, whose soul-journey away from nature and towards the 'philosophic mind' will seem pointlessly pessimistic:

> Is the light vanished from our golden sun,
>   Or is this daedal-fashioned earth less fair,
> That we are nature's heritors, and one
>   With every pulse of life that beats the air?
> Rather new suns across the sky shall pass,
> New splendour come unto the flower, new glory to the grass.

The conclusion confirms Wilde's intention of 'rewriting' the "Immortality" ode, and elevating the egotistic poet and his lover to their proper level. After death, they will add their vibrations to the music of the spheres – for without 'us' that music would inevitably jar. This significant order of precedence – 'we' are not one with the world, the world is one with 'us' – dominates the final stanza:

> We shall be notes in that great Symphony
>   Whose cadence circles through the rhythmic spheres,
> And all the live World's throbbing heart shall be
>   One with our heart; the stealthy creeping years
> Have lost their terrors now, we shall not die,
> The Universe itself shall be our Immortality.

Setting aside, then, those shorter pieces which are largely exercises in taste or technique, we can see the rudiments of a characteristically Wildean pattern. Three poems show the artist languishing in his latter-day garden close. One, "Charmides" – 'the most perfect' of the volume – implies an equation of sexual knowledge with intellectual knowledge, and associates these with the breaking of religious and social taboos: a complex of attitudes which was soon to enter Wilde's own life. The remaining two poems confront the great Romantic theme of modern man's estrangement from nature, and hence from self, and suggest antithetical pagan solutions to it. "Panthea" is a rhetorical poetic answer: division is inevitable, but so is posthumous reunion. "Humanitad" proposes a recovery of the Greek ideal of harmony between body and soul – a harmony which is purely mortal, but which cannot be reached, even so, until (as Wilde was to argue in "The English Renaissance") we heave the spirit from its marsh of medievalism and inaugurate a new Renaissance founded on a new Hellenism.

These two alternatives duly take charge of the Romantic and critical halves of Wilde's later work. The pantheistic alternative has no bearing on the lyrical dramas, but its influence is present in the fairy tales, and its absolutism is reflected in all of Wilde's Romantic endeavours. The new Hellenism flourishes and proliferates in "The Soul of Man", "The Critic as Artist", and *Dorian Gray*, dwindling to practical proportions in the comedies. The remainder of Wilde's poetry was unaffected by these ideas. Although *The Sphinx* and *The Ballad of Reading Gaol* are of technical and psychological interest, all of his most thoughtful work was to be in prose.

II   Prose – the Post-lapsarian Form: "L'Envoi"; "The English Renaissance of Art"; "The Rise of Historical Criticism"

Although verse figured less prominently in Wilde's future, the poet's aims and attitudes lingered. Indeed, the three phases into which Edouard Roditi divided Wilde's poetic endeavours span his whole career and demonstrate radical changes in his approach to verse composition: 'From a sometimes absurdly self-assured loftiness . . . the poet had progressed [by the time of *The Ballad of Reading Gaol*] to a far more lyrical and intimately symbolic art where experience of his own life rather than of traditional art was his true subject matter.'[36] Roditi also posits a parallel shift from a poetic to a prose sublime: Parnassian lyrics and Romantic dramas give way to mythopoeic fiction and argumentative criticism. Though Roditi's exposition is confused here and there (for example, he treats Wilde's first blank verse drama, *The Duchess of Padua*, as prose), his account is convincing in general terms, and finds support, besides, in a remark in "The English Renaissance of Art": 'There is indeed a poetical attitude to be adopted towards all things, but all things are not fit subjects for poetry.' The 'harsh' and the 'disturbing' should never be admitted into 'the secure and sacred house of Beauty', Wilde says. If an artist wishes to treat 'the social problems of the day', then he will do so, 'as

Milton nobly expressed it, with his left hand, in prose and not in verse, in a pamphlet and not a lyric'.[37] While such an attitude is clearly not a nineteenth-century prerogative, it closely resembles the late-Romantic tendency to reserve poetry as 'the Holy of Holies'.[38] According to Roditi, Wilde eventually chose the Romantic's only poetic alternative to this verse sublime, which was to regard any and every subject as potentially sublime, taking treatment as the sole test. This view, also, finds support in the shape of Wilde's career, most notably in the change from Impressionist lyrics to poems in prose and the prose-poetry of *Salomé* which were based on French 'pure' poetics. It might also be justified by parts of the *Ballad*. Its weakness is that it leads Roditi to treat the tales and dialogues primarily as significant technique, and the anti-sublime comedies merely as specimens of 'self-degradation'.

Indeed, under closer scrutiny, Roditi's theory appears to be based on certain assumptions which are foreign to Wilde's interests and temperament. For an aesthete, the distinction between 'the experience of traditional art' and 'the experience of his own life' will not seem particularly useful. Much of Wilde's work, whether in verse or prose, was clearly devoted to showing that the two experiences could often, or should always, be one and the same. Rather than simply giving up poetry together with the Aesthetic attitudes which had dominated it, Wilde translated the aestheticism of his early verse into the far more intelligent and informed critic's stance – that awareness of art's diverse aims and methods that he developed in book reviews and dialogues. Clearly, he was still searching for a satisfactory form, or forms, of personal sublime, and it is interesting to see how devices from certain early poems are transformed in the critical dialogues; but the poet-lover's fantasies yield to an ideal of philosophic culture approached by means of the critical spirit. The change of allegiance was never complete or whole-hearted, but it echoes, even in its ambivalence, certain cross-currents in Romantic theory. In 1811, Schelling had heralded 'the poet-prophet who will sing the greatest of all epics, of which the theme will be the journey back to the lost paradise, or golden age, which is the restoration of a lost unity of the human intellect with itself and nature'.[39] No such work was for the moment forthcoming (Wordsworth's English epic of poetic growth and sensibility being still unpublished), and Schelling's judgement that the time was not ripe may reflect, M. H. Abrams says, 'the circumstance that he himself had begun a nature epic, but then had given it up'. Wilde's poetic projections of ecstatic reunion with the golden age had similarly lacked conviction and instead of impetuous self-centred passion he now offered a programme of gradual individualistic culture. For all their rhetoric, "The Critic as Artist" and "The Soul of Man" elaborate the new Hellenism from a specifically critical standpoint. As it happened, Schelling's hoped-for epic had been anticipated, in philosophic form, by Hegel's *Phenomenology of the Spirit* (1807), and it is the Hegelian prose tradition rather than the tradition of the English or German poet-prophet that stands behind Wilde's new sublime.

In the midst of so much theory it would be unwise to overlook the practical aspect: poetry seldom pays, and Wilde earned more from verse as a lecturer than he ever did as a poet. However, criticism is not especially lucrative either; and Wilde had little time to devote to it until he was well established in the brief sinecure, or virtual sinecure, of the editorship of the *Woman's World,* in which his wife, Constance, appears to have assisted him.

In 1883, besides, Wilde was not immediately beset with financial worries. He settled in Paris with the remaining proceeds of his American lecture tour, aiming at serious work. He refused one invitation, to Rome, on the grounds that he intended not 'to stir from my little rooms over the Seine till I have finished two plays. This sounds ambitious, but we live in an age of inordinate personal ambition and I am determined that the world shall understand me'. The drama is 'the meeting place of art and life' and would occupy a large proportion of his time in future.[40] All that emerged was a revision of *The Duchess of Padua,* the refusal of which by Mary Anderson was soon followed by the failure of *Vera* in New York in August. Fortunately he had other ambitions to fall back on. 'The rhythmical value of prose has never been fully tested,' he wrote to Sherard, sending him a copy of "L'Envoi" to show what he had in mind. 'I hope to do some more work in that *genre,* as soon as I have sung my Sphinx to sleep, and found a trisyllabic rhyme for catafalque.'[41]

The Sphinx was Wilde's only poetic endeavour in Paris, and its relationship with "L'Envoi" (written in the United States in 1882) neatly embodies his modified literary priorities. Unpublished until 1894 (back in London, Wilde was still searching for a rhyme[42]), *The Sphinx* is a prosodic tour-de-force which irritated lovers of Tennyson's *In Memoriam* (Wilde pointed out that the true precedent for his couplets was Elizabethan), but owed far more to Flaubert's *La Tentation de Sainte Antoine* (1874) or Rossetti's "The Burden of Nineveh" than to the laureate. Apart from its value as a technical exercise (the poem seems to have been started at Magdalen), its main purpose was to allow Wilde to play charades with the Muse-Sphinx of personality. "L'Envoi", no less self-conscious, is also semi-autobiographical mythopoeia, a tour-de-force of cadenced prose intended to preface a friend's lyrics[43] but effectively upstaging them. Its manner shows the influence of Pater's criticism, and in 1883 Wilde would have had his advice freshly in mind: 'Why do you always write poetry? Why do you not write prose? Prose is so much more difficult.'[44] The anecdote did not appear in print until 1890, by which time Wilde could have been seen to have profited by it; but the context in which it did so – his appreciation of Pater's *Appreciations*–points back to Wilde's first period. 'In Mr Pater,' he says, 'as in Cardinal Newman, we find the union of personality with perfection'. Eight years earlier, Wilde had presented this union as the motive force of the Aesthetic Movement, making it the chief theme of his lecture, "The English Renaissance of Art".[45] His allusion to it now, at the height of his critical career, is only superficially surprising, for the lecture contains the seeds of many future works and formed the theoretical basis for the critical dialogues.

Within the 'English Renaissance', 'personality' and 'perfection' are represented by the 'spirit of romance' and the 'Hellenic spirit'. The characteristics of the former are 'its variety of expression and the mystery of its vision', those of the latter 'its clearness of vision and its sustained calm'. Wilde tends to juggle with definitions here: 'What is romance but humanity?'; 'What is medievalism, said Mazzini, but individuality?'. Still, the English Renaissance of art emerges as a kind of aesthetic equivalent to Arnold's golden mean: a blend of spontaneous individualism and calm detachment, medievalism and Hellenism, in which what might become narrow in its view and over-intense in its emotional response is tempered by clarity of conception and the discipline of formal control. To this golden mean it adds, however, a distinct personality: 'whatever of artistic value the intricacy and complexity and experience of modern life can give'. Classically formal, it is 'romantic' – and therefore, in Wilde's terms, modern – in choosing 'the momentary situation of life' and 'the momentary aspect of truth'.

The implication is that here we have the perfected voice of the century. Yet the figures who constitute the 'Renaissance' – Whistler, Albert Moore, Rossetti, Swinburne, Morris (and Morris & Co.), Burne-Jones – often speak with rather different voices, and Wilde's definition may be traced to his admiration for Keats, in whom 'the artistic spirit of this century first found its absolute incarnation'. Keats's qualities – 'the calmness and clearness of his vision, his unerring sense of beauty and his recognition of a separate realm for the imagination' – found an echo in the Pre-Raphaelites whose subject-matter, though non-Hellenic, was handled with that 'love of definite conception', that antipathy to 'the transcendental spirit', which marks not merely 'Greek' but 'all great art'.[46] The artist, Wilde declares, can find 'no escape from the bondage of the earth', nor does he desire any;[47] and successive works confirm this idea. 'The mystery of the world,' says Gilbert in "The Critic as Artist", 'is not the invisible but the visible.' Even *Salomé*, superficially Symbolist, and therefore putatively expressive of 'the essence of the transcendental spirit', is devoted to the glories of what can be seen. In *De Profundis*, Wilde recalled his steadfastness to 'the concrete', observing that he had been, like Gautier, one 'pour qui le monde visible existe'.[48] Towards the end of that letter, he predicted a 'Mystical' element in his future, but on his release into the concrete world, the concrete soon reasserted its familiar dominion.

The lecture contains, then, a number of Wilde's most important aesthetic convictions. Love of the concrete should never be confused with trivial realism, which is an insidious growth of subjectivity. The true artist recognises that all art is formally objective and therefore ideal. 'Art never harms itself by keeping aloof from the social problems of the day: rather, by so doing, it more completely realises for us that which we desire.'[49]

Already Wilde sees the possibility, realised in "The Critic as Artist", of turning Plato from a moral philosopher into an aesthetician: the artist, we learn, is 'the spectator of all time and all existence', so that, while inevitably 'the child of his age', he will realise that 'for him no form is obsolete, no subject out of date'. His sense of artistic selection will enable him to treat any and all in ways which will reveal their 'beautiful life'. Here, already, is the theoretical basis, in Wilde's own work, for that shift to Roditi's second variety of sublime.

A further corollary of this argument for objectivity was to be developed in "The Critic as Artist" and "The Decay of Lying". The artist's perfect poise is often disturbed by the 'restless modern intellectual spirit'. 'Only a few, escaping from the tyranny of the soul, have learned the secret of those high hours when thought is not.'[50] The importance of oriental influences upon western art lies here: 'the East has always kept true to art's primary and pictorial traditions'. This foreshadows the conclusion in "The Critic as Artist" – again founded in Plato – that the truly moral arts are those that 'touch us', not those that 'teach us'.

Finally, the paradox of *Dorian Gray* is already formulated. Art has often been called an escape from 'the tyranny of the senses', Wilde says, but 'it is an escape rather from the tyranny of the soul'.[51] (That Wilde's 'soul' combines both intellectual and spiritual qualities affords a further point of comparison with the protagonist of Hegel's *Phenomenology* of the 'spirit', or 'mind'.) And the lecture provides readymade one of the aphorisms comprising the novel's Preface: 'One should never talk of an immoral poem: poems are either well written or badly written, that is all.' The only change necessary in 1891 was to substitute 'book' for 'poem'.

Although the lecture is principally devoted to the creative arts, both fine and decorative, it also reveals Wilde's early concern for the critical faculty. 'In nations, as in individuals, if the passion for creation be not accompanied by the critical, the aesthetic faculty also, it will be sure to waste its strength aimlessly.'[52] Goethe, observes Wilde, felt the need to protest against the dominating claims of the understanding, but the nineteenth-century artist must protest rather against 'the claims of sentiment or mere feeling'. This conviction eventually shaped the comedies.

The earliest significant evidence of Wilde's critical interests, however, is to be found in the ambitious and unsuccinct essay, "The Rise of Historical Criticism", entered for the Chancellor's Essay Prize at Oxford in 1879.[53] Its theme is civilisation's gradual emancipation from the influence of primitive superstition, inhibiting cultural traditions, and religious dogma by means of the cultivation of the critical instinct. Wilde defines historical criticism as partly a faculty and partly an attitude. It is one aspect of 'that complex working towards freedom which may be described as the revolt against authority, . . . part of that speculative spirit of innovation, which in the sphere of action produces democracy and revolution, and in that of thought is the parent of philosophy and physical science'.[54] Its importance lies less in 'the results that it attains' than in 'the tone of thought which it represents, and the methods by which it works'. The 'material despotisms of Asia' and the 'stationary civilisation of Egypt' cannot sustain it, while in China 'free criticism is as unknown as free trade'. Its beginnings are to be found among the Greeks, to whom 'we owe all that moves in the world except the blind forces of nature'; for, ever since their migration to the Aegean, their race has been characterised by the 'search for light', and 'the spirit of historical criticism is part of that wonderful Aufklärung or illumination of the intellect which seems to have burst on the Greek race like a great flood of light about the sixth century B.C.'.[55]

Much of the essay is concerned with the relation between myth, mythopoeia and fact. At an early stage, Wilde argues the inadequacy of ancient attempts to rationalise inherited myth and present the resultant 'dry husk' as historical fact. In his rhetorical conclusion he deliberately chooses two myths from the two dominant western European cultures – Greek and Christian – and interprets them symbolically. Here is the first:

> It was the fashion of early Italian painters to represent in medieval costume the soldiers who watched over the tomb of Christ, and this, which was the result of the frank anachronism of all true art, may serve to us as an allegory. For it was in vain that the Middle Ages strove to guard the buried spirit of progress. When the dawn of the Greek spirit arose, the sepulchre was empty, the grave-clothes laid aside. Humanity had risen from the dead.[56]

The education of the modern spirit by ancient thought sent Columbus to seek the new world and launched Copernicus on his new astronomical theory, the one following Aristotle, the other, Pythagoras. At this point the second image appears:

> Out of the melancholy sea of medievalism rose the free spirit of man in all that splendour of glad adolescence, when the bodily powers seem quickened by a new vitality, when the eye sees more clearly than its wont and the mind apprehends what was beforetime hidden from it.[57]

The resurrection of Christ comes to represent for the Renaissance the rebirth of humanity; the birth of Venus, the surfacing of 'the free spirit of man' after its long though temporary immersion in the sub-critical, retro-evolutionary state.

The former image was adapted in "Shakespeare and Stage Costume" to convey the imaginative reality of archaeology for the Renaissance mind. The latter, of Venus rising, suggests both the poem, "Vita Nuova" (roughly contemporary with the essay) and the story which seems to have grown out of it, "The Fisherman and his Soul". The 'argent splendour of white limbs' glimpsed by the poem's world-weary fisherman may be a racial as well as a personal vision promising cultural as well as psychological rejuvenation:

'Across the drear waste of a thousand years the Greek spirit and the modern spirit join hands.'[58] Although the argument is not fully worked out, Wilde suggests through these images that the critical spirit can bring about just such a fusion – perhaps, even, an identification of divine and profane love, sense and soul, for the spiritual rebirth of Christ and the physical birth of a new Venus herald the same cultural state. Significantly, the redemptive, reintegrating power of criticism projected at the end of "The Critic as Artist" and in "The Soul of Man under Socialism" is anticipated by Wilde's concluding sentence here:

> In the torch race which the Greek boys ran from the Cerameican field of death to the home of the goddess of Wisdom, not merely he who first reached the goal but he also who first started with the torch aflame received a prize. In the Lampadephoria of civilisation and free thought let us not forget to render due meed of honour to those who first lit that sacred flame, the increasing splendour of which lights our footsteps to the far-off divine event of the attainment of perfect truth.[59]

Between 1882 and 1890 Wilde was to divide his time largely between short stories and occasional criticism. In both genres he built on the technical basis established in "L'Envoi", experimenting with the formal possibilities of the modern Endymion's makeshift. He also began to consider the imaginative possibilities of the lapse into thought, the fall from the pastoral state. In the high society stories, the theme is carried to no definite conclusion. In *The Happy Prince*, the keynotes are 'personality' and 'perfection' and the relation in which action places them. The lapse itself is only intermittently an issue. In *A House of Pomegranates*, Wilde continues to ring the changes on 'states of nature', but the lapse now becomes the central theme. Though still working in an 'ideal' and essentially pastoral, or non-intellectualising, form, Wilde brings the artist up to date. Works expounding the 'modern' viewpoint of the critic follow in quick succession: "The Portrait of Mr W. H.", *The Picture of Dorian Gray*, the critical dialogues, "The Soul of Man under Socialism". The unfinished verse plays, *A Florentine Tragedy* and *The Cardinal of Avignon*,[60] represent a continuing attempt to find a convincing format for romantic aspirations in verse, but their fragmentary state tells its own tale. Wilde's last and intensest expression of the romantic sublime was a play written in prose, *Salomé*, at a point when his critical interests had already yielded a fresh approach to drama, 'the meeting place of art and life', in the shape of contemporary comedies of manners. Pater's admonitory paradox may well have been crucial in awakening Wilde's critical sense of his own capacities.

III Fiction as Ingratiation – First Attempts at a Social Pastoral: "Lord Arthur Savile's Crime", "The Canterville Ghost", "Lady Alroy", "The Model Millionaire"

Wilde's four smart stories have the easy charm of frankly occasional writing. Two appeared in a fashionable journal and marriage gazette, two in a weekly that wedged brief fictions between parliamentary problems and the racing news.[61] They were not collected until 1891. Critics agreed that the new volume, *Lord Arthur Savile's Crime and Other Stories*, would not add much to its author's reputation. Wilde himself must have known it, yet he had changed nothing but one title and added only a set of subtitles which parody Whistler's – a gesture which may have been intended to continue the Wilde-Whistler battle of wit (Whistler's acidulous *Gentle Art of Making Enemies* had appeared the previous year), and which draws Wilde's bits of narrative gossamer into conscious competition with the painter's 'minimal' art.

This is especially true of "The Sphinx without a Secret – *An Etching*" (formerly "Lady Alroy") and "The Model Millionaire – *A Note of Admiration*", neither of which is more than an expanded epigram. The latter has been compared with James's story "The Real Thing", but the difference in scope between them hardly warrants it. The only resemblance is the assumption that the painter's model is a willing accomplice in art's illusionism. James's artist cannot make use of Major and Mrs Monarch because they are just what they look and can never be or look otherwise. Wilde's, instead of unsuccessfully extending kindness to a genteel couple out-at-elbows, profitably humours a rich man's whim to be painted as a beggar. Wilde may have taken the idea from his "Note in Black and White on Mr Whistler's Lecture":

> Popular is he, this poor peripatetic professor of posing, with those whose joy it is to paint the posthumous portrait of the last philanthropist who, in his lifetime, had neglected to be photographed, – yet, he is the sign of the decadence, the symbol of decay. For all costumes are caricatures.[62]

However, his 2,000 words really hang on the closing epigram – 'Millionaire models . . . are rare enough; but, by Jove, model millionaires are rarer still!' – which neatly discredits the 'great truths of modern life' stated with pragmatic conciseness at the opening: 'Romance is the privilege of the rich, not the profession of the unemployed. . . . It is better to have a permanent income than to be fascinating.' Social appearance and personal reality are often at odds, but here everyone benefits from life's oddity: the millionaire gets his thrill, the painter gets a fine price, the young man kind to a beggar gets his girl. In this ideal, or ironic, social pastoral, money buys poetic justice.

"The Sphinx without a Secret" is even thinner, although it plays with one of Wilde's persistent themes, modern life's want of mystery. Lady Alroy is a poor impression of Pater's Mona Lisa – 'a Gioconda in sables'–and a pale reflection of Wilde's unborn Salomé–'a moonbeam in grey lace'. Here the reference to Whistler is specific, for Wilde had written to him from America asking, 'The Moon-Lady, the Grey Lady, the beautiful wraith with the beryl eyes, our Lady Archie, how is she?' Whistler had begun a portrait of Lady Archibald Campbell, *The Grey Lady*, which he destroyed unfinished,[63] but a completed portrait survives. Its title, *Arrangement in Black: Lady in a Yellow Buskin*, was a topical archaism: the picture was first exhibited in 1884, in June of which year Lady Archie's pastoral production of *As You Like It* opened. (Wilde reviewed the revival in 1885.) The full-length figure is shown wearing a fur hat and tippet, and turning away with an ambiguous smile into a shadowy background (see plate 5).

The point of Wilde's story is its emptiness. The scene is set for mystery, only to be invaded by prosaic common sense and formless accident. Instead of being a 'woman in white' shrouded in secrets, Lady Alroy is a fashionable hostess in 'a tea-gown looped up by some strange moonstones that she always wore', bored stiff. The whiff of Wilkie Collins is a false scent: the suspect is merely a living exponent of Wildean mythopoeia fighting the good fight of fancy against annihilating fact. The bemused lover fails to solve this simple secret, and, while he cools his heels in Norway, she catches a fatal chill at the Opera. The landlady of her former hideaway can only tell him plain truth: 'She simply sat in the drawing room, sir, reading books, and sometimes had tea'; and the narrator is equally disenchanting: 'Lady Alroy was simply a woman with a mania for mystery. She took these rooms for the pleasure of going there with her veil down, and imagining herself a heroine. She had a passion for secrecy, but she herself was a Sphinx without a secret.' The story may have developed a hint from Henry James,[64] but its chief purpose is to prove Wilde's contention that 'Nowadays it is only the unreadable that occurs', and it points straight towards the mythopoeic practice of "The Portrait of Mr W. H." and the precepts of "The Decay of Lying".

Slight as they are, these sketches are essentially metaphorical: a *jeune premier* and a Society belle circumvent conventional blocks to self-fulfilment. The two longer pieces similarly form a pair which represents, among other things, Wilde's debut as a fashionable writer rather than as a mere personality. Changing direction from the lyrics, reviews, one essay of minority interest, and the unsuccessful verse drama which had comprised his output since *Poems*, Wilde now tries his hand at three popular conventions: detective story, ghost story, and fairy tale. In the anecdotes about the millionaire and the 'Sphinx', elements of the first and the third are traceable. In "Lord Arthur Savile's Crime" and "The Canterville Ghost" all three are developed and refashioned by Wilde's characteristic irony. "Lord Arthur

Savile's Crime", for instance, takes up two of them at once. The blend of detective story and fairy tale works so well that without the ironic subtitle Wilde's double motive might pass unnoticed. While entertaining others with a parody of Society romance, he amuses himself by guying a serious Victorian, and personal, theme: the elusive equation between one's duty to society and one's duty to oneself.

"Lord Arthur Savile's Crime–A Study of Duty": *The Self-sufficient Hero*
In terms of the detective story, Wilde's hero is both sleuth and criminal. Tipped off by Podgers the palmist, an informer from the psychic 'underworld', he sets out in search of the destined murder victim. His only clue – false, as it transpires – is that it will be 'a distant relation'. After two unsuccessful attempts to keep homicide within the family, Lord Arthur decides to rely on intuition. Now the fairy tale takes over. No sooner has the hero, despondent at his task and despairing of the maiden who waits beyond it, determined (like the hero of Tennyson's "Maud") that 'there is always some war in which a man can give his life' and that he should let 'Destiny' reveal 'the doom assigned' to him, than he is nudged by the hand of providence. Strolling along the Thames Embankment, he lights at once upon his object. The triumphant detective finds that the informant is identical with the victim; the able felon tips him into the river. The long-delayed marriage can now take place unthreatened, and the couple live happily for 'some years', devout believers in the chiromantic art.

From this fusion of the two traditions Wilde creates an imaginative metaphor identifying the criminal 'underworld' with the world of the unconscious. The personality's two halves are expressed by reference to light and landscape: daytime and the innocence of countryside or Park are contrasted with night and the city's corruption. Building on this basis, Christopher Nassaar has argued that the story is a fable of initiation which introduces Lord Arthur to his darker self, personified by Podgers, whom he must vanquish before he can pass on to unite himself with Sybil, the ideal part of his nature, thus reaching 'the higher innocence'. The notion that Wilde's detective story encloses a hunt for the hero's real self is a striking one, and receives strong support from the various parallels with *Dorian Gray*. However, Nassaar chooses to emphasise the 'Naturalist' settings in which the real world of evil, the 'demon universe' that enveloped Wilde, finds its characteristic expression. For him, there is something almost sacramental about the hero's nocturnal wanderings:

> Before 12:00 p.m., Arthur's world is a beautiful but tainted one. It is dominated by the moon and an exquisite star-spangled 'hollow purple dome'; but it also contains such disturbingly unaesthetic elements as barges, a turbid stream, and shrieking trains. After 12:00 p.m., this world begins to fade away – lights go out, the roar of the city grows faint – and entirely fabulous dreamworld of silver and shadow emerges, wrapped in the religious aura of the huge, lofty dome of St Paul's. The time for his salvation has come.[65]

But there are dangers in treating so facetious a story as coherent psychology or symbolism, particularly when Wilde uses good and evil as decorative elements in an aesthetic entertainment. Aloofness from the true force of virtue or evil is, however, characteristic of literary pastoral, and I suggest that Wilde gives us a sophisticated exercise in that manner.

Lord Arthur, like Dorian Gray, has hitherto lived an upper-class idyll 'exquisite in its freedom from sordid care, its beautiful boyish insouciance'. After his consultation with Podgers, he dashes out into the night. First he comes to the Park, 'whose sombre woodland seemed to fascinate him'. Like an Adam already fallen into knowledge, he 'leaned wearily up against the railings, cooling his brow against the wet metal, and listening to the tremulous silence of the trees'. Soon he makes his way through 'a labyrinth of sordid houses' and emerges at dawn in Piccadilly. Returning home, he meets some 'white-smocked carters' riding 'with their rough, good-humoured voices and their nonchalant ways' to sell their produce at Covent Garden market. The pastoral reference, absent from the parallel passage in *Dorian Gray*, is here specific: 'Rude as they were, with their heavy, hob-nailed shoes, and their awkward gait, they brought a little of Arcady with them. He felt that they had lived with Nature, and that she had taught them peace.' They are ignorant of the city's 'splendour' and 'shame', its 'fierce, fiery-coloured joys, and its horrible hunger, of all it makes and mars from morn to eve', and he envies them 'all that they did not know'. Significantly, however, this feeling drains away with his morning bath-water: the 'exquisite physical conditions' of his sumptuous bathroom 'had dominated him, as indeed often happens in the case of very finely-wrought natures, for the senses, like fire, can purify as well as destroy'.

The midnight catastrophe perfects the self-consciously aesthetic pastoral by invoking the example of Whistler. The painterly lyrics with which Wilde had experimented in the early 1880s are thriftily adapted here to a prose context. "Impression du Matin" (1881), for instance, contains 'country waggons', the dome of St Paul's which 'loomed like a bubble', and the river with its barges. Far from being 'unaesthetic', the barges are virtually the hallmark of the Whistlerian nocturne; and Lord Arthur's sudden change of mood – or the city's sudden self-transformation – resembles nothing so closely as Nature's magical apotheosis at the climax of the "Ten O'Clock" lecture:

> And when the evening mist clothes the riverside with poetry, as with a veil, and the poor buildings lose themselves in the dim sky, and the tall chimneys become campanili, and the warehouses are palaces in the night, and the whole city hangs in the heavens, and fairyland is before us – then the wayfarer hastens home; the working man and the cultured one, the wise man and the man of pleasure, cease to understand, as they have ceased to see, and Nature, who, for once, has sung in tune, sings her exquisite song to the artist alone.[66]

It is surely into this world, the amoral world of pastoral or 'fairyland', that Lord Arthur is briefly initiated. He passes not from the world of aristocratic innocence into the world of Naturalist guilt and squalor so much as from the pastoral state of self-ignorance into the equally secure state of art-pastoral (a phase through which Dorian Gray also passes). The dreamlike vision of Wilde's 'nocturne' is the cultural equivalent of the London seen by the Arcadian carters, 'a London free from the sin of night and the smoke of day, a pallid ghost-like city, a desolate town of tombs'. Such a vision can be reached only by the Whistlerian artist, or by someone whose nature is no less 'finely-wrought'; and when Lord Arthur attains to it he is suddenly confronted with the truly unaesthetic Podgers – 'the fat, flabby face, the gold-rimmed spectacles, the sickly feeble smile, the sensual mouth' – whom he pushes into the river. (One remembers that Wainewright, Wilde's next criminal subject, admitted to having murdered a woman because 'she had thick ankles'.) The river, acting this once, like Whistler's Nature, in accord with moment and mood, reveals under aesthetic conditions even the final trace of the victim: 'a tall hat, pirouetting in an eddy of moonlit water'. Already we can see that Wilde's characteristic epiphanies tend to occur when masterful instinct is ratified by art.

After such skilful avoidance of any real moral confrontation, Wilde produces the inevitable happy ending. Even the tell-tale traces of crime disappear – for a corpse would be as disturbing here as in a pastoral by Boucher. But, as in most murder mysteries, the resolution is disappointing: the comic brainwave passes, its energies dissipate. If idle domestic bliss is really a 'higher innocence', it is most uninviting. Indeed, what we are shown is less progression than regression. For a while, it seems that the hero will be changed by contact with life's perilous demands: 'one would have said that Nemesis had stolen the shield of Pallas, and shown him the Gorgon's head. He seemed turned to stone, and his face was like marble in its melancholy.' Soon, however, he is saved by providential irony, comic twin to poetic justice. He turns the goddess of knowledge's paralysing mirror upon her own, visiting the prediction upon the predicter. And so, for the ideal social sweethearts, 'romance was not killed by reality', and their future stretches away into the sunset, perfect. They retire to a sort of country Camelot;[67] but as Lord Henry Wotton later observes, 'anybody can be good in the country. There are no temptations there. That is the reason why people who live out of town are so absolutely uncivilised. . . . They stagnate.'[68]

From these elegant evasions we may choose to infer a projection of Wilde's domestic plight and his ambiguous attitude towards it. Podgers then becomes, as Nassaar suggests, far more than a palmist, far closer than a 'distant relation'. We are at present so accustomed to full frontal exposure of sexual behaviour that Wilde's undeceptive 'poses' may seem merely embarrassing. Joyce felt something of this as early as 1906. Of *Dorian Gray* he observed: 'Wilde seems to have had some good intentions in writing it – some wish to put himself before the world – but the book is rather crowded with lies and epigrams. If he had had the courage to develop the allusions in the book it might have been better.'[69] It might have. Lord Arthur's escape into the country, like Wilde's various escapes into art, was achieved, we suspect, only at the expense of killing off (permanently 'submerging') half of his vital forces. But that very absence of adequate biographical detail which invites such speculation also denies it critical weight. We tend to overlook the fact that Wilde instinctively worked in images: even the Wildean epigram can be viewed as an attempt to make thought emblematic. Perhaps there is something naïve, then, in assuming that Wilde's weakness lay in not speaking out directly about his "problem". Art and personality are rarely such straightforward matters. The real underlying significance of "Lord Arthur Savile's Crime" is that here, for the first time, Wilde considers something of the effects of the unconscious upon personality and behaviour, and does it with remarkable comic poise. The psychic and the metropolitan underworld briefly fuse in an image of ugliness and chaos, and while he is exposed to it Lord Arthur remains unsure whether he is hunter or hunted, hero or villain, sane or mad.

Of course, it is only at the frivolous level that everything comes right. The preposterous contortions of the 'duty' theme make the rigid social norms look grotesque: morally, everything goes wrong, and self and society could not be further apart than they are here. Lord Arthur is obliged to win Society's palm by flouting society's most serious taboo. The irony lies in the fact that the desired ideal – perfect union between a sturdy man of action and an alluring virgin spared all nastiness – is a sentimental figment of a smug paternalistic culture, while the ideal which suffers – the right of any individual to society's protection from assassination at the whim of his fellows – is crucial to any civilised state. Allusions to *Hamlet* and to Wilde's own revenge tragedy compound the absurdity, and Wilde revels in the resultant sophistries:

> Many men in his position would have preferred the primrose path of dalliance to the steep heights of duty; but Lord Arthur was too conscientious to set pleasure above principle. . . . He was no mere dreamer or idle dilettante. Had he been so, he would have hesitated, like Hamlet, and let irresolution mar his purpose. But he was essentially practical. Life to him meant action, rather than thought. He had that rarest of all things, common sense.

In modern eyes, Laertes, not Hamlet, is the real hero. The only true 'common sense' shown in the play appears in Claudius' and Laertes' capable plot to murder the prince. The vagaries of the high-born humanist are eclipsed these days by the man of action's moral efficiency:

> For a moment he had a natural repugnance against what he was asked to do, but it soon passed away. His heart told him that it was not a sin but a sacrifice; his reason reminded him that there was no other course open. He had to choose

between living for himself and living for others, and terrible though the task laid upon him unboubtedly was, yet he knew that he must not suffer selfishness to triumph over love.

As Lord Henry Wotton later observes, 'It was the passions about whose origin we deceived ourselves that tyrannised most strongly over us. Our weakest motives were those of whose nature we were conscious.' Lord Arthur, we are told, did not possess a 'heart corroded by the shallow, fashionable egoism of our day, and he felt no hesitation about doing his duty'. He follows the exemplary egoism of instinct.

If Wilde's comic gloss on *Hamlet* is romping social satire, his treatment of *The Duchess of Padua* is less forthright. This early essay in the 'Jacobethan' tradition follows a classic revenge pattern. Guido has sworn to avenge his father but falls in love against his oath. When confronted by Moranzone, who insists that he accomplish the murder of his beloved's husband, he hesitates so long that she finally does the deed herself, whereupon Guido frantically rejects her. Lord Arthur conducts his affair in true Victorian style: 'he would never let her know what he was doing for her sake, and would keep the secret of his self-sacrifice hidden always in his heart'. By contrast with such decisiveness, Guido's poetic procrastination is the self-spoken epitaph of the social loser:

> I can endure no longer
> The dreadful oath, the strange and weird old man.
> The awful mission and the awful sign
> Are become dreams, shadows, and unreal things,
> But half remembered and but half believed:
> How can I carry murder in my heart
> When Love sits there upon his golden throne?[70]

Wilde understandably cut these feeble lines. I give them here because they summarise the relationship between story and play, showing how a romantic poetic extreme, self-admittedly fatal even within its own closed context, was adapted to a modern society setting. (*Vera* didn't escape either. One of Lord Arthur's partners in attempted crime is Count Rouvaloff, 'a young Russian of very revolutionary tendencies', formerly Colonel of the Imperial Guard in *Vera*, now reputed to be a Nihilist agent, though ostensibly researching the undercover life of Peter the Great.) The conditions chosen are admittedly absurd. Still, by imposing an anti-social labour through which the hero must prove his worth, Wilde is courting, if only in general terms, the norm's assent to the Romantic's exceptional personality. If only the exception can ape the norm in all the right ways, nothing will go amiss for him. Even his sins, if sins they are, will look splendid – so splendid, indeed, that modesty will forbid their publication: 'he was very anxious not to murder Lady Clementina in any way that might attract public attention, as he hated the idea of being lionised at Lady Windermere's, or seeing his name figuring in the paragraphs of vulgar society-newspapers'. The Romantic hero, it seems, is still all-deserving, and in deserving cases justice and poetic justice are co-extensive. Indeed, poetic justice may have extended even to the unfortunate Podgers. Wilde's numerous hints of his financial troubles raise the question of whether he may have been leaning on the parapet pondering suicide, so that by pushing him – even on purely egocentric impulse – Lord Arthur would be doing him a good turn.

In Wilde's comic world of the 1890s 'the dandy is self-sufficent and needs no pardon'.[71] In this contemporary aesthetic pastoral, halfway house between Romantic tragedy and modern comedy of manners, the Romantic egotist is equally self-sufficient. Pardon and trespass are cancelled by poetic justice; egotism is self-sacrifice for a socially laudable end; Romantic longing is the prerogative of the ostentatiously eligible young. In two further collections, *The Happy Prince* and *A House of Pomegranates*, Wilde extended his scope and freed his imagination, but he still chose to retain the pastoral framework with its transfiguring window upon, or against, the world.

"The Canterville Ghost – A Hylo-Idealistic Romance" : the Redemptive Heroine

In Chapter 4 of *The Portrait of a Lady* (1881), the transatlantic heroine opens her European inquiries by asking, 'Please tell me, isn't there a ghost?' The heir of Gardencourt observes sadly, 'I might show it to you, but you'd never see it. The privilege isn't given to everyone; it's not enviable. It has never been seen by a young, happy, innocent person like you. You must have suffered first, have suffered greatly, and gained some miserable knowledge. In that way your eyes are opened to it.' When at length Isabel has shared with her dying cousin the full extent of her miserable relationship with Osmond, the ghost appears briefly to her as a sign that Ralph now lies dead upstairs, and that the cycle he spoke of is now complete.

Wilde's socialite ghost story contains reversals of these two scenes, though whether it was intended as a recognisable parody of James is another matter. Vivian's stylistic objections to James in "The Decay of Lying" suggest sufficient impatience, and Wilde's own numerous echoes of the novel a sufficient admiration, to make successful parody feasible; but Wilde most probably recognised that parody, no less than 'the real thing', requires the willing sacrifice of egotism to a fastidious objectivity for the frugal reward of 'imperceptible "points of view"', and such sacrifice never tempted him.

Parody or not, the story is relentlessly topical. 'Innocents Abroad', glib reminiscences of New World life, 'an entirely new and original ghost',[72] and a Romantic virgin-heroine are combined in an entertainment which starts out as a high-class spoof of spooks (Wilde gleefully gives the pedigree of one of the Ghost's choicest victims) and ends up as an allegory of reconciliation between guilt and innocence, old world and new.

After the establishment of the Society for Psychical Research in 1882, interest quickly grew in the possibility of demonstrating 'the objective existence of phantasmata', and Wilde uses this interest, or lack of it, as the basis for his characterisations of the old and the new worlds. The established cultural prejudice and superstition of an ancient family is contrasted with the scepticism affected by practical republicans and members of the 'Free American Reformed Episcopalian Church'. Thus Canterville Chase becomes a kind of preposterous parallel to Northanger Abbey. Instead of a ghost too few there is one too many; instead of too much 'sensibility' there is too lit le. Whereas Catherine Morland does all she can to discover a non-existent horror by exercising her imagination, the Otis family sets out at first to disbelieve in all ghosts, then to treat the resident ghost as a tiresomely disorganised lodger. As the Ghost puts it, they are 'evidently people on a low, material plane of existence, and quite incapable of appreciating the symbolic value of sensuous phenomena'.

In 1891 came the intellectualising subtitle which draws attention to this aspect of the plot. The 'hylo-idealist' is the heroine, Virginia, who rescues the Ghost from his purgatory by believing in him and retaining that belief until he can find death. The idea can be paralleled by such fairy tales as "The Frog Prince", and Virginia has a fairy-tale innocence combined with a forthright ignorance reminiscent of Isabel Archer or Carroll's Alice. Indeed, the literary sources for the story are more varied than they might appear. For the Ghost's character, Wilde seems to have drawn hints from the two principal sources of "Pen, Pencil and Poison" – the life of Thomas Griffiths Wainewright and De Quincey's parody-essay "Murder Considered as one of the Fine Arts".[73] Gothick melodrama, Coleridge, and Tennyson are also laid under contribution. When Virginia first sees the Ghost, he is posing as the spasmodic hero of "Maud", sitting at a window and 'watching the ruined gold of the yellow trees fly through the air',[74] and observing how nature emulates the ghostly scene in "Christabel" by setting 'the red leaves dancing madly down the avenue'.[75] Their dialogue pits dandiacal aestheticism against the astringent frankness of Carroll's child-heroine:

> 'Mrs Umney told us, the first day we arrived here, that you had killed your wife.'
>
> 'Well, I quite admit it,' said the Ghost petulantly, 'but it was a purely family matter, and concerned no one else.'
>
> 'It is very wrong to kill any one,' said Virginia, who at times had a sweet Puritan gravity, caught from some old New England ancestor.
>
> 'Oh, I hate the cheap severity of abstract ethics! My wife was very plain, never had my ruffs properly starched, and knew nothing about cookery. Why, there was a buck I had shot in Hogley Woods, a magnificent pricket, and do you know how she had it sent up to table? However, it is no matter now, for it is all over, and I don't think it was very nice of her brothers to starve me to death, though I did kill her.'

Virginia's status as *ingénue* is clinched by her offering the Ghost a sandwich, and by her fondness for painting sunsets in watercolours. (Wilde habitually regarded a taste for sunsets as 'painfully natural': his parody *ingénue* in *Lady Windermere's Fan* is 'devoted to sunsets'.) Her status as redemptive heroine becomes clear when she stands resolute before the Ghost's interpretation of the prophecy in the library window: 'you must weep for me for my sins, because I have no tears, and pray with me for my soul, because I have no faith, and then, if you have always been sweet, and good, and gentle, the Angel of Death will have mercy on me. You will see fearful shapes in darkness, and wicked voices will whisper in your ear, but they will not harm you, for against the purity of a little child the powers of Hell cannot prevail.' There is an unexpected sexual substratum in this which the inappropriate reference to 'a little child' (Virginia is of marriageable age) does nothing to dissipate. However, at Virginia's reappearance it is soon forgotten. Wilde now opens every Gothick stop to prepare for his artificial conclusion:

> Just as they were passing out of the dining-room, midnight began to boom from the clock tower, and when the last stroke sounded they heard a crash and a sudden shrill cry; a dreadful peal of thunder shook the house, a strain of unearthly music floated through the air, a panel at the top of the staircase flew back with a loud noise, and out on the landing, looking very pale and white, with a little casket in her hand, stepped Virginia.

Such phrases as 'looking very pale and white' are careless, but carelessness is not inseparable from emptiness, and the fairy-tale format which now takes over has a validity independent of Wilde's self-indulgence. Virginia takes the family to look at the skeleton in the wainscot, and, as she kneels beside it in prayer, they see the fulfilment of the prophecy: the old almond tree has blossomed in the moonlight (marking the start of a sequence of sympathetically blossoming flora in Wilde's prose tales).

> 'God has forgiven him,' said Virginia gravely, as she rose to her feet, and a beautiful light seemed to illumine her face.
> 'What an angel you are,' cried the young Duke, and he put his arm round her neck and kissed her.

The pun defines the extent of this ideal, ironic, and ultimately patronising relationship. Virginia's vocabulary is basically moral, the Duke's basically social. The happy ending, with its sentimental mercenary marriage, is perfected by the Ghost's gift of a casket of jewels — an old-world dowry which may be financial or moral, depending on one's view of the story — and by her receiving 'the coronet, the reward of all good little American girls'. Her fastidious father does not object to the title, but does try, without success, to restore the jewels to the Cantervilles. Indeed, even Virginia's wish to keep only the casket he deplores as an 'alarming sympathy with medievalism', explicable only by 'the fact that she was born in one of your London suburbs after Mrs Otis had returned from a trip to Athens'.

A visit to Athens at so impressionable an age, a sympathy with medievalism, a reputation as a 'wonderful amazon', and a figure 'as lithe and lovely as a fawn' combine to make the heroine inclusively 'modern' as well as ideally pastoral. Her marriage achieves a corresponding cultural fusion: the fresh moral vision of the new world redeems the inherited misdeeds of the old. In the final scene – an optimistic and Gothicised echo, perhaps, of Warburton's interview with Isabel in the Coliseum – Wilde repeats the marriage of modern with historical. The couple stroll into 'the ruined chancel of the old abbey. There the Duchess sat down on a fallen pillar, while her husband lay at her feet smoking a cigarette and looking up at her beautiful eyes.' He asks what passed between the Ghost and herself, insisting that 'a wife should have no secrets from her husband'. She tells him merely that 'He made me see what Life is, and what Death signifies, and why Love is stronger than both.' With this the Duke professes himself content: 'You can have your secret as long as I have your heart'. Instinctive understanding of the forces represented by the Ghost belongs to the new world, not the old; but the marriage combines the best of both: the pastoral peace of the aristocracy and the moral insight of the Puritan. This conclusion is the feminist's answer to Lord Arthur: here the wife 'sacrifices' herself and keeps the details from her husband. For readers of the *Court and Society Review* such symmetry was doubtless important.

The American *ingénue* with Puritan principles and a large dowry reappeared in *A Woman of No Importance* to beard the aristocracy in its crumbling den; but by this time Wilde had evolved a consistent philosophy of dandyism and had begun to experiment with a revival of Restoration comic techniques. Surrounded by idlers far more effective as examples of the unscrupulous neo-Hobbesian hedonist than the Ghost could ever have been, even in his Regency days, the styleless prig from overseas can seem only the 'country wife' of the piece. There is no fusion of the two cultures; rather, there is mutual repulsion. English society, decides Hester Worsley, 'lies like a leper in purple', and she takes her future husband and his guilt-ridden unmarried mother to 'countries over sea, better, wiser, and less unjust', where they presumably inaugurate a post-lapsarian republican idyll financed by a large fortune. This play marked Wilde's last use of the ingenuous American. Significantly, it offers the only decisive proof of Mr Otis's naïve hunch that 'the laws of nature are not going to be suspended for the British aristocracy'.

IV. More Versions of Pastoral

Rarely studied as serious literature, though sometimes as miniature *tours de force*, Wilde's two collections of fairy tales have escaped extensive comment.[76] One reason for this – especially in the case of *The Happy Prince and*

Other Tales – is their supposed genesis in the Tite Street nursery. Perhaps the young Wildes did witness their father's improvisations; perhaps they heard the finished versions. But Cyril was only three and Vyvyan two years old when *The Happy Prince* appeared. If their pleasure was a stimulus, their comprehension can hardly have been a standard for composition.

The point is significant in view of disagreements about Wilde's intended audience and of dissatisfaction with the volume's ambiguous tone. Edouard Roditi, for instance, noticed that the simplicity of *The Happy Prince* which Yeats admired and thought due to its oral beginnings was really a highly sophisticated effect designed to charm highly sophisticated people.[77] For Roditi, however, this simplicity amounted to no more than 'an adult imitation of childish thinking', product of 'some deeply-rooted awkwardness or sense of guilt as an artist', so that Wilde's equivocal purpose in the stories would be to appeal to 'the Papas and Mamas of the upper-class nurseries of the late Victorian era' while satisfying a private urge towards intellectual slumming – 'simple pleasures' being 'the last refuge of the complex'.[78]

Wilde's own account of his aims is unambiguous. With one exception, all of his recorded remarks about the tales make it clear that they were not primarily children's stories. The exception occurs in a letter to Gladstone, to whom he sent a copy of *The Happy Prince*. Addressing the practical Premier and champion of Irish nationalism whose help he was later to solicit when trying to arrange a Civil List pension for Lady Wilde, he disparaged his book as 'only a collection of short stories' which were 'really meant for children'.[79] But to a fellow-author he spoke of them as 'studies in prose, put for Romance's sake into a fanciful form: meant partly for children, and partly for those who have kept the childlike faculties of wonder and joy, and who find in simplicity a subtle strangeness'.[80] Writing to another poet and playwright, he called them 'an attempt to mirror modern life in a form remote from reality – to deal with modern problems in a mode that is ideal and not imitative'. (This description anticipates the precepts of "The Decay of Lying", which was written the same year, 1889.) 'They are, of course,' he continued, 'slight and fanciful, and written, not for children, but for child like people from eighteen to eighty'.[81] And two years later, after *A House of Pomegranates* had baffled the press, he declared acidly, 'I had about as much intention of pleasing the British child as I had of pleasing the British public'.[82]

This seems straightforward enough; but one element is predictably missing from Wilde's summaries. For all their appeal as bedtime tales and their interest as moral or technical callisthenics, the stories have a highly subjective basis. Roditi noted this without specifying its nature. Richard Ellmann offers a simple biographical gloss: 'Wilde cancelled his nightmare of being found out with light-hearted dreams of pardon and transfiguration'.[83] Professor Ellmann believes that the fairy-tale element permeated Wilde's work, and such a view is bound to favour the devil's-advocate approach.

The notion of Wilde gaily rehearsing before his infant heirs a bowdlerised allegory of his future downfall is appalling and no doubt fantastic, but suggestive nevertheless. For, from the biographical, if not quite from the literary perspective, The Happy Prince can look very like a child's garden of egos, a collection of wise saws upon which its author was too clever to act, but which plainly preached the folly of that cult of personality which led him, at first deliciously, towards prison.

Wilde's own perspective on these matters broadened at Reading, where he recognised that much of his work, including The Happy Prince, had offered portents which he had not understood.[84] Apparently the artist, like Podgers, was blind to his own clairvoyance. This fact discounts conscious autobiographical parallels, at least in any systematised form, and weakens the quasi-psychoanalytic approach to a corresponding degree. Nassaar's theory – that both collections of fairy tales trace a growth from a childish to a higher innocence – is attractive in that it anchors these ambiguous volumes to a Romantic tradition pursued by Wilde with no less devotion than misgiving. Even so, searching for psychological rather than artistic motive – setting diagnosis above literary analysis – has its dangers. Robert Ross may have changed Wilde's life radically in 1886; but Wilde's Romantic (and, according to Rupert Croft-Cooke, his homosexual) proclivities were apparent several years earlier.[85] If biographical speculation is at all relevant here, one might argue no less plausibly that the recent birth of two sons brought the author-father to reflect on the qualities of childhood.[86] From this, it would have been small distance to a literary reconsideration of that condition which in Romantic eyes was synonymous with childhood: the psychic golden age, the state of pastoral self-ignorance, or innocence.

In A House of Pomegranates this became Wilde's main theme, but in The Happy Prince several elements vie for predominance. At first glance, some of the tales seem mere retreats from Nonconformist dullness or Decadent soul-weariness to a world of fancy where flowers talk, where both stars and walk-ons may be creatures or fireworks, and where even the seasons occasionally show a keen sense of the ethics of reward and punishment. But this kindergarten has its resident serpent: comic irony, two-faced agent of the 'fortunate fall'; and Wilde makes full use of it. The appearance of the humans in "The Remarkable Rocket", for instance, is as brilliant, as vapid, and as brief as a firework's career in an evening's festivities. The story of "The Devoted Friend", a 'story with a moral' concerning two humans, is a linnet's well-meaning fable of true friendship. The egotistical Water-rat tolerates the narrative at first, but loftily pooh-poohs it as soon as he learns of its didactic purpose. Thus, Wilde's unlikely cast ultimately serves a serious function. Their preposterous world is depressingly true. Humans and non-humans appear equally flawed. There is no retro-cultural pastoral condition available, no way out from personality even in fantasy: cynicism, self-importance, sentimentality, stupidity, and avarice exist even among lizards, rockets and roses. Occasionally idealism also exists, but unless sanctified by the intervention of divine love it fares no better than in the ordinary world. Anthropomorphism leads not back to nature, but back to man.

What, then, is the value of creating this fabulous world at all? The answer is partly that here Wilde can accommodate children at their true Romantic level. If *Poems* reveals the youth straining for adult inflexions, the fairy tales are the work of an adult fascinated by the young. Children stand for purity and simplicity – 'all those things', as Cecil Graham says in *Lady Windermere's Fan* to a roomful of dimwits and dandies, 'that we men have lost'. They show an instinctive understanding of the forces of nature; they can bring springtime to a garden merely by their presence; they 'cry for the moon'; they alone have the imagination, or the candour, to compare the Happy Prince's statue with the angels seen 'in our dreams', defying pedagogic disapproval; they are identified with flowers because of the beauty, freedom, and natural organic growth of their personalities.

This view of childhood obviously owes something to Blake and Wordsworth, both of whom would have disliked it. It is related also to Wilde's praise of the child-like personality in "The Soul of Man under Socialism" and to his later argument (in *De Profundis*) that Christ 'took children as the type of what people should try to become. He held them up as examples to their elders, which I myself have always thought the chief use of children, if what is perfect should have a use.'[87] Wilde did the same. Like his various poems in prose, the tales are essentially parables; but instead of presenting images of the desirable, they emerge, as often as not, sermons by a sceptic to the relentlessly unconverted. While the Biblical parable is intrinsically didactic and incidentally narrative, Wilde's parables tend to be intrinsically narrative and only incidentally didactic, even though their 'moral' basis, in the general sense of the word, is unmistakable. Hence the confusion and dissatisfaction over Wilde's narrative tone. For the evangelist's static conviction Wilde substitutes the multiple perspective of the over-educated modern to whom 'a moral' is a childish commodity. The only story with an explicit moral is "The Devoted Friend", which admonishes its readers' never to tell a story with a moral. Wilde's characteristic morals are anti-morals.

I suggested earlier that part of the function of the pastoral world in *The Happy Prince* was to accommodate the Romantic child. It is also a screen for the intellectual subversive. Wilde makes 'the child as swain'[88] at home; but to balance this ideal figure he introduces the comic child-sage, prominent in "The Devoted Friend" and "The Happy Prince". A year later, as if to bear out his conviction that 'to be premature is to be perfect',[89] Wilde cast 'Cyril' and 'Vivian' as the iconoclastic disputants of "The Decay of Lying"; but this is only a hint of the potential for creative subversion that he perceived in the young. His review of Mark Twain's article "English as She is Taught" (1887) is clearly the precursor of the narrative child-sage:

Though the Oracles are dumb, and the Prophets have taken to the turf, and the Sibyls are reduced to telling fortunes at bazaars, the ancient power of divination has not yet left the world. Mr Mark Twain's fascinating article, in the current number of the Century Magazine, on "English as She is Taught" in his native country, throws an entirely new light on that *enfant terrible* of a commercial civilisation, the American child, and reminds us that we may still learn wisdom from the mouths of babes and sucklings. For the mistakes made by the interesting pupils of the American Board-Schools are not mistakes springing from ignorance of life or dulness of perception; they are, on the contrary, full of the richest suggestion, and pregnant with the highest philosophy. No wonder that the American child educates its father and mother, when it can give us such luminous definitions as the following:

Republican, a sinner mentioned in the Bible.
Demagogue, a vessel containing beer and other liquids.
The Constitution of the United States, that part of the book at the end which nobody reads.
Plagiarist, a writer of plays.[90]

The ingenuous young American who in "The Canterville Ghost" had redeemed an elder generation now becomes the child who schools its betters. Age and authority are suddenly far more insidious threats than cultural provincialism. Even the over-educated dandy, far removed from childhood, one might think, realises the folly of listening to people older than himself.[91]

What, then, are we left with? The review's 'child-philosopher' has great comic potential, and the prospect of writing a book to be bought by other Papas and Mamas and read to their children, only to reveal the child as the true mentor, clearly appealed to Wilde. On the other hand, the pure imaginative response of children is artistically static. It defies narrative development, and in its sporadic absence Wilde succeeds no less well – perhaps all the better – in tackling one of the child's, and the artist's, earliest lessons: the proper balance between egotism and altruism. We can say, also, that these five brief tales 'put for Romance's sake into a fanciful form' establish Wilde's characteristic stance. Two tales offer ideal conclusions ("The Happy Prince" and "The Selfish Giant"). Alternating with these are two which end sceptically ("The Nightingale and the Rose" and "The Devoted Friend"). The fifth parodies aspects of both, and with unflagging irony laughs off the entire question. The Remarkable Rocket is a transcendent egotist, an over-reacher, who maintains himself in a paradise of one by wilful self-ignorance. When at last he achieves an obscure blast-off, he has no audience but himself. Though born to great things, he opts for self-destructive egotism, and holds by it. Taken as a whole, the collection shows Wilde opting, at present, for nothing in particular – a precaution, or whim, which makes all the more striking the potential parallel between the Rocket's comic climacteric and Wilde's own fate.

Such parallels are the critics' amusement. Meanwhile the author's amusement tends to pass unnoticed: there are various indications that the Rocket was intended as a portrait of Whistler.

V.   The Happy Prince and Other Tales

"The Happy Prince"
The title-story of *The Happy Prince and Other Tales* brings together two types of carefree egotist each of whom discovers through personal experience the superior claims of altruism over that hedonistic impulse which is presented as the natural, happy, and therefore 'innocent' motive for behaviour. The Prince's life was perfectly happy in the walled garden of the palace of Sans-Souci. Now, after his death (we overlook the fact that he must have died young), those less fortunate than he have set up his likeness as an image of the desirable. Complete happiness suggests perfection of form – so the innocent hedonist is replaced by a gilded statue. For all its outward perfection, however, the statue can suffer; and from his new pedestal the Prince sees the ugly realities previously shut out from his world. His penance is to stand as a monument to that perfect happiness which he now realises to have been imperfect and illusory, and to strip away his beautiful surface until he becomes blind and ugly, 'little better than a beggar', and fit only for the rubbish heap, at which point divine love transfigures him.

Two related elements impinge on this redemptive pattern: the innocent hedonism of the Swallow, and the pompous egocentricity of the utilitarian Town Councillors and the speciously intellectual Professors.

The Swallow is a natural and capricious egotist. He amazes his friends by falling in love with a reed (' "she has no money and far too many relations;" and indeed the river was quite full of Reeds'), and delaying his migration by six weeks. Her company, however, soon proves trying: she has 'no conversation'; she flirts with the wind; she is 'too attached to her home' – no domestic virtue in a wife whose husband is devoted to travel – and so he leaves her. When he arrives in the Happy Prince's town, his first thought is 'I hope the town has made preparations'. When he decides to put up between the golden feet of a statue, and feels a drop of water which apparently has fallen from a cloudless sky, he complains, 'What is the use of a statue if it cannot keep the rain off?' And when the Prince explains why he is weeping – 'I can see all the ugliness and all the misery of my city, and though my heart is made of lead I cannot choose but weep' – his only reaction is politely veiled surprise that the Prince 'is . . . not solid gold'.

This egotism threatens the Prince's altruistic plans at first, but the Swallow is convinced of the Prince's earnestness by the beauty of his face in sorrow. After he has given away the Prince's sapphire eyes, as commanded, the Swallow regales him with fantastic travellers' tales 'of the King of the

Mountains of the Moon . . . of the great green snake that sleeps in a palm-tree . . . of the pygmies who sail over a big lake on large flat leaves, and are always at war with the butterflies'.[92] The Prince replies,' . . . you tell me of marvellous things, but more marvellous than anything is the suffering of men and of women. There is no Mystery so great as Misery.' In *De Profundis*, Wilde recalled the casual way in which he had made use of a similar phrase;[93] even so, the Prince's aphorism marks the Swallow's initiation into moral beauty. Winter is at hand, but he stays on and flays the statue of its golden skin, flake by flake, to bestow it on the poor: 'the living always think that gold can make them happy'. As a result, the Swallow is at last reduced to a state worse than that suffered by the Prince's beneficiaries. When he comes to take his leave, the Prince supposes that he is setting off at last for Egypt. The truth marks the Prince's own perfect initiation into sorrow: 'At that moment a curious crack sounded inside the statue, as if something had broken. The fact is that the leaden heart had snapped right in two. It certainly was a dreadfully hard frost.'

This 'practical' explanation is the cue for the Town Councillors' reappearance. Appalled at the condition of the statue, they decide to replace it, also to issue a proclamation forbidding the death of birds in the vicinity. The Art Professor justifies the demolition in a parody of his own lip-service to anti-utilitarian values: 'As he is no longer beautiful he is no longer useful'. The Councillors fail to justify it at all: 'the Mayor held a meeting of the Corporation to decide what was to be done with the metal. "We must have another statue, of course," he said, "and it shall be a statue of myself." "Of myself," said each of the Town Councillors, and they quarrelled. When I last heard of them they were quarrelling still.' The poet sees essentials, but the pedant and the public servant see only the outsides of things. Eventually, the image of the innocent but now enlightened egotist will be replaced by a monument to the captious egotism of a Tweedledum and Tweedledee bureaucracy.

In this 'ideal form', however, poetic justice ministers to its own. Utilitarian and aesthetic values are alike discredited by an element of the miraculous: the foundrymen cannot melt down the leaden heart. When God commands that he be brought the two most precious things in the city, an angel visits the 'dust-heap' and bears away metal heart and dead bird for apotheosis. Yet, in spite of the idealised ending, the beauty of the acts of self-sacrifice seems marred by the obtuseness of their objects. When the Prince sacrifices his eyes, the Chattertonian playwright freezing in his garret concludes, ironically, 'I am beginning to be appreciated . . . this is from some great admirer!', while the little match-girl cries, 'What a lovely bit of glass!' The tales which follow confirm that self-sacrifice is justified less by practical results than by its role in perfecting the giver – an idea developed in "The Soul of Man" and *De Profundis*. Charity, it seems, begins, and ends, at home.

"The Selfish Giant"

The story presents another extraordinary egotist, another walled garden, and another example of newly awakened compassion leading to transfiguration. Wilde took the winter-blossoming trees and thawing human heart from his Aesthetic lyric, "Le Jardin des Tuileries", but there are also suggestions of Shakespeare's sonnet XCVII – 'And thou away, the very birds are mute' – and of Meredith's *The Egoist*, in which Sir Willoughby, who wants to build a wall to exclude the world from his park and his life, is described as the 'original male in giant form', and where a white-flowering cherry tree acts as a revelatory vision.

During the Giant's absence from home, the children play in his garden. On his return, he is annoyed to find his privacy thus invaded and builds a wall to preserve it. By doing so he interferes with a fundamental law of nature. This, at least, is the implication of Wilde's metaphor, which posits a kind of conscientious withholding of labour on the part of flora and fauna to account for the non-appearance of the seasons in due order. The birds do not care to sing in the garden, because there are no children; the trees do not blossom, as there are no birds; the Giant's new noticeboard, 'TRESPASSERS WILL BE PROSECUTED', saddens the flowers and they decide to remain underground. 'But the Spring never came, nor the Summer. The Autumn gave golden fruit to every garden, but to the Giant's garden she gave none. "He is too selfish," she said.'

Pathetic fallacy can go no further, and the Giant is greeted one morning by music: the children have found a hole in the wall and returned to the garden, and so the birds are singing. All the trees but one are blossoming, and each bears a child. Under the only barren tree stands a child too small to climb into its branches. At this sight, 'the Giant's heart melted' and the penitential winter leaves him. He places the child in the tree; it kisses him; he knocks down the wall. He grows old in the company of successive generations of happy children until, one winter morning, he sees 'a tree quite covered with lovely white blossoms. Its branches were golden, and silver fruit hung down from them, and underneath it stood the little boy whom he had loved.' The child bears the nail-prints of the Crucifixion, and explains to the enraged Giant that they are 'the wounds of love'.

> 'Who art thou?' said the Giant, and a strange awe fell on him and he knelt before the little child.
> And the child smiled on the Giant, and said to him, 'You let me play once in your garden, to-day you shall come with me to my garden, which is Paradise.'
> And when the children ran in that afternoon, they found the Giant lying dead under the tree, all covered with white blossoms.

By comparison with the Happy Prince's penance, the Giant's is a mere token; and although he re-establishes contact with the mysterious forces of nature by placing the child in the tree, he neither knows the symbolic significance of his action, nor even that the Crucifixion has taken place. Yet the bare tree is a traditional symbol for the rood, and the Giant's action unwittingly confirms that pain and sorrow necessarily precede redemption. The 'wounds of love' cause the white flowers of love to spring, and, once the Giant understands this, his corpse is strewn with them by the elemental powers.

"The Nightingale and the Rose"

Something of the romantic primitivism found in "The Selfish Giant" pervades "The Nightingale and the Rose", although it makes no use of Christian machinery. Wilde called it 'the most elaborate' of the set, and it is richly suggestive. It dramatises one of the main themes of the poems – the opposition of romantic commitment through passionate action to the relative safety of philosophic contemplation – and shows the relationship between egotism and altruism in various shifting lights.

The most important factor in the story is the characterisation of the Nightingale as a Romantic artist. Even the unappreciative Student speaks of her art, while the narrator and the Nightingale herself know that she is a Romantic: 'Night after night I have sung of him though I knew him not: night after night have I told his story to the stars and now I see him. His hair is dark as the hyacinth-blossom, and his lips are red as the rose of his desire; but passion has made his face like pale ivory and sorrow has set her seal upon his brow.' When the Nightingale's unseen ideal moves from her lyric art into her life, where it becomes incarnate in the Student, she identifies herself completely with the true lover's condition. The Student thinks that a red rose will gain him the attentions of the Professor's daughter, and the Nightingale, though appalled at the price of it, determines to provide one, singing all night long with her breast against a thorn of the barren rose-tree. The Student, a sound sleeper despite his amatory frustrations, finds the perfected flower blowing at noon under his window: 'Why, what a wonderful piece of luck! . . . It is so beautiful that I am sure it has a long Latin name'. He runs off to be rejected by the Professor's daughter, to whom the Chamberlain's nephew has given jewels – 'and everybody knows that jewels cost far more than flowers'. We know the futility of the Nightingale's sacrifice but the ironic juxtapositions in this scene still shock:

> 'Well, upon my word, you are very ungrateful,' said the Student angrily; and he threw the rose into the street, where it fell into the gutter, and a cartwheel went over it.
> 'Ungrateful!' said the girl. 'I'll tell you what, you are very rude; and after all, who are you? Only a Student. Why, I don't believe you have even got silver buckles to your shoes as the Chamberlain's nephew has;' and she got up from her chair and went into the house.

The Student is the natural egotist, puffed up by learning. He combines the vices of the philistine, the materialist, and the reviewer:

> 'She has form,' he said to himself as he walked away through the grove – 'that cannot be denied to her; but has she got feeling? I am afraid not. In fact, she is like most artists: she is all style without any sincerity. She would not sacrifice herself for others. She thinks merely of music, and everyone knows that the arts are selfish. Still, it must be admitted that she has some beautiful notes in her voice. What a pity it is that they do not mean anything, or do any practical good.'

In many ways, this is Wilde's succinctest piece of social criticism. What seems an improbable context actually heightens its dramatic effect, since the speech is as much characterisation as satirical commentary; but it also shows Wilde's double, or ambiguous, purpose. On the one hand, the Student is an individual, a bookworm who has acquired all the arrogance of pedantry without any of the humility of self-knowledge. His art-criticism is a string of *non sequiturs*, his sentiment an absurdity: 'I have read all that the wise men have written, and all the secrets of philosophy are mine, yet for want of a red rose is my life made wretched.' Like the philistines to whom Gautier addressed the Preface to *Mademoiselle de Maupin*, he is also a cynic and a hypocrite to whom beauty is a closed book. Love, he decides, 'is not half as useful as Logic, for it does not prove anything, and it is always telling one of things that are not going to happen and making one believe things that are not true'. In a word, love is impractical, and since, 'in this age to be practical is everything', he decides to 'study Metaphysics. So he returned to his room and pulled out a great dusty volume and began to read.' Clearly, the Student's values are wrong on every count, a tissue of hopeless inconsistencies. He betrays his calling. He bears no relation to Wilde's true contemplative ideal, as becomes evident when his words are compared with the following passage in "The Critic as Artist", where Wilde adapted them to express a more general social truth: 'It takes a thoroughly selfish age, such as our own, to deify self-sacrifice. It takes a thoroughly grasping age, such as that in which we live, to set above the fine intellectual virtues, those shallow emotional virtues that are of immediate practical benefit to itself.'

If, on the one hand, the student is a cloistered pedant, on the other he represents the workaday world, deaf to nature and impervious to Romantic imagination. By casting a bird as the archetypal Romantic artist, Wilde can express the two ideas simultaneously. The Student is the modern 'fallen' intellectual as the Romantic perceives him – one upon whose ears the Nightingale's song falls like charming gibberish. But he is also the typical anti-poet: instead of exercising 'negative capability', taking wing with the Nightingale into 'fairy lands forlorn', his musings in the grove are wholly unmetaphorical. He is a time-serving Victorian pragmatist. Like the Town Councillors in "The Happy Prince", he is too occupied with external forms to notice essences.

In these generalised Romantic attitudes, there is more than a touch of quasi-Wordsworthian sentiment, especially in the anti-intellectual ending. As it happens, Wilde's Commonplace Book records, under the heading 'Wordsworth', three quotations from "The Tables Turned", including the famous stanza, 'One impulse from a vernal wood'. Perhaps the Student would do well to 'come forth into the light of things', but the adjuration to 'let Nature be your teacher' would be uncharacteristic of Wilde at any time, and particularly in a prose parable in 'fanciful form'. It is hard to see Wilde's 'brown bright nightingale amorous'[94] completing a moral trinity with Wordsworth's unliterary linnet and the throstle who is 'no mean preacher', and surely it is no accident that Wilde's third bird hero should be a literary linnet whose moralistic fable of devoted friendship is a comical flop. Whatever fascination Romantic primitivism held for Wilde was clearly not to be wasted on the Student. He was irretrievable – 'almost as bad as the girl he thinks he loves'. The story belongs to the Nightingale – 'the true lover, if there is one. She, at least, is Romance, and the Student, like most of us, is unworthy of Romance.'[95]

The Nightingale is in fact a development of her predecessor in "The Burden of Itys": her song-spell is woven to justify her own ideal rather than that of a ventriloquising poet. Wilde takes pains to conjure the right atmosphere. Even the sentence describing her flight through the wood recalls the moonlight love-song, 'Now sleeps the crimson petal',[96] while much of her dialogue is modelled on *The Song of Solomon*: 'passion has made his face like pale ivory and sorrow has set her seal upon his brow'. But here a macabre element supervenes. *The Song of Solomon* was an important influence on the prose poetry of *Salomé*, and there are several significant similarities between the story and the play. The narrative opening, for instance – the Student's lovesick speeches alternating with the asides of the Nightingale – is not unlike the opening exchanges of *Salomé*, similarly pregnant with irony and expressive of the same themes: misplaced romantic passion and its tragic incommunicability. The red rose-tree uses similies which reappear in Salomé's speech about Iokanaan's mouth – 'My roses are . . . as red as the feet of the dove, and redder than the great fans of coral that wave and wave in the ocean-cavern' – while the bird's successive appeals to the white, yellow, and red rose-trees, followed by a horrifying and bloody death for an ideal of love, parallel Salomé's courtship and execution. Moreover, both works are dominated by moonlight. The very building of the red rose 'by music out of moonlight' crystallises the poetic ambiguity of the mood: it suggests the obsessive climax of the hedonistic play, and also something of Tennyson's Camelot, an eerie spiritual city 'built / To music, therefore never built at all, / And therefore built for ever'.

Such an unlikely mixture of allegiances makes the story a kind of fulcrum in Wilde's internal autobiography. It is not yet clear whether the true Romantic, acting on impulse in pursuit of 'moments' or ideal projections, is silly suicide, heroic martyr, or anarchistic murder. *Vera* suggested the second; *The Duchess of Padua*, the second and third. *Salomé* contains all three. In the Nightingale's case, only suicide or martyrdom is in question, and in our attempt to choose between them Wilde's summary of his career in *De Profundis* may prove helpful. Here he rationalised his longstanding fascination with the image of the moon, defining it as the presiding planet of modern art:

> We call ourselves a utilitarian age, and we do not know the use of any single thing. We have forgotten that Water can cleanse, and that Fire can purify, and that the Earth is mother to us all. As a consequence, our Art is of the Moon, and plays with shadows, while Greek art is of the Sun, and deals directly with things.[97]

For much of his career, the Romantic absolute was the only thing to which Wilde accorded anything approaching elemental power, and this absolute is generally accompanied by some reference to the moon. In *De Profundis* he also repeated his convicition that much modern art spoke with the voice of Marsyas, the faun whose art was his undoing; and the Nightingale (like her predecessor, the 'wingèd Marsyas' of "The Burden of Itys") suffers a fate no less painful. She also exercises something of that power over natural objects which Orpheus possessed. At her 'last burst of music', the 'white Moon . . . forgot the dawn, and lingered on in the sky. The red rose heard it, and it trembled all over with ecstasy, and opened its petals to the cold morning air. Echo bore it to her purple cavern in the hills, and woke the sleeping shepherds from their dreams. It floated through the reeds of the river, and they carried its message to the sea.' According to Herbert Marcuse, Orpheus represents the reverse of 'the performance principle', a phrase which might well qualify the Student's life. Orpheus' is 'the voice which does not command but sings; the gesture which offers and receives; the deed which is peace and ends the labour of conquest. . . . The images of Orpheus and Narcissus reconcile Eros and Thanatos. They recall the experience of a world that is not to be mastered and controlled but to be liberated.'[98] This, I think, gives a clue to the proto-Symbolist aspect of the story. I do not suggest that Wilde had such ideas consciously in mind, any more than I would suggest that *Salomé* was a deliberate rewrite of certain details in an unpretentious tale. The fact is, however, that Wilde habitually associated certain images and words with certain moods and notions. From the standpoint of Wilde's inner monologue, which the story articulates partially, the Nightingale – like the Young Syrian in *Salomé*, like Salomé herself, perhaps, or like Wilde in poetic mood – is a further manifestation of the last Endymion, a poet-lover pouring the passion of her perfect vision into the unhearing ears of a corrupt, prudish and practical age which cannot comprehend her commitment. She may or may not be the prototype of the Orphic liberator, but she clearly reaffirms the familiar Romantic conviction that Eros and Thanatos are inseparable.

If these remarks shed some light on Wilde's thinking, they do not, after all, determine whether the Nightingale is a true Romantic hero – whether her self-sacrifice, like that of the Happy Prince and the Swallow, sanctifies. She dies fulfilled, ignorant of her gift's futility, blinded by belief. Since the Student cannot conceive of her being useful, she has not been useful. It is the common fate of the martyr, but Wilde prefers non-committal irony. We are left with two alternative inferences: that self-sacrifice for altruistic motives is futile and wasteful, or that self-sacrifice in pursuit of a personal vision – 'everybody knows that the arts are selfish' – is as egotistical as any other form of self-realisation, including staying alive. In the remaining stories, Wilde moves perceptibly closer to the pragmatists, and in the last we see the Nightingale's voluntary martyrdom explicitly parodied: it is the least beguiling pose.

"The Devoted Friend"

Despite its overall comic form, "The Devoted Friend" contains the extremest example of willing altruism exploited by practised selfishness. The pessimistic parable of the devoted friend is encased within a dramatic framework including an induction, an epilogue, and various interruptions. Within this framework, which is both parodic and didactic, Wilde snipes every character from some point of view – the sentimental feather-brained Duck, the crusty misogynistic Water-rat, the well-intentioned Linnet, the gross hypocritical Miller and his wife. Their good-hearted little son, the child-sage of the piece, escapes only because in this venal adult world he is automatically ignored.

The one key to this moral chaos is Wilde's ubiquitous irony, upon which the author's chief point – the point made by the story as a whole, not just the point of the central parable – wholly depends. The Linnet, having failed to make clear her idea of devoted friendship, thinks that a story will make it plainer. But the Water-rat sees in the story only the reflection of his own egotistical nature, taking for granted its comeliness there as in all contexts. He reinforces the ambiguity of the story's title, and proves the folly of anyone's taking seriously the genre of the 'story with a moral'. Wilde the narrator makes a unique appearance in the first person, but merely to disclaim responsibility. The story, and the mistake, belong to the Linnet. Wilde is only the means by which we hear how the Linnet's harrowing tale fails to touch those who could profit most by it. When the Water-rat learns that the story was supposed to have a moral, he becomes indignant at such an outmoded literary monstrosity, and shouts ' "Pooh," like the critic' whose *avant-garde* notions of fiction he espouses. When the downcast Linnet admits what has happened – 'The fact is that I told him a story with a moral' – the Duck replies, 'Ah! that is always a very dangerous thing to do'. The final line, in Wilde's own voice – 'And I quite agree with her' – is the story's greatest irony, since the Duck is the archetypal benign self-satisfied mother who gets things right only by accident. She tells her children, ' "You will never be in

the best society unless you can stand on your heads," . . . and every now and
then she showed them how it was done.' Wilde implies, however, that babes
and ducklings are still the sources of the purest and most upright values: 'The
little ducks paid no attention to her. They were so young that they did not
know what an advantage it is to be in society at all.' At the same time, the
story of Little Hans's exploitation and death illustrates with new force the
dangers of such ingenuous purity of motive, and the piece as a whole, though
clearly full of humanitarian sympathy, is also self-defensive and shows a
certain respect for the machinations of the worldly-wise. Maybe egotism is
not such a bad thing if ingenuous altruism is so blatantly unsuccessful. There
are even hints of the paradoxical and temporising dandy, most notably in the
Miller's sophistries, which sould like a combination of Gilbert in "The Critic
as Artist" and Lord Darlington in *Lady Windermere's Fan*.[99]

It was this ambiguous manner that Roditi disliked, and in "The Devoted
Friend" Wilde is even more elusive than before. If the story is understood as
having been written for children, then the force of the irony is lost. Wilde,
however, seems to take for granted that children will see the essentials as
clearly as the Miller's son does. The Romantic child does not read stories
with morals, it stars in them. Adults, by contrast, may respond to them in
three different ways. The simplest will accept the parable at face value as a
reinforcement of the everyday ethics that they themselves instil into
children, and beyond which many adults never develop. Their intellectual
contribution will be correspondingly small. Wilde's ironic commentary will
appeal to a further group, who are capable of finding stimulation and
amusement in the pose of the egotist without ignoring the uncomfortable
truth contained within the parable. They will realise, however, that the
parable is not 'a story with a moral' in the Linnet's sense, but a literary device
which has no moral except the futility of telling stories with a moral. To this
group, a story can have as many morals as readers, or as many morals as those
readers are prepared to recognise. The third group would comprise people
like the Miller and the Water-rat, natural egocentrics without literary
sense – a daunting prospect which, as the Linnet finds, leaves small scope for
critical ingenuity. Wilde refuses to opt for one of these alternatives, and his
refusal leaves the reader uneasy. Clearly, Little Hans, not the Miller, is the
truly devoted friend; but, equally clearly, his devotion, so praiseworthy by
the standards of 'a thoroughly selfish age', is stupid and pointless.

There are two possible sources for "The Devoted Friend", and these, if
Wilde knew them (as he surely must have), give additional point to the self-
conscious literary manipulation in it. They are both folk variants: Andersen's
"Little Claus and Big Claus" and Grimm's "Lucky Hans". In the latter, a
silly peasant begins with a gold-hoard and trades it away for increasingly
worthless articles until, left with nothing, he is as cheerful as ever. Lucky
Hans's dumb confidence, however, is no more than a travesty of business
sense – he genuinely believes that he gets the best of every deal – and his
story, like many folk tales, is hardly more than a cumulative anecdote about

the survival, or success, of the fittest. Andersen's story combines two clichés: everybody loves a winner, and everybody roots for the underdog. Little Claus is a diminutive *homme moyen sensuel* of considerable greed who vanquishes a bigger and stupider neighbour of identical aspirations. Admittedly, refinement of moral attitude is foreign to most folk tales, but even Andersen's revision, for all its sophisticated simplicity of style, is full of grossness and cruelty. If "The Devoted Friend" is Wilde's response to this – a more realistic account, though in 'fanciful form', of the true balance of power in everyday life – it can only be regarded as subtly refining the cruelty of the original. Here, everything goes wrong for the underdog. Wilde's Little Claus has good intentions in place of native guile, and the initiative belongs entirely to the Big Claus, whose virtuous friend crawls, a blind and willing sacrifice, to the altar of self-interest, where he dies by misadventure.

"The Remarkable Rocket"

This story might be described as the *Earnest* of the volume, since it parodies all the major themes while deftly avoiding commitment to any conclusion at all. Egotism, self-fulfilment, the Romantic imagination and its passionate absolutes – Wilde sends them up sky-high for the pleasure of watching them fall in a shower of stars.

The Rocket is a genuinely original comic creation, although it is hard to resist the idea that it had its origin in the pyrotechnics of the Ruskin–Whistler trial, caused by Ruskin's derisive estimate of *Nocturne in Black and Gold: The Falling Rocket*, and resulting in a negligible victory for the arrogant and testy Whistler. The Rocket's manner also recalls certain *mots* of Wilde's dating from his own verbal skirmishes with the 'Butterfly': 'Popularity is the only insult that has not yet been offered to Mr Whistler';[100] 'The only thoroughly original ideas that I have ever heard him express have had reference to his superiority over painters greater than himself';[101] 'Admirable as are Mr. Whistler's fire-works on canvas, his fire-works in prose are abrupt, violent, and exaggerated.'[102]

Relentlessly anti-public, the Rocket cultivates an élite of one, and maintains (or fabricates) the exceptional attitude towards everything. His only resource against life is the consciousness, which he has long developed, of 'the immense inferiority of everybody else'. He believes that the King's son's marriage has been arranged to coincide with his ascent. He ridicules 'common sense', which dictates that he keep himself dry, because he is 'uncommon'. He claims a Romantic nature and plentiful imagination, both predictably eccentric.[103] The Fire-balloon enthuses about the Prince's wedding–'when I soar up into the air I intend to tell the stars all about it. You will see them twinkle when I tell them about the pretty bride' – but the Rocket's egotism is far too great to admit his being out-Apolloed by a social inferior. The Fire-balloon's neo-Keatsian imagery stirs no joy in him, merely the scornful sneer of a Malvolio confronted with tipsy domestics: 'Ah! what a trivial view of life! . . . but it is only what I expected. There is nothing in you; you are hollow and empty.' His own Romanticism takes the form of projecting unforeseen disasters for the newlyweds, a prospect so moving that 'he actually burst into real tears', which prove his undoing.

The Rocket is not, of course, a Romantic, merely a pathological egotist. The Romantic of the story is the Catherine Wheel, in whose very form martyrdom is implicit. She believes that 'love is not fashionable any more, the poets have killed it. They wrote so much about it that nobody believed them, and I am not surprised. True love suffers, and is silent.' She is a parody of Wilde's Aesthetic pose in "The Garden of Eros": whereas the last Endymion had bewailed that true poets were few and 'all romance is flown', the Catherine Wheel reiterates, 'Romance is dead'. She is also a parody of the Nightingale, stuck through with the necessary nail in place of the thorn: She 'had been attached to an old deal box in early life, and prided herself on her broken heart'. Habituated to one emotion, she admires the Rocket's tears intensely: 'He must have a truly romantic nature . . . for he weeps when there is nothing at all to weep about'.

For all her sentimentality, she does at least perform on time, whereas the Rocket's affectation of sentiment proves fatal. He misses the Coronation display because he is too wet; and when he does finally 'go off', making himself 'very stiff and straight' and experiencing 'a curious tingling sensation all over him', which leaves small room for doubt about Wilde's studied appeal to the post-pubescent understanding, his only possible witnesses are two small boys quite innocent of the exhibition, since, with the perfect tact of the ideal bedtime audience, they have fallen asleep.

Certain details can again be traced to Andersen. "The Collar", for instance, with its punning inanimates and its writers' joke about the *tabula rasa*, shows close similarities. If this was indeed a conscious source, then Wilde showed it his customary irreverence. Andersen's moral fable concerns a shirt-collar, soiled with long wear, which yearns to be made into clean white paper. His wish is granted, but the paternalistic narrator records upon that very piece of paper the tell-tale chronicle of the collar's life. Wilde, sceptical father of future sophisticates, takes a leaf from Andersen's book, but only to add lustre to the little anarchic charge he has twisted within it.

It is, of course, anarchy with a difference. Nothing could be further from the heroics of *Vera* or *Salomé,* or the exquisite urbanity of Lord Henry Wotton. The Rocket has no pretensions to a philosophical position. He may not, for that matter, be intended as a portrait of the independent Whistler – although Wilde, who noted that many of Whistler's portraits 'are pure works of fiction',[104] would have been the first to perceive the autobiographical potential in painting someone else. (He treated the idea seriously in *Dorian Gray*.) And the note of the inner monologue is surely there – above all, the suspicion that the emotional impulse is at last perilously close to an elaborate joke which, if taken seriously, can deceive those who give way to it, frustrating the urge towards that self-expression of which it extends such fair promise, and betraying them instead into ignominious defeat. The Rocket barely contrives to convince himself of his ultimate triumph, and his absurd stance – Student playing Nightingale in front of a mirror – convinces no one else. The conflicting claims have become hopelessly blurred; the only recourse is to laughter.

Wilde continued to explore these questions in less 'fanciful' form, but his study of the Rocket, a small and early masterpiece, was perhaps his most penetrating self-portrait to date.

VI. *A House of Pomegranates* The Death of Pastoral

Three of these stories had been written by 1890,[105] so that in spite of its date (late 1891) this collection marks a transition between the themes and manner of *Poems* and *The Happy Prince* and the mature myth-making of *Dorian Gray* and *Salomé*: indeed, Wilde apparently considered sending "The Fisherman and his Soul" to *Lippincott's Monthly*, until the first *Dorian Gray* came to him and he thought better of it.[106]

Although the fall from nature is recognisable in all four stories, its treatment varies considerably. "The Young King" and "The Star Child", which are closest in manner to the earlier volume, oppose the private paradise of physical beauty to the moral beauty which seems to attend its renunciation: both heroes come into their kingdom only after public penance for their anti-social narcissism. "The Birthday of the Infanta" and "The Fisherman and his Soul" develop more explicitly pagan and pastoral metaphors. Here, too, personalities come of age; but imaginary conflicts between the Greek ideal and the Christian ideal, or between the state of nature and the state of art or civilisation, are still susceptible to historical probabilities. These stories are elegies, not parables. They contain no miraculous transfigurations.

In "The Decay of Lying" Wilde had claimed that the task of the artist, particularly the prose artist, was to 'rewrite history'. "The Fisherman and his Soul" and "The Star Child" are genuinely timeless, exercises in a form that is 'ideal not imitative', but the other two stories suggest recognisable historical settings. Here Wilde follows the example of Pater's *Imaginary Portraits* (1887) – 'or imaginative portraits, as we prefer to call them'[107] – treating a pivotal moment in cultural history as the basis for psychological narrative. Thus the pastoral state, implicit or explicit, becomes a metaphor for a stage in the individual's development, a state of self-unconsciousness similar in many ways to that in which the child still believes itself to be unique. The crucial, and sometimes fatal, moment arrives when others intrude into the paradise of one. Throughout Wilde's work recurs the implication, now serious, now comic, that paradise belongs to the self-sufficient singleton.

In all this the love theme plays its part. Romantic images of love are among the most obvious forms of self-projection. When the four love-affairs – with princess, mermaid, or self – break down, the pastoral is over, the invasion of knowledge begins. If *A House of Pomegranates* could leave any doubt that in mythic terms knowledge and self-knowledge are synonymous, its successor, *Dorian Gray*, dispels that doubt, repeating the pattern with an explicit visual gloss and completing the metaphor of the fall by reference to the idea of 'modernity'. Dorian, a monster of egoism, clings to his pastoral image while simultaneously attempting to achieve in his own life the ideal of all-encompassing knowledge and experience. Wilde restates this ideal in "The Critic as Artist", where the image of the Romantic *peregrinatio*, the journey towards complete knowledge and final reintegration of the fragmented personality, is combined with the evolutionary metaphor of social Darwinism. Heredity makes possible the idea of 'concentrated race experience', and the true critic is he who will reach through fastidious self-culture that state which Schelling, Schiller and Hegel variously posited as the goal of philosophic endeavour. In the novel, heredity adds one strand more to Dorian's complex fantasy of self-realisation by 'the experimental method' – a scheme feasible, even in fiction, only under pastoral camouflage.

Such intellectual or critical solutions to the post-lapsarian state are necessarily alien to the 'ideal form' of mythopoeic romances and *Märchen*. Here, feeling and instinct are given pride of place, while thought or knowledge most often seem intruders from a different world. Wilde studiously preserves this literary decorum, so that even fatalities detract little from the last Endymion's diehard conviction that 'to feel is better than to know'.

"The Young King"

Like "The Birthday of the Infanta", this story explicitly contrasts palace and woodland, and associates the splendours of art and of its concomitant civilisation with a sophistication of 'natural' human values. However, the hero's conscientious (and very Victorian) rejection of *Joyeuse*, Wilde's definitive palace of art, is ambiguous and fraught with complications. The imagery of the piece is no less confusing – Christianity battles with Hellenism, the image of Tannhäuser eclipses that of Narcissus; even so, it seems to offer the only real clue to Wilde's intentions, and also confirms the volume's debt to *Poems*.

Three Wildean images are here superimposed: Narcissus, Tannhäuser, and the artist-martyr, and each has its group of verbal echoes.

Narcissus is not mentioned by name in the story, but his presence haunts it. Soon after the Young King is brought to his ancestral palace, he is described as 'lying there, wild-eyed and open-mouthed, like a brown woodland Faun, or some young animal of the forest newly snared by the hunters', and it is not long before he is known to be passing much of his time in gazing at likenesses of Adonis and Endymion, or, 'so the tale ran, pressing his warm lips to the marble brow of an antique statue' of Antinous. If all this suggests the lines in

"The Burden of Itys" describing Narcissus, it also recalls a quite different piece. In his review of the Grosvenor Gallery exhibition (1877), Wilde carefully digressed on the type of Greek adolescent boy depicted in Renaissance painting, and spoke of 'those wild-eyed, open-mouthed St. Johns of the "Incoronata Madonna"' of Correggio.[108] The reuse of the phrase in so different a setting is striking. (In "The Burden of Itys" Narcissus was to have replaced Christ in the poet's mental picture-gallery.) If we accept Marcuse's definition of Narcissus as the type that 'lives by the aesthetic reality principle: his life is beauty, his existence contemplation',[109] then the Young King, who gazes 'as one in a trance' at antique carvings and finds in physical beauty 'an anodyne from pain', represents a rustic Narcissus suddenly confronted with a whole heritage of beauty in the unfamiliar shapes of art. Even his chamber is hung with 'rich tapestries representing the Triumph of Beauty', and he identifies himself with this setting, as with his long-obscured family heritage, by ordering a magnificant coronation regalia. His three dreams bring about the invasion of knowledge (or, in more modern terms, release suppressed guilt); and, once conscience is awakened, the image of Narcissus and the 'aesthetic reality principle' give way to an image of Tannhäuser and a public penance, followed by an image of Christ, glorious in self-abnegation. The Young King decides that his true regalia consists of his goatherd's cloak and staff and a symbolic crown of thorns – 'a spray of wild briar that was climbing over the balcony' – all of which undergo miraculous transformation once he has withstood the mockery of lords, clergy and commons. The ideal of the story reverses the ideal of the earlier poem: perhaps this is why it fails to convince. The three dreams are brilliant pieces of image-making – at times they have a heraldic, almost a surrealist or hallucinatory vividness. It is disillusioning to find that such self-justifying purple passages debouch into a pantheon of conscience where Ruskinian ethics and the church-furnishings of the Oxford Movement vie for predominance.

The second strand of imagery concerns Tannhäuser, whose story Wilde appears to have adapted to his own needs by means of various substitutions. In place of the Venusberg, the mountain of love, we find *Joyeuse*, the palace of art. Instead of Venus herself, art objects engross the hero, notably pagan glorifications of male beauty. Instead of a vision of his former chivalric self – which, in "Laus Veneris", Wilde's likeliest and nearest source, reveals to 'Christ's knight' his fallen state and drives him to Rome – the Young King has three dreams which picture the fallen state of his realm. He wakes to reality at the sight of his own face in a mirror, and, unable to outface conscience, he rejects external beauty and proceeds to his coronation like a sinner seeking absolution. (The vision in the mirror is another instance of a reversal of something in *Poems*. In "Humanitad" lines 289–94, it is 'self-slain humanity' which is shocked into its true condition by seeing its own image as an agonised Christ-face – a shock with precipitates strong Hellenist counter-action.) Like the Pope in the Tannhäuser legend, the Bishop here is obstructionist. Unlike the legend, Wilde yields his miracle at once: the staff sprouts, the crown blossoms, and the sun weaves a tissue of light around the 'beggar', who returns home with angelic countenance.

The mistress – or minion – art, has been rejected. And yet, in terms of the narrative framework, this rejection achieves little. The king's subjects are not merely unappreciative, like the poor in "The Happy Prince", but hostile: unjust employers, they feel, are preferable to unemployment. The king ignores their objections, his face saddened and his eyes on higher values, but Wilde gives no indication of future benefits in this for the state. 'Home' for the Young King is still presumably the palace of art, and it is hard to avoid the conclusion that, like the Soul in Tennyson's poem, he wants the glory of renunciation without giving up the chance of later reoccupation.

Perhaps the story really hinges on the conflict between public and private obligations, a subject which touched Wilde closely. The Young King's self-sacrifice may signify a recognition that the practical or symbolic demands of the public sector outweigh, for the public figure, all private preferences. It is an uncharacteristic conclusion, and the third strand of imagery, the trinity of Christ, poet, and martyr, points to a more subjective, and perhaps a truer, interpretation. Here we find various ideas and phrases from earlier work twisted together in a complicated pattern, all of them colouring the Young King's transfiguration. First we must consider a passage from "The English Renaissance" (1882): 'While the incomplete lives of ordinary men bring no healing power with them, the thorn-crown of the poet will gild its own thorns, and his pain, like Adonis, be beautiful in its agony; and when the poet's heart breaks it will break in music.' This was an adaptation of some lines in "The Garden of Eros" (202–10) describing Burne-Jones, whose lilies, roses, and other medievalisms are prominent in Wilde's cathedral scene. Part of it reappeared in 1884 in a poem, "To L. L.", which is apparently a quasi-recollection of Wilde's infatuation for Lily Langtry: 'Well, if my heart must break, / Dear Love, for your sake, / It will break in music, I know, / Poets' hearts break so.' Second, we must recall "The Artist's Dream", in which fame proved a bitter blessing, and the laurel crown turned to a thorn-crown which left red wounds on the poet's brow. The Young King's coronation bears traces both of beautiful heartbreak and of aesthetic stigmata, and appears to reconcile optimistically these contradictory accounts of the artist's lot. His chosen thorns sprout golden leaves, while red roses replace the wounds he might have felt. The blossoming of lilies from his goatherd's staff confirms that it is the 'natural' rather than the clerical or aristocratic condition which brings benediction upon the individual. From this it is not hard to infer that the artist is of all men closest to nature, even if others take his creations to furnish the palace of art. The breaking of the artist's heart in music confirms the involuntary complicity in his nature between 'natural' impulse and perfect expression.

What does all this amount to? We are back, admittedly, with Wilde's inner monologue. The imagery is not wholly articulate. But it appears that the poet or artist is a modern Adonis gored by life and a modern Christ whose Passion is fame. Like the 'English Renaissance' itself he embodies pagan and 'medieval' (or Christian) forces. Like the rites of Adonis, the Passion of Christ, or the purifying 'elemental' powers mentioned in *De Profundis*, he brings renewal and 'healing power'. If he is martyr, he is also mythic hero. In either case, he consults his own perfection: his audience, his congregation, or his subjects will not understand him. Nine years too soon, it is Wilde's Reading self-portrait.

Finally, there are the similarities to Pater's Duke Carl. In his review, Wilde summarised the motif of this piece as 'the passion for the imaginative world of art',[110] and this is clearly the common starting point. Duke Carl is an eager, instinctive, and largely untutored precursor of the *Aufklärung* who becomes a legend in his own time by making a marriage in the style of King Cophetua, finally perishing, as the hypothesis goes, with his bride-to-be on their wedding eve, when, through following his motto, "Go straight to life!", they are trampled underhoof by a victorious army advancing across his diminutive realm. Like Duke Carl's death, the Young King's birth is traditionally picturesque (his mother, a princess, made a bohemian marriage soon stealthily annulled by poison and intrigue). Wilde's hero, like Pater's, lives in a period of cultural ferment (the Bishop and the palace suggest France, but the other details suggest Rome in the early Renaissance). Both are crucially influenced by a great painting from Italy; undergo lone artistic revelations is upper rooms; rely on the sympathetic collusion of a young companion in a plot which is ostensibly subversive but actually crucial to personal development. (Duke Carl, immured by court etiquette, contrives to escape in pursuit of his Apollonian ideal by arranging his own funeral and attending the ceremony disguised as a minstrel before setting out. The Young King 'would chafe at the tedious court ceremonies' and wander in the 'new world' of his palace as if seeking 'a sort of restoration from sickness'.) In both stories this trick or plot alienates the ruler from his subjects. (Duke Carl's empty coffin remained 'as a kind of symbolical "coronation incident"' for them, while the Young King is even more remote from the people after his coronation than before it: 'no man dared look upon his face, for it was like the face of an angel'.) Finally, the Christ-image of Wilde's story is matched by the word 'Resurgam' inscribed on Duke Carl's empty coffin – a prophecy fulfilled once in the flesh, and a second time in the spirit through such figures as Lessing and Goethe.

Striking as these parallels are, it must be admitted that they only accentuate the differences between the two writers. Pater's story is founded in fact, and although his disposition no doubt influenced the choice of subject, the subject is thereafter paramount. Wilde's story is a fiction based on fictions, and remains imperfect because insufficiently objectified. We are not surprised to read in *De Profundis* that, when he wrote the line 'Is not He who made misery wiser than thou art', he had considered it 'little more than a phrase'.[111] Wilde continues to pace the uncertain path from egotism to altruism, bent here into the artist's magic circle, the precinct of the palace of art.

"The Birthday of the Infanta"

So long as I myself am *identical* with nature, I understand what a living nature is as well as I understand my own life. . . . As soon, however, as I separate myself . . . from nature, nothing more is left for me but a dead object. [Schelling[112]]

Implicit in all four stories, this idea is here demonstrated as a literal truth. The scene opens with two of Wilde's favourite motifs: the significant birthday, and the garden – glorious but over-ripe, poised for a fall.

The Infanta is just twelve, an age at which she stands on the brink of official womanhood without having experienced anything of ordinary childhood. Normally 'she was only allowed to play with children of her own rank, so she always had to play alone, but her birthday was an exception'. It is but one exception of many, since the court itself is a permanent and conscious exception to every social norm, a community whose instincts seem destined to run à rebours. Opposed to joy, laughter, and all spontaneous feeling, the court elevates pain into pageantry and suffocates life by ceremonial.

The sense of languor and decay extends to the garden, which is symbolically (and would have been architecturally) a continuation of the palace:

The purple butterflies fluttered about with gold dust on their wings, visiting each flower in turn; the little lizards crept out of the crevices in the wall, and lay basking in the white glare; and the pomegranates split and cracked with the heat, and showed their bleeding red hearts. Even the pale yellow lemons, that hung in such profusion from the mouldering trellis and along the dim arcades, seemed to have caught a richer colour from the wonderful sunlight, and the magnolia trees opened their great globe-like blossoms of folded ivory, and filled the air with a sweet heavy perfume.

This is a miniature Eden, but an Eden of art. It has less of the dew-fresh atmosphere of the 'first fair morn' than of the mellowing glaze of literary pastoral. The butterflies seem to be paying court visits rather than mundanely feeding. The lemons in the dim arcades are reminiscent of Marvell's 'golden lamps in a green night' – Wilde had quoted the line in his comments on Spencer Stanhope's picture *Eve Tempted* in 1877[113] – but the serenity of Marvell's garden is threatened here by the pomegranates, which admonish that all is not, or will not be, well. (The image of the split pomegranate recurs in *Salomé*, again connoting calamitous infatuation.)

When we first meet the Infanta, she is still sufficiently 'natural' to prefer the sunny garden to the shuttered palace, even if the garden is essentially an outdoor palace in which everyone behaves very much as he would inside.

But Wilde's description of her appearance, taken from Velázquez, presents a figure as much doll-like as child-like, as much art as nature, and in so formal a portrait the real flower strikes an incongruous note:

> Her robe was of grey satin, the skirt and the wide puffed sleeves heavily embroidered with silver, and the stiff corset studded with rows of fine pearls. Two tiny slippers with big pink rosettes peeped out beneath her dress as she walked. Pink and pearl was her great gauze fan, and in her hair, which like an aureole of faded gold stood out stiffly around her pale little face, she had a beautiful white rose.

The uneasy blend of art and nature sets the tone of the story. The Infanta and her playmates are products of an adult society and ape its manners. Even when they seem to react spontaneously, Wilde's irony disabuses us: 'the children got so excited that they stood up upon the benches, and waved their lace handkerchiefs and cried out: *Bravo toro! Bravo toro!* just as sensibly as if they had been grown-up people.'

Wilde characterises his actors by turning them into an audience. Although, as we soon learn, the Infanta has no knowledge or understanding of real human passions, she is moved to tears by the puppet-play of *Sophonisba* (a lurid saga of love and political intrigue in which the heroine is saved from forced marriage by taking poison sent by her true betrothed), so good is the acting and so 'natural' the puppets' gestures. The adults react no less perversely. The Chamberlain and the Grand Inquisitor are amused by the sham cruelty of the bullfight, reluctantly affected by the puppets. This may reflect merely Wilde's theory that the 'feigned ardours and unreal rhetoric' of art wield more power than direct experience does, but it is more probably a characterisation of the courtiers. The Grand Inquisitor seems to resent the capacity of 'things made simply out of wood and coloured wax, and worked mechanically by wires' to be 'so unhappy and meet with such terrible misfortunes'. He finds the puppets' sufferings 'intolerable' – perhaps because for such as he the pain of inanimates is a frustration, an immorality.

The Dwarf appears at the height of the merry-making and cuts his capers while we still regard him, as the court does, wholly from the outside. It is not until later that we appreciate his relationship to the natural world, but in retrospect his entrance and the treatment he receives reveal the court's attitude towards nature. Nature is innately grotesque, the grotesquer the better, and no different in kind from art, ceremonial, or mountebankery, since all serve to entertain. The Dwarf bursts upon the already comic proceedings like a clumsy bucolic anti-masque: 'When the children laughed, he laughed as freely and joyously as any of them, and at the close of each dance he made them each the funniest of bows, smiling and nodding at them just as if he was really one of themselves, and not a little misshapen thing that Nature, in some humourous mood, had fashioned for others to mock at.'

Thus far the narrative tone has supported the court's values with minimum ironic underpinning. The Infanta's parting gesture marks a turning point: she throws her white rose to the Dwarf as 'a jest', governed in this, as in everything, by mixed motives. She recalls how the great ladies throw bouquets to a famous *castrato*, and wishes to copy them, but she also knows that it will annoy her chaperone. The Dwarf responds with an unwitting travesty not only of the operatic star but also of the prima ballerina and the chivalric champion, and undermines the Infanta's gravity so completely that she has to be led indoors.

Once the court has retired for siesta, nature becomes vocal. Animals and birds are given interior monologues, and the flowers, beseemingly mute in the presence of their betters, vent their petty snobbery and false refinement in an amusing parody of court life below stairs. The flowers, who behave like talking fashion dummies, resent the Dwarf: he is ugly, he is mobile, and he is the centre of attention. Theirs is the note of Wilde's later dowagers and dandies, the advocates of aristocratic inaction, who find life an elaborate chore and are seldom roused except by what is 'painfully natural'.

The birds ('mere vagrants like the gipsies') are kinder. The Dwarf's consideration for them makes him exceptional, just as the nightingale's dowdy exterior belies her inner quality: 'Why, even the nightingale herself, who sang so sweetly in the orange groves at night that sometimes the Moon leaned down to listen, was not much to look at after all'. The Dwarf is a further example – Wilde's last – of the innocent romantic who fails to survive the touch of reality and the shock of self-knowledge. He survives slightly longer than the Nightingale in "The Nightingale and the Rose", who died in blissful ignorance, and he falls with a difference; but the fall is none the less fatal – an aesthetic equivalent of original sin. The knowledge to which he is exposed is less the knowledge of good and evil in the external world than the knowledge of beauty and ugliness, specifically in oneself.

The talking flowers form part of a series of literary echoes which provides a mimic commentary on the Dwarf's ill-fated trespass. The two most obvious sources are *Through the Looking-Glass* (1872) and "Maud" (1855), which Carroll had parodied. The scene in the 'high Hall-garden' where the neurotic hero of "Maud" awaits a glimpse of the 'passionless, pale cold face' became a scene in which the sensible Alice awaits the arrival of the Red Queen, a virago of discipline famed for indiscriminate decapitation. Tennyson had placed his waiting hero in the balmy garden where he listened to the sounds of the dance inside, the flowers combining in choric commiseration. Wilde's hero awaits the end of the heroine's siesta so that she can come to watch *him* dance, and the flowers are totally antagonistic. In so bizarre a reversal, poetic fallacy can only work against the hero, and, as if to stress the enormity of the Dwarf's expecting anything of the Infanta, Wilde inserts a vignette which dramatises two stanzas from "Now sleeps the crimson petal" (the song already used in "The Nightingale and the Rose"), and casts the full glare of the Spanish sunlight on the Dwarf's 'moonstruck' infatuation:[114]

the old Sundial . . . could not help saying to the great milk-white Peacock, who was sunning herself on the balustrade, that every one knew that the children of Kings were Kings, and that the children of charcoal-burners were charcoal-burners, and that it was absurd to pretend that it wasn't so; a statement with which the Peacock entirely agreed, and indeed screamed out, "Certainly, certainly," in such a loud, harsh voice, that the gold-fish in the basin of the cool splashing fountain put their heads out of the water, and asked the huge stone Tritons what on earth was the matter.

The ironic contrast between the Dwarf's predicament and that of the unconscious wounded hero, watched over by solicitous Princess Ida who reads 'deep in the night', is obvious.

In another respect, the story is closer to Carroll. The palace is really a 'looking-glass house', entered by 'a little private door' reminiscent of the door that opened Alice's adventures underground. Indeed, the Dwarf's progress is not unlike a visit to the underworld, since the looking-glass house – the palace of art – is a lifeless realm. Even its doorkeepers are lifeless – antique statues that gaze at him 'with sad blank eyes and strangely smiling lips' and who partake of what Wilde called 'that calm which despair and sorrow cannot disturb but intensify only'.[115]

The detailed descriptions that follow have often been criticised as tedious lists of 'aesthetic furnishings' or 'bric-à-brac' better suited to a sale catalogue.[116] Wilde himself presumably valued them: 'In style,' he commented, '(in *mere* style, as honest Besant would say) it is my best story.'[117] Moreover, they are integral to the characterisation and theme, pointed contrasts with the Dwarf's memories of the forest. Before entering the palace he projects in true bucolic fashion an idyll for the Infanta and himself: he will bring her tame wood-pigeons, show her 'the great wise tortoises', and weave for her, not 'a belt of straw and ivy buds', but 'a necklace of red bryony berries that would be quite as pretty as the white berries that she wore on her dress'. He will also dance for her – and in his relationship to dance we see the surest sign of his integral pastoral consciousness. As Frank Kermode has said,

Dance is the most primitive, non-discursive art, offering a pre-scientific image of life, an intuitive truth. Thus it is the emblem of the Romantic image. Dance belongs to a period before the self and the world were divided, and so achieves naturally that 'original unity' which modern poetry can produce only by a great and exhausting effort of fusion.[118]

The Dwarf's dancing is of this character – it is precisely his lack of self-consciousness that the court enjoys and misunderstands– and Wilde now reveals that he knows a series of seasonal dances, a cycle of natural ceremonial wholly different from the dance of Our Lady which had so impressed the Infanta: 'All the wild-dances he knew, the mad dance in red raiment with the autumn, the light dance in blue sandals over the corn, the dance with white snow-wreaths in winter, and the blossom-dance, through the orchards in spring' – a repertoire which not only defines his communion with nature but also reveals the full extent of the court's self-impoverishment. Dance inside the palace, certainly dance of the Dwarf's kind, is inconceivable. The repeat performance, like the first, was to have taken place in the garden.

For everything in the palace partakes of death. It is more than a looking-glass house, a mirror image of nature. It is a schematic reversal of nature, a place where lifeless copies replace graceful living things. Sun and stars – ironically the gloom-loving king's favourite devices – are embroidered, together, on black velvet. The tapestries, with horses and hounds whose verisimilitude frightens the Dwarf, were woven to divert an incarcerated madman. There is an ebony cabinet on which Holbein's *Dance of Death* is aptly engraved. In contrast to the 'dappled bee-haunted cells' of the foxglove, the chestnut's 'spires of white stars' and the hawthorn's 'pallid moons of beauty', the walls of the final room are covered with Lucca damask 'patterned with birds and dotted with dainty blossoms of silver'. The furniture is 'massive silver, festooned with florid wreaths, and swinging Cupids; in front of the two large fireplaces stood great screens broidered with parrots and peacocks, and the floor, which was of sea-green onyx, seemed to stretch far away into the distance.' Closing off this room, with its exotic symbols of pride and its metallic love-gods in arrested motion, is the mirror.

Wilde may have based the Dwarf's encounter with the mirror on an episode in *The Water-Babies* (1863). When Tom is taken by Grimes to sweep chimneys at the great house, he loses his way among the flues and descends into a white bedroom containing a beautiful girl lying asleep. Having surveyed the wonderful chamber, he suddenly sees 'standing close to him a little ugly, black, ragged figure, with bleared eyes and grinning white teeth. He turned on it angrily. What did such a little black ape want in that sweet lady's room?' Kingsley's scene slips from precarious romance into rollicking comedy. Tom, we learn, has never seen a cheval-glass before, but 'for the first time in his life' he realises he is dirty; and in his attempt to climb back up the chimney he upsets the fire-irons, awaking the girl who 'screamed as loud as any peacock', whereupon a classic chase ensues. Wilde avoids all mention of the word 'mirror', leading the reader through the Dwarf's bewilderment and final comprehension, and introducing a final pastoral reference. We have been told earlier that the Dwarf plays 'the pipe that Pan loves to hear'. Now, puzzling over his reflection, he wanders unconsciously into synaesthesia: 'Was it Echo? He had called to her once in the valley, and she had answered him word for word. Could she mock the eye, as she mocked the voice? Could she make a mimic world just like the real world?' There are two distinct points here. The reference to Echo suggests that the Dwarf's pastoral reality is identical with that of Greek myth. But his speculation about Echo is in itself intriguing. If Echo were indeed a mirror held up to nature, then Echo's 'mimic world' would be an unexpected pastoral definition of art – the mirror in which the Dwarf discovers his objective self.

Wilde's work is, of course, full of mirrors; but a mirror at the centre of a palace of art immediately invites comparison with "The Lady of Shalott". The parallel is less tenuous than might at first appear, nor is this the last that we shall hear of Tennyson's presence in the story. Considering the possibility that the Infanta might be bored with him in the forest, the Dwarf had earlier counted over a list of sights that might interest her. Certain details in it recall the procession that passes under the Lady of Shalott's window – an insignificant resemblance were her fate not a mirror image of the Dwarf's. For her, Lancelot is too vivid a sight to behold only in the mirror: this once, she must defy the spell and look at life directly. The mirror of imagination cracks, the web of art floats away; the Lady drifts downstream to the worldly city of Camelot (worldly, at least, in this context), where she is found dead on arrival. The Infanta is an equally disturbing intrusion into the Dwarf's life, a life also in its way spellbound. His search for her shatters in similar fashion his self-sufficient world – the primitive world where instinct is one with motive and observation one with imagination – and the mirror's 'curse' proves equally fatal. In Tennyson's design, life is the assassin, the Lady the hapless artist-victim. In Wilde's, the victim is the pastoral hero. Art, paradoxically, by holding its mirror up to nature, is no high idealist but a murderer, a Medusa, 'heartless' and 'witless' as some have claimed nature to be, the apparently cruel standard of an undoubtedly cruel civilisation. The only kind word spoken by a human – the Chamberlain's brief elegy over the Dwarf's body – is hardly less formal than Lancelot's cursory chivalry over the Lady's corpse.

It is sometimes argued that the Infanta is a juvenile version of the fatal woman who theoretically figures in *Vera*, *The Duchess of Padua*, and *Salomé*.[119] In such a case, the Infanta's resemblance to Salomé would presumably be in the form of a further mirror image: Salomé falls in love with Iokanaan and dances for him, while the Dwarf dances for the Infanta and falls in love with her. Salomé dies, having come face to face with the reality of a romantic dream built around Iokanaan, while the Dwarf follows the same pattern in relation to the Infanta, who shares some of Salomé's disposition and inhabits comparably sterile surroundings. The resemblance is striking as far as it goes; but of itself it does not validate the fatal-woman theory, especially in a story which has more in common with literary pastoral than with Decadence. If the Infanta is really a *belle dame sans merci*, then we might look for her predecessor in Marvell's "Little T. C. in a Prospect of Flowers" who 'only with the roses plays' and whose eyes give promise of driving 'In Triumph over hearts that strive'. The likelier influence, however, is the Tennysonian 'high-born maiden': having veered from "Maud" to "The Princess", Wilde turns back again to "Maud" in order to complete his pastoral parallel to Tennyson's garden scene. The Infanta appears just in time to applaud the Dwarf's 'acting' – his death-spasm – the immediate cause of which is her thrown favour, the white rose.

In "Maud", as the hero agonises in the garden, the white rose whispers sympathetically, 'She is late'.

In conclusion, I shall point to one more parallel with Tennyson, which brings together the ideas of the high-born maiden, the romantic and untried youth, and the power of innocence over ugliness and death. The scene concerned occurs in "Gareth and Lynette" (1872), the first and most idealistic of *The Idylls of the King*. Although the comparable scene in Wilde's story is relatively slight, there is sufficient resemblance to make a conscious echo probable – the more probable in that the essentials in Wilde are reversed, to ironic and pathetic effect. Gareth, an unfleshed knight disguised as a kitchen-knave, accompanies a frosty and snobbish maiden, Lynette, to the tower in which her kin are held captive. He vanquishes four knights, the last of which is 'Night' or death, a champion in black armour at the sight of whom 'even Sir Lancelot through his warm blood / Felt ice strike'. Gareth, the unspotted idealist, cleaves the knight's helm open, 'and out from this / Issued the bright face of a blooming boy / Fresh as a flower new-born' – an image of rebirth for the faithful. At this, the company 'made merry over Death, / As being after all their foolish fears / And horrors only proven a blooming boy.' Gareth marries the lady. As Wilde had made the Dwarf's solo scene with the mirror tragic instead of comic, so here he turns Tennyson's heroic scene into comical play-acting:

> After a prolonged combat, during which several of the hobby-horses were gored through and through, and their riders dismounted, the young Count of Tierra-Nueva brought the bull to his knees, and having obtained permission from the Infanta to give the *coup-de-grâce*, he plunged his wooden sword into the neck of the animal with such violence that the head came right off, and disclosed the laughing face of little Monsieur de Lorraine, the son of the French ambassador at Madrid.

The Dwarf is not directly associated with the bullfight, but he is clearly presented as an incorrigible travesty of a courtly admirer. Though committed to no more ambitious chivalric quest than to find the Infanta – his relationship to her balancing that of Gareth to Lynette – he penetrates into the realm of death, bearing her token. Here he comes face to face with an opponent no less fearsome than Gareth's – himself – against whom he is defenceless.

"The Fisherman and his Soul"

During the autumn of 1889 Wilde was evidently considering sending this story to the American magazine *Lippincott's Monthly*, but he changed his mind in favour of the first *Dorian Gray*, written during the first part of 1890 and published in the June number.[120] The change of plan was perhaps as much a matter of length as of style and suitability – *Dorian Gray* filled the entire number – although the somewhat 'byzantine' mythopoeia of "The

Fisherman" (Wilde used the word of *Salomé*, which the story anticipates in some details)[121] may have struck him as unsuitable for simultaneous publication on both sides of the Atlantic.

There are, however, close links between the two tales. Each explores the relationship between the hedonistic impulse, posited as innocent, and the established cultural beliefs and superstitions which trespass upon it. Each identifies as 'the soul' that destructive and contaminating influence which initiates the pagan nature into the evil of the external world as of the inner personality, and each uses for the purpose the device of the *Doppelgänger*. Dorian metaphorically cuts himself off from his 'soul', the portrait, while the Fisherman cuts off his soul literally: 'He took the little knife with its handle of green viper's skin, and cut away his shadow from around his feet, and it rose up and stood before him and looked at him, and it was even as himself.'[122]

Wilde acknowledged to Henley his French debts in *The Happy Prince*,[123] and they are even more obvious here. The mythopoeic fabric of the tale, like that of *Salomé*, owes much to Flaubert. We catch a glimpse of the dancer from the portal of Rouen cathedral, who dances 'sometimes on her hands and sometimes on her feet', and in the Circassian in the litter we see a sketch for Salomé herself: she smiles from between the muslin curtains, and the Soul, like the Young Syrian in the play, murmurs, 'I have never seen anyone so pale'. The Emperor with his ring, his wealth, and his Nubian executioner anticipate Herod, while the Fisherman's dying affirmation of love over the Mermaid's corpse has several points in common with Salomé's last speech to Iokanaan's head.

Like the world of *Salomé*, the Fisherman's world is a timeless realm in which priests of a medieval turn of mind – that condition that Wilde said 'belongs not to time but to temperament'[124] – exist together with Fauns, Merfolk, Tritons, Gryphons, and Dragons. The Soul describes other strange men and creatures encountered on its wanderings: the dog-faced Agazonbae; the horsefooted Sibans; the crocodile-worshipping Krimnians; the Aurantes, who bury their dead in the tops of trees; and the Magadae, who seem to have anticipated Max Beerbohm in being born old and growing younger daily, dying when they are little children. These fancies Wilde borrowed from, or invented in emulation of, Mandeville and Herodotus, whom he praised in "The Decay of Lying" for their enlightened indifference to fact. Their purpose, apart from the charm of the tall story and the traveller's tale, is to make the contemporary world an impossible anachronism, to create conditions in which issues of contemporary relevance can be examined with complete artistic objectivity.

The Fisherman flirts with demonism, as with literary history: the witch to whom he applies for help to rid himself of his soul combines fragments from *Macbeth* and Christina Rossetti's "Goblin Market", while the Devil himself, 'dressed in black velvet, cut in the Spanish fashion', might have stepped out of Wilde's own Spanish story. But the main point of the scene at the witches' sabbath is to establish the Fisherman's essential innocence. Wilde makes sure of the point by romanticising the lure of the undersea pagan pastoral. The Fisherman is like a Greek statue about to enter a Turner seascape full of clustering siren arms: 'Bronze-limbed and well-knit, like a statue wrought by a Grecian, he stood on the sand with his back to the moon, and out of the foam came white arms that beckoned to him, and out of the waves rose dim forms that did him homage.' The departure of the Soul, as the Fisherman plunges away to the sound of Triton fanfares, is the most interesting dramatic point in the story. Wilde creates an impossible historical perspective, but a consummation devoutly to be wished by the committed Hellenist. The Soul stands on the shore, as if watching the reversal of the chronological development from pagan to Christian culture, left behind in redundancy: 'And the Soul stood on the lonely beach and watched them. And when they had sunk down into the sea, it went weeping away over the marshes.'

The Fisherman's new life is intrinsically undescribable, a *vita nuova* inaccessible to the modern mind, but briefly suggested by Wilde's earlier poem of that name: 'When lo! a sudden glory! and I saw / The argent splendour of white limbs ascend, / And in that joy forgot my tortured past.' (The limbs of the poem may be Venus's, but the poet is significantly a fisherman smitten with *taedium vitae*.) The new life underwater, then, shifts the emphasis of the narrative to the adventures of the Soul, whose progression towards evil is represented by the three appeals that it makes to the Fisherman. It offers him first 'the Mirror of Wisdom', then 'the Ring of Riches', for possession of which, it implies, it has done murder. Finally it offers him a dancer, and the Fisherman, remembering the Mermaid's lack of feet (though forgetting their superfluity in her) – also remembering, perhaps, his whirling dance with the witch on the moonlit hilltop – succumbs to what he thinks harmless curiosity. The Soul's tactics are neatly handled. First, in its innocence, it offers something of real worth, the Mirror of Wisdom in which the beholder sees everything but himself. The Fisherman, however, is committed to an exclusive romantic love, a love which might be regarded as a manifestation of 'the Mirrors of Opinion' in which the beholder sees nothing but himself. By comparison, the offer of the Ring of Riches is canny, but crude, and that of the dancer highly politic, almost Machiavellian. Once the Soul has betrayed him, however, and he **discovers how corrupt** it has become in its absence, he withstands all further temptation, whether evil, sensuous (the Salomé dancer), or good (missionary work to right wrongs and alleviate 'the world's pain'). His heart is 'so compassed about with love' that the Soul can find no entry there, and he retires to a house of wattles and waits there for two years for the Mermaid's reappearance.

The full significance of the Fisherman's pagan quest emerges when we consider Wilde's use of two further literary sources. Flaubert's influence is pervasive, but largely stylistic. The contributions of Andersen and Tennyson, however, are directly relevant to the Hellenist argument. The witch, the white arms in the surf, the dramatic use of legs, tails, and dancing, all occur in some form in Andersen's story "The Little Mermaid", but Wilde characteristically reverses its three essentials: the setting is the land, not the sea; the protagonist is male, not female; and the issue is not the acquisition of an immortal soul as a means to an ideal romantic love, but the attempt to get rid of one for the same purpose. The echo of Tennyson confirms this irony. Already there is, from the Christian point of view, the contradiction of the Fisherman being not a 'fisher of souls' but a spurner of his own soul. This substitution of pagan for Christian assumptions is completed by an adaptation of Victorian poetry's most celebrated death scene, "The Passing of Arthur" (1870) from *The Idylls of the King*, and its use here balances the use of "Gareth and Lynette", the first of the idylls, in "The Birthday of the Infanta". After the last battle in the west, when Arthur's corpse is taken out to sea in a barge by the weeping queens, the watchers hear 'faint / Sounds, as if some fair city were one voice / Around a king returning from his wars.' The cry transforms what seemed like defeat into what seems like victory. The death of the Mermaid reverses this outcome. History provides no after-life for pagan anachronisms. Wilde tells us that a great cry comes from the sea, and the Mermaid's corpse is borne towards the shore by black waves. 'White as the surf it was, and like a flower it tossed on the waves. And the surf took it from the waves, and the foam took it from the surf, and the shore received it, and lying at his feet the young Fisherman saw the body of the little Mermaid.' Instead of the serene resignation of Arthur confronted with the collapse of his earthly hopes, the Fisherman's reaction is hysterical sobbing. 'And to the dead thing he made his confession. Into the shells of its ears he poured the harsh wine of his tale. . . . Bitter, bitter was his joy, and full of strange gladness was his pain. . . . From the palace of the Sea-King came the cry of mourning again, and far out upon the sea the great Tritons blew hoarsely on their horns. . . . And his Soul besought him to depart, but he would not, so great was his love. . . . And the sea covered the young Fisherman with its waves.'

The Fisherman's anti-spiritual quest for the grail of self, the perfection of the personality through joy and love alone, fails. Wounded, however, by the part of himself that he had cast off, he comes to understand suffering, and, at the moment when his heart breaks 'through the fulness of love' and the sea overwhelms him and takes its revenge on his faithless body, soul and heart are mingled and the pagan harmony that he had sought by means of self-amputation is paradoxically, yet inevitably, completed. The pattern finds a close parallel in Wilde's own life, as he realised in *De Profundis*.

At this point in the story, Wilde reintroduces the Priest, and with a certain courteous distaste. He goes forth in the morning to bless the sea, 'for it had been troubled. And with him went the monks and the musicians, and the candle-bearers, and the swingers of censers, and a great company.' When he sees the Fisherman and the Mermaid lying clasped in the surf, he makes the sign of the cross, and refuses the blessing he had intended. 'Accursed be the

Sea-folk, and accursed be all they who traffic with them.' He orders the
bodies to be laid in barren, unhallowed ground, with no sign placed to
identify the grave. Three years later, the disturbing fragrance of some white
flowers on the altar causes him to speak not of God's wrath, as he had
intended, but of the love of God, moving people to tears; and when he learns
that the flowers came from the site of the grave, 'he trembled, and returned
to his house to pray'. Once again, the power of love conquers, for

> in the morning, while it was still dawn, he went forth with the monks and the
> musicians, and the candle-bearers and the swingers of censers, and a great
> company, and came to the shore of the sea, and blessed the sea, and all the wild
> things that are in it. The Fauns also he blessed, and the little things that dance in
> the woodland, and the bright-eyed things that peer through the leaves. All the
> things in God's world he blessed, and the people were filled with joy and
> wonder.

Thus, at last, pagan and Christian were formally reconciled, if only by a testy
priest obliged to reconsider.

Wilde speaks of 'God's world' and takes for granted the basic metaphysical terms of Christianity. But the blessing is not an act justified by divine law
or authoritarian dogma. It is a gesture of acceptance through love which is
called forth by the miraculous sign that springs from the lovers' grave. It
repairs nothing except the Priest's own blindness. The flowers do not
reappear; the field lies relentlessly barren; the sea-folk no longer come into
the bay, 'for they went to another part of the sea'. The story is no more anti-
theist than any of Wilde's work, but it is strongly opposed to that doctrinaire
puritanism in which he saw the chief bane of modern life and against which
Dorian Gray was to be an energetic campaigner.

In the story which grew out of "The Fisherman", Wilde rehabilitated his
critical ideal of the new Hellenism in a fictional form. The new Hellenism's
great achievement was to make the soul indefinitely and transcendentally
porous, bringing man to that state in which 'sin is impossible', not because he
makes 'the renuciations of the ascetic' but because it will be impossible to
wish for anything 'that can do the soul harm, the soul being an entity so
divine that it is able to transform into elements of a richer experience, or a
finer susceptibility, or a newer mode of thought, acts or passions that with
the common would be commonplace, or with the uneducated ignoble, or
with the shameful vile'. This is the critic's utopia as opposed to the pagan
Romantic's – no less unthinkable, in its way, than it would be for modern
man to reverse the evolutionary process and live naked at the bottom of the
sea.

There is, in fact, a suggestion, if no more, of biological metaphor in the
story. Wilde may have had Kingsley's *The Water-Babies* in mind (already an
influence on "The Birthday of the Infanta"). This Christian pastoral shows
its child hero cleansed of the grime and suffering of modern life by contact

with a timeless water-underworld peopled by *putti* with gills. Notes in Wilde's Commonplace Book show, however, that he had been reading accounts of research on basic organic structures, and was interested in the parallels drawn between 'the protoplasmic hierarchy' – the development of differentiation of function in lower forms – and moral and social organisation in more advanced creatures. While it is unlikely that Wilde would base a fairy tale on Herbert Spencer, the biological metaphor summarises the tale's moral foundation. For all its beguiling appearance, the Fisherman's return to the sea is a retro-cultural step leading to self-destruction, and it is immoral because it denies the potential inherent in the more highly developed organism. This conclusion is admittedly implicit, but it is confirmed by *Dorian Gray*, where stepping outside the moral flow and outside history, time, and the aging process are explicitly equated.

"The Star Child"

This, the least unified of the four tales, is also the least original. Overtly Biblical in style (though similar in certain details to Flaubert's "St Julien L'Hospitalier"), it is a parable of pride with aesthetic glosses which follows a simple and familiar redemptive pattern. If the story of the woodcutters, the star, and the gold-wrapped foundling (mixing suggestions from Grimm with suggestions from the New Testament and George Macdonald's *The Golden Key*) seems a curious prelude to purgatorial scenes coloured by *The Arabian Nights*, there is nevertheless an underlying theme which holds the piece together and relates it to the remainder of the volume. This theme, which offers a further perspective on the pastoral condition, is itself composite, blending the myth of the gold to be found where a shooting star falls with the myth of Wordsworth's "Immortality" ode.

Two woodcutters, forced into unfamiliar parts of the forest by a snowstorm, are bewailing their lot when they see a shooting star come to earth close to them. Instead of the legendary crock of gold, they find only a child wrapped in a cloth of gold tissue worked with stars. One of them takes it home, where it is cared for and grows more beautiful daily; but, in return for the love it is given, the Star-Child shows only ingratitude and pride, maiming defenceless creatures and eventually rejecting even its own mother, who has sought continuously for it since its strange birth, because she is a beggar and ugly. At this point, his beauty leaves him; he becomes reptilian to look at, and searches without success for the woman he has spurned. Three years pass. He approaches a city, where he is first refused entry, then sold into slavery under an 'evil magician' whose motiveless malice is directed by the power, as yet undeclared, of a benevolent fate. There follow three trials of his newly awakened sense of charity and humility. Then the Star-Child is miraculously restored to his former beauty and followed through the streets like a triumphant king, but he refuses the crown offered him since his only aim is to find his mother and beg her forgiveness. At this point, he sees her in the crowd and by her side the leper to whom, in his three trials under the magician, he had shown kindness at the expense of beatings. He humbles himself before them, and when they raise him up he sees that they are his parents, and a king and queen. The Star-Child is duly crowned, and rules kindly and justly; 'Yet ruled he not long, so great had been his suffering, and so bitter the fire of his testing, for after the space of three years he died. And he who came after him ruled evilly.'

The Child's birth is ambiguous: did he fall with the star, or was he merely revealed by the star's fall? In either case, traces of 'heaven, which is our home' wrap him around in his infancy, and his beauty seems to mark him out as super-terrestrial. But, as in many of Wilde's works, perfect physical beauty is shown to be 'incompatible with mental development and a full recognition of the evil of things'.[125] It is as if the Star-Child, unlike Wordsworth's babe, has come from a realm in which human values are irrelevant. He is not morally unsullied but god-like in the Apollonian manner, perfectly beautiful and pitiless; and, the longer he is exposed to life on earth, the further what could once have been an innocent delight in perfect beauty for its own sake, or as a natural manifestation of the god-like state, develops into vulgar narcissistic vanity. In order to live by the terms of an earthly life, the Star-Child must don another skin, resemble the snake and the toad that he reviled, and be reviled in turn. Apollonian egotism cannot be accommodated in human life – it becomes there the equivalent of the serpent in the garden which offers the perfect soul the chance to sin – and the Star-Child must learn this before he can regain the outward form which indicates his other-worldly origins. His beauty duly returns after his third act of charity to the leper, and the ecstatic welcome given him by the citizens is reminiscent of Christ's entry into Jerusalem on Palm Sunday; but his real trial consists in not being misled a second time by those who judge by outward appearances. Only the forgiveness of those whom he has wronged can restore his lost patrimony on earth: by washing the beggar-woman's feet and clasping the feet of the leper he imitates the penitence of the Magdalen and the humility of Christ, and thus shows himself the willing servant and conscious offspring of all humanity.

Not surprisingly, Wilde's parable, unlike Wordsworth's, ends bitterly. The Star-Child completes the redemptive cycle only by forsaking the countryside and taking up his destiny among men in the city. The three trials involve his symbolic reconciliation with the nature that he had spurned and maimed; he favours the woodcutter's family; but, as in "The Young King" there is a distinct movement away from pastoral origins towards some reluctantly and belatedly recognised position as erring member of a complex moral organism. The Star-Child, however, never reaches the 'years of philosophic mind', nor can the kernel of his experiences be passed on like Wordsworth's. He banishes the evil magician and fosters a brief interlude of justice and harmony; but when he dies, burned out by 'the fire of his testing', evil returns and there is no suggestion of a second coming followed by a second imperfect messianic example. Like the death of the Fisherman and the

Dwarf, the Star-Child's death ends a pattern which is archetypal yet exceptional. The true value of the pattern can be learned only by following it.

3 Crime and Egotism (1)

I. Criticism as Ingratiation—Chatterton, Wainewright, and the Aesthetics of Crime: Essay on Chatterton; "Pen, Pencil and Poison", "The Portrait of Mr W. H."

Of Wilde's various unpublished fragmentary writings, the Chatterton MS. is by far the most interesting. It throws new light on at least two of his better known critical pieces, and they, considered from this perspective, suggest a fresh interpretation of his critical work as a whole. Wilde has often been criticised for failing to fulfil his own 'Intentions', but much of the work collected under that title, besides much that was left out, took on its present form precisely because its premises were unrealisable in practice.

Wilde's early work had been full of rhetorical romantic impossibilities, and the first sign that he had begun to consider such issues in a rational or critical context is his interest in Chatterton, which appears to date from 1886. In that year Wilde and Herbert P. Horne, editor of the *Century Guild Hobby Horse*, launched a scheme to erect a monument to Chatterton in the poet's school, Colston's, in Bristol. The scheme aborted, and Chatterton received no public tribute of any kind except a lecture given by Wilde at Birkbeck College, London, on 24 November. No written record of the lecture has survived beyond a notebook containing a brief holograph introduction augmented by clippings from printed biographies, and, if these notes were intended to form the basis of the article announced for the October number of the *Hobby Horse*, Wilde must have reconsidered, for the article never appeared.

The conjecture surrounding Wilde's Chatterton venture is increased by a series of apparently coincidental links between Chatterton, Tasso, and Thomas Griffiths Wainewright, subject of "Pen, Pencil and Poison". In the *Foreign Quarterly Review* (July 1842) there appeared an anonymous and lengthy review of an experiment in biographical criticism. The book, *Conjectures and Researches concerning the Love, Madness, and Imprisonment of Torquato Tasso* (New York, 1842), purported to be an objective investigation of the relationship between Tasso and the Princess of Este, but the reviewer spent only a fraction of his space on Tasso, using the excellence of the author's research techniques to justify his own digression into an analogous English case, the mistreatment of Chatterton. The defender of

Tasso was one Richard Henry Wilde; the defender of Chatterton, Robert Browning.

Born in Dublin in 1789, Richard Henry Wilde lived most of his life in the United States, where he became a congressman and later something of a poet and Italian scholar (the *Tasso* presents 'a well-documented but romantic argument'[1]). I have found no direct evidence to connect Wilde with his American namesake,[2] but, if a family connection had existed, Lady Wilde would certainly have known of it and mentioned the book or article, or both. One thing is certain: if Wilde had chanced on the article, he could not have known that it was Browning's work. The only written evidence to support Browning's authorship dates from 1895, and remained unpublished until 1933. It occurs in a diary of Edith Cooper, who, with her aunt, Katherine Bradley, comprised the author 'Michael Field'. The pair met Browning as early as 1885, when he had enthused about Chatterton, but Wilde seems not to have known 'Michael Field' until several years later. He reviewed their play *Canute the Great* in *The Woman's World* in 1888, but his letter of 1890 suggests only a slight literary acquaintance.[3]

In spite of so much uncertainty about direct influence, Browning's essay is of interest here for its technique. Donald Smalley has called it an example of 'special-pleading in the laboratory', and it is a precursor, if not a progenitor, of Wilde's pseudo-forensic essays and dialogues. Browning seems to have believed that he was interpreting facts objectively, when he was actually 'rewriting history', as Wilde later claimed the great Elizabethan dramatists had done. Eventually Browning developed this approach in the overt fictions of his dramatic monologues, but in this early essay he is indifferent to the boundary between fiction and fact:

> A comparison of the Essay with its sources shows that into . . . the biographical data Browning read a thoroughly unhistorical revelation of spiritual redemption and courageous conflict with the forces of darkness. He evolved from Chatterton's pathetic story of moody pride, frustration, and suicide the plan and the protagonist of an edifying moral drama. . . . Browning worked, by forcing factual detail to argue against itself, to give substance and plausibility to a plot and a hero of his own invention. . . . Even his assurance to Julia Wedgwood that he had invented nothing in *The Ring and the Book* scarcely parallels his presenting the Essay in a sober quarterly review as a factual study that proposed to correct the mistakes of Chatterton's previous biographers.[4]

Browning's conclusion shows him modestly unrepentant; indeed, unaware. 'Thus much', he writes, 'has been suggested by Mr Wilde's method with Tasso. . . . Let others apply in like manner our enquiry to other great spirits partially obscured and they will but use us – we hope more effectually – as we have used these able and interesting volumes.'[5] Wilde may well have taken Browning at his word. In "Pen, Pencil and Poison", which 'corrects' the moralistic 'mistakes' of Wainewright's previous biographer, W. Carey Hazlitt, he largely avoids Browning's 'special-pleading'. But in "Mr W.H."

Cyril Graham, Wilde's forger-critic, virtually reincarnates 'the marvellous boy', and the opening paragraph of the story echoes that of the Chatterton draft:

> I insisted that his so-called forgeries were merely the result of an artistic desire for perfect representation; that we had no right to quarrel with an artist for the conditions under which he chooses to present his work; and that all Art being to a certain degree a mode of acting, an attempt to realise one's personality on some imaginative plane out of reach of the trammelling accidents and limitations of real life, to censure an artist for a forgery was to confuse an ethical with an aesthetical problem.

Browning's hypothetical influence on these two works is the more interesting in that, whatever their personal significance for Wilde, they are formally exercises in critical detachment. Chatterton's fate, if not Tasso's, admonishes the would-be Romantic, in life no less than in art. It may be coincidental that 1886, the year of Chatterton, was also the year of Robert Ross. On the other hand, Wilde did abandon work on Chatterton and suspend definitive critical statement on the compatibility between 'crime and culture' until three years later, by which time he had developed the serviceable mask of the book reviewer. This may have been a simple matter of practicalities, or it may have been a matter of technique – which, for Wilde, was essentially personality. Certainly, his career soon developed into a series of objective artistic or critical statements, all of which rested on prior calculation of the personal risk of ignoring their unalluring anti-Romantic truths; and it is apt that the much-delayed pronouncement on Chatterton should finally occur in a fiction whose objective form encloses the Romantic artist-as-critic's conclusions about the true relation between personal and factual truth.

A final fascinating point of comparison with the Browning article emerges from Donald Smalley's commentary. Not only does Wilde substitute, both in "Pen, Pencil and Poison" and in "Mr W. H.", an aesthetic for an ethical purpose, but, in addition, he later adapts, as Browning apparently had done, an early treatment of Chatterton to essentially dramatic ends. Browning's fictionalised Chatterton becomes the hero of his play *The Return of the Druses*, and approximates not only the career of Wilde's Shakespearean critic, Cyril Graham, but even, in many details, of Wilde's own career:

> Did Browning think of letting Chatterton reveal his truth upon the stage? In any event, Diabal, like Chatterton, (1) takes his first false step in youth, (2) resorts to imposture because the world will otherwise refuse him the exercise of his talents, (3) succeeds in his deception only because of his intellectual superiority to his credulous audience, (4) finds that his followers prize the accidental rather than the real merit of his work, (5) suffers because he cannot claim as his own his achievements in a borrowed guise, (6) struggles manfully to free himself from the effects of his first false step, (7) makes a partial return to the

POSTLETHWAITE ON "REFRACTION."

Grigsby. "HELLO, MY JELLABY, YOU HERE! COME AND TAKE A DIP IN THE BRINY, OLD MAN. I'M SURE YOU LOOK AS IF YOU WANTED IT!"
Postlethwaite. "THANKS, NO. I NEVER BATHE. I ALWAYS SEE MYSELF SO DREADFULLY FORESHORTENED IN THE WATER, YOU KNOW!"

1 Oscar Wilde, *photo* Sarony, New York (1882)

2 'Postlethwaite on Refraction', *Punch* (1881)

1 The Critic as up-stager of art:
an early but definitive pose
dating from the American
lecture tour of 1881-2. As yet,
the art-work in question is merely
a plaster backdrop in pseudo-
Renaissance style, but Wilde's
stance, like his Aesthetic
lectures, gives promise of the
doctrines of "The Critic as Artist"

2, 3 (overleaf)
Two interpretations by Du Maurier
of Aesthetic egotism.
Postlethwaite, Prigsby, and
Maudle (see plate 14) were
Punch's representative Aesthetic
triumvirate, Grigsby the hilarious
back-slapping establishment.
Wilde took light revenge in a
draft of *The Importance of Being
Earnest* with his shady solicitor,
Gribsby, cut in the final three-act
version.

DISTINGUISHED AMATEURS.—2. THE ART-CRITIC.

Prigsby (contemplating his friend Maudle's last Picture). "THE HEAD OF ALEXIS IS DISTINCTLY DIVINE! NOR CAN *I*, IN THE WHOLE RANGE OF ANCIENT, MEDIÆVAL, OR MODERN ART, RECALL ANYTHING QUITE SO FAIR AND PRECIOUS; UNLESS IT BE, PERHAPS, THE HEAD OF THAT SUPREMEST MASTERPIECE OF GREEK SCULPTCHAH, THE ILYSSUS, WHEREOF INDEED, IN A CERTAIN GRACIOUS MODELLING OF THE LOVELY NECK, AND IN THE SUBTLY DELECTABLE CURVES OF THE CHEEK AND CHIN, IT FAINTLY, YET MOST EXQUISITELY, REMINDS ME!"

Chorus of Fair Enthusiasts (who still believe in Prigsby). "OH, YES—YES!—OF COURSE!—THE ILYSSUS!!—IN THE ELGIN MARBLES, YOU KNOW!!! *HOW TRUE!!!!*"

ALWAYS READY TO LEARN, AND DEEPLY IMPRESSED BY THE EXTENT OF PRIGSBY'S INFORMATION, OUR GALLANT FRIEND THE COLONEL TAKES AN EARLY OPPORTUNITY OF VISITING THE BRITISH MUSEUM, IN ORDER TO STUDY THE HEAD AND NECK OF

THE ILYSSUS!

3 'Distinguished Amateurs – 2. The Art-Critic' *Punch* (1881)

4 *Andromaque*, IV, v, from Girodet's illustrations to Racine's *Théâtre* (1813). According to Jules Barbey D'Aurevilly, whose study of Beau Brummel, *Du Dandysme* (1845), significantly influenced Wilde, the 'ravishing, impertinent, and very modern attitude of Pyrrhus listening to Hermione's imprecations' embodies the true dandy's characteristic stance towards modern life

5, 6, 7 Lady Archibald Campbell: as painted by Whistler in *Arrangement in Black: Lady in a Yellow Buskin* (c. 1883); and as she appeared in two pastoral productions directed by William Godwin – 6, as Orlando from *As You Like It* (produced 1884, revived 1885); and 7, as Perigot (with Amaryllis) from Fletcher's *The Faithful Shepherdess* (produced 1885). The two engravings appeared in Lady Archie's piece, "The Woodland Gods" – a description of her dramatic experiments – which opened the first number of the *Woman's World* under Wilde's editorship (November, 1887)

[v]

9 Charles Ricketts and Charles Hazlewood Shannon (from William Rothenstein's *English Portraits* (1898), further contenders for the originals of Basil Hallward and Dorian Gray. Together they designed *A House of Pomegranates*. Ricketts designed several more of Wilde's books, and 'forged' a portrait of Mr. W. H.

8 Beardsley's frontispiece to John Davidson's *Plays* (1894), showing Wilde as a placid Dionysus 'with many vine-leaves' (contemporary homosexual slang), his legs apparently tied together

10 Gustave Moreau's *L'Apparition* (1876), the water-colour admired by Dos Esseintes, hero of J.-K. Huysmans' *À Rebours* – the novel which, according to Wilde, both was and was not 'the book that poisoned, or made perfect, Dorian Gray.'

11 Holman Hunt's wood-engraving, *The Lady of Shalott,* for Moxon's *Poems of Alfred Tennyson* (1859). The design is possible source for Beardsley's first Salomé drawing (12). The Lady of Shalott is herself a prototype of Wilde's Sybil Vane and of various characters in *Salomé*.

12 'j'ai baisé ta bouche, Iokanaan' (1893), the drawing which secured Beardsley the commission from John Lane to illustrate the play that he would have preferred to translate

13 Programme flier by Francis Sourbié for the French production of *Salomé* at the Théâtre le Globe MCDV, Paris, in 1972, with an all-male cast — the classic Freudian view of Iokanaan's (and, by implication, of Wilde's and Beardsley's) internal landscapes: voyeurism, castration fears, and sado-masochism.

15

MAUDLE ON THE CHOICE OF A PROFESSION.

Maudle. "How CONSUMMATELY LOVELY YOUR SON IS, MRS. BROWN!"

Mrs. Brown (a Philistine from the country). "WHAT! HE'S A NICE, MANLY BOY, IF YOU MEAN THAT, MR. MAUDLE. HE HAS JUST LEFT SCHOOL, YOU KNOW, AND WISHES TO BE AN ARTIST."

Maudle. "WHY SHOULD HE BE AN ARTIST?"

Mrs. Brown. "WELL, HE MUST BE SOMETHING!"

Maudle. "WHY SHOULD HE BE ANYTHING? WHY NOT LET HIM REMAIN FOR EVER CONTENT TO EXIST BEAUTIFULLY?"

[*Mrs. Brown determines that at all events her Son shall not study Art under Maudle.*

14, 15 Two views of the social usefulness and desirability of the 'new Hellenist': Du Maurier's signed cartoon and an engraving sent anonymously to

ways of Truth, but (8) achieves a final victory over falsehood, the moral
impulses of his nature triumphing over the intellectual, only in his last
moments.[6]

Although it is unlikely that Wilde would have constructed for himself so
exact a schema, his Chatterton notes sufficiently show that he had considered
most of these issues, and imply his awareness of their autobiographical
application:

> The conditions that precede artistic production are so constantly treated as
> qualities of a work of art that one is sometimes tempted to wish that all art were
> anonymous. For every true artist, even the portrait painter or dramatist, be his
> work absolutely objective in presentation, still reveals himself in his manner.
> Even abstract forms such as music and colour have much to tell us about the
> nature of him who fashioned them, and take the place of the biographer.
> Indeed, in some cases it is almost better for us not to search too curiously into the
> details of an artist's life – the *incompleteness* of Keats's life for instance blinds
> many of his critics to the *perfection* of his song – and it is well on the whole that
> we know so little about Shakespeare. [Quotes here Matthew Arnold's sonnet
> on Shakespeare.] Yet there are cases where the nature of the artist is so bound up
> with the nature of the man that art criticism must take account of history and
> physiology in order to understand the work of art. And this is specially true in
> the case of Chatterton.[7]

This passage bears in some way on almost everything that Wilde
subsequently wrote, the most obvious results being the dramatisation of its
central premise in the figure of Basil Hallward and the adaptation of its
technique of 'special-pleading' in "Pen, Pencil and Poison", a 'study in
green'[8] of Wainewright the homicidal artist-forger.

Wilde's principal source, W. Carey Hazlitt's *Essays and Criticisms of
Thomas Griffiths Wainewright* (1880), served him much as Richard Henry
Wilde had served Browning, with one important difference. Whereas
Browning saw a chance to assert a redeeming moral pattern, Wilde
deliberately avoids anything of the kind: the true critic's duty lies, among
other things, in disarming the moralist. Obliged to concede to the average
reader that Wainewright was 'far too close to our own time for us to be able
to form any purely artistic judgment about him', and continuing ironically
that it was 'impossible not to feel a strong prejudice against a man who might
have poisoned Lord Tennyson, or Mr Gladstone, of the Master of Balliol',
Wilde insists even so that 'there is no essential incompatibility between crime
and culture' and that 'one can fancy an intense personality being created out
of sin' – premises which underlie *Dorian Gray* and *Salomé*. Following up
Hazlitt's remark that Wainewright may have precipitated De Quincey's
parody essay "Murder, Considered as One of the Fine Arts" (*Blackwood's
Magazine*, 1824), Wilde concludes on a defiantly irresponsible note: 'To be
suggestive for fiction is to be of more importance than a fact.'

Evidently De Quincey's piece was itself suggestive: traces of it appear in "Lord Arthur Savile's Crime" and "The Canterville Ghost", besides its shadowy presence in the background of "Pen, Pencil and Poison". However, the two men share only the assumption that art is independent of ethics, and even here they are opposed. De Quincey makes it the basis for an amateurs' guide to the outstanding examples of imaginative murder, that 'fine art' whose object, he concludes, is to purge the beholder by exciting pity and terror. For Wilde, art and crime are not comically comparable but entirely separate, incompatible as thought and action are. Wainewright's crimes may have infused 'a strong personality' into his work, but Wilde is more interested in them from the psychological than from the aesthetic viewpoint. The differences are accentuated by style. Both works are essentially exercises, but Wilde's poker-faced prose, in spite of ironic signals, is basically more straightforward than De Quincey's modest proposals, and distinguishes what is essentially a serious inquiry of considerable subjective importance from an entertainment balanced on the precarious premise that few of the best philosophers die quietly in their beds. Wilde's occasional mischievous flicker may betray the solemn obituary manner –

> There is something dramatic in the fact that this heavy punishment [deportation to Tasmania] was inflicted on him for what, if we remember his fatal influence on the prose of modern journalism, was certainly not the worst of his sins. . . .
>
> De Quincey says that Mrs Wainewright was not really party to the murder. Let us hope that she was not. Sin should be solitary, and have no accomplices. . . .
>
> In 1852 he died of apoplexy, his sole living companion being a cat for which he had evinced extraordinary affection. . . .

– but the mischief is calculated. The last of these quips, with its laconic 'sole living companion', is intended to finesse convention. Wilde, the roving joker, palms a quotation from the prejudiced, punctilious Hazlitt (who had acknowledged his source for it), and produces it at the pseudo-moral climax to clinch the rubber for objective aesthetics. In Hazlitt, the remark had served merely to show how the inhumane assassin retained his love of cats.

The year after De Quincey's essay was published, Wainewright produced a characteristically whimsical pamphlet entitled 'Some Passages' in the Life of Egomet Bonmot, Esq., edited by Mr. Mwaughmaim, and now published by ME. (1825). This work, consisting largely of Bonmot's death-bed 'confessions' recorded by his 'other self', Mwaughmaim, has a certain air of Chattertonian dissembling about it, though it could never be regarded – as Wilde regarded the Rowley poems – as an example of true artistic objectivity. Bonmot's Byronic contempt for the current fashion in moral strip-tease may well dwarf the Wildean dandy's fastidious distaste for the 'broken heart' that will 'run to many editions',[9] but, the more energetically Wainewright postures, the more he emphasises the transparency of the disguise:

> – Oh, then full soon 'twas plainly seen that I
> Could be right eloquent of misery –
> For, roaming all th'astonished world about,
> I turned my heart and bowels inside out –
> Displaying these in all their yearning mood
> Whilst t'other showed the colour of my blood. –
> Troth, thought I, what though nature meant to hide,
> 'Twill please the folks to show 'em what's inside,
> For whether what is shown gives pain or nor,
> The major part o' the world cares not a jot;
> So there be hints of some all-nameless crime,
> Or hideous secret lurking in the rhyme.

Wainewright's obscene exhibitionism under his stage-alias is a perverse act of pride: like Baudelaire's dandy, whose origins lie in the Regency period, his boast is that he can shock without ever being shocked. The fact that contemporary conditions enable him to combine the dandy's aim of *épater le bourgeois* with the critical satirist's aim of *épater l'artiste* (or, more precisely, *l'artiste manqué*) is Wainewright's one piece of good fortune.

Wilde disliked Wainewright's flair for the grotesque. However, as Bonmot continues his account of the surest way to gain public attention, the curious parallel with Wilde's situation emerges:

> The hideous secret that I spoke about,
> Though hinted at, should never quite pop out –
> Brimful of darkness let it seem to be –
> Something abhorrent to humanity –
> Incest, for instance, or, at *least*, adultery:–
> Then, 'mid the crushing weight of mighty woe,
> Some phrase's ambiguity may show
> The author with the hero of his tale
> Vaguely identified:– and 'twill not fail
> To take the public if on FATE's decree
> Is laid the burden of delinquency.

In the age which relished General Napier's telegram and *Lady Audley's Secret*, and fizzled out in *Il Segreto di Susanna*,[10] there is little point in restricting Wilde to specific hypothetical analogues. Even so, Bonmot's egotism is a striking precedent for much of Wilde's attitudinising. The epigraph to his pamphlet – a line from Virgil: 'Me, Me, adsum qui feci – in Me convertite'[11] – finds, for example, a forlorn echo in *De Profundis*: 'It is not everyone who cries, "I, I," that can enter the Palace of Art.'[12] The joke extends even to his epitaph, which was to read:

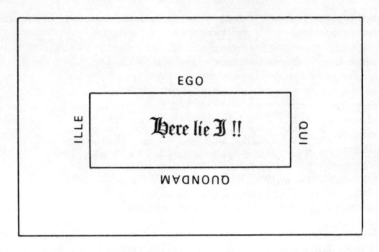

Finally, Bonmot lets fall the obligatory hint when he casually wonders whether his opinion of 'the sex' is causing the Muses deliberately to set obstacles in his path to fame. It was left for Wilde to point out, in his appreciation, that Wainewright, like Gautier and like Wilde himself, 'was fascinated by that "sweet marble monster" of both sexes that we can still see at Florence and in the Louvre'.

Although "Pen, Pencil and Poison" argues a discreet position beyond which Wilde had already ventured by the time it was published, it remains a test case. Many of the details of Wainewright's imprisonment and subsequent exile were to be matched by Wilde's own experiences, and the essay sounds intermittently prophetic: 'The permanence of personality is a very subtle metaphysical problem, and certainly the English law solves the question in an extremely rough-and-ready manner.' Wilde consistently opposes Hazlitt by regarding Wainewright as a cultivated and intelligent individual who has fallen foul of the law. Hazlitt, while recognising 'a psychological phenomenon of unsurpassed magnitude and curiosity', also declares it to be

> one of the most singular and deplorable cases of intellectual obliquity and deformity that I can call to mind. . . . In Wainewright . . . I realize a man who had no genuine sympathy with Nature or with Art. He was a heartless and callous voluptuary, who was prepared to trample on the noblest and tenderest feelings of humanity in the unpitying pursuit of his own selfish purposes. He was a villain of the true melodramatic stamp, but a thousand times more devilish and dangerous than any hero of melodrama.

For Hazlitt, Wainewright's shrugging off of the murder of Helen Abercrombie as merely the result of her 'thick ankles' is simply more fuel to the hell-fire. For Wilde, it is a sign of two of the artist's necessary virtues: wit, and deceit.

To the moralist, Wainewright is a citizen; to the artist-as-critic, a personality. Personality creates the artist, and while genius separates him in quality from ordinary people, personality separates him in kind. In such circumstances, ethical assessments of individual worth are inadequate, since they ignore the various ways in which the artistic impulse – in itself idealistic, presumably, and innocent – may seek expression. This attitude, inferable from "Pen, Pencil and Poison", is explicit in the notes on Chatterton. Was Chatterton 'a mere forger with literary powers', or was he 'a great artist'? Wilde opts for the latter view. 'Chatterton may not have had the moral conscience which is truth to fact, but he had the artistic conscience which is truth to Beauty. He had the artist's yearning to represent, and if perfection of representation seemed to him to demand forgery, he needs must forge.' Wilde insists that this course was not the result of arrogance or perversity but came rather from 'the desire of artistic self-effacement. He was the pure artist – that is to say his aim was not to reveal himself but to give pleasure – an artist of the type of Shakespeare and Homer, as opposed to Shelley or Petrarch or Wordsworth.'

It is a singular vision that can identify as an objective workman 'the father of the Romantic movement in literature, the precursor of Blake, Coleridge and Keats', but the assertion matches Wilde's own repeated claim that 'subjective form' is undesirable, and that modern art has progressively coarsened at the touch of ham-handed autobiographers. Wainewright's response to this tendency was to transform himself, in Hazlitt's phrase, into a 'literary Cerberus' with three daunting pseudonyms: Janus Weathercock, Egomet Bonmot, and Van Vinkvooms. 'A mask', Wilde remarks, 'tells us more than a face. These disguises intensified his personality.' Chatterton's case was analogous. He was 'essentially a dramatist and claimed for the artist freedom of mood. He saw that the realm of the imagination differed from the realm of fact. . . . He loved to let his intellect play, to separate the artist from the man.' This, Wilde says, explains his 'extraordinary versatility'. He knew that 'a great genius can affect anything'.[13]

These remarks tell us more, perhaps, about Wilde than about Chatterton, and they show the extent of the change of tactics represented by "Pen, Pencil and Poison". Wilde's defence of Chatterton springs from genuine conviction, or from the even more dynamic desire for it.[14] "Pen, Pencil and Poison" is wholly objective. Here Wilde practises none of 'that "whitewashing of great men", as it has been called, which is so popular in our own day, when Catiline and Clodius are represented as honest and far-seeing politicians, when *eine edle und gute Natur* is claimed for Tiberius, and Nero is rescued from his heritage of infamy as an accomplished dilettante whose moral aberrations are more than excused by his exquisite artistic sense and charming tenor voice.'[15] On the other hand, ethical prejudice is inadmissible in aesthetic issues: 'It is only the Philistine who thinks of blaming Jack

Absolute for his deception, Bob Acres for his cowardice, and Charles Surface
for his extravagance, and there is very little use in airing one's moral sense at
the expense of one's aesthetic appreciation.'[16] These attitudes from earlier
criticism are combined in the conclusion to "Pen, Pencil and Poison", where
science joins history and art to form an ethically impervious trio: 'Nobody
with the true historical sense ever dreams of blaming Nero, or scolding
Tiberius, or censuring Caesar Borgia. These personages have become like
the puppets of a play. . . . We have nothing to fear from them. They have
passed into the sphere of art and science, and neither art nor science knows
anything of moral approval or disapproval.'

Wilde's attempt to ingratiate himself with the public at one remove seems
on the whole to have misfired. Admittedly slight, the essay struck Arthur
Symons, for example, also as pointless: 'A pretentious, affected writer does
not become interesting merely because he commits a murder.'[17] Perhaps
Symons found it objectionable to base an analysis of the artistic temperament on a subject better fitted to some 'notable criminals' series; but if he did
he must have overlooked the irony implicit even in the essentially serious
opening:

> It has constantly been made the subject of reproach against artists and men of
> letters that they are lacking in wholeness and completeness of nature. As a rule
> this must necessarily be so. That very concentration of vision and intensity of
> purpose which is the characteristic of the artistic temperament is in itself a mode
> of limitation. To those who are pre-occupied with the beauty of form nothing
> else seems of much importance.

However, Wilde says, there are exceptions to this rule: Milton, Goethe,
Rubens and Sophocles spring to mind. To offer as climax to this list the
figure of Thomas Griffiths Wainewright – 'not merely a poet and a painter,
an art-critic, an antiquarian, and a writer of prose, an amateur of beautiful
things and a dilettante of things delightful, but also a forger of no mean or
ordinary capabilities, and as a subtle and secret poisoner almost without rival
in this or any age' – is to push bathos to the brink of farce; and thus it is no
surprise that, when he found that this type of technique failed to attract the
right sort of attention, Wilde turned to more directly dramatic means: "Mr
W. H.", a dialogue within a story, and the two critical dialogues themselves.
'We are born in an age', mourns Gilbert, 'when only the dull are treated
seriously, and I live in terror of not being misunderstood.'[18] Through the
mask of the critical protagonist (Regency forger and murderer, Socratic
conversationalist, would-be Shakespearean critic or *fin-de-siècle* voice of the
'Tired Hedonists' club and contributor to the '*Retrospective Review*') the
artist scans his own future.

II. Shakespeare, the Woodland Gods, and Gautier's 'Perfidious Sphinx': *As You Like It* and "Shakespeare and Stage Costume"

Wilde's first London article, "Shakespeare on Scenery", appeared on 14 March 1885, in the *Dramatic Review*, a new weekly to which Shaw and William Archer also contributed. The article argues briefly that Shakespeare, for all his brilliant verbal scene-painting, deplored the practical limitations of Elizabethan theatres. Shakespeare would have welcomed with alacrity the technical refinements of the modern theatre, and this, Wilde says, is the best justification for 'archaeology', or historically accurate design.

The issue was topical. Archaeology in easel-painting had already been popularised by Alma-Tadema, Leighton, and Poynter, and by the mid-1880s Irving's Shakespearean revivals at the Lyceum Theatre were equally celebrated. Moreover, the architect and designer E. W. Godwin, who had worked on the interior of Wilde's Tite Street house, contributed seven articles on the subject between February and October, and Wilde's piece, which appeared midway through the sequence, was clearly intended to support Godwin's side of the debate.

During the following month Wilde assembled much documentation and published the resulting essay, "Shakespeare and Stage Costume", in the *Nineteenth Century* in May. Allegedly a reply to an article by Lord Lytton (December 1884), it is really an independent defence of archaeology on aesthetic premises. Godwin's main aim had been to clarify the archaeologists' theory and defend his own application of it in various productions. Wilde uses Lytton merely to define better his own sense of direction, and, perhaps, as a means of getting so respectably into print. Lytton's article is principally a review of London opinion of Mary Andersen's performance as Juliet, and his only reference to archaeology occurs in a footnote. Of the first scene (for which he admits to having arrived late) he wrote: 'The "public place" in Verona seemed to us faultless. . . . I say this without reference to the archaeology of it. The attempt to archaeologise the Shakespearean drama is one of the stupidest pedantries in an age of prigs.' Lytton published nothing further on the subject, and it was William Archer who responded to Wilde's essay with a short piece under the slightly weary title "Is Shakespeare Also among the Archaeologists?" (*Dramatic Review*, 23 May 1885). Archer's view is conditioned by his notion of Wilde as dress-reformer turned drama critic, 'an aesthetic Teufelsdröckh' entering 'in his own sprightly fashion . . upon the whole Shakespearean clothes-philosophy'. Wilde's 'conclusion' will be seriously disputed by no one, he claims, but his premises are untenable. The conclusion in question is simply that the critics have not given archaeology a chance to show its paces: 'If they will not encourage, at least they must not oppose, a movement which Shakespeare of all dramatists would most have approved; for it has Truth for its aim, and Beauty for its result.'

By the time *Intentions* appeared, Wilde had grown tired of the essay, although if he included it there as a make-weight he made a virtue of the necessity. Retitled "The Truth of Masks – *A Note on Illusion*", it now represents the Janus-head of criticism. 'Not that I agree with everything that I have said in this essay,' he adds. 'There is much with which I entirely disagree. The essay simply represents an artistic standpoint, and in aesthetic criticism attitude is everything.' When arranging for a French translation of *Intentions*, Wilde substituted "The Soul of Man". Perhaps he felt the redundancy of preaching in Paris the truth of masks, but he must also have realised that "Mr W. H." had exhausted in more shapely fashion the aesthetics of the Shakespearean subject and its relation to the ethics of the critic.

The evidence used in "Shakespeare and Stage Costume" falls into three classes: that drawn from the text of the plays, that drawn from historical sources, and the kind of interpretative statement which appeals purely to the reader's aesthetic sense. I have no space to summarise the elaborate argument, but it was evidently intended to vindicate the critic and his subject from scepticism such as Archer's, and it constitutes Wilde's first organised essay in 'the philosophy of the superficial'. Not only does Shakespeare draw many outstanding metaphors from dress, but in addition, Wilde says, 'the whole of the Philosophy of Clothes' is contained in Lear's scene with Edgar, 'a passage which has the advantage of brevity and style over that prolonged struggle between the Scotch dialect and the German irregular verb which is such an exciting quality in *Sartor Resartus*'. Moreover, the Renaissance itself was fascinated by archaeology, which afforded a way of filling 'with the new wine of romanticism forms that else had been old and outworn'. There was a keen interest in every kind of costume, and even Shakespeare's indifference to anachronism was counterbalanced by his frequent provision of precise historical details. Thus, 'in mounting a play in the accurate costume of the time, according to the best authorities', a designer is 'carrying out Shakespeare's own wishes and method'.

To support these propositions, Wilde compares two recent productions of *As You Like It*: one, inartistically elaborate, at the Haymarket Theatre; the other, an outdoor performance mounted by E. W. Godwin and Lady Archibald Campbell, which demonstrated, among other things, the effectiveness of costumes conceived integrally with the setting (see Plates 6, 7). Lady Archie outlined her aims in the first number of the restyled *Woman's World* (November 1887) under the Arcadian title, "The Woodland Gods" – a phrase which suggests, as does the argument, Wilde's guiding hand. Realism has reached its zenith, she claims; but 'on the pastoral stage . . . we may pass from the realisation of the actual to the realisation of the ideal'. The setting was a woodland attached to Coombe House, Richmond-on-Thames, and Lady Archie took the part of Orlando. Unlike

Hamlet, Romeo, and even Shylock, this role had never been undertaken by a woman. 'Yet', she says, 'one can feel that it might have been written for one of those youths who in Shakespeare's time played women characters'.

It is, in fact, upon the androgynous nature of Lady Archie's performance that Wilde seems most disposed to dwell, particularly in his notice for the *Dramatic Review* (6 June 1885). He opens his remarks with a quotation from Swinburne: 'the golden book of spirit and sense, / The holy writ of beauty'. Later, he applied these lines to Pater's *Marius the Epicurean*, but here they refer to Gautier's *Mademoiselle de Maupin*, the androgynous Romantic novel celebrated in Swinburne's sonnet, and whose central episode uses an amateur production of *As You Like It* as a means of revealing to the hero the true sex of the disguised heroine.

Maupin has dressed herself as a man and taken the name Théodore de Sérannes in order to see more of the world. In due course, she finds herself at a château where the hero, D'Albert, and his mistress, Rosette, are staying with a party of friends. Having exhausted the gamut of rustic entertainments, they decide to stage a play. D'Albert chooses *As You Like It* and commandeers Orlando. Rosette is given the female lead, Rosalind, but a sudden caprice forbids her to compromise her delicacy by dressing as a man. No lady wishes to seem less modest than her hostess, so that the production is threatened, whereupon Théodore, previously cast as Jaques, offers to play Rosalind. His appearance in female costume creates a great stir, and D'Albert, whose consternation has daily kept pace with his infatuation for someone whom objective evidence presents as a man, becomes increasingly sure that his passion is not 'unnatural'. (Beardsley was evidently sceptical about D'Albert's self-communings, depicting him as a bulbous-hipped exquisite.) Until then, D'Albert recalls, his romantic feelings had seemed ever more monstrous: 'Mes rêves de tendresse si doucement caressés . . . devaient donc se métamorphoser en ce sphinx perfide, au sourire douteux, à la voix ambiguë, et devant lequel je me tenais debout sans ôser entreprendre d'expliquer l'énigme!'[19] Now, every detail of the rehearsals confirms his happy suspicions: Théodore's appearance in doublet and hose, for instance, seems subtly awkward. Eventually the undeclared lovers play their own roles under cover of Shakespeare's, with Rosette, now cast as Phoebe, completing the trio of *double entendres*. D'Albert is certain that Théodore fully realises the situation, and that 'à travers le voile de ces expressions empruntées, sous ce masque de théâtre, avec ses paroles hermaphrodites, il faisait allusion à son sexe réel et à notre situation réciproque'.[20]

The original Maupin had been no less ambivalent. Madeleine D'Aubigny, wife of le Sieur de Maupin, died at thirty-seven after leading an extraordinary life as opera-singer, duellist, and bisexual Don Juan. She was as capable of laying flat three adversaries in an evening's duelling as of achieving notable success in Campra's opera *Tancrède* (1702): 'sa voix "ambiguë" de contralto, sa beauté virile et sa grace digne d'une véritable femme, avaient fait merveille dans le rôle travestie de Clorinde'.[21]

'Yet,' Wilde pursues, 'lovely as Gautier's description is, the real presentation of the play last week at Coombe seemed to me lovelier still.' Not only did it have 'all those elements of poetry and picturesqueness which *le maître impeccable* so desired', but in addition it had the charm of open woodland and open air. Lady Archie's Orlando was

> a really remarkable performance. Too melancholy some seemed to think it. Yet is not Orlando love-sick? Too dreamy, I heard it said. Yet Orlando is a poet. And even admitting that the vigour of the lad who tripped up the Duke's wrestler was hardly sufficiently emphasised, still in the low music of Lady Archibald Campbell's voice, and in the strange beauty of her movements and gestures, there was a wonderful fascination, and the visible presence of romance quite consoled me for the possible absence of robustness.

The 'low music' and the 'strange beauty of her movements and gestures' with their 'wonderful fascination' were to be transferred to Sibyl Vane, whose voice in *Romeo and Juliet* was 'very low at first, with deep mellow notes', and then, as the play proceeded, began to evoke impressions of distant musical instruments, recalling the curious palimpsest of visual and aural effects in the review – the Elizabethan foresters with their 'whoop and shout', the distant horn of Hugo or Verlaine, the 'faint wreaths of blue mist' which gave the scene a Japanesque quality and demonstrated 'the aesthetic value of smoke'. Though lacking the physical vigour of the original Maupin, Lady Archie's performance of the pastoral hero *en travestie* must have been one of the principal stimuli for Wilde's two imaginative projections of idealised Shakespearean actors: she is the progenitor not merely of Sibyl Vane but also of Willie Hughes. Mr W. H.'s relationship with the great dramatist combined 'spirit and sense' in subtle proportion, while in his fleshly encounter with the mysterious 'Dark Lady' (added to the extended version) we may trace a hint of Gautier's 'perfidious' or Wilde's 'false' sphinx, the monster whose teasing smile and ambiguous tones 'wake foul dreams of sensual life' and make the poet 'what I would not be'.[22]

A fortnight before the review of *As You Like It*, Wilde contributed a notice of "*Henry IV* at Oxford" (*Dramatic Review*, 23 May 1885). Its concluding epigram sums up his attitude to Shakespearean performance, and confirms its importance in the critic's imaginative realm: 'While we look to the dramatist to give romance to realism, we ask of the actor to give realism to romance.' Wilde the critic is essentially Wilde the self-dramatist, and his remark points straight to "The Portrait of Mr W. H.", which leads in turn to Dorian's cerebral affair with 'all the heroines of romance' summed up in one actress, Sibyl Vane.

III. "The Portrait of Mr W. H." The Wishful Thinker as Criminal

> That is what the highest criticism really is, a record of one's own soul. It is more fascinating than history, as it is concerned simply with oneself. It is more delightful than philosophy, as its subject is concrete and not abstract, real and not vague. It is the only civilised form of autobiography, as it deals not with the events, but with the thoughts of one's life; not with life's physical accidents of deed or circumstance, but with the spiritual moods and imaginative passions of the mind. ["The Critic as Artist", part I; *Works*, 1027.]

Wilde's Shakespearean fiction was first published in July 1889 in *Blackwood's Magazine*, the journal previously associated with De Quincey and Waine-wright. Wilde acknowledged Robert Ross's half-share in the story,[23] though certain articles in the *Dramatic Review* and the *Woman's World* (Lady Archibald Campbell, Amy Strachey on child-actors, and others[24]) may have contributed something.

The story reflects Wilde's current prose endeavours. It borrows the socialite tone and setting of the four smart stories of 1887, adapts mythopoeically the historical evidence used in "Shakespeare and Stage Costume", and develops the special-pleading of the Essay on Chatterton. Moreover, its aesthetic and critical premises reappear throughout *Intentions*. The artist as liar and the critic as cultured autobiographer, the two central protagonists of the critical dialogues, are cast together here in a literary detective story – with one significant adjustment. With the artist-forger and the artist-liar four months behind him, Wilde moves to consider the modern Chatterton, the critic who rewrites history in his own image. As in "Lord Arthur Savile's Crime", the 'objective form' of detective fiction covers a hunt for the self. From within its elaborate stage-set of ironic narrative, pseudo-memoir, paradoxical peripeteia, and dramatic dialogue and *dénouement*, "Mr W. H." presents the scientific value of evidence, the ethical value of literal truth, and the aesthetic value of personal conviction as the irreconcilable constants in the critic's dialectic.

"Pen, Pencil and Poison" was Wilde's first study of an artistic personality. "Mr W. H." is his first study of the effect of one artistic personality upon another, and it clearly influenced "The Critic as Artist" (first published in July and September 1889), in which he argues that the two epoch-making events in the history of art are the discovery of a new technique and the discovery of a new personality. Willie Hughes transformed the Elizabethan drama as Antinous and Charmides transformed Greek art and philosophy, and Wilde makes further claims which place him at the head of the modern Romantic tradition.

"The Portrait of Mr W. H." exists in two substantially different versions. In the first, the narrative is more prominent, the theory less elaborately documented, the curiosity value of the evidence correspondingly emphasised, and the calculated self-revelation of the narrator is absent. The second version, which remained unpublished during Wilde's lifetime, offers theoretical houseroom to the Dark Lady and develops the narrator's autobiographical testimony.

Before examining the fascinating second version, it will be as well to summarise the argument of the first. The theory invented by Wilde's critical Chatterton, 'the youngest and the most splendid of all the martyrs of literature' as the narrator calls him, is that Mr W. H. must have been someone who had a decisive influence on Shakespeare's dramatic art, and whose personality was capable of filling 'the soul of Shakespeare with terrible joy and no less terrible despair'. This assertion depends on two debatable premises: that the tone of the sonnets is, for the sensitive reader, not only a reliable but also a conclusive guide to the circumstances surrounding their composition, and that the artist's temperament is congenitally subservient to beauty, whether corporal or ideal. The second version makes this quite explicit:

> I was about to leave the room when Erskine called me back. "My dear fellow," he said, "let me advise you not to waste your time over the Sonnets. I am quite serious. After all, what do they tell us about Shakespeare? Simply that he was the slave of beauty."
> "Well, that is the condition of being an artist," I replied.

The conviction held by each of the three characters in turn is that Mr W. H. was a boy actor called Will Hughes, or Hews (a name revealed by italicised puns in the Quarto text), the sonnets' chief personage being identical with their dedicatee. How Shakespeare met him is unexplained, but the encounter made him the first interpreter of the great Shakespearean female roles. When the dramatist urges him to 'multiply' himself, he is expressing his wish that Willie Hughes will place his beautiful form and chameleon-like personality at art's disposal, and the 'marriage of true minds' is a compact with Shakespeare's 'Muse' – not the 'slight' genius of the sonnets but the dramatic muse. Mr W. H.'s incomplete commitment to Shakespeare appears in his temporary allegiance to the 'rival poet', which draws from Shakespeare the bitter concession, 'I grant thou wert not married to my Muse'. (Wilde overlooks the fact that drama is traditionally the province of two muses, but a great poet is presumably eligible for poetic licence.) The discovery of Mr W. H.'s name is 'comparatively nothing', but the discovery of his professional relationship with Shakespeare is 'a revolution in criticism'. The Friend's character, his histrionic gifts, his love of attention, his incapacity to feel devotion while yet exciting it in others, are all consistent with the actor's capricious nature, and are further confirmed by comparison with the proud youth in "Venus and Adonis" and the deceitful youth in "A Lover's Complaint", both of whom were modelled on him.

The theory is rounded off by some further biographical speculations connecting Mr W. H. with a copy of *Edward II*, the play written by Marlowe (the 'rival poet') especially for him, extant in the library at Cassel ('the only copy in existence, as Mr Bullen tells us'), and with the presentation of Shakespeare's death-mask to an actor in Germany in 1617 by a member of the English ambassador's suite, 'pale token of the passing away of one who had so dearly loved him'. The hypothesis that Mr W. H. survived Shakespeare and spread his art through Europe leads to Wilde's final critical claim on behalf of Willie Hughes:

> Indeed, there was something peculiarly fitting in the idea that the boy-actor, whose beauty had been so vital an element in the realism and romance of Shakespeare's art, had been the first to have brought to Germany the seed of the new culture, and was in his way the precursor of the *Aufklärung* or Illumination of the eighteenth century, that splendid movement which, though begun by Lessing and Herder, and brought to its full and perfect issue by Goethe, was in no small part helped on by a young actor – Friedrich Schroeder – who awoke the popular consciousness, and by means of the feigned passions and mimetic methods of the stage showed the intimate, the vital, connection between life and literature.[1893 text.]

This specific echo of the conclusion to "Duke Carl of Rosenmold" places the story within the tradition of the Paterian 'imaginary portrait', the critical fiction which creatively rewrites history. Even so, Wilde's purpose is in one respect antithetical to Pater's, since the more "Mr W. H." appears to correspond with objective historical research, the more subjective it becomes in essence – a paradox discussed and exemplified in "The Decay of Lying".

Wilde sent the manuscript of the enlarged version to Charles Ricketts in the summer of 1893. Ricketts had "forged" a picture of Mr W. H. for Wilde in 1889 and was to design the new volume, using the picture as frontispiece. Various projects, including *The Sphinx*, delayed the venture, and when Wilde again approached his publishers, Elkin Mathews and John Lane, they were in the process of terminating their partnership. Their reluctance to take on the new "Mr W. H." may have arisen from commercial considerations, but they may, also, have remembered the adverse criticisms of *Dorian Gray* in 1890 and wished to keep away from an equivocal subject, the one refusing to issue it 'at any price' and the other undertaking it only if he 'approved of it'.[25] This must have been particularly irritating for Wilde, after his revision of *Dorian Gray* and his caution in the first "Mr W. H.", for it seems probable that 'the greatest mystery in modern literature' appealed to him precisely because, as a public property, it offered a sufficiently objective form in which he might reach an imaginative conclusion on historical premises which was at the same time aesthetically and psychologically satisfying to himself.

The basis of the work has been defined as the Wildean paradox (used also in the prose poem "The Teacher of Wisdom") that the effort of conversion saps conviction. This idea does support the narrative framework, bringing about the various reversals between the three characters and providing Wilde with a convenient means of introducing and concluding the story; but it is not the motive force, nor does it bear any direct relationship to the additional material. This falls into three classes: authentic historical evidence, biographical speculation based on textual interpretation, and other, more impressionistic material which develops the theory beyond its original literary and historical scope and relates it to the wishful thinker's plight and the modern mode of subjective criticism.

The most important historical additions concern the influence of boy actors on drama and the influence of neo-Platonic thought during the Renaissance. After making the obvious point that the use of boy actors gave rise to the widespread dramatic convention of women dressing as men, also to the theme of sexual ambiguity prominent from Lyly onwards, Wilde takes the argument a step further. If sex is indeed an element in artistic creation, he says, then it might be urged 'that the delightful combination of wit and romance which characterises so many of Shakespeare's heroines was at least occasioned if not actually caused by the fact that the players of these parts were lads and young men, whose passionate purity, quick mobile fancy, and healthy freedom from sentimentality can hardly fail to have suggested a new and delightful type of girlhood or womanhood'. To those who would object that only a woman can do justice to these roles, Wilde would reply that this view denies the art of acting all objectivity and that the Elizabethan stage, unlike the modern, never suffered from too close an identification of the actor with the role. (Nevertheless, this argument reverses Wilde's earlier contention that Shakespeare regularly complained about the inadequacy of his female leads.) 'The very difference in sex between the actor and the part' offered one more demand upon 'the imaginative capacities of the spectators', and such demands were among the great strengths of Shakespeare's stage. To these same conditions, Wilde argues, is due Shakespeare's apparently exaggerated anxiety about the early fading of Willie Hughes's youth and beauty: the artist's universal regret over such things is heightened by the dramatist's desire that Mr W. H. will engender 'copies' of himself before it is too late ('when chins grew rough and voices harsh much of the charm and grace of the performance must have gone').

Wilde adds the section on neo-Platonic thought, in particular its conception of friendship, to develop more fully his theory of 'the marriage of true minds' between actor and dramatist. Emphasising the contemporary fascination with such books as Ficino's translation of the *Symposium*, he argues that the friendship between Shakespeare and Mr W. H. was largely ideal. Over and above the 'subtle element of pleasure, if not of passion' which accompanied their 'artistic comradeship' there was 'the Soul, as well as the language, of neo-Platonism'. This emerges clearly in the imagery of the sonnets. Childbirth, the union of the two sexes in one person and of the tangible and the ideal in one personality, the suggestion of an almost mystical 'marriage' – all these place the poems in the tradition deriving from the *Symposium*:

> In its subtle suggestions of sex in soul, in the curious analogies it draws between intellectual enthusiasm and the physical passion of love, in its dream of the incarnation of the Idea in a beautiful and living form, and of a real spiritual conception with a travail and a bringing to birth, there was something that fascinated the poets and scholars of the sixteenth century. . . . Love had, indeed, entered the olive garden of the new Academe, but he wore the same flame-coloured raiment, and had the same words of passion on his lips.

Mr W. H.'s children are to be the progeny of his friendship with the poet, for, as Diotima says, 'friends are married by a far nearer tie than those who beget mortal children, for fairer and more immortal are the children who are their common offspring'.

All of this tends, as one might expect, to confirm the power of personality. The fusion, in the quotation above, of Dantesque love with neo-Platonic theory reminds us of that union of medieval and Greek influences which was responsible for the distinctive quality of the nineteenth century 'English Renaissance', that movement whose motto was 'La personnalité, voila ce qui nous sauvera'. We therefore learn without surprise that the Romantic movement is directly indebted to Willie Hughes. To him we owe Shakespeare's pre-eminence as the first great modern artist who recognised the full significance of personality, not only in the artist, but to the artist also. The beautiful personality – that combination of physical, mental and spiritual qualities which seems to express an involuntary kinship with art – is in fact the main causeway between life and art. In particular, the actor, who 'uses all means at once' in his appeal to the audience, and who is not limited like the musician, the sculptor or the painter, is 'Art's most complete, most satisfying' instrument. In such completeness lies danger, Wilde concedes: 'Those arts are happiest that employ a material remote from reality, and there is a danger in the absolute identity of medium and matter, the danger of ignoble realism and unimaginative imitation.' Yet Shakespeare was an actor himself; his plays contain 'the most perfect rules for acting that have ever been written'; his work depends upon theatric presentation, 'and we cannot marvel that he worshipped one who was the interpreter of his vision, as he was the incarnation of his dreams'. Willie Hughes, in fact, stood to Shakespeare as Pico della Mirandola stood to Marsilio Ficino, the only difference being that Shakespeare had the good fortune to meet Mr W. H. at a point in his career when he could be of maximum artistic benefit to him. Nashe railed at Shakespeare for 'reposing eternity in the mouth of a player', but this very determination marks the vital link between the Renaissance and the modern spirit, proving the primacy in modern art of personality.

The premises governing Wilde's interpretation of Mr W. H. govern also his interpretation of the Dark Lady. Her identity is of no interest, beyond the fact that it remains a mystery. Her importance lies solely in her relationship

to the 'marriage' of actor and dramatist. Any attempt to explain the Dark
Lady on a biographical basis must be speculative at best, but Wilde's
explanation of her role in Shakespeare's life is highly so. In part, no doubt, it
depends on his view of Mr W. H.'s androgynous personality and of the
'essentially male' culture of Renaissance England. In other respects, it
appears to introduce further highly subjective themes, formalised to fit the
established narrative. There is an element of the ridiculous in offering a
speculative interpretation of a speculative interpretation of a speculative
relationship, and I do so with some reservations. However, the various ideas
which make up Wilde's Dark Lady episode find such striking echoes in his
own career that speculation is justified merely on the basis of what might
seem coincidence.

Though the implications of the Dark Lady theory are complicated, its
'facts' are soon summarised. 'Two things were certain: she was much older
than the poet, and the fascination that she exercised over him was at first
purely intellectual.' When she sought, in addition to 'enslaving the soul of
Shakespeare', to 'snare the senses of Willie Hughes', Shakespeare aped the
language of passion to lure her away, knowing 'the weakness of the boy-
actor's nature, his susceptibility to praise, his inordinate love of admiration'.
Shakespeare finds, however, that disguise is a wickedness, that 'a comedy in
real life' turns serious, and that his feigned love is a Nessus' shirt, 'a plague-
stricken and poisonous thing' that he cannot throw away. He soon realises
that 'his genius is nothing to her compared to the physical beauty of the
young actor', and so he cuts himself free, returning soon afterwards to
Stratford. When he reappears in London, her influence over Willie Hughes
seems to have ended, though it was shortly succeeded by that of the rival
poet. (This account depends on transferring sonnets CXXVII–CLII to their
'proper place' between sonnets XXXIII and XL.) Nevertheless, her over-
shadowing of their ideal friendship was responsible for Shakespeare's
composition of the sonnet on lust, 'Th'expense of spirit in a waste of shame'.
Wilde calls this 'the greatest sonnet ever written'.

If, as Wilde suggests, Willie Hughes marks the beginnings of the
Romantic movement in literature, then the Dark Lady might be regarded as
another "first" – the first fatal woman, acquisitive, lustful, and destructive of
the Romantic poet (though not, at this early stage of the genre, all-
consuming). In this, she has certain points in common both with the Sphinx
of Wilde's poem of that name and with Lord Alfred Douglas, although her
similarities to the Romantic *femme fatale* are less important than the fact that
Wilde conceived of her as an intruder into an ideal artistic relationship. She is
a generic outsider – 'possibly the profligate wife of some old and wealthy
citizen', but unquestionably one to whom art and intellect mean nothing.

As early as *Poems*, Wilde had pondered the penalties of a fall from aesthetic
grace, while in *De Profundis*, often repetitive of the matter and manner of his
early work, he returned to the subject with new vehemence. The only work
of which it forms the theme, however, is *The Sphinx*, unique in having

retained Wilde's interest for some fifteen years. Begun at Magdalen, almost finished in Paris in 1884, it was finally published in 1894 with Ricketts' designs. *The Sphinx* is Wilde's reply to *La Tentation de Sainte Antoine* (1874). (He was hoping, late in 1888, to translate Flaubert's piece into English.[26] Nothing came of this, but the work could still beguile him in 1898 when, 'torn' by that 'tiger, Life', he languished in the desert of anonymity.[27]) The creature lurks in the corner of the 'student's cell', staring him out of self-possession: 'You wake in me each bestial sense, you make me what I would not be./You make my creed a barren sham, you wake foul dreams of sensual life'. The 'creed' is ostensibly Christian: the hidden personality, a serpent of old Nile, lures the Anglo-Catholic from his beads. But the creed could as plausibly be art, and the Sphinx the metaphorical culprit for the invasion of art's imaginative realm by the flesh.

When Wilde began *The Sphinx*, his relationship with his own Muse-Sphinx of personality had hardly begun. By 1894 he had met and become dominated by the personality which, besides his own, had the profoundest effect on his life: Alfred Douglas. At first sight, Douglas might appear a living model for Mr W. H. – the capricious, unstable youth, naturally histrionic, always seeking attention, sexually ambiguous, something of an artist in his own right, and capable of eliciting from Wilde such declarations as 'You are the atmosphere of beauty through which I see life'.[28] But Wilde did not meet Douglas until 1890,[29] and it is significant that the 1893 narrator, newly eloquent about the 'presence' that has accompanied him unrecognised all these years, insists that it has remained unincarnate and unseen. Mr W. H., in other words, was never a portrait from life, only a premonition. Only the unreadable occurs.[30]

If Douglas, however coincidentally, had much in common with Mr W. H.,[31] he had scarcely less in common with the Dark Lady. 1893, the year of the Dark Lady – or, more precisely, the year of the manuscript in which she appears – was also the year in which Douglas's interruptions of Wilde's work first reached crisis proportions.[31] (As early as 1891, however, Wilde had ruefully inscribed Douglas' copy of *Intentions* 'To Bosie, in memory of the higher philosophy'.[32]) Further evidence linking Wilde, Douglas and Shakespeare emerged in the trials. Wilde was called upon to vindicate passages in his own work, notably *Dorian Gray* and a letter, and a sonnet by Douglas. The letter began, 'Your sonnet is quite lovely, and it is a marvel that those red rose-lips of yours should have been made no less for music of song than for madness of kisses. Your slim gilt soul walks between passion and poetry.'[33] Wilde described the letter as a 'prose poem' and 'like a little sonnet of Shakespeare'. He further asserted that "Mr W. H." had not been written, as counsel implied, to show that Shakespeare's sonnets were 'suggestive of unnatural vice', but to show the reverse: 'I objected to such a perversion being put upon Shakespeare.' The sonnet by Douglas upon which Wilde was asked to comment tells of 'two loves', one representing romantic heterosexual love, the other implied homosexual love, 'the love that dares not speak its name'. Elucidating that now notorious phrase, Wilde invoked Plato, Michelangelo and Shakespeare, dwelling on the Platonic conception of an intellectual affection between an older and a younger man, and repudiating the sexual insinuation. Similarly, when asked whether he had ever 'adored a young man madly' as Basil Hallward had, he replied, 'No, not madly; I prefer love – that is a higher form', acknowledging with regret that the 'whole idea' for Basil's infatuation had been taken from Shakespeare's sonnets.[34] Douglas' sonnet could well have shared the same inspiration. Both of its 'loves' are male figures, but in other respects it recalls the poem in which Shakespeare apparently contrasts Mr W. H. with the Dark Lady: 'Two loves I have of comfort and despair, / Which like two spirits do suggest me still: / The better angel is a man right fair, / The worser spirit a woman coloured ill.' ("In Praise of Shame", another queried sonnet, and "To Shakespeare" were also written in 1893, as was "The Sphinx", only fruit of Douglas' brief sojourn in Egypt, where his family, no less than Wilde, hoped that he would stay for a year or more as an attaché.[35])

Wilde's interpretations of Douglas' work may be as subjective as his interpretations of Shakespeare. They may also owe much to the circumstances. (He maintained that 'shame' in the second sonnet meant 'modesty', though this was apparently Douglas' own gloss.[36]) However, it would be cynical to suppose that all of Wilde's evidence about his work and his beliefs was purely opportunist, and impossible to separate what might have been from what was not. Once again, De Profundis strikes the relevant note. Commenting on Douglas' pathological hatred of Queensberry, Wilde also disavows any physical bond: 'That your father might have had your body, which did not interest me, and left me your soul, which did not interest him, would have been to you a distressing solution of the question. You scented the chance of a public scandal and flew to it.'[37] Moreover, he leaves no doubt about how closely Douglas' character could approach to that of the anti-intellectual profligate projected in the Dark Lady:

> Of the appalling results of my friendship with you I don't speak at present. I am thinking merely of its quality while it lasted. It was intellectually degrading to me. You had the rudiments of an artistic temperament in its germ. But I met you either too late or too soon, I don't know which. When you were away I was all right. . . . While you were with me you were the absolute ruin of my Art, and in allowing you to stand persistently between Art and myself I give to myself shame and blame in the fullest degree. You couldn't know, you couldn't understand, you couldn't appreciate. I had no right to expect it of you at all. Your interests were merely in your meals and moods. Your desires were simply for amusements, for ordinary or less ordinary pleasures. . . . One half-hour with Art was always more to me than a cycle with you. Nothing really at any period of my life was ever of the smallest importance to me compared with Art. But in the case of an artist, weakness is nothing less than a crime, when it is a weakness that paralyses the imagination. . . . You said that you were under 'no intellectual obligation of any kind' to me. I remember that when I read that

statement, I felt that it was the one really true thing you had written to me in the whole course of our friendship. [The 'statement' refers to Douglas' most nearly dramatic venture in collaboration with Wilde: the unsatisfactory prose translation of *Salomé*.] I saw that a less cultivated nature would really have suited you much better. I am not saying this in bitterness at all, but simply as a fact of companionship. . . . When I compare my friendship with you to my friendship with such still younger men as John Gray and Pierre Louÿs I feel ashamed. My real life, my higher life was with them and such as they.[38]

Evidently, Douglas sometimes fulfilled the role of the Dark Lady as well as that of Mr W. H. Given that the fatal (or nearly fatal) woman can be interpreted – not least in Wilde's romantic dramas – as the objectification of impulses that the male writer distrusts or suppresses in himself, it would have been a relatively simple act of critical transvestism for Wilde to project a degrading temptress who disrupts the artist's Platonic dream.

In spite of these autobiographical elements, 'objective form' remains the true mode of the serious artist. Wilde would have us believe that 'the form' of "Mr W. H." and 'the form alone, is eloquent'.[39] Placing the Dark Lady in his hypothetical plot enables him to summarise the entire 'romance' traced by the sonnets. Shakespeare invites Willie Hughes onto the stage to interpret his heroines. A woman visits the playhouse and becomes infatuated with the young actor. At first she arouses Shakespeare's intellectual curiosity, but when he detects her passion for Willie Hughes, he feigns passion to divert her from him. Falling victim to his own device, Shakespeare extricates himself from the degrading situation only by returning to Stratford. When he comes again to London, she has disappeared. Willie Hughes is now lured away to play Gaveston in Marlowe's *Edward II*, 'filling up' the rival's 'line' with his 'countenance'. On Marlowe's death, he returns to Shakespeare. 'Evil rumour has now stained the white purity of his name, but Shakespeare's love still endures and is perfect. Of the mystery of this love, and of the mystery of passion, we are told strange and marvellous things, and the Sonnets conclude with an envoi of twelve lines whose motive is the triumph of Beauty over Time, and of Death over Beauty.'

If it is remarkable that Wilde succeeded in shaping so coherent a narrative from the chaos of the Quarto text, the form in which he arranges it is no less so: 'a drama and a soul's tragedy of fiery passion and noble thought' in four acts or scenes. Nothing could be more apt than a dramatic scenario for embodying a theory about Shakespeare's principal dramatic inspiration. Equally apt, as an example of autobiographical transposition, is Wilde's use of the four-act as opposed to the five-act form – a change warranted not merely by nineteenth-century dramatic practice but, indeed, by Wilde's own comedies, two of which had been produced by 1893, and all of which are concerned with the relationship between idealised love, trespass, and compassionate forgiveness. One might also point out that Wilde's phrase 'a soul's tragedy' is the borrowed title of a play by Browning, the first part of which was written in blank verse, the second part in prose, to reflect the change in the hero's circumstances. Besides recalling the dramatic treatment to which Browning adapted his Chatterton theme, this final coincidence suggests the relationship between the poetic 'romance' of Shakespeare's sonnets and the prose romance constructed around them by the latter-day critic, condemned to live in 'an age of prose'.

Wilde's reference to Pater's essay on "Love's Labour's Lost" suggests his increasing critical objectivity. He compares the early comedy to the sonnets, remarking that both contain 'that half-sensuous philosophy that exalts the judgment of the senses "above all slower, more toilsome means of knowledge"', and repeats Pater's suggestion that Berowne is 'a reflex of Shakespeare himself "when he has just become able to stand aside from and estimate the first period of his poetry"'.[40] Wilde, too, is making adjustments. The earlier Romantic extremes – 'For, sweet, to feel is better than to know' – are replaced here by the emphasis on criticism as a method of self-analysis: witness the reasons offered for the narrator's sudden loss of conviction in the theory: 'I had gone through every phase of this great romance. I had lived with it, and it had become part of my nature. How was it that it had left me? Had I touched upon some secret that my soul desired to conceal? Or was there no permanence in personality?' The problem of 'the permanence of personality', discreetly sounded in "Pen, Pencil and Poison", here becomes central. Wilde moves from the historical 'distance' previously recommended into the present day, all within the space of a few lines. At one moment, the narrator is sitting in 'the round theatre with its open roof and fluttering banners', watching history re-create itself in the manner of "The Critic as Artist". At the next, 'it was in this century that it had all happened. I had never seen my friend, but he had been with me for many years, and it was to his influence that I owed my passion for Greek thought and art, and indeed all my sympathy with the Hellenic spirit.'

By 1890, Wilde had begun to take account of the influence of the unconscious: 'Our weakest motives,' Lord Henry muses, 'were those of whose nature we were conscious. It often happened that when we thought we were experimenting on others we were really experimenting on ourselves.'[41] The second "Mr W. H." enlarges on this, and on the associated premises of "The Critic as Artist", making it the justification for impressive criticism. Very often art yields its truths accidentally, but criticism organises their personal significance:

> Consciousness, indeed, is quite inadequate to explain the contents of personality. It is Art, and Art only, that reveals us to ourselves.
>   We sit at the play with the woman we love, or listen to the music in some Oxford garden, or stroll with our friend through the cool galleries of the Pope's house at Rome, and suddenly we become aware that we have passions of which we never dreamed, thoughts that make us afraid, pleasures whose secret had been denied us, sorrows that have been hidden from our tears. The actor is unconscious of our presence: the musician is thinking of the subtlety of the fugue, of the tone of his instrument; the marble gods that smile so curiously at

us are made of insensate stone. But they have given form and substance to what
was within us; they have enabled us to realise our personality. . . .
        . . . our conscious life [is] the least important part of our development. The
soul, the secret soul, [is] the only reality.

In both "Mr W. H." and its successor, *Dorian Gray*, personality is revealed
and perfected by a work of art, a portrait. In the novel the hero's likeness
becomes a picture of his soul that he takes increasing pleasure in spoiling – so
revenging himself on the painter's ideal conception of him. In the critical
romance it is the portrait of another which first shows the narrator his own
soul, and the element of sympathetic sensibility which is the inner spring of
criticism works at the unconscious level to reveal, rather than to destroy,
ideal beauty. The contrast was present also in Wilde's life: the more reckless
his behaviour became, the more sophisticated his theory of subjective
criticism grew.

The narrative frame returns to complete the story and to dispel subjective
speculation by reason. The narrator, having written in passionate support of
the theory, and now finding himself unaccountably drained of conviction,
visits Erskine, whom he finds stubbornly reconverted. Shocked by the very
change he had worked to produce, the narrator cries, 'Don't be carried away
by mere sentiment in this matter. Whatever romance may have to say about
the Willie Hughes theory, reason is dead against it.' For the moment, the
paradox develops no further. The master and the disciple merely change
places. 'The things about which one feels absolutely certain are never true.
That is the fatality of faith, and the lesson of romance.'[42] The two men lose
contact with one another until, two years later, the vital twist occurs. Just as
Cyril Graham had written a suicide note by which he hoped to convert
Erskine to the Willie Hughes theory, so Erskine now writes to the narrator
implying that he too is about to kill himself for the cause. The narrator soon
discovers that Erskine's letter was a mere dramatic gesture: he used his
imminent death from consumption as a means of trying to expiate his
scepticism towards Cyril Graham, also to reconvert the narrator. In the 1893
version, Wilde added at this point a significant anti-Romantic *caveat*.
The survivor of the trio can scarcely believe that Erskine would suppose him
susceptible to 'the pathetic fallacy of martyrdom': 'Martyrdom was to me
merely a tragic form of scepticism, an attempt to realise by fire what one had
failed to do by faith. No man dies for what he knows to be true. Men die for
what they want to be true, for what some terror in their hearts tells them is
not true. The very uselessness of Erskine's letter made me doubly sorry for
him.'

Even so, Erskine's presence lingers on: he bequeaths to the narrator the
forged portrait. Its return at the end of the story reminds us that the topic of
the opening conversation had been literary forgeries, and that the narrator,
safely identifiable with Wilde at that point, had insisted that Chatterton's

so-called forgeries were merely the result of an artistic desire for perfect representation; that we had no right to quarrel with an artist for the conditions under which he chooses to present his work; and that all Art being to a certain degree a mode of acting, an attempt to realise one's own personality on some plane out of reach of the trammelling accidents and limitations of real life, to censure an artist for a forgery was to confuse an ethical with an aesthetical problem.

This definition pulls the story as a whole into focus with its 'criminal' background. Chatterton, we now perceive, committed suicide 'for an artistic theory' – as a direct result of being artistically misunderstood – not because he had been 'found out' by Horace Walpole. At the same time, his 'martyrdom' contained within it those doubts or 'terrors' which demand the absolute gesture. The narrator in his early scepticism found Cyril Graham's suicide for a literary theory 'incredible', but Graham's case is virtually identical with Chatterton's, except that Graham is critic, not artist – or rather, he is critic as artistic felon, creating the vital evidence for his theory in an attempt to prove both the theory and the unimportance of proof: 'The only apostle who did not deserve proof was St Thomas, and St Thomas was the only apostle who got it.' Artistic truth will always be at the mercy of a trial by objective veracity, and it will always be the philistine who requires, and misconducts, such trials.

The final scepticism of the narrator matches the initial scepticism of Erskine, with one important modification. When the story opens, Erskine has never given any credence to Graham's theory, but by the end of it the narrator is aware that his own sensibility has been subtly refined by contact with an absorbing cerebral romance, and concedes, 'sometimes, when I look at it, I think there is really a great deal to be said for the Willie Hughes theory of Shakespeare's Sonnets'. Still, the additional subjectivity of the 1893 version is balanced by increased objectivity in the closing pages. Wilde had already demonstrated in drama and fiction that the romantic impulse was often suicidal, and he now shows its fatal effects even in theoretical criticism. The impetuous Romantic cannot survive the discrepancy between intuitive truth and rational scepticism. (Much the same might be said of Wilde, whose premonitions about the Dark Lady, or Douglas, or both, proved disastrously accurate.) Having gazed on a vision of ideal beauty, he is run down by the hounds of his own dialectic. Every martyr dies of a one-track mind. But the true critic, whose medium, no less than the artist's, is 'to a certain degree a mode of acting', fully appreciates 'the truth of masks'. He will distinguish with fine precision between objective and subjective form. He will be capable of adopting either with equal ease. But his special prerogative will be to survive both the onslaughts of romance and 'the trammelling accidents and limitations of real life' by recasting everything in the mould of his own personality. At once artist, actor, model, and medium, he is 'the only begetter' of true 'copies'–his own Mr W.H..

IV. "The Decay of Lying"⁴³: The Redeeming Falsehood

The widespread discussion of Wilde's critical dialogues in recent years has resulted in general agreement about their importance for his own artistic development, though with the reservation, in some cases, that *Intentions* was aptly named. The dialogues are polemical restatements of ideas first mooted in early work and crystallised through contact with various later stimuli: "The Decay of Lying" has its origins in "The English Renaissance" but was influenced by conversations with Whistler and published at the height of the controversy over realism and romance in fiction, while "The Critic as Artist" elaborates ideas in the early poems and reflects Wilde's experience as a professional book reviewer.

Both works amply bear out Roditi's idea that Wilde moved from an unsatisfactory poetic sublime to a highly idiosyncratic prose sublime; but one interesting aspect of their technique, closely connected with Roditi's idea, has not been remarked: namely, the traces of the last Endymion's stage properties. This is particularly noticeable in "The Decay of Lying", Wilde's formal 'defence of prose'. A work which embodies its own recommended principles is, perhaps, intrinsically poetic, and Wilde adds to this poetic conception many of the trappings of conventional verse: pictorial and imaginative digressions, personification, lavish use of metaphor, rhetorical hyperbole. It is the programme, however, which fixes it in the tradition of Wilde's own poetic attempts, for the dramatic setting, like that of "The Critic as Artist", is an adaptation of the setting of Wilde's most 'Aesthetic' poem, "The Garden of Eros", an implicit comment on the redirection of his interests.

"The Decay of Lying" opens in the library of a country house where Vivian is busily ignoring Nature in order to correct the proofs of an article which deplores Nature's tyranny over modern art. (This is an amusing comment on Wilde's own recent endeavours: the composition in town of a set of narrative myths picturing the irretrievable loss of man's original harmony with nature.) The dialogue's theme is thus the same, essentially, as that of "The Garden of Eros": 'Spirit of Beauty, tarry still a-while, / They are not dead, thine ancient votaries'. As Wilde develops it, however, the prose piece reverses the course taken by the poem. A self-indulgent lament over 'an age of prose' is superseded by a sophisticated exercise in practical aesthetics. A similar reversal is effected by the settings. The poem opens in a woodland at evening, with the conventional bucolic invitation to a companion to share its pleasures. After listing various deficiencies, and fewer compensations, in the modern world, it concludes at dawn by laying aside the transient charms of poetic reverie in favour of a return to ordinary life: 'How we have lived this night of June!' The dialogue, which takes place in daylight, also opens with a perfect pastoral landscape, and continues with an invitation which, by modern standards, is sufficiently bucolic: 'Let us go and lie on the grass and smoke cigarettes and enjoy Nature.' Cyril's implication that books are a dull and endless strife is countered by Vivian's argument that Wordsworth found under the Lake District's stones the sermons that he had placed there; but when the conversation ends the two men do leave the library: 'let us go out on to the terrace,' Vivian suggests, 'where "droops the milk-white peacock like a ghost," while the evening star "washes the dusk with silver". At twilight nature becomes a wonderfully suggestive effect, and is not without loveliness, though perhaps its chief use is to illustrate quotations from the poets.' Having developed Whistler's theories of nature's suggestiveness, Vivian asserts the superiority of literature over painting (and of Wilde over Whistler) with supreme nonchalance; but the remark has an added irony, as have the quotations chosen. The first, from a song in Tennyson's "The Princess", had recently appeared dressed as prose in Wilde's pastoral tale "The Birthday of the Infanta".[44] The second, which silently places *Poems* of 1881 on a level with the laureate, confirms that nothing looks so like continuity as self-borrowing. 'Awake,' cried the nymph enamoured of hubristic Charmides, the raper of knowledge, 'already the pale moon / Washes the dusk with silver'. But while the pastoral youth is both metaphorically and literally dead to nature, a corpse thrown up on the seashore, the modern critic steps out to peruse the landscape with the eye of a subtle connoisseur.

"The Critic as Artist", which also contains a significant quotation from *Poems*,[45] reproduces the time sequence of the poem exactly, beginning in the evening, breaking off for supper (it was published in two instalments), and concluding at dawn. This time, however, the setting is urban – a library overlooking Green Park – and when the conversation ends, the two men admire the townscape from a specifically painterly point of view: 'Piccadilly lies at our feet like a long riband of silver. A faint purple mist hangs over the Park, and the shadows of the white houses are purple.' The reversal is complete. Just as life reasserted its superiority over poetical fantasy in "The Garden of Eros", so Gilbert is obliged to admit that even the trained critical intelligence cannot retain utopian pan-cultural visions for very long. Tiring of thought, the talkers exchange Parnassus for Piccadilly (one of Wilde's favourite alliterative antitheses), and go to look at the roses in Covent Garden market.

"The Decay of Lying" was 'meant to bewilder the masses by its form. *Au fond* it is of course serious.'[46] Although he does not refer to it, Wilde must have known Arnold's essay "On the Study of Celtic Literature" (1867),[47] for the dialogue's tone is set and maintained by the voice of the irresponsible and fantastic Celt, fact-hater and verbal mage, whose Flaubertian image of 'the solid, stolid British intellect', stuck like the Sphinx in a desert of boredom, beguiled and taunted by the chimera of fantasy with her 'false, flute-toned voice', summarises not just Vivian's argument but also Wilde's own relationship with his reluctant public. The element of self-justification goes deep: the author defends his own prose technique in poems in prose, tales,[48] and the dialogues themselves, deliberately equating the artist and the social liar as two of a kind, performers who seek to give pleasure.

In keeping with these aims, Wilde adopts a frivolous form of dialectic. The 'child-philosopher' is transferred from mythopoeic fiction to criticism which advocates mythopoeia. Giving his young sons' names to the disputants and making the younger son the *magister* and the elder the *discipulus* of a Socratic dialogue enables Wilde to define the proper relationship between youth and age, rebel and establishment, and to create equivalents to those revealing accidents with language quoted by Twain in his article on the American child. Cyril and Vivian get all their terms "wrong". They systematically contradict and misappropriate the accepted meanings of words at crucial points in the argument – particularly the would-be critic, Vivian. Far from being 'mistakes springing from ignorance of life or dulness of perception', these errors are 'full of the richest suggestion' and 'pregnant with the highest philosophy'. They help to regenerate art by chipping from the communal vocabulary the accretions of habit.

This procedure leads into various studied absurdities, including the suggestion for a primer, 'When to Lie, and How', which would prove 'of real practical service to many earnest and deep-thinking people'.[49] The premise for all Vivian's theories, however, is an aesthetic interpretation of the 'fortunate fall'. Nature, 'as Aristotle says somewhere', has 'good intentions' which she cannot 'carry out'. The artist therefore replaces Nature's intentions with his own *Intentions*, thus justifying his existence: 'It is fortunate . . . for us that Nature is so imperfect, as otherwise we should have no art at all. Art is our spirited protest, our gallant attempt to teach Nature her proper place.' With Nature's authority discredited, Wilde (or rather, Vivian[50]) makes four claims which constitute the 'new aesthetics'. First, art is entirely autonomous and does not necessarily reflect the concerns of its age. All bad art comes from 'returning to Life and Nature and elevating them into ideals', the reason being that 'when Art surrenders her imaginative medium she surrenders everything'. Second, 'Life imitates Art more than Art imitates Life', because the creative imagination offers forms for self-realisation. Third, a corollary to this (added in 1891) states that 'external Nature' also imitates Art, since the senses by which we apprehend it can reproduce only those effects that Art has taught them to notice. Fourth, 'lying, the telling of beautiful untrue things, is the proper aim of Art'.

When Wilde formulated these doctrines, *Dorian Gray* and *Salomé*, which are the fullest realisations of them, were as yet unwritten, and the dialogue should be seen not just as a personal manifesto but also in the broader context of the dispute over literary realism.[51] This came to a head in 1888 and 1889 with the prosecutions of Henry Vizetelly, elderly translator and publisher of Zola. In the *Fortnightly Review* for January 1889, there appeared (simultaneously with "The Decay of Lying", and in the same issue as "Pen, Pencil and Poison") a complaint of precisely the kind criticised by Vivian: 'How can we expect the young to escape spring blights if that beautiful and natural guard against them, the sense which calls the mantling blush to the cheek, is broken down by literature that is wantonly purulent?' Wilde does not distinguish between Realism and Naturalism. Zola, for Vivian, is wrong simply 'on the grounds of Art': morals or social determinism are different issues. *Robert Elsmere*, quite different in subject matter from Zola and unexceptionably decent, is no less at fault because no less deficient in the transfiguring imagination. Vivian dexterously shows 'Truth' to be what is – anything susceptible to the 'scientific' method; while 'Lying' is what should be – answerable only to the imagination. Vivian invokes Plato the idealist to refute Plato the Republican: 'Just as those who do not love Plato more than Truth cannot pass beyond the threshold of the Academe, so those who do not love Beauty more than Truth never know the inmost shrine of Art.' Vivian, insisting that 'as a method, Realism is a complete failure', takes neither side in the moral controversy, yet his Celtic whimsy – 'Like Emerson, I write over the door of my library the word "Whim" ' – paradoxically upholds the beneficial functions of fiction, 'lying', for civilised society. While Realism panders to the unregenerate imagination, Romance redeems it by freeing it from what is.

V. "The Critic as Artist": The new Eden of Criticism

In his review of *Dorian Gray*, published six months after *Intentions* had appeared, Pater spoke of the conversational character of much of Wilde's writing and praised his mastery of dialogue which is 'really alive' and through which 'he carries on, more perhaps than any other writer, the brilliant critical work of Matthew Arnold'.[52] Pater remained silent about his own influence on Wilde's criticism (though he did discreetly dissociate his idea of Epicureanism from Lord Henry's). "The Critic as Artist", however, marries Pater's technique of 'impressive' criticism to critical premises which can be traced back to "The Function of Criticism at the Present Time" and *Culture and Anarchy*. A short digression on male prose writers in a review of "English Poetesses" (1888) suggests Wilde's view of his debt to Arnold. 'We have', he concluded, 'a few, a very few, masters, such as they are. We have Carlyle, who should not be imitated; and Mr Pater, who, through the subtle perfection of his form, is inimitable absolutely; and Mr Froude, who is useful; and Matthew Arnold, who is a model.'[53] It is precisely as 'a model' that Arnold appears the following year in "The Critic as Artist" – a lay figure whose impractically staid anatomy the artist decks out in carnival costume and frog-marches off towards the utopian frontier of 'doing as one likes'.[54]

Even by the late nineteenth century, the dialogue was not fully naturalised as an English literary form.[55] Wilde, accomplished classicist and voluble Celt, may have adopted it the more readily for that. He certainly handles it with a keen sense of its rich literary traditions from Plato and Lucian to Sidney, Dryden, and Landor, using the old 'battle of the books' as a conversational pretext for reversing the attitudes of the last Endymion and launching a full-scale Apology for Criticism which, true to Horatian precept, simultaneously instructs and delights.

If much of the delight lies in Wilde's Paterian re-creation of literary and historical episodes, most of the instruction consists in his urbane debunking of Arnold. Arnold's critical premises issue piecemeal from Wilde's *discipulus*, who is ominously called Ernest and seldom contrives to make a valid point. Ernest's errors, or Arnold's ideas, thus become the target for Gilbert, the creative iconoclast; and, after a feeble show of resistance to intellectual pressure ('Don't degrade me into the position of giving you useful information. . . . We are born into an age when only the dull are treated seriously and I live in terror of not being misunderstood'), Gilbert settles to the task of educating Ernest by imparting much 'useless' information. (The title of the 1890 version of the dialogue is "The True Function and Value of Criticism; with some Remarks on the Importance of Doing Nothing".)

Arnold's main point in "The Function of Criticism" had been that true criticism must be 'a disinterested endeavour to learn and propagate the best that is known and thought in the world'. While recognising the value of the critical spirit in correcting racial prejudice or jingoist self-satisfaction, he did not expand on its practical functions. *Culture and Anarchy*, by contrast, was a practical 'Essay in Political and Social Criticism'. Criticism, now called 'culture', is the answer to political and religious strife, a conveyor of 'sweetness and light', a path leading to a golden state resting on the virtuous mean: 'the State, or organ of our best self, of our national right reason'. This 'best self' required the repression of the urge to 'do as one likes'. Personal grievances and prejudices were to be sunk in the interests of the social corporation. Singly, men were citizens; collectively, the State.

Wilde takes the opposite view.[56] A healthy state depends on the health of individuals, which depends in turn on full self-realisation. Therefore, while Gilbert eventually lists the public benefits attendant on individual critical awareness, he first insists that criticism ignore the calls on it from the practical sphere. This is the only point of Arnold's left unchallenged by the 'new Hellenism'. Arnold had argued that the Hellenist was 'terribly at ease in Zion', that the Platonic conception of self-knowledge and self-culture took insufficient account of 'sin', which 'thwarts all our efforts' to see things 'in their reality' and 'in their beauty'. The Hebraist virtue of 'strictness of conscience' must therefore be added to the Hellenist's 'variety of consciousness' to produce a modern workable balance. Wilde considered that any latter-day programme must accept Goethe's judgement that 'all eras in a state of decline and dissolution are subjective',[57] and he turned to an ideal of enlightened subjectivity for which Pater had given the lead: 'That the end of life is not action but contemplation – *being* as distinct from *doing* – a certain disposition of the mind, is, in some shape or other, the principle of all the higher morality.'[58] Wilde paraphrases this: the critic's vocation is 'not *doing*, but *being*, and not *being* merely, but *becoming*'. In this he follows Goethe, whom Arnold himself had quoted: 'To act is so easy, as Goethe says, to think is so hard!' Wilde uses the distinction to summarise the two halves of his dialogue, devoted to 'the importance of doing nothing' and 'the importance of discussing everything'; but its force is felt throughout, emerging most clearly in Gilbert's defence of the critic's true work:

> Perhaps you think that in beholding for the mere joy of beholding, and contemplating for the sake of contemplation, there is something that is egotistic. If you think so, do not say so. It takes a thoroughly selfish age, like our own, to deify self-sacrifice. It takes a thoroughly grasping age, such as that in which we live, to set above the fine intellectual virtues those shallow emotional virtues that are of immediate practical benefit to itself. . . . It is so easy for people to have sympathy with suffering. It is so difficult for them to have sympathy with thought.

'The aristocracy of the intellect', as Wilde called it, has a social obligation to secure itself from the claims of 'the democracy of suffering';[59] for, 'where self-culture has ceased to be the ideal, the intellectual standard is instantly lowered, and, often, ultimately lost'.

The critic's first requisite is not Arnold's dispassionate eye, but 'a temperament exquisitely susceptible to beauty and to the various impressions that beauty gives us'. Art is intensification of personality, and personality in the critic will therefore be a revelatory, not an intrusive, element. The other necessary qualities further contradict Arnold. Wilde's critic will be neither 'fair' nor 'sincere' nor 'rational'. 'Art lives only by prejudice', claimed Zola,[60] and the critic will reflect this truth by his own approach. Fairness is impossible: 'The man who sees both sides of a question is a man who sees absolutely nothing at all.' Reason is out of place: it is not the faculty to which art appeals. 'If one loves Art at all, one must love it beyond all other things in the world, and against such a love, the reason, if one listened to it, would cry out.' Sincerity, 'dangerous' in small quantities, is 'fatal' in large. The true critic will be sincere 'in his devotion to the principle of beauty' but this will lead him to 'realise himself in many forms, and by a thousand different ways', thus proving that 'we are never so true to ourselves as when we are inconsistent'. For 'what is mind but motion in the intellectual sphere?'

The critic's meticulous subjectivity will have two principal results. It will produce work which is 'the only civilised form of autobiography, as it deals not with the events, but with the thoughts of one's life' and is thus 'a record of one's own soul'. The critic will interpret himself through the work before him, as Wilde did in "Mr W. H.". It will have also a public effect. The critic, through constant exposure to his cultural and intellectual heritage, will become the microcosmic vehicle for the culture of the race. He will interpret the work before him according to the clarity with which he has interpreted himself.

> For who is the true critic but he who bears within himself the dreams, and ideas, and feelings of myriad generations, and to whom no form of thought is alien, no emotional impulse obscure? And who the true man of culture, if not he who by fine scholarship and fastidious rejection has made instinct self-conscious and intelligent . . . develops that spirit of disinterested curiosity which is the real root, as it is the real flower, of the intellectual life, and thus attains to intellectual clarity, and, having learned 'the best that is known and thought in the world', lives – it is not fanciful to say so – with those who are the Immortals.

Thus Wilde reaches Arnold's ideal by the Paterian route. For Pater's Duke Carl had speculated on these very topics while seeking to effect single-handed a Hellenic *Aufklärung* in his obscure principality:

> He began to see that it could be in no other way than by action of informing thought upon the vast accumulated material of which Germany was in possession: art, poetry, fiction, an entire imaginative world, following reasonably upon a deeper understanding of the past, of nature, of one's self – an understanding of all beside through the knowledge of one's self.[61]
> Surely, past ages, could one get at the historic soul of them, were not dead but living, rich in company, for the entertainment, the expansion of the present: and Duke Carl was still without suspicion of the cynic afterthought that such historic soul was but an arbitrary substitution, a generous loan of oneself.[62]

Wilde's critical self-projection is no worse for the 'cynic afterthought'. Confronted at the outset, it justifies the entire dialogue. 'By the Ilyssus, says Arnold somewhere, there was no Higginbotham. By the Ilyssus, my dear Gilbert, there were no silly art congresses bringing provincialism to the provinces and teaching the mediocrity how to mouth. . . . The Greeks had no art critics.' This, Ernest's first serious suggestion, is a mere pastoral fiction, fraught with 'all the vitality of error and all the tediousness of an old friend'. Regardless of the list of distinguished Greek critics that might be cited, the idea of a golden age of art is wishful thinking, nostalgic self-projection. If we indulge it 'our historical sense is at fault', because any century which produces art is thus far a self-conscious century, and 'self-consciousness and the critical spirit are one'.

In due course, Gilbert 'proves' that criticism, far from confining itself to commentary on the work of others, can 'lie' and 'rewrite history' no less than art can, and may, indeed, be more creative than art. But in the present context, his most significant point is that criticism stands to art as art stands to life: the sophisticated arranger of relatively raw materials. Gilbert takes Arnold's suggestion that the present age was better fitted to criticism than to enduring artistic creation[63] and develops it into a consciously post-lapsarian position. Subjectivity may be the note of the age, but 'a further development of the habit of introspection may prove fatal to that creative faculty to which it seeks to supply fresh material. I myself am inclined to think that creation is doomed. It springs from too primitive, too natural an impulse.' Creation is *naïv* by comparison with the modern, self-divided and self-dividing activity of criticism, its *sentimentalisch* successor. 'It is to the future that criticism belongs.'

This proposition is characteristically justified by reference to form. 'The artists', says Gilbert, 'reproduce either themselves or each other, with wearisome iteration. But Criticism is always moving on, and the critic is always developing.' Nor is the critic limited to 'the subjective form of expression'. Drama, epos, narrative and dialogue are at his disposal. Indeed, dialogue justifies by its very form that postscript to "Shakespeare and Stage Costume" added in 1891 to turn it into "The Truth of Masks": 'just as it is only in art-criticism, and through it, that we can apprehend the Platonic theory of ideas, so it is only in art-criticism, and through it, that we can realise Hegel's system of contraries'. By 'Hegel's system of contraries' Wilde evidently meant his dialectical system, summarised in a note in the Commonplace Book: 'The normal condition of progress in thought is this: first a narrow definiteness, an uncompromising dogmatism. Then the antagonism and criticism to which they give rise. Lastly the intellectual synthesis and union.'[64] The dialogue form is a physical equivalent to this, and Wilde's implication that the conscientious critic will be a kind of intellectual Antaeus wrestling with complete knowledge corresponds to Hegel's sequence of aliases, or *Geister*, that 'gallery of pictures' through which the Spirit of the *Phenomenology* passes in order to achieve 'the becoming of knowledge' and so return into itself.[65] Whereas the *sentimental-isch* artist was unhappily divided against himself and alienated from nature, the critic is voluntarily self-fragmented, and through this very condition completes the Romantic *peregrinatio* towards total cognition. Predictably, Wilde pictures this state as a wholly Hellenist Zion where 'sin' has no place:

> And when we reach the true culture that is our aim, we attain to that perfection of which the saints have dreamed, the perfection of those to whom sin is impossible, not because they make the renunciations of the ascetic, but because they can do everything they wish without hurt to the soul, and can wish for nothing that can do the soul harm, the soul being an entity so divine that it is able to transform into elements of a richer experience, or a finer susceptibility, or a newer mode of thought, acts or passions that with the common would be commonplace, or with the uneducated ignoble, or with the shameful vile.

In *Poems*, Wilde, like Schelling, had identified the fall into knowledge with the conquest of Greek paganism by Christianity. In *A House of Pomegranates*, he treated the fall from various imaginative points of view. Now he expresses Schelling's notion of redemptive philosophy – 'the progressive history of self-consciousness'[66] – in purely aesthetic terms in an amoral critical context.

Within this Romantic metaphor an aptly subversive irony lies hidden. Gilbert has already argued that the true critic will be the touchstone of a society's accumulated value, and that this involves 'doing nothing'. Plato, 'with his passion for wisdom', and Aristotle, 'with his passion for knowledge', would both have agreed that 'it is to do nothing that the elect exist'. In a utilitarian society, however, art and thought are disruptive forces: 'Society often forgives the criminal but it never forgives the dreamer'. Romantic thinkers compounded this relatively mild offence. Coleridge's reading of the mystics convinced him that 'all the products of the mere *reflective* faculty partook of DEATH'.[67] Schelling and his contemporaries regarded 'the very act of taking thought' as 'an evil' because it was an onslaught on the primordial unity.[68] Wilde echoes this view: 'All thought is immoral. Its very essence is destruction. If you think of anything, you kill it. Nothing survives being thought of.'[69] Thus, the critic is a professional assassin, but one in whose criminality all the most responsible members of society willingly share. Only the ignorant are innocent.

The most obvious objection to Wilde's whole proposition is that Gilbert's 'elect spirits' will 'grow less and less interested in actual life, and will seek to gain their impressions almost entirely from what art has touched'. This is because art offers expressive form, while life offers merely chaos. Such a view may well seem little less than a new form of pastoral, a mere exaggeration of Pater's suggestions in the Conclusion to *The Renaissance* and the logical extension of his remark that art is 'a sort of cloistral refuge from a certain vulgarity in the actual world'.[70] We should go to art 'for everything', Gilbert declares, for 'Art cannot hurt us'; but he does not argue that art, in present circumstances, is enough. Goethe, Wilde had noted, 'owed his sublime cheerfulness to his scientific training – "for those who do not walk delicately in the sunlit air", or "garlanded with white poplar run races in the prime of spring when the plane whispers to the pine", the Greek attitude can only be gained by a recognition of the scientific basis of life.'[71] Science is the missing factor from the modern equation, and Gilbert's attempt to support his argument by reference to theories of heredity is the logical development of Wilde's interest in the artistic implications of social Darwinism. 'In the modern attempt to rest morals on a scientific basis,' he had noted, 'as well as in Baudelaire's cry, "O Seigneur: donnez–moi la force et le courage/De contempler mon coeur et mon corps sans dégoût", a return to the old Hellenic ideal $Z\acute{\eta}\nu$ $\kappa\alpha\tau\grave{\alpha}$ $\phi\acute{\upsilon}\sigma\iota\nu$ can be seen'.[72] Gilbert unexpectedly treats science as the answer to a critic's prayer. 'It was reserved for a man of science [Darwin] to show us that "sweet reasonableness" of which Arnold spoke so wisely, and, alas! to so little effect', Gilbert says, and he interprets with characteristic idiosyncrasy the moral implications of genetic determinism:

> By revealing to us the absolute mechanism of all action, and so freeing us from the self-imposed and trammelling burden of moral responsibility, the scientific

principle of Heredity has become, as it were, the warrant for the contemplative life. It has shown us that we are never less free than when we try to act. It has hemmed us round with the nets of the hunter, and written upon the wall the prophecy of our doom. We may not watch it, for it is within us. We may not see it, save in a mirror that mirrors the soul. It is Nemesis without her mask. It is the last of the Fates, and the most terrible.

Wilde had touched on these ideas in the first *Dorian Gray*, and expanded them in the second, where Lord Henry's curiosity about Dorian's ancestry leads him into some genealogical inquiries which fix his impression of Dorian's unique temperament. In the novel, heredity has a doom-laden quality, as has the soul-mirror which interprets it. In pure criticism, however, its effects are beneficial. What enables the critic to 'live these countless lives' is the imagination, and 'the imagination is the result of heredity. It is simply concentrated race-experience.'

If there is a trace in all of this of doing rather than thinking, it is the result, perhaps, of criticism still seeming to the Romantic egotist an elaborate and glorious second-best. The desire to realise the modern personality in life, not thought – the desire responsible for Dorian Gray – overflows into Wilde's criticism as inevitably as his critical theories permeated the novel. Gilbert justifies the apparent discrepancy by appealing to the pressures of latter-day scepticism. Religion and philosophy, he decides, are both exhausted:

> The courts of the city of God are not open to us now. Its gates are guarded by Ignorance, and to pass them we have to surrender all that in our nature is most divine . . . We cannot go back to the saint. There is far more to be learned from the sinner. We cannot go back to the philosopher, and the mystic leads us astray. . . . To the aesthetic temperament the vague is always repellent. . . . Like Aristotle, like Goethe after he had read Kant, we desire the concrete, and nothing but the concrete can satisfy us.

Roditi called Wilde 'a rare Aristotelian among the many Platonists and neo-Platonists of nineteenth century aesthetics',[73] but Wilde did not subscribe to the common opposition of the two thinkers. For him, both were idealists, the ideal of the one being 'actual and immanent' while that of the other was 'potential and transcendent'.[74] The modern critic will tend, in fact, to fuse the two. His temperament requires an 'actual and immanent' ideal, but many of his assumptions are utopian, bearing witness to an ideal 'potential and transcendent'. The solution to this situation, Gilbert suggests, is to consider Plato's findings in a new context:

> The problems of idealism and realism, as [Plato] sets them forth, may seem to many to be somewhat barren of result in the metaphysical sphere of abstract being in which he places them, but transfer them to the sphere of art, and you will find that they are still vital and full of meaning. It may be that it is as a critic of beauty that Plato is destined to live, and that by altering the name of the sphere of his speculation we shall find a new philosophy.

The origins of "The Critic as Artist" lie in Wilde's "English Renaissance" lecture, so it is no surprise that Gilbert cites that movement as the modern manifestation of the 'new Philosophy'. Decorative arts, the movement's real strength, are concrete and 'actual' yet also abstract and 'ideal' in form because not literally imitative. Daily contact with such arts – 'the arts that touch us, not the arts that teach us' – will fulfil Plato's educational theory. The individual will develop a 'fine instinctive taste' which will grow into the 'critical and self-conscious spirit' that he will ultimately 'salute and recognise as a friend with whom his education has made him long familiar'. As Wilde noted in "The Decay of Lying", those who 'do not love Plato more than Truth cannot pass beyond the threshold of the Academe', and 'those who do not love Beauty more than Truth never know the inmost shrine of Art'. In "The Critic as Artist", the shrine is all-encompassing. Perhaps remembering the remark that 'The Beautiful . . . is higher than the Good: the Beautiful includes in it the Good' (Goethe, as quoted by Carlyle),[75] Wilde makes a similar point with a biological metaphor: 'Aesthetics are higher than Ethics' because 'to discern the beauty of a thing is the finest point to which we can arrive. . . . Ethics like natural selection, make existence possible. Aesthetics, like sexual selection, make life lovely and wonderful, fill it with new forms, and give it progress, and variety and change.' 'The true culture which is our aim' will, like beauty itself, 'heal the spirit that is wounded, and "bring the soul into harmony with all right things" '.[76] In that state, ethics will have been superseded by aesthetics. We shall be at ease in Zion – 'the finest point to which we can arrive' – the new Eden of the Hellenist 'critic of beauty'. The nineteenth century has a long way to go: 'I need not say how far,' Gilbert remarks. But the Wildean critic, ideal blend of comprehensive thinker and imaginative creator, is uniquely qualified to point the way, and does so, as always, by a dramatic form of self-projection.

VI. "The Soul of Man under Socialism": The Artist as Legislator

This is Wilde's only formal polemic after the Aesthetic lectures of 1881–2, and, although it replaces their bland showmanship by a new aggressiveness, result of various attacks in the Press,[77] it is, in form at least, the least satisfying of his mature pieces. This is partly due to its occasional character. It breaks Wilde's rule in having been written more because other people are what they are than because the artist is what he is, and the critic has clearly forgotten, for the moment, that 'it is only the intellectually lost who ever argue'.[78] Nevertheless, the piece is highly significant in Wilde's development. If "The Critic as Artist" can be thought of as his theoretical response to Arnold, the "The Soul of Man" is his 'practical' response, an essay in 'social and political criticism' which praises rebellion and anarchism as life forces and draws up a specimen constitution for the utopian land where the proper aim of life for all is 'doing as one likes'. 'In good democracy,' says Prince Paul to the idealistic Czarevitch in *Vera*, 'every man should be an aristocrat, but these people in Russia who seek to thrust us out are no better than the animals in one's preserves, and are made to be shot at, most of them'.[79] Wilde's ideal state assumes a norm of universal aristocracy; or, to put it another way, it will be a one-class society in which the norm will be unaffected idiosyncrasy, sign of that healthy individualism which does not seek to make claims upon others.

As Donald Stone has observed,[80] individualism was topical in the 1880s in a variety of contexts. Had Wilde known of Nietzsche, he would have sympathised with his pursuit of 'the theme of the anti-political individual who seeks self-perfection far from the modern world' no less than he sympathised with Pater's Marius, or even more with his Duke Carl, whose search for the 'new Hellas' is echoed in several of Wilde's works and probably gave to the essay's individualism its utopian name. George Moore in *Confessions of a Young Man* (1888) claimed that he had undertaken 'the rescue and individualisation of the ego' in fiction, but Wilde disapproved of artists treating art as if it were merely 'a mode of autobiography', and the total absence of Moore's name from his work, even from the list of Realist miscreants in "The Decay of Lying" (a position to which several of Moore's early novels fully entitled him), is perhaps in itself an eloquent denial of influence. In economics and politics, 'individualism' was synonymous with Tory *laissez-faire*. As Sidney Webb put it, 'There is no resting place for stationary Toryism in the scientific universe. The whole history of the human race cries out against the old-fashioned Individualism.'[81] Wilde objects to the *status quo*, but envisages a future state in which science and socialism will support a brand-new and true individualism. His argument may owe something to the short pamphlet "Anarchism and State Socialism" (1889), in which Shaw made the point that slavery degrades those who dominate no less than those who are dominated. He clearly agreed with a further remark of Shaw's (made in his review of Nordau's *Degeneration* in 1895): 'The whole progress of the world is from submission and obedience as safeguards against panic and incontinence, to wilfulness and self-assertion made safe by reason and self-control.' But Wilde had already come to this conclusion himself some years earlier: it forms the basis of "The Rise of Historical Criticism" (written in 1879).

One specific source for "The Soul of Man" may be located in the work of W. K. Clifford. Wilde's Commonplace Book contains jottings on Clifford's lectures, published posthumously in 1879,[82] two of which are immediately relevant. The first, "Conditions of Mental Development" (dating from 1868), is interesting for its anticipation of points in Pater's Conclusion to *The Renaissance* (1873) and its conclusion implies a criticism of contemporary society made overt and argumentative by Wilde. Clifford's metaphor is characteristically Darwinist, and the principles of social Darwinism were hardly central to Wilde's, still less to Pater's, aesthetics. However, they both developed the ideas expressed in the following paragraph and Wilde no doubt relished Clifford's parting paradox which rounds off the lecture:

> To become crystallised, fixed in opinion and mode of thought, is to lose the great characteristic of life, by which it is distinguished from inanimate nature: the power of adapting itself to circumstances. This is even more true of the race. There are nations in the East so enslaved by custom that they seem to have lost all power of change except the capability of being destroyed. Propriety, in fact, is the crystallisation of a race. And if we consider that a race, in proportion as it is plastic and capable of change, may be regarded as young and vigorous, while a race which is fixed, persisting in form, unable to change, is as surely worn out, in peril of extinction, we shall see, I think, the immense importance to a nation of checking the growth of conventionalities. It is quite possible for conventional values to get such power that progress is impossible, and the nation only fit to be improved away. In the face of such a danger, *it is not right to be proper*.[83]

In due course, Wilde transferred these ideas into his society comedies, where the dandy embodies the principle of plasticity and the critical voice of change. In the essay, he concentrated on the stasis produced by authoritarian interference with the lives of individuals and with the artist's freedom of expression.

> If a man of science were told that the results of his experiments, and the conclusions that he arrived at, should be of such a character that they would not upset the received popular notions on the subject, or disturb popular prejudice, or hurt the sensibilities of people who knew nothing about science; if a philosopher were told that he had a perfect right to speculate in the highest spheres of thought, provided that he arrived at the same conclusions as were held by those who had never thought in any sphere at all – well, nowadays the man of science and the philosopher would be considerably amused.

But it is not so long, Wilde says, since science and philosophy were both subjected to the authority of 'brutal popular control', while imaginative art is still so. The beneficial effects which would follow the overthrow of popular control – habit – may be glimpsed in the transformation of functional art accomplished by the Aesthetic movement. 'The public clung with really pathetic tenacity to what I believe were the direct traditions of the Great Exhibition of international vulgarity, traditions that were so appalling that the houses in which people lived were only fit for blind people to live in.' Beautiful things began to be made; the public cried out against them but the work went on; 'and now it is almost impossible to enter any modern house without seeing some recognition of good taste, some recognition of the value of lovely surroundings, some sign of the appreciation of beauty'.

The second of Clifford's essays of relevance to "The Soul of Man" is "On the Scientific Basis of Morals" (1875), which deals with the relationship between individual and social responsibility. 'The basis of our moral feelings,' Wilde notes, 'may be found in the desire for self-preservation. But this preservation of *self* is not the individual self but what Clifford calls the tribal self: individualism, private property, and a private conscience, as well as the nominative case of personal pronouns, do not appear till late in all civilisations: it is the tribal self which is the first mainspring of action, and canon of right and wrong.'[84] Wilde also notes, 'Not to conform is simply a synonym for progress', and 'Progress is simply the instinct for self-preservation. Knowledge rendered active by self-preservation produces higher forms of civilisation. Higher freedom – the impulse to escape from the confines of any -ism, is essentially self-preservation.'[85] And again, 'Progress in thought is the assertion of individualism against authority, and progress in matter is differentiation and specialisation of function: those organisms which are entirely subject to external influences do not progress any more than a mind entirely subject to authority.'[86] In "The Soul of Man" these precepts are pressed into the service of the new Individualism.

> Individualism does not come to man with any sickly cant about duty, which merely means doing what other people want because they want it; or any hideous cant about self-sacrifice, which is merely a survival of savage mutilation. In fact, it does not come to man with any claims upon him at all. It comes naturally and inevitably out of man. It is the point to which all development tends. It is the differentiation towards which all organisms grow. It is the perfection that is inherent in every mode of life, and towards which every mode of life quickens. . . . To ask whether Individualism is practical is like asking whether Evolution is practical. Evolution is the law of life, and there is no evolution except towards Individualism. Where this tendency is not expressed, it is a case of artificially arrested growth, or of disease, or of death.

However, the aim of individualism is not self-indulgence, or any form of selfishness. Authority will be done away with because 'it is only in voluntary organisations that man is fine'. As a result, man will become unselfish and natural. 'Selfishness is not living as one wishes to live, it is asking others to live as one wishes to live. And unselfishness is letting other people's lives alone, not interfering with them. Selfishness always aims at creating around it an absolute uniformity of type.' However, Individualism, like art, does act as 'a disintegrating force'. It seeks 'to disturb monotony of type, slavery of customs, tyranny of habit, and the reduction of man to the level of a machine.' Art and individualism, indeed, are synonymous. Wilde adds a definition of 'egotism' which is at odds with his sympathetic use of it elsewhere, but supports nevertheless his claims on behalf of individualism. 'Nor will men be egotistic as they are now. For the egotist is he who makes claims upon others, and the Individualist will not desire to do that. It will not give him pleasure.' Under such utopian conditions, doing as one likes will never coincide with doing as other people dislike.

The practical functions of Wilde's projected state are soon summarised. Science will remove pain and disease; machinery will provide the slave labour indispensable to any highly organised civilisation; the government, ceasing vain attempts to govern, will occupy itself with the provision and distribution of the necessaries of everyday life. In accordance with the beliefs of the artist, soon-to-be-acknowledged legislator and already self-expressive individual, every citizen will be left free to follow the path to self-perfection: 'The form of government that is most suitable to the artist is no government at all. . . . The past is what man should not have been. The present is what man ought not to be. The future is what artists are.' Under such conditions, men will do their work, no matter what form it takes, with joy, as Ruskin and Morris had insisted they should. Private property will be abolished – not because it is the outcome and symbol of an unfair system of employment or trade, but because it represents, to the individual who amasses it no less than to the individual who cannot, a false and burdensome ideal. In a few cases, Wilde concedes, notably in the lives of certain artists, private property has been an advantage, even a necessity, and its existence has therefore advanced at times the culture of the world. But in general it has encouraged men to place their faith in objects or symbols external to themselves instead of in themselves merely. The abolition of private property will help to rectify this, and will also free society from some of its most hypocritical virtues: philanthropy, charity, altruism. From the point of view of individualism, all humanitarian remedies, no matter how fine their motivations, are a part of the disease they set out to cure, and it is sentimental, insincere, and grotesque to praise them. Such sympathy, Wilde claims, is 'the least fine mode' because there is an element of selfish terror in it. When our lives are no longer burdened with 'the tedious necessity of living for others', a humanitarian obligation that socialism will dispel, we shall be free to cultivate the wider and more difficult sympathy with 'the entirety of life' and to exemplify the truth of the proposition that self-culture, not self-sacrifice, is 'the primary duty of man'.

To bring this imaginary construct into focus with prevailing moralities, Wilde invokes the example of Christ; but even Christ's position represents no more than one of the stations on man's pilgrimage towards self-perfection. Christ neither challenged the established order of society nor proposed any system of social reform, and thus had to realise himself through pain and self-sacrifice. But 'Pain is not the ultimate mode of perfection', even though the world has far more often idealised pain than it has idealised pleasure. Pain is 'merely provisional and a protest. It has reference to wrong, unhealthy, unjust surroundings. When the wrong, and the disease, and the injustice are removed, it will have no further place. It was a great work, but it is almost over. Its sphere lessens every day.' By contrast, the new Individualism will challenge authority and does seek to establish a healthier programme for society. It will realise itself through joy. Christianity may assist it in this, but such assistance is not essential; for the conditions in which

Christianity is founded 'will be done away with, and human nature will change':

> Man has sought to live intensely, fully, perfectly. When he can do so without exercising restraint on others, or suffering it ever, and his activities are all pleasurable to him, he will be saner, healthier, more civilised, more himself. Pleasure is Nature's test, her sign of approval. Whe.. man is happy, he is in harmony with himself and his environment. The new Individualism, for whose service Socialism, whether it wills it or not, is working, will be perfect harmony. It will be what the Greeks sought for, but could not, except in Thought, realise completely, because they had slaves, and fed them; it will be what the Renaissance sought for, but could not realise completely except in Art, because they had slaves, and starved them. It will be complete, and through it each man will attain to his perfection. The new Individualism is the new Hellenism.

If there is a further suggestion here of the Romantic *peregrinatio* towards a new Eden, it receives a measure of support from Wilde's characteristic interpretation of the teaching of Christ. Although the new Hellenism is destined to supersede Christianity in the ordinary course of the human spirit's evolution, the two creeds will often find themselves at one. ' "Know thyself!" was written over the portal of the antique world. Over the portal of the new world, "Be thyself" shall be written. And the message of Christ to man was simply "Be thyself" '.' Christ's teaching, Wilde argues, was the refinement of individualism. He recognised no claims of family or society, nor any external influence prejudicial to self-perfection. The story of the young man of many possessions illustrates this at a simple level: 'private property hinders Individualism at every step'. The story of the woman taken in adultery demonstrates it more subtly. When she poured costly perfumes over Christ's hair, 'his friends tried to interfere with her, and said that it was an extravagance, and that the money should have been expended on charitable relief of people in want, or something of that kind'. Christ disagreed, pointing out that the spiritual wants of man were even more pressing than his very evident material wants, and that 'in one divine moment, and by selecting its own mode of expression, a personality might make itself perfect'. Even so, Wilde concedes, 'it is a question whether we have ever seen the full expression of a personality, except on the imaginative plane of art. . . . Most personalities have been obliged to be rebels. Half their strength has been wasted in friction.' When we do see the true personality of man, it will be 'a marvellous thing'. It will grow organically, 'flowerlike'. It will be uncontentious, yet wise. 'It will have nothing. And yet it will have everything, and whatever one takes from it, it will still have, so rich it will be.' It will love others for their differences, and help all 'as a beautiful thing helps us, by being what it is'. It will be 'as wonderful as the personality of a child'. Under the new Hellenism, everybody will be an individualist, and so everybody will be, in the true meaning of the word, an artist: 'self-schooled, self-scanned, self-honoured, self-secure'.[87]

Wilde did not confront these issues again until 1897. Imprisonment, bankruptcy, disgrace and personal bereavements forced him to acknowledge that the 'great work' of pain was not so nearly over as the essay had suggested; and, when all of the conditions necessary to the realisation of a Hellenic ideal had been taken from him, Wilde reverted, no less characteristically, to an individualism based on the opposite extreme – the reality of pain and sorrow, and the perfection of the personality through them. The central section of *De Profundis* reverses the argument of "The Soul of Man". If, by the standards of "The Critic as Artist", the essay was a valiant effort to place the utopian ideal of self-culture into a practical rather than a purely contemplative framework, by the standards of *De Profundis* it propounds the philosophy of someone out of touch with his soul. Christ now appears to Wilde to be the finest example of the fully realised personality, the man whose life most nearly approaches the perfection of a work of art because inner substance and outer form are entirely and mutually expressive. 'Behind Joy and Laughter there may be a temperament, coarse, hard, and callous. But behind Sorrow there is always Sorrow. Pain, unlike Pleasure, wears no mask.'[88] But it remains a source of encouragement to him to remember having suggested that the criminal and the sinner may both find their perfection in characteristic but anti-social behaviour: 'Personality is a very mysterious thing. A man cannot always be estimated by what he does. He may keep the law, and yet be worthless. He may be bad, without doing anything bad. He may commit a sin against society, and yet through that sin realise his true perfection.' This idea, toyed with in "Lord Arthur Savile's Crime", considered more seriously in "Pen, Pencil and Poison", incorporated into *Dorian Gray* and dramatised in *Salomé*, makes the essay pivotal in Wilde's development.

4 Crime and Egotism (2)

I. *The Picture of Dorian Gray*: Art, Criticism, and Life – The Trinity of Self

Wilde's second 'imaginary portrait' is in many ways his most complex work. It may be, in part, ' a study of various Victorian art movements',[1] a dramatisation of Ruskin's and Pater's tutelary influences,[2] a rehash of Poe,[3] a crib from Stevenson,[4] a cento of *Vathek, Vivian Grey, Melmoth the Wanderer, Mademoiselle de Maupin, A Rebours, Le Peau de Chagrin, Margery Merton's Girlhood*, Lefébure's *History of Lace*, and the handbook to the South Kensington Museum.[5] Ultimately, Wilde is his own most important influence, and his multiple presence in the book effectively belies the simple tale with a moral, or simple lack of morals, dismissed by many early reviewers and certain later critics.

Central to the design is Dorian's portrait. Mallarmé thought that it became 'the book itself',[6] but the book itself is really a triple portrait of the artist as a young man. In the relationships between the central trio we find Wilde's most serious statements. Something of this emerges in letters. In public, Wilde felt the need to defend himself against charges of immorality: 'The painter, Basil Hallward, worshipping physical beauty far too much, as most painters do, dies by the hand of one in whose soul he has created a monstrous and absurd vanity. Dorian Gray, having led a life of mere sensation and pleasure, tries to kill conscience, and at that moment kills himself. Lord Henry Wotton seeks to be merely the spectator of life. He finds that those who reject the battle are more deeply wounded than those who take part in it.' If the public requires a moral tag, Wilde will provide one: 'All excess, as well as all renunciation, brings its own punishment.' What the public will not have realised is the subjective significance of the proposition.

In the same statement, Wilde insisted on the novel's imaginary basis. 'Life by its realism is always spoiling the subject-matter of art. The supreme pleasure in literature is to realise the non-existent.'[7] Such assertions have not prevented speculation about the original sitters for so provoking a 'picture'. There is an account, almost certainly apocryphal, of Wilde's visits during the 1880s to a studio where he supposedly conceived the idea for the story.[8] John Gray and Alfred Douglas are obvious candidates for the hypothetical 'real' Dorian. Even Charles Ricketts and Charles Shannon might have posed as artist and sitter respectively: according to Rothenstein's double portrait (see

Plate 9), they closely resembled Wilde's Basil and Dorian, and they shared an artistic establishment in Chelsea. There is, however, no definite evidence to support any of their claims,[9] and the most obvious and most likely source for Wilde's experimental modern hero is the same as that for his idealised Elizabethan dramatic hero: his own wishful thinking. 'The supreme pleasure in literature is to realise the non-existent.' Another letter, to one Ralph Payne, supports this view: 'The book that poisoned, or made perfect, Dorian Gray', Wilde admitted, 'does not exist: it is a fancy of mine merely. I am so glad that you like that strange coloured book of mine; it contains much of me in it. Basil Hallward is what I think I am: Lord Henry what the world thinks me: Dorian what I would like to be — in other ages, perhaps.'[10] This succinct account, to which surprisingly little attention has been paid,[11] forms the basis of my argument.

The first version of Dorian Gray, published in 1890 in *Lippincott's Monthly*, differs from the 1891 volume as a longish short story generally differs from a novella: it concentrates on a single line of exposition and minimises incidentals. Apart from servants, waiters, and the like, there are only three characters besides the central trio, and none of the three — Sibyl Vane, Alan Campbell, and Lord Henry's wife — appears more than once. Wilde's 'art-decorator's' prose is also functional. As in "The Birthday of the Infanta", it serves as an aid to characterisation. The notorious chapter about Dorian's collections is one of the few passages in the 1890 version to reveal something of the inner workings of his personality.

But the most publicised difference between the 1890 and 1891 texts concerns Basil's feelings for Dorian. Pater had observed that certain expressions were open to misinterpretation,[12] and Wilde duly emended them; but his attitude seems to have been ambiguous from the start. Basil 'worships' Dorian. He is possessed by the image of him, and admits (in the 1890 version) that he had 'never loved a woman — I suppose I never had time'. Yet his love for Dorian — 'for it was really love — had something noble and intellectual in it'.[13] Wilde changed this to 'The love that he bore him — for it was really love — had nothing that was not noble and intellectual in it', continuing, 'It was such a love as Michael Angelo had known, and Montaigne, and Winckelmann, and Shakespeare himself. Yes, Basil could have saved him.' This change is significant beyond the obvious disclaimer. Dorian's list of intellectual lovers matches that which appears in the second "Mr W. H." (dating from 1893) though absent from the first (1889). (It also matches that given by Wilde during his third trial, after passages from *Dorian Gray* had been quoted to support the prosecution's allegations of immorality, in an attempt to justify 'the love that dares not speak its name' in the nineteenth century.) Moreover, the 1891 *Dorian Gray* anticipates the second "Mr W. H.", in which a section on neo-Platonism was introduced, by arguing, through Lord Henry, the application of Platonic theory to the modern artist, Basil:

From a psychological point of view, how interesting he was! The new manner in art, the fresh mode of looking at life, suggested so strangely by the merely visible presence of one who was unconscious of it all; the silent spirit that dwelt in dim woodland, and walked unseen in open field, suddenly showing herself, Dryad-like and unafraid, because in his soul who sought for her there had been wakened that wonderful vision to which alone are wonderful things revealed; the mere shapes and patterns of things becoming, as it were, refined, and gaining a kind of symbolical value, as though they were themselves patterns of some other and more perfect form whose shadow they made real: how strange it all was! He remembered something like it in history. Was it not Plato, the artist in thought, who had first analysed it? Was it not Buonarotti who had carved it in the coloured marbles of a sonnet-sequence? But in our own century it was strange.[14]

The one crucial parallel that Lord Henry understandably fails to draw is with Wilde's Shakespearean trio, though it is clear enough that Wilde associated them intimately in his own mind. Basil's love for Dorian and its capacity to 'save' him recalls Shakespeare's all-forgiving love for the fickle Mr W. H.,[15] and his faith in Dorian as an ideal could have negated, if Dorian had allowed it to, the terrible passions and evil dreams to which the influence of the artist's rival, Lory Henry, exposed him. Furthermore the power of the unconscious over Dorian, a theme elaborated in the 1891 version is analogous to the Dark Lady theory added to the second "Mr W. H.".

These details, however, are less important than the overall structural resemblances. Both works are based on all-male trios, and both are principally concerned with the relationship between art and life, theory and feeling. Dorian Gray not merely takes over the central situation of "Mr W. H.", but dramatises Wilde's current artistic and personal conflicts. Basil, Dorian, and Lord Henry embody Wilde's three most highly developed literary manners – romantic mythopoeia, social pastoral, and utopian criticism – but they also re-interpret the roles of Wilde's three Shakespearean protagonists: Basil being cast as the worshipping and idealising artist, Dorian as the capricious inspiring youth who involuntarily stimulates a fresh era in art, and Lord Henry as the 'rival poet' whose medium, with significant modification, is criticism, and whose working material is the personality of others.

This relationship is much clearer in the first version, and it seems likely that, quite apart from the details noted by Pater, Wilde shared Basil's anxiety that those who gazed at a portrait might spy out the artist's secret. Basil is unmistakably the artist (mentioned again in "The Critic as Artist") to whom a rare personality suggests a new manner, and Lord Henry the critical swashbuckler, the proud sail of whose full paradox sweeps away the sitter towards a full awareness of himself as a being, not just a model. Basil's conventional medium is art; Lord Henry's rival and ultra-modern medium is life itself, and his subject is Dorian. He plays on Dorian as on 'an exquisite violin' (Shakespeare had so played on Willie Hughes) and his 'poisonous theories' which Dorian unwisely and uncritically puts into practice, 'just as I do everything that you say, Harry', make 'the lad . . . largely his own creation'. Lord Henry, a covetous sybarite fledged in the Paterian cloister, prefers the experimental or 'scientific' method, but the subject matter provided by science seems to him 'trivial and of no import'. 'Human life' is the one thing worth study; and so, like the 'true critic', but with none of his purity of motive, Lord Henry lives vicariously on the emotions and experiences of other people: 'One's own soul and the passions of one's friends – they were the two fascinating things in life.'[16] Between Lord Henry and Basil, Dorian makes a more independent Willie Hughes, defining a new relationship between life and art. If Willie Hughes, who first suggested the identification of perfection with personality, was the first recognisable ancestor of the Romantic movement, as Wilde's narrator had suggested in "Mr W. H.", then Dorian articulates that movement's *dernier cri*. Basil sees in him the epitome of a new school which, like the 'English Renaissance' of Wilde's lecture, will combine 'all the passion of the Romantic spirit' with 'all the perfection of the spirit that is Greek.' But Lord Henry tells him later 'Life has been your art, Your days have been your sonnets,' and Dorian assents wearily. 'Yes, life has been exquisite.' He has devoted his life to the quasi-Paterian, or 'modern', aim of seeing (in Alfred Douglas' words) that 'the moment holds a madrigal',[17] and his wish-fulfilment via the portrait enables such a life to continue without ethical or legal interference from others.

In his early dramas, Wilde had feared that even the briefest romantic ecstasies tended to cost too much. Guido may reassure the dying Duchess that he has no regrets: 'have I not / Stood face to face with beauty; that is enough / For one man's life'; 'Why, in this dull and common world of ours / Men have died looking for such moments as this / And have not found them';[18] but the dramatist still felt it necessary to place poetic justice on the side of those who venture. Ripeness may come too soon; adaptability, as Prince Paul shows, is all. In *Dorian Gray* the supernatural steps in and saves the hero from adapting. Lending his 'countenance' to 'fill up' Lord Henry's critical life-drama, he becomes 'the type that the age has been looking for, and is afraid that it has found'. Directly responsible for Hallward's new artistic vision, and thus for the furtherance of modern art as a whole, Dorian finally transcends art as 'Art' by establishing life as the quintessentially modern art form even though it is necessarily transitory, and even though, when the personal influence inevitably fades – as the actor must die – the formal works of 'Art' will remain, not merely as the actor's or model's epitaph but as the true and enduring record of the age. For the portrait does change back; and though it is unwise to press for too specific an allegorical pattern, the reinstatement of the artist's ideal matches, appropriately enough, Wilde's interpretation of the twelve-line sonnet (CXXVI) as Shakespeare's last word in the Willie Hughes story: 'An envoi . . . whose motive is the triumph of Beauty over Time and of Time over Beauty.'

Passing from Wilde's account of Shakespeare's sonnets to his account of his own novel, it is not difficult to fit the unadmitted trio to the admitted. Basil is 'what I think I am': the serious artist possessed by an ideal of beauty imperfectly understood until he sees its physical incarnation, but lifted by it into a wholly new phase in his art. While this influence is restricted to his art, the 'romance' is fruitful. As Basil, and Wilde himself in the Preface, insist: 'The artist can express everything'. As soon as Basil allows the feeling to impinge on his life, where it can find only incomplete expression, he is doomed by it. 'There was something tragic,' Dorian muses, 'in a friendship so coloured by romance.' Lord Henry is 'what the world thinks me': the dandiacal mental athlete, the sceptical voluptuary who finds cynicism (as Wilde said of it in *De Profundis*) 'fascinating from its intellectual side', and who is committed to nothing except remaining uncommitted – above all, uncommitted to serious passion. He has been seen as 'a jab at Pater', but there is no need to read in Lord Henry's philosophy of inaction any criticism of *The Renaissance* when the author of *Vera, The Duchess of Padua, The Happy Prince, A House of Pomegranates*, and "The Critic as Artist" saw such virtue in postponing self-commitment. Dorian, finally, is 'what I would like to be – in other ages, perhaps', Wilde's one serious romantic egotist in modern dress. Just as Basil had painted Dorian in all sorts of mythical and historical guises (including all of those admired by the Young King), so Wilde himself now faced the problem of embodying his own 'non-existent' ideal in a contemporary setting – the ultimate test of its dubious viability. Basil's contemporary portrait is 'one of the greatest things in modern art' and the artist's masterpiece; but it dislocates his sense of abstract beauty, destroys his artistic objectivity, and, by a curious reversal of the Pygmalion story, takes on a life of its own at the price of the artist's life.

Within this pattern, Wilde's enduring dilemma undergoes definitive resolution. The egotistic romantic impulse, the impossible quest for the grail of self through art or through expressionistic action, is at odds with the sceptical critical faculty which refuses to accede to it, knowing such desires to be suicidal. Caught in the crossfire between these cohabiting antagonists is the artist, painted here as the worshipper and slave of beauty. But, in the words of the Wildean critic himself, 'There is nothing sane about the worship of beauty. It is too splendid to be sane. Those of whose lives it forms the dominant note will always seem to the world to be pure visionaries.'[19] The visionary's world is a no man's land, doubly vulnerable from the theoretician and the man of action, as Basil learns. 'Sometimes,' Wilde wrote in 1886, before he had developed his critical stance, 'I think that the artist's life is a long and lovely suicide, and I am not sorry that it is so.'[20] With a clearer view of the alternatives, he now took warning. After *Dorian Gray*, he moved back into the history-myth of *Salomé*, objectified through its woman hero; developed the autobiographical motive in the second "Mr W. H.", objectified by the conventions of aesthetic and textual criticism; and passed into the social compromise of stage comedy. Thus the novel stands at the crossroads, or more properly at the trivium, of personality – that fateful spot where the Muse-Sphinx must, and does, solve its own riddle.

Related to this motif of the tripartite personality is Dorian's development out of a state of pastoral self-ignorance. Pastoral images of countryside and garden are juxtaposed with dandiacal expositions of the 'new hedonism' and the novel fuses the symbolism of the fairy-tales with the philosophy of Wilde's utopian criticism. Beauty, however, not thought, is still the revelatory quality. For Dorian, as for the Young King, the Dwarf, and the Star-Child, personal beauty, present or absent, initiates the pastoral personality into the truth about itself.

This is the principal significance of the notorious book lent by Lord Henry, the hero of which attempted 'to realise in the nineteenth century all the passions and modes of thought that belonged to every century except his own, and to sum up, as it were, in himself the various moods through which the world-spirit had passed'. In a manuscript version Wilde gave the title of this book as 'Le Secret de Raoul' and its author as 'Catulle Sarrazin'.[21] In the published versions it was untitled and anonymous. In public letters he insisted that the book did not exist, and in private he both denied a specific model and acknowledged the partial influence of *À Rebours*.[22] The influence is there, but Wilde's and Huysmans' heroes have little in common other than a set of elaborate artistic tastes. The above summary of the mysterious protagonist's life bears scant relation to the pathetic attempts of Des Esseintes to keep illness, the present, and the bourgeois at bay, though it does resemble the cultural ideal of Pater's Duke Carl or of "The Critic as Artist": 'To realise the nineteenth century, one must realise every century that has preceded it and that has contributed to its making. To know anything about oneself one must know all about others. There must be no mood with which one cannot sympathise, no dead mode of life that one cannot make alive.'[23] This is the creed that Dorian briefly embraces, and which makes him, for as long as he remains true to it, Wilde's only perfect specimen of the Marcusean Narcissist, whose 'life is beauty, whose existence is contemplation'.

Between the true critic and 'the type the age has been looking for', as defined by Lord Henry and exemplified by Dorian, there is, however, one crucial difference. The Wildean or neo-Hegelian critic was to relive history through his aesthetic sensibility, while the cultivated hedonistic egotist was to 'rewrite history' according to his own real or postulated appetites. The critic lives wholly in thought. For him the revelatory medium is 'imagination', the concentration of 'race-experience' in its purest form: 'The great events of the world take place in the brain. The great sins of the world take place in the brain also.'[24] But the egotistical hedonist with his modern sensibility – 'too intellectually subtle and too curious of exquisite pleasures to accept any speculations about life in exchange for life itself'–finds contemplation unsatisfying. Life is his only conceivable medium, and the 'experimental method' the only profitable way of exploring it.

Pater had outlined the 'experimental method' in the celebrated Conclusion to *The Renaissance* (1873), returning to it with more caution in *Marius the Epicurean* (1885), and *Gaston de Latour* (published serially, June–October 1889). In the third chapter of the unfinished romance (August 1889), entitled "Modernity", Pater had explored the prospect, for an impressionable youth of the sixteenth century, of 'the worship of physical beauty' becoming 'a religion, the proper faculty of which would be the bodily eye.' But Gaston feels reservations:

> Might that new religion be a religion not altogether of goodness, a profane religion, in spite of its poetic fervours? There were 'flowers of evil', among the rest. It came in part, avowedly, as a kind of consecration of evil, and seemed to give it the beauty of holiness. Rather, good and evil were distinctions inapplicable in proportion as these new interests made themselves felt. For a moment, amid casuistical questions as to one's indefeasible right to liberty of heart, he saw himself, somewhat wearily, very far gone from the choice, the consecration of his boyhood.[25]

Gaston's boyhood state had been a dreamy, half-questioning absorption with the church around which his early years had been passed. A visit to Ronsard wakes him to life, but Montaigne's tutelage proves the formative influence. Although the school of Ronsard 'was soon to pay the penalty of that immediate acceptance, that intimate fitness to the mind of its own time, by sudden and profound neglect . . . like magic youth, or magic beauty, turned by magic's own last word into withered age', Gaston has genuinely loved the poet's lyrics. Even so, it is the philosopher's deliberate unpretentious egotism in which he recognises 'the pattern of the true intellectual life of everyone'.[26] These successive influences at work upon Gaston operate simultaneously upon Dorian. Lord Henry's garden speech offers the instinctual and the philosophic approaches to life in one accessible creed, and Dorian's escape from the 'consecration of his boyhood' is accomplished within minutes.

The relationship between Dorian's development and Lord Henry's influence was modified in the 1891 version. Originally, Lord Henry dilated on his theories only before Dorian and Basil. The trio could therefore be regarded as an eccentric clique, and the impetus for Dorian's backsliding – or for his climb out of the pastorally perfect state into 'modern' inclusive consciousness – could be supposed to come almost entirely from within himself. In the 1891 version, seeking to make the 'moral' less obtrusive, Wilde expanded the social setting so that Dorian's egotism in its everyday manifestation seems, if not 'the pattern of the true intellectual life of everyone', at least the norm of civilised contemporary life. Dorian's acceptance of Lord Henry's theories therefore appears little more than an exaggerated instance of the socialisation of the gifted individual. Only the artist remains an awkward anti-social exception.

Like "The Birthday of the Infanta", the novel opens with a series of deliberate ambiguities. Entering the studio in which Basil works and Lord Henry lounges, we sense at once its interpenetration with the adjacent garden. The room brims with 'the rich odour of roses'; Lord Henry glimpses 'the gleam of the honey-sweet and honey-coloured blossoms of the laburnum' bowed with the Edenic burden of its beauty; 'the fantastic shadows' cast by moving birds against the curtains remind him of the paradox of arrested motion beloved of the 'pallid jade-faced painters of Tokio'. Even the 'dim roar' of the distant city resembles an organ's pedal note. Art and nature lie together here with incestuous freedom, and the intimacy of their mutual identification fixes the scope and manner of the novel.

As soon as the topic of Basil's absent sitter occurs, Lord Henry expounds a social satirist's view of the 'state of nature': 'Beauty, real beauty, ends where intellectual expression begins.' If Hegel could include in his *Bildungsgeschichte* a section devoted to phrenology, Wilde, not to be outdone, it seems, will include in his *Bildungsroman* a physiognomic corollary to the doctrine of the original lapse into thought:

> The moment one sits down to think, one becomes all nose, or all forehead, or something horrid. Look at the successful men in any of the learned professions. How perfectly hideous they are! Except, of course, in the Church. But then in the Church they don't think. A bishop keeps on saying at the age of eighty what he was told to say when he was a boy of eighteen, and as a natural consequence he always looks absolutely delightful.

Lord Henry is confident that Dorian will bear out his theory:

> Your mysterious young friend, whose name you have never told me, but whose picture really fascinates me, never thinks. I feel quite sure of that. He is some brainless, beautiful creature, who should be always here in winter when we have no flowers to look at, and always here in summer when we want something to chill our intelligence.[27]

This calculated flippancy summarises the underlying premise of the novel and the visual metaphor by which it is expressed. Like the Star-Child, Dorian begins to lose his mysterious gift of beauty once his latent egotism is consciously developed; or rather, the loss is transferred to the portrait which, as long as Dorian lives, presents a sub-human figure, 'wrinkled and loathesome of visage', more repulsive even than the Star-Child's reptilian skin. This process begins as soon as Dorian stirs to Lord Henry's panegyric on youth and the physical world – as soon, in Lord Henry's terms, as Dorian begins to think.

The ambiguous relationship between art and nature is maintained throughout the early chapters. Basil makes his confession of Dorian's importance to him as 'a motive in art' in the garden, not in the studio. Upon re-entering the studio at the beginning of chapter 2,[28] the men see Dorian sitting at the piano, leafing through Schumann's *Forest Scenes*, which he asks Basil to lend him. (Of these we hear no more. The next book with which Dorian is associated is *Manon Lescaut*, lying in Lord Henry's library.) Dorian's immaturity is pointedly exaggerated in this chapter, accentuating one of the ironies of Basil's portrait: the 'half-parted lips and the bright look in the eyes' (again recalling the Young King and the Narcissus of "The Burden of Itys") are produced by the critic's persuasive invitation to self-knowledge. Wilde makes doubly sure of the point. While Basil stays inside to finish the picture, Dorian escapes into the garden from the 'stifling' air of the studio (as Salomé escapes, with analogous results, from the banquet). He buries his face in the 'great cool lilac-blossoms, feverishly drinking in their perfume as if it had been wine'. Lord Henry tells him:

> 'You are quite right to do that. Nothing can cure the soul but the senses, just as nothing can cure the senses but the soul.' . . .
> Dorian Gray listened, open-eyed and wondering. The spray of lilac fell from his hand upon the gravel. A furry bee came and buzzed round it for a moment. Then it began to scramble all over the oval stellated globe of the tiny blossoms. He watched it with that strange interest in trivial things that we try to develop when we are stirred by some new emotion for which we cannot find expression, or when some thought that terrifies us lays sudden siege to our brain and calls on us to yield. After a time the bee flew away. He saw it creeping into the stained trumpet of a Tyrian convolvulus. The flower seemed to quiver, and then swayed gently to and fro.[29]

Later, both Basil and Dorian become convinced that Lord Henry's influence was pernicious, perhaps wilfully so; but here Wilde's imagery suggests that the instrument is less important than the moment, and that, while Lord Henry recognises the moment's psychological promise, the intellectual pollination that he effects is as inevitable to any complex personality as the simplest cyclical processes are to nature. Clearly, Lord Henry's assertion that the only nature that can be said to be spoiled is one whose development has been arrested can be countered by arguing that his hedonistic theory and his delight in playing upon 'the lad's unconscious egotism' leads to an *impasse* in Dorian's moral growth. But, at this first meeting between them, no such growth has yet begun. Dorian does not understand Basil's devotion, nor does he appear to care much for Basil's art or his own prominence in it. To the unfallen personality, the distinction between art and nature is either incomprehensible, as it was to the Dwarf, or has not yet acquired that intensity and clarity which are the consequence of regarding them as the polarities of civilised life. Wilde accordingly commences the 'fall' in the studio, pursues it in the garden, and completes it back in the studio. Basil's portrait is the instrument of revelation, but Lord Henry's seductive picture of the fruits awaiting youth and beauty is the immediate cause of Dorian's looking at his own likeness with new eyes. As a result of what he hears and sees, he wishes for a division between art and nature so extreme and so unnatural that it inevitably causes the total disintegration of personality. It is the fate of Basil's modern dress portrait to record, after the fashion of Pater's *Imaginary Portraits*, the crucial moment of cultural and psychological transition.

Only after the portrait has been hidden away, however, does Dorian's development enter its most interesting phase. As Nassaar has pointed out, Wilde deliberately consigns the corrupted picture to the scene of Dorian's boyhood innocence, the schoolroom at the top of the house. In the 1890 version, the housekeeper, Mrs Leaf, makes a point of calling her employer 'Master Dorian' although she feels that this is no longer appropriate, makes allusions to his boyish taste for jam, and provides further comic business of the kind. In the 1891 version the specifics were removed but the implicit contrast remained. While the image of his awakening ignorance festers obscenely in the surroundings where knowledge first touched him, its avatar lives out, in the adult apartments below, a life of sophisticated experimentation. The physical removal of the portrait, first from its creator, then from the presence of its owner and subject to a secret hiding-place, matches the increasing dichotomy within Dorian's personality. Basil saw in his Dorian-vision a potential re-incarnation of the harmony of soul and body, but Dorian, following Lord Henry's rival aesthetic, soon reaches the point at which he involuntarily rejoices in driving them further and further apart. Once more, physical and moral beauty appear incompatible. On the one hand,

> while he was but too ready to accept the position that was almost immediately offered to him on his coming of age, and found, indeed, a subtle pleasure in the thought that he might really become to the London of his own day what to Imperial Neronian Rome the author of the *Satyricon* once had been,[30] yet in his inmost heart he desired to be something more than a mere *arbiter elegantiarum*, to be consulted on the wearing of a jewel, or the knotting of a necktie, or the conduct of a cane. He sought to elaborate some new scheme of life that would have its reasoned philosophy and its ordered principles, and find in the spiritualising of the senses its highest realisation.[31]

On the other hand, he would

> creep upstairs to the locked room . . . and stand, with a mirror, in front of the portrait that Basil Hallward had painted of him, looking now at the evil and ageing face on the canvas, and now at the fair young face that laughed at him from the polished glass. The very sharpness of the contrast used to quicken his sense of pleasure. He grew more and more enamoured of his own beauty, more and more interested in the corruption of his own soul.[32]

The Young King's implied narcissism in an upper room of the palace here becomes explicit and perverse, as does the earlier suggestion of the influence of his ancestry. Indeed, Dorian speculates on the subject, walking past his

ancestors' portraits and trying to determine the balance of their composite
influences within him. He realises that literary forebears are 'nearer, perhaps,
in type and temperament' than genetic ancestors, and that they act upon one
'certainly with an influence of which one was more absolutely conscious'.
He appreciates also that 'Psychical environment is as important as physical:
we cannot lay the ghosts of dead creeds';[33] but he feels that the uncertainty of
mere genetic influence magnifies its grotesque potential:

> He used to wonder at the shallow psychology of those who conceive the Ego in
> man as a thing simple, permanent, reliable, and of one essence. To him, man
> was a being with myriad lives and myriad sensations, a complex multiform
> creature that bore within itself strange legacies of thought and passion. . . . Had
> the lover of Giovanna of Naples bequeathed to him some inheritance of sin and
> shame? Were his own actions merely the dreams that the dead man had not
> dared to realise?[34]

Only a few months after publication of the first *Dorian Gray* Wilde
suggested in "The Critic as Artist" that heredity, by annihilating the notion
of free will, became 'as it were the warrant for the contemplative life'.
Dorian, in so far as he consciously evaluates its role in his life, tends to regard
it as the warrant for 'doing as one likes' in deed rather than merely in
thought. In this, as in his choice of the schoolroom as soul-depository, there
is a substantial degree of cultural rebellion. 'The pride of rebellion,' Wilde
tells us, 'is half the fascination of sin', and he repeated in various contexts his
conviction that disobedience is the first step in the growth of a man or a
nation. Dorian's schoolroom was the place of his habitual banishment by an
unsympathetic guardian; and whether or not Dorian's is one of those
personalities half of whose strength 'is wasted in friction',[35] his preference
for the 'splendid sins' of history clearly stunts his growth towards inclusive
culture. Those moments when he feels that 'history was merely the record of
his own life . . . as it had been in his brain and in his passions' are firmly
associated with wrong-doing.

Pater's warning against acquiescing 'in any facile orthodoxy of Comte or
of Hegel or of our own' has its initial effect on Dorian— 'of the asceticism
that deadens the senses, as of the profligacy that dulls them' his philosophy
was to know nothing. It was to 'teach man to concentrate himself on the
moments of a life that is itself but a moment'. It was never to arrest his
intellectual development. But Dorian avoids 'facile orthodoxy' only to fall
into facile unorthodoxy. Like the Fisherman, he sees the possibility of a
hedonistic ideal for the realisation of which the soul is an irrelevance or an
embarrassment, and by a supernatural trick he cuts himself off from it. The
portrait will bear the burden. But, as Wilde later wrote, 'To reject one's own
experiences is to arrest one's own development. To deny one's own
experiences is to put a lie into the lips of one's own life. It is no less than a
denial of the Soul.'[36] Dorian passes through Catholicism, mysticism, and
Darwinism — a group of interests not unparalleled in Wilde's own

career – but in wishing to create for himself worlds 'in which things would have fresh shapes and colours, . . . in which the past would have little or no place, or survive, at any rate, in no conscious form of obligation or regret', he denies the complexity of history and perverts its message. Eventually, suspended in time by the trick with the portrait, suspended in 'history' – in his own development – by wilful egocentricity, Dorian comes to regard the story of Tannhäuser as 'the presentation of the tragedy of his own soul'.

The recognition comes to him at the opera, but Wilde probably had Swinburne's version of the legend in mind as much as, if not more than, Wagner's. Elucidating his purpose in "Laus Veneris", Swinburne commented:

> To me it seemed that the tragedy began with the knight's return to Venus – began at the point where hitherto it had seemed to leave off. The immortal agony of a man lost after all repentance – cast down from fearful hope into fearless despair – believing in Christ and bound to Venus – desirous of penitential pain, and damned to joyless pleasure – this, in my eyes, was the kernel and nucleus of the myth comparable only to that of the wise and foolish virgins, and bearing the same burden.[37]

Dorian's uncritical pursuit of the 'new hedonism' propounded by Lord Henry matches Tannhäuser's imperfect religious dedication. Tannhäuser is 'Christ's knight, / No blinkard heathen stumbling for scant light'. Dorian also has his ideal, the ideal of perfect culture, the reintegration of 'sense' and 'soul', from which he is diverted into a false quest for the grail of self. The old schoolroom is his Venusberg, the portrait his Venus, self-consuming and all-consuming. The novel shows the romantic egotist's relation to that motto which was soon to become the quintessence of dandyism: 'To love oneself is the beginning of a lifelong romance.'[38] Dorian's worship of the portrait turns to fascinated loathing. Beauty and youth are rejected (in the 1891 version) as 'a mask' and 'a mockery'. But his one 'real' attempt to repent of his sordid life – his conceited decision to 'spare' the rustic Hetty Merton – is as ineffectual as Tannhäuser's. Lord Henry, his lay–confessor, flippantly quotes from the Bible and mocks him for being absurdly 'boyish', and Dorian returns home to find the image of his soul looking even fouler than before.

The Sibyl Vane episode is the chief (in the 1890 text the only) instance of Dorian's self-destructive vanity at work beyond the central triangle. He wants 'to place her on a pedestal', he tells Lord Henry, 'and make the world worship the woman who is, mine'. The prominent note of 'worship' throughout the 1890 version becomes the more interesting in the light of manuscript variations: Wilde veered between two forms of Sibyl's surname, 'Vane' and 'Fane'. Violet Fane was a character in *Vivian Grey* (1826), one of Wilde's putative sources, and he knew a Violet Fane as early as 1880. (Violet Fane was the pseudonym of Mrs Singleton, whose contributions to *The*

Woman's World included, in 1888, a verse-confection entitled "The Mer-Baby".) 'Vane' is the name of the leading actor in Reade and Taylor's play *Masks and Faces* (dating from 1852), revived in 1885 in London and noticed in the newly established *Dramatic Review*, to which Wilde had contributed. A sentimental comedy set in eighteenth-century London, the piece relies for its main interest on the actress, Peg Woffington, who is being courted simultaneously by Sir Charles Pomander, donor of 'three hundred a year – house – coach – pin-money – my heart – and the et ceteras', and Ernest Vane, 'that pastoral youth who means to win la Woffington by agricultural courtship, who wants to take the star from its firmament and stick it in a cottage'. Woffington agrees to have her portrait painted by a pathetic incompetent jack-of-all-arts, and, when he despairs of his work and slashes it with a palette knife, she stands in for her image, placing her face behind the hole in the canvas and thus saving the painter's professional credit, besides discrediting the claptrap of visiting critics who pontificate on the differences between art and nature. Finally, Vane's wife, Mabel, seeking out her husband, sees what she takes to be the image of her rival and declares, 'Oh that she were here, as this wonderful portrait is; and then I would plead to her for my husband's heart!', whereupon, emulating Galatea, Hermione, and Walpole's Gothick statue of Alfonso, all combined, Woffington sheds a tear. Mabel is frightened, but Woffington steps down from the picture-frame, and being herself instead of merely playing herself, swears to relinquish all claim on Vane and break her influence over him. The strength and nature of this influence appear in the first scene:

POMANDER: All this eloquence might be compressed into one word – you love Mrs Margaret Woffington.

VANE: I glory in it.

POMANDER: Why not, if it amuses you? We all love an actress once in our lives, and none of us twice.

VANE: You are the slave of a word, Sir Charles Pomander. Would you confound black and white because they are both colours? Actress! Can you not see that she is a being like her fellows in nothing but name? Her voice is truth, told by music: theirs are jingling instruments of falsehood.

POMANDER: No – they are all instruments; but hers is more skilfully tuned and played upon.

VANE: She is a fountain of true feeling.

POMANDER: No – a pipe that conveys it, without spilling or retaining a drop.

VANE: She has a heart alive to every emotion.

POMANDER: And influenced by none.

VANE: She is a divinity to worship.

POMANDER: And a woman to fight shy of. No – no – we all know Peg Woffington: she is a decent actress on the boards, and a great actress off them.[39]

CRIME AND EGOTISM (2)

Wilde's susceptibility to names – the comedies, for instance, show name-changes in almost every draft – extended beyond his work, and he often dwelt on the names of recent acquaintances in his letters to them. Whatever the balance of emphasis – whether Sibyl is a sham temple to which men bring the text of their own false oracle, or whether she is merely a passive instrument swung by the changing wind of Dorian's favour – Wilde significantly used 'Fane' at three turning points in the manuscript: when Dorian first mentions her to Lord Henry; when Lord Henry reminds him that he had spoken of her as 'all the heroines of romance'; and in the newspaper report of the inquest. This suggestion of 'worship' is made plain in both the 1890 and the 1891 version when Lord Henry, like Pomander, deflates his friend's romantic bubble with a sceptical aphorism:

> 'Ordinary women never appeal to one's imagination. They are limited to their century. No glamour ever transfigures them. One knows their minds as easily as one knows their bonnets. One can always find them. There is no mystery in any of them. They ride in the Park in the morning, and chatter at tea-parties in the afternoon. They have their stereotyped smile, and their fashionable manner. They are quite obvious. But an actress! How different an actress is! Harry! why didn't you tell me that the only thing worth loving is an actress?'
> 'Because I have loved so many of them, Dorian.'
> 'Oh, yes, horrid people with dyed hair and painted faces.'
> 'Don't run down dyed hair and painted faces. There is an extraordinary charm in them, sometimes,' said Lord Henry.
> 'I wish now I had not told you about Sibyl Vane.'
> 'You could not have helped telling me, Dorian. All through your life you will tell me everything you do. . . . And now tell me – reach me the matches like a good boy: thanks – what are your actual relations with Sibyl Vane?'
> Dorian Gray leaped to his feet, with flushed cheeks and burning eyes. 'Harry! Sibyl Vane is sacred!'
> 'It is only the sacred things that are worth touching, Dorian,' said Lord Henry, with a strange touch of pathos in his voice.[40]

In recounting Dorian's treatment of Sibyl, Wilde draws together several images from related works, notably "Mr W. H.", "The Fisherman and his Soul", and "The Critic as Artist". Like the Fisherman, Dorian has separated himself from his soul in order to follow a self-projecting myth. Filled with a new sense of his own beauty which has cast him in the fairy-tale role of 'Prince Charming', he anticipates joyfully his entry with Sibyl into a pastoral world of art – a realm unique in its combination of the richness of experience with the safety of innocence, lying within the bounds of knowledge but capable of being traversed repeatedly 'without hurt': 'I want the dead lovers of the world to hear our laughter and grow sad. I want a breath of our passion to stir their dust into consciousness, to wake their ashes into pain.' When Sibyl breaks from this world, in which she has always lived, and shows a preference for real life, of which she thinks Prince Charming a fine example, Dorian is bitterly disillusioned. Sibyl (the details of whose situation

are a remarkable mirror image of the Dwarf's) accepted make-believe, like
the Lady of Shalott, because spellbound by ignorance of anything else.
Lancelot of stage-door-Johnnies, Dorian breaks the enchantment and makes
the mirror look cracked and paltry. Wilde enlarged the sub-plot in the 1891
version by a chapter showing Sibyl's drab home and impossible mother, a
tattered relic of 'the palmy days of the British Drama'. Extra grounds for her
willing absorption in fantasy are hardly needed, however, and the reference
to Tennyson is already explicit in the 1890 text:

> I believed in everything. . . . The painted scenes were my world. I knew
> nothing but shadows, and I thought them real. . . . You taught me what reality
> really is. To-night, for the first time in my life, I saw through the hollowness,
> the sham, the silliness of the empty pageant in which I had always played. . . .
> You brought me something higher, something of which art is but a reflection.
> You had made me understand what love really is. . . . I have grown sick of
> shadows. [41]

'Shadows'also returns us to "Mr W. H.", in which Wilde had discussed the
special theatrical meaning attached to the word in Shakespeare's day – 'the
best in this sort are but shadows'; 'Life's but a walking player, a poor
shadow/ That struts and frets his hour upon the stage' – as virtually a
synonym for 'actor' or 'stage personage'. I have suggested that Basil
reproduces something of Shakespeare's idolisation of Mr W. H., and that
once Dorian awakes to his full personality he deserts the artist for his rival.
Dorian follows a similar pattern with Sibyl. As Shakespeare had worshipped
the interpreter of his timeless creations, so Dorian chooses to worship an
actress as the human embodiment both of his romantic daydream and of his
flirtation with 'history'. Interestingly enough, it is after her performance as
Rosalind – in her boy's costume she had 'never looked lovelier' – that
Dorian first kisses her. He watches her interpret 'all the heroines of romance'
(his list is in fact wholly Shakespearean), and comes to grief, like Basil, once
his ideal touches the modern and the actual and steps out of the frame of art.
Like Basil's ideal (Dorian), like Shakespeare's ideal (Mr W. H.), Dorian's
ideal (Sibyl) throws over art for life. However, 'the boy player of Rosalind
had nothing to gain from marriage, or from the passions of real life' – so, at
least, Wilde's Shakespearean critic had informed us. Lord Henry uses
precisely the same argument to persuade Dorian that his egotistical
indifference to Sibyl's suicide is natural and fitting to the occasion:

> It often happens that the real tragedies of life occur in such an inartistic manner
> that they hurt us by their crude violence, their absolute incoherence, their
> absurd want of meaning, their entire lack of style. They affect us just as
> vulgarity affects us. They give us an impression of sheer brute force, and we
> revolt against that. Sometimes, however, a tragedy that possesses artistic
> elements crosses our lives. If these elements of beauty are real, the whole thing
> simply appeals to our sense of dramatic effect. Suddenly we find that we are no

longer the actors, but the spectators of the play. Or rather, we are both. We watch ourselves, and the mere wonder of the spectacle enthralls us. . . . you must think of that lonely death in the tawdry dressing-room simply as a strange lurid fragment from some Jacobean tragedy, as a wonderful scene from Webster, or Ford, or Cyril Tourneur. The girl never really lived, and so she has never really died. To you, at least, she was always a dream. . . . The moment she touched actual life, she marred it, and it marred her, and so she passed away.[42]

Dorian is reassured. He feels that Lord Henry has explained him to himself, and henceforth he concentrates on himself and becomes his own art-ideal.

In "The Critic as Artist", Wilde had remarked of heredity: 'We may not watch it, for it is within us. We may not see it, save in a mirror that mirrors the soul' – an image taken from "The Fisherman and his Soul". *Dorian Gray* combines the symbolism of the pastoral tale with the scientific pretensions of the critical dialogue. While the Fisherman disports himself with the Mermaid, his Soul returns to him periodically, at first tempting him with 'the Mirror of Wisdom' in which everything in the world is reflected except the beholder. Eventually, more experienced in the world's ways, the Soul successfully lures the Fisherman to land by other means, only to be rejected in its turn. Dorian's portrait becomes his soul-mirror of wisdom. When it shows him the evil in his nature, he cuts himself off from its presence, but decides to keep watch over it, like the solipsistic actor-spectator of Lord Henry's misleading exposition: he will become the modern or *sentimentalisch* artist-in-life. 'This portrait would be to him the most magical of mirrors. As it had revealed to him his own body, so it would reveal to him his own soul.' Meanwhile the public, the conscious, Dorian prefers the 'mirrors of opinion' in which nothing but the beholder is reflected, and his bargain with the portrait, like the Fisherman's undersea life, enables him to defy the true mirror's message – that truth offered by 'soul' to 'sense', or to the conscious by the unconscious. He stands 'with a mirror, in front of the portrait that Basil Hallward had painted of him, looking now at the evil and ageing face on the canvas, and now at the fair young face that laughed back at him from the polished glass. The very sharpness of the contrast used to quicken his sense of pleasure. . . . He mocked the misshapen body and the failing limbs.'

However, as Wilde commented in "The Critic as Artist", when comparing the visual arts with literature,

The statue is concentrated to one moment of perfection. The image stained upon the canvas possesses no spiritual element of growth or change. If they know nothing of death, it is because they know little of life, for the secrets of life and death belong to those, and those only, whom the sequence of time affects, and who possess not merely the present but the future, and can rise or fall from a past of glory or of shame.[43]

The proper state for the portrait is the perfect representation of the crucial moment – time frozen – and the true balance is restored when Dorian, finding self-love and self-hate at last in equipoise ('For very love of self himself he slew'[44]), decides to destroy it with a knife: 'As it had killed the painter, so it would kill the painter's work, and all that that had meant.' However, as Wilde has told us in the Preface, 'It is the spectator, and not life, that art really mirrors'.[45] Only the self can destroy its self-projection. Wilde's final *tableau* reveals Dorian's self-portrait, his study in life, lying almost unrecognisable on the floor, while Basil's study from life, the real portrait, stands inviolate beside it.

The sudden and yet inevitable restitution has given rise to various ingenious interpretations, the most esoteric of which, perhaps, is that Dorian committed 'astral suicide'.[46] Wilde's own version, taken from Poe – that 'when Dorian kills conscience he kills himself' – is the simplest. More recently, Christopher Nassaar has argued that the novel is a symbolic account of the decline of Aesthetic art at the hands of Decadence. Suggestive as this theory is in some particulars, especially in its interpretation of Sibyl Vane, it really applies only to the 1891 text, since much of the Naturalist material on which it depends was not present in the 1890 version. It is weakened, too, by overcircumstantial argument: Basil's resemblance, such as it is, to Nassaar's various Pre-Raphaelite contenders is diminished, not increased, by the little we are told of his ideals, subjects, and technique.[47] But the real flaw in this interpretation lies in its definitions of Pre-Raphaelitism, Aestheticism, and Decadence – especially of the last, which leads to what I take to be a misunderstanding of the novel. To summarise: the portrait takes on, following Dorian's experiences, those qualities detected by Pater beneath the teasing mask of the *Mona Lisa* and defined by him as integral to the modern consciousness. It becomes, in other words, a modern Giocondo. Dorian rejects the 'Greek grace' of Sibyl Vane as Pater had rejected the 'white Greek goddesses and beautiful women of antiquity'. Only the evil embodied by Lord Henry can satisfy the modern sensibility, and through his spiritual ventriloquism – he projects 'his evil soul' into Dorian – his disciple becomes a Decadent masterpiece. As Leonardo had called mimes and flute-players to protract the subtle expression on his model's face (Pater records the story), so Lord Henry's surrogate talents serve the modern painter. Basil's admission that Dorian had been to him, before they had ever met, 'a dream of form in days of thought', matches Pater's account of Leonardo's preoccupation with 'the smiling of women', for 'From his childhood we see this image defining itself on the fabric of his dreams; and but for express historical testimony, we might fancy that this was but his ideal lady, embodied and beheld at last.'

However intriguing these parallels are, they do not account for the conclusion of the novel. Granted that Dorian learns to seek beauty in evil – granted even the premise that 'while aesthetic art . . . presents the soul as being essentially pure, decadent art sees it as being evil and derives pleasure from that evil' – it is plainly untrue that Decadent art sets out to be ugly. In so far as Decadent art had a unified and coherent aim, it might be defined in Baudelaire's phrase 'trouver le beau dans l'horrible', to find beauty in the ugliness of external or internal experience by subjecting it to the discipline of artistic form. Wilde himself, in public defence of his book, quoted Keats's remark that Shakespeare took as much delight in creating an Iago as an Imogen,[48] and repeated it in other contexts. Dorian's portrait cannot fulfil both requirements at once. It cannot be both literally hideous, as we are encouraged to suppose it, and also a masterly distillation of the visual effects of vice. It is not, in fact, 'beautifully horrible' art, but beautiful art turning mysteriously, and temporarily, into horrible life. When the picture changes back again, the sitter's defacement of his soul-portrait amounts to no more than wilful graffiti scrawled over the artist's invulnerable Platonic dream.

The logical end of the 'demonic' theory is to project a terrible doom for Lord Henry, who 'has placed his soul entirely in his art – Dorian – and when Dorian dies he loses it'.[49] Yet the fact remains that, however bleakly Lord Henry's future may stretch without his best friend and his uncompanionable wife, he, at least, survives – whereas the crusading egotist dies once he recognises the whole of himself; the sleeping-beauty actress dies once kissed to life; and the artist makes a third who dies when his human ideal defaces his imaginative ideal. But the critic, his rival, never confronts or knows the horror of the portrait – 'the real Dorian' – and Wilde takes pains to make clear that Lord Henry thinks Dorian 'perfect' precisely because he has not changed. He sees him as 'the type of the age', but having once typecast him he becomes incapable of penetrating his character. He cannot credit that Dorian should have turned to crime. 'The wilful sunbeams of life' do not commit crimes and he treats Dorian's hint that he murdered Basil as mere affectation – 'posing for a character that doesn't suit you'. To replace so unlikely a confession, he proposes for the disaffected lover a death both pseudo-romantic and full of arty pathos, an urban parody of the drowned Ophelia: 'I dare say he fell into the Seine off an omnibus, and that the conductor hushed up the scandal. Yes: I should fancy that was his end. I see him now, lying on his back under those dull-green waters, with the heavy barges floating over him, and the long weeds catching in his hair.' If these, too, are self-conscious pictorial echoes, then they could provide an amusing epitaph on the Victorian painter who confuses art with life. Has Basil's literal Pre-Raphaelite art died a natural death by misadventure in Symbolist Paris, picked off by 'one of the trammelling accidents of real life'? Has he gone there to finish 'a great picture that I have in my head', as he tells Dorian he intends to do, only to end up as an almost invisible component in a Whistlerian nocturne? Lord Henry's picture is perhaps most suggestive in parodying Wilde himself: it reminds us of the death of Little Hans, the affectionate masochist of "The Devoted Friend", that least optimistic of Wilde's earliest set of ego-parables.

If, then, Lord Henry's soul is indeed as dead as the artist and his model, it must have perished from other causes. Though Dorian was 'largely his own

creation' at first, 'the lad' emancipates himself from his mentor's influence
and demonstrates the truth of Wilde's comforting critical doctrine that
'when a work is finished it has an independent life of its own, and may
deliver a message far other than that which was put into its mouth to say'.[50]
Lord Henry never realises the irony of telling his 'creation' that he represents
to him 'all the sins that you have never had the courage to commit'. The
revelation of Dorian's full character would have shocked him no less than it
shocked Basil. Perhaps this is why it never occurs. The real Muse-Sphinx of
every conscientious egotist must be the enigma of his own personality, and,
if the book is indeed built on a consciously autobiographical triangle, then
one, at least, of the trio ought to survive. The likeliest candidate for this
honour (or ignominy) is not the Platonising artist who cannot come to terms
with life, nor the passionate egotist whose desires and attempts to gratify
them overstep the bounds not only of the socially acceptable but also of the
physically possible. The likeliest candidate is the critic, sceptical artist in
modern life, who moves with the social tide and duly graduates into stage
comedy – most refined of social metaphors – where romance and egotism
are subjected to intellectual authority, where the riddling sphinx of
personality, so mute or so menacing in private contexts, is teased into
repartee by the chimera of dandiacal epigram, and where nobody dies at all.

II.   Rise and Fall of the Woman Hero: (i) *Vera, or The Nihilists* and *The Duchess of Padua*

Usually discussed as technique, these prentice pieces are by no means so
lacking in intellectual content as is generally supposed. As the beginnings of
Wilde the dramatist they would command a certain attention. As the
beginnings of Wilde the self-dramatising egotist they command rather
more. With *Salomé* they comprise the greater part of his Romantic drama,
and the strident internal conflicts expressed in them, though temporarily
gagged by irony or muffled by mythopocic distances in the narrative and
critical endeavours of the 1880s, broke out again in *Salomé*, where, in their
Romantic form at least, they were silenced once and for all.

They have also some claim to artistic originality, of conception if not of
execution. It may be coincidence that neither contains more than one female
character, or perhaps Wilde despaired of writing anything worthy of Henry
Irving and concentrated on capturing a leading actress instead. (Later, with
greater self-confidence and, perhaps, more pressing financial problems, he
did offer *The Duchess of Padua* to Irving, to no effect.[51]) However, this was
the decade when the 'woman as hero' emerged in the novel and the drama,[52]
and Wilde's three romantic female leads are convincing specimens of this
class. Family tradition was conceivably a factor in this. The heroic female
sublimely active in a male world may have been stimulated by Lady Wilde's

example. The details of her career as Speranza, champion of Irish nationalism, must have constituted Wilde's earliest and vividest exposure to professional mythopoeia, a blueprint for literary treatment of Romantic anarchism. Certainly his own career was launched from her London salon when various manifestations of the New Woman were beginning to make their mark, and one of Guido's speeches contains a mixture of romance and art-criticism which seems to skirt autobiography, even if the persistent note of 'we women' is temporarily submerged in Victorian courtly sentiment:

> DUCHESS:Love will bring music out of any life.
>   Is that not true?
> GUIDO: Sweet, women make it true.
>   There are men who paint pictures, and carve statues,
>   Paul of Verona and the dyer's son,
>   Or their great rival, who by the sea at Venice,
>   Has set God's little maid upon the stair . . .
>   Or Raphael whose Madonnas are divine
>   Because they are mothers merely; yet I think
>   Women are the best artists of the world,
>   For they can take the common lives of men
>   Soiled with the money-getting of our age,
>   And with love make them beautiful.[53]

Whatever prompted Wilde's choice of the woman hero, he evidently found in Vera, Beatrice, and Salomé figures expressive of that Romantic conflict which occurs when the exceptional personality, as it must, seeks self-perfection in despite of law and duty. Wilde's observation of 1890 about the great tragic masterpieces of Athens and England was anticipated by his own dramatic practice a decade before:

> those figures of Greek or English drama that seem to possess an actual existence of their own, apart from the poets who shaped and fashioned them, are, in their ultimate analysis, simply the poets themselves, not as they thought they were, but as they thought they were not; and by such thinking came in strange manner, though but for a moment, really so to be.[54]

In 1887, two tragedies the wiser, Wilde played with self-fulfilment in "Lord Arthur Savile's Crime". In the lyrical dramas, he developed something resembling a personal myth, similar in shape to that Victorian favourite, Perseus and Andromeda. The ego is the distressed maiden; duty or restraint the rock to which she is fastened; disobedience or rebellion the ravening monster which guards her or threatens her destruction; while the individual will, expressed through anarchic courage, is the saving heroic force. Once more, however, Wilde transforms familiar picture into critical paradox. The hero delivers the captive not so that she can flee the monster, but so that she can embrace it without embarrassment. Rebellion and self-expression become virtually synonymous. Capitulation to the *status quo* means a despicable betrayal of self. Naturally, Wilde ensures that the *status quo* never appeals. In this single point his Romantic and critical works agree.

Vera, The Duchess of Padua, Salomé, and the unfinished plays[55] all contain this idea, and in the first three a clear progression is visible. As Wilde takes the compulsion towards anarchy more seriously, so he becomes less concerned, on behalf of his protagonists, about self-preservation or the good opinion of others. Finally, Salomé cuts loose: we no longer sense the dramatist waiting in the wings with the nimbus of martyrdom in his hands.

For his first play, *Vera*, Wilde chose a subject sufficiently topical to prevent its London production for diplomatic reasons.[56] Yet, as he explained to Marie Prescott, its American star, 'It is a play not of politics but of passion. It deals with no theories of government, but with men and women simply; and modern Nihilistic Russia, with all the terror of its tyranny and the marvel of its martyrdoms, is merely the fiery and fervent background in front of which the persons of my dream live and love.'[57] Publicity prose, perhaps, but accurate criticism. Vera's vow 'To strangle whatever nature is in me; neither to love nor to be loved; neither to pity nor to be pitied; neither to marry nor to be given in marriage, till the end is come' is threatened by her awakening love for Alexis, apparently a Nihilist conspirator but in fact the son of the reigning Czar. When the Nihilists assassinate the Czar, Alexis ascends the throne with the hope of reforming the government on juster principles. Vera is chosen by lot to shoot him as a traitor to the cause. Instead, she commits suicide under the final curtain, claiming to have 'saved Russia'. By giving her life for his, she averts the likelihood of a tyranny run by political extremists; but she also preserves intact both her unfulfilled love and her vow to annihilate all feeling. From one point of view, her suicide betrays her oath to duty. From another, it preserves the spirit of it while betraying only the word. From a third, it is the logical extreme of the Nihilist code of self-effacement. It is also the supreme act of the Romantic individual's independent will. Vera is a traitor and no traitor, to love and to Nihilism, and she emerges a hero as well.

While Vera acts the heroic martyr's part, her aristocratic antagonist, Prince Paul, cultivates the anti-heroism of modern life with dandified cynicism. He has, however, one point in common with the Nihilists whom he despises: his amoral egotism is a sophisticated form of individualistic anarchy. In cutting his political losses and joining the rebels, he remains essentially consistent. His contempt for everyone but himself and good cooks ensures him a plausible, if uncomfortable, transition from aristocratic to proletarian subversion.

Prince Paul, like Wilde, has given thought to perfecting life as an art form, but he fails to find that perfection when he accepts an ignominious and inaesthetic compromise. Vera, for whom life is at first valuable only as a form through which to realise her ethical and social idealism, makes her own life perfect by ending it, with unerring dramatic instinct, at the perfect moment. Whereas Prince Paul is weakly anarchic in word, Vera is doubly anarchic in deed. She relinquishes the shallow anarchism of the Nihilists for a new and complex anarchy which demands a triple renunciation – of love, of allegiance, and of life itself. The play edges gingerly towards a confrontation between art and ethics, and embodies suspicions that Wilde is still unwilling to endorse by his own behaviour: commitment brings fulfilment and perfection of form, while detachment and indifference undermine and destroy. It also embodies reservations about the grand gesture and the place of expediency. The path to self-fulfilment would seem to lead through the anarchic extreme, but the price is high. Prince Paul lives to coin new epigrams. Vera may save Russia, but she solves the problem of how to keep a spotless conscience only by rubbing the problem off the blackboard.

For his second play, *The Duchess of Padua*, Wilde turned to the Elizabethan revenge tradition, which offered a combination of full-blooded Romantic individualism, gorgeousness of setting and extravagance of plot, speech, and character. Romantic death from *Romeo and Juliet* and madness from *The Duchess of Malfi* are ushered in by bad weather from *Julius Caesar*. Guido, in love with Beatrice, is bound by a family vendetta to kill her husband, the Duke. While he hesitates, Hamlet-like, the Duchess is overcome with revulsion for her savage and cynical consort and commits the murder herself. By so doing, she estranges Guido's affections, then loses heart and has him arrested for the crime. When she denounces him in open court, no one believes his protestations of innocence. He refuses to implicate the Duchess and is incarcerated to await execution. Beatrice now feels remorse more strongly than fear, and reconciles herself to Guido and to her guilt by visiting his cell, insisting that he escape, and taking poison. Guido refuses to leave, stabs himself, and completes the anarchic sequence. Both characters escape the social consequences of personality. Rather than bearing the ignominy of compromise – self-submission to outside authority – they choose Romantic death.

Vera had portrayed civil anarchy. *The Duchess of Padua* presents a kind of private anarchy contained, as in many of its models, within the confines of an autonomous court. The tyrannical Duke is murdered for personal, not political, reasons. Nor, even, is the court a microcosm of the state. In a trial scene borrowed, with amendments, from *The White Devil* and *The Merchant of Venice*, the course of legal justice is repeatedly diverted in favour of the truths of poetic justice, in which art and ethics conveniently combine.

The principals may scorn compromise, but it still holds attractions for the author. Wilde's final gesture is not merely Romantic, but anarchic within the framework of his own play. Guido and Beatrice throw their lives away with rhetorical abandon, but Wilde himself is obviously ill at ease with such unqualified self-sacrifice. 'They do not sin at all who sin for love', Guido assures the dying Duchess. She quietly demurs: 'No, I have sinned, and yet Perchance my sin will be forgiven me. / I have loved much.' In a supporting stage direction, the Lord Justice arrives before the final tableau to drag Guido's cloak from the Duchess's lifeless face, now revealed to the audience as 'the marble image of peace, the sign of God's forgiveness'. Wilde has moved a step further towards complete commitment in action, but, as Richard Ellmann has said of his later ironic mode, he still has 'an eye on the door left open for the witless law'.[58]

III.   Rise and Fall of the Woman Hero: (ii) *Salomé* [59]

Le poète est celui qui regarde [André Gide].

The germ of Salomé may be traced partly to "Pen, Pencil and Poison", but more particularly to "The Soul of Man", where Wilde made his most cogent statement of the artist's utopian and anarchic duty:

> Art is the most intense mood of Individualism that the world has known. I am inclined to say that it is the only real mode of Individualism that the world has known. Crime, which, under certain conditions, may seem to have created Individualism, must take cognisance of other people and interfere with them. It belongs to the sphere of action. But alone, without any reference to his neighbours, without any interference the artist can fashion a beautiful thing; and if he does not do it solely for his own pleasure, he is not an artist at all.[60]

Published only a few months before he began work on *Salomé*, this passage defines Wilde's conscious attitude towards so strange a subject. Indeed, the play bears out surprisingly fully his chief critical 'intentions'. It fulfils the anti-Naturalist aesthetic of "The Decay of Lying" and the historical disinterestedness urged in "Pen, Pencil and Poison" ('It is exactly because Hecuba is nothing to us that her sorrows are so admirable a motive for tragedy'). It emulates *Dorian Gray* by fulfilling one of the critic-as-artist's requirements: 'People sometimes say that fiction is getting too morbid. As far as psychology is concerned, it has never been morbid enough. We have merely touched the surface of the soul.'

Following these precepts, Wilde 'rewrote history'. Herod combines features from all three Biblical Herods.[61] Iokanaan is no longer the Baptist familiar through European iconography. Salomé is emancipated from her mother's authority, and the remainder of the cast, though glancing at times towards Maeterlinck, Flaubert, J. C. Heywood, or Wilde's earlier fables, is largely invention.[62] Under cover of this artistic objectivity, Wilde confronts issues dodged in *Dorian Gray* or skirted in previous plays and stories, showing the definitive truth of masks.

His precautions prevented neither official censorship[63] nor critical disapproval. *Salomé* was received as a silly puppet-show, or 'an arrangement in blood and ferocity, morbid, *bizarre*, repulsive, and very offensive in its adaptation of scriptural phraseology to situations the reverse of sacred'.[64] Wilde had anticipated such a response. A year earlier, after his experience with reviews of *Dorian Gray*, he had written: 'What is morbidity but a mood of emotion or a mode of thought that one cannot express? The public are always morbid, because the public can never find expression for anything. The artist is never morbid. He expresses everything. . . . To call an artist morbid because he deals with morbidity is as silly as to call Shakespeare mad because he wrote *King Lear*.'[65]

Salomé was to 'express everything' – a test case for Wilde the self-analyst as for Wilde the technician, who turned to French, perhaps for extra distance.[66] To this extent the play is more reliant on foreign models than *Dorian Gray* had been, although it also distils *Vera* and *The Duchess of Padua*, blending the themes of revenge and romantic self-fulfilment in a manner which suggests that it stands to *The Duchess of Padua*, in particular, as Jacobean stood to Elizabethan tragedy. A white devil for heroine, a court ruled by lust and cynicism, dry wit, romantic suicide, a pitiless climax (vengeful but explicitly amoral), and some astonishing love speeches are manipulated by an author who is now the dispassionate spectator of his characters, though far from disinterested privately about the principles at stake.

The female hero – 'a young woman affronting her destiny'[67] – is portrayed as the supreme egotist of a cast imprisoned by indifference or introspection, exemplars of Pater's claim that 'experience, already reduced to a swarm of impressions, is ringed round for each one of us by that thick wall of personality through which no real voice has ever pierced on its way to us, or from us to that which we can only conjecture to be without.'[68] Characters either ignore each other, misunderstand each other, or are repulsed by each other. Herod and Herodias live in mutual contempt. The Young Syrian and the Page linger in an advanced state of homosexual misunderstanding. The Syrian ignores the Page, Salomé ignores the Syrian. Salomé invests Iokanaan with the romance of the inaccessible. Iokanaan sees in her the abominations of the untouchable. She is intoxicated by the sound of his voice and hypnotised by the sight of him. He refuses to look at her, even to listen to her, decends into his womb-like, or tomb-like cell, and does not reappear alive. The intimate remains incommunicable, but the imperious ego requires self-fulfilment through communication – specifically through love. This discrepancy makes the play, in every sense. Climax to a century of largely prudish artistic solipsism, *Salomé* is, among other things, an orgasmic metaphor through which the unspeakable erupts in brief and devastating triumph.

The action of the play consists of a battle of wills. Herod wants most to avoid trouble, Herodias to keep face, Iokanaan to remain untouched. Yet Herod indulges dangerous whims, revenging himself on others; Herodias' dignity is merely a sterile pose; and Iokanaan wraps himself in arrogance and meanness of spirit. Salomé opposes them all and vanquishes them on their own ground. She is proud and virginal, but refuses to regard isolation or purity as ends in themselves. She indulges her whims, but neither regrets them nor avoids their consequences. She is 'a dreamer' by Herodias' cynical standards, and thus one of the 'sick people', yet her ultimate indifference to life results from having got the only thing that she desired, not, as in Herodias' case, from having tired of all available alternatives. These positive qualities define her uniqueness and her position as hero of a largely anti-heroic cast.

Admittedly, one's view of Salomé must depend on one's view of Iokanaan, who has provoked much disagreement. The conventional view is surely the least tenable. A Baptist who makes historically verifiable predictions about Christ's arrival, a figure revered by hindsight and the only representative of recognisable spiritual values, has no place in Wilde's scheme. Indeed, Wilde took precautions against the predisposition towards it. As a prophet, Iokanaan is a failure. Most of his prophecies are not fulfilled, and when they are they tend to undergo ironic reinterpretation. Nor can Iokanaan be given the credit for the mysterious outcome of divine will, for the unexpected recurs throughout *Salomé* and actions regularly give the lie to words.[69] His self-esteem is unattractive, almost blasphemous: 'Back, daughter of Sodom! The temple of the Lord God must not be profaned.' With his bombast, his priggishness, and his prurient anatomisation of Herodias, he can hardly be taken seriously as the voice of the new spiritual kingdom. Even his well-meaning 'quotations' from the scriptures are inaccurate, and his menacing presence, from which Salomé alone is immune, is chiefly the produce of his incomprehensibility. At most he is a male sphinx, though no-one knows whether he had a secret or not, and his total effect might be compared with that of the soap-box orator described by Lord Henry Wotton:

> I was going through the Park last Sunday, and close by the Marble Arch there stood a little crowd of shabby-looking people listening to some vulgar street-preacher. As I passed by, I heard the man yelling out that question to his audience ['What does it profit a man if he gain the whole world and lose his own soul?']. It struck me as being rather dramatic. London is very rich in curious effects of that kind. A wet Sunday, an uncouth Christian in a mackintosh, a ring of sickly white faces under a broken roof of dripping umbrellas, and a wonderful phrase flung into the air by shrill, hysterical lips — it was really very good in its way, quite a suggestion. I thought of telling the prophet that Art had a soul but that man had not. I am afraid, however, that he would not have understood me.[70]

Wilde did not cast his prophet literally as 'a vulgar street-preacher' (Laforgue, in his "Salomé", did[71]); but the passage is 'quite a suggestion' and perhaps lingered in his memory.

I shall return to *Dorian Gray* later. Meanwhile, it is worth noting how *Salomé*'s best-known critic, Richard Strauss, reacted to Iokanaan. Taken to task by a friend who thought that he had not 'experienced the faith of the savage Precursor in the slightest degree', and by another who found the themes allotted to the prophet 'decidedly commonplace', the composer protested, '"Oh, no! no! I don't think so at all!" But after a while he conceded rather lamely: "Besides, I didn't want to treat him too seriously. You know, Iokanaan is an imbecile. I've got no sympathy at all for that kind of man. I would have preferred above all that he would appear a bit grotesque." '[72] Norman del Mar's judgement – that Strauss's failure to give Iokanaan's music 'the necessary sublimity' was 'integral to the whole of [his] genius' – may have much to recommend it; nevertheless it is based on the false assumption that 'the lofty passages of Wilde's text' are direct Biblical quotations, not deliberately picturesque hybrids.

Critics have often amused themselves with Wilde's French, comparing it to Ollendorf, 'the Berlitz of that age',[73] or seeing in the play as a whole a 'primer' for the 'Philistine' who wishes to wear 'the lion's skin' of *avant-garde* culture.[74] Much remains to be said about the complexities of *Salomé*'s composition and translation. It is more important, here, to point out that the play realises two of Wilde's critical 'intentions'. The justification of its characters is 'not that other people are what they are, but that the author is what he is',[75] while the prose style, by unifying plot, atmosphere and character, produces that harmony of feeling with structure that Wilde had earlier called 'imaginative form'.

Herod's court fall into two groups, the cynics and the dreamers, descendants of the author's critical-Romantic conflict. Herodias, the Roman ambassador, and the soldiers belong to the first group; Salomé, Iokanaan, the Young Syrian, and the Page to the latter. Herod is caught between the two. The cynics talk plain prose without imagery or symbol. (When the soldiers describe the tetrarch's wines as 'red like blood' and 'yellow like gold', these are rare metaphoric flights.) The dreamers speak figuratively more often than not, either in fantastic visual metaphors or with visionary or apocalyptic undertones. The two attitudes, worldly cynicism and symbolist fantasy, take their extreme form in Herodias and her Page. Herodias disbelieves in miracles because she has 'seen too many'. The Page sees symbols and threats in everything, and cannot do or say or hear anything without the fear that 'something terrible might happen'.

The contrast is established in the opening lines. Isolation transforms apparent conversation into something very like monologue, and the scene becomes a string of self-contained, almost Absurdist, *non sequitur*s:

YOUNG SYRIAN: How beautiful Princess Salomé is tonight!
PAGE: Look at the moon. The moon looks very strange. You'd think it was a woman rising from a tomb. She is like a dead woman. You'd think she was looking for dead men.
YOUNG SYRIAN: She looks very strange. She is like a little princess who wears a yellow veil and has silver feet. Like a little princess whose feet are like little doves. You'd think she was dancing.
PAGE: She's like a dead woman. She moves very slowly.
(*Noise in the banqueting hall.*)

FIRST SOLDIER:	What a racket! Who are those animals bawling?
SECOND SOLDIER:	The Jews. They're arguing about their religion.
FIRST SOLDIER:	Why do they argue about their religion?
SECOND SOLDIER:	I don't know. They always do. For instance, the Pharisees claim there are angels, and the Sadducees say that angels don't exist.
FIRST SOLDIER:	I think it's ridiculous to argue about such things.[76]

The visitors to Herod's court are as spiritually bankrupt as its inmates. While orthodox Jews wrangle over degrees of heterodoxy, the Cappadocian declares the gods of his country to be dead, chased out by the Romans, and the Nubian regards god-worship as a matter of relentless and ineffectual human sacrifice. Into this spiritual desert enters first Iokanaan's voice, proclaiming the downfall of pagan beliefs, then Salomé – so much of a pagan that she does not even know who Elias was.

The crucial psychological action is schematic, almost ritualistic. Salomé appeals three times to Iokanaan, is three times rejected, cursed, and left to contemplate revenge. Followed by the whole court, the tetrarch enters in search of her. Salomé hardly speaks for some time: her motive forms silently. Meanwhile, Iokanaan's voice assaults Herod and Herodias, until, pricked by his wife's contempt and his own lust, the tetrarch vanquishes pride and succeeds in persuading Salomé to dance. Unknown to him, the dance expresses both her defiance of Herod's advances and her mocking courtship of Iokanaan. When she refuses any reward other than Iokanaan's head, Herod is appalled, but finally surrenders. Salomé seizes the head, taunts it, laments over it, and, with the moonlight quenched, utters her final words to it in utter darkness.

Wilde's long fascination with the moon reached its climacteric in *Salomé*. Here it is a symbol, a structural device, and a device of characterisation. Though physically absent from the set,[77] it becomes a symbolic reference point for individual responses to Salomé.[78] The Young Syrian sees a little princess with a yellow veil and silver feet; the Page sees a dead woman; Herod sees a 'drunken woman looking everywhere for lovers'; Herodias sees merely the moon, though she does remark that the disputing Jews are 'mad' because 'they have been looking at the moon too much'. The cloddish soldiers appear not to see the moon at all – aptly enough, since the executioners of the supreme undisciplined individualist ought never to perceive her symbolic aspect.

Salomé sees the moon as a virgin, a sympathetic presence aloof from the fleshly excesses of the court, and it inspires the lyric grace of the Young Syrian's descriptions of her, as of her first impression of Iokanaan – 'a silver moonbeam'. She is sure that he is 'chaste, like the moon'. However, Salomé never looks at the moon once she has looked at Iokanaan, and, as her character develops, so Herod's view of the moon changes. He thinks he sees it turning red, as Iokanaan prophesied it would, and later envisions it as 'reeling across the sky', drunken and naked, shaking off its cloud-coverings.

He is still obsessed with the moon when he tries to press Salomé to pearls or peacocks instead of Iokanaan's head:

> Salomé, you know my white peacocks, my beautiful white peacocks that walk in the garden between the myrtles and the great cypresses. Their beaks are gilded, and the grain that they eat is gilded also, and their feet are coloured with purple. The rain comes when they cry, and when they strut about the moon shows herself in the sky. . . . Well, I will give you fifty of my peacocks. They will follow you everywhere, and you in their midst will be like the moon in a great white cloud. . . . I have a necklace of pearls in four rows. You'd think they were moons fettered with silver beams, fifty captive moons in a mesh of gold.[79]

Salomé, too, develops the moon imagery, referring to it in her first love speech to Iokanaan, in which white predominates, and in her second, which anticipates the moonless darkness at the end of the play. Even Wilde's stage direction for her final speech with the head, when moon and stars are obscured, has symbolic significance. Herod's ultimate panic takes the form of a fear of light. 'Put out the torches,' he cries. 'Hide the moon! Hide the stars!' Wilde suggests a cloud, the moon and stars duly disappear. The darkness heralds Salomé's eclipse – not by divine intervention, however, but by Herod's jealous and neurotic rage.[80] A last ironic ray of moonlight picks out her motionless form as the soldiers rush forward, but by this time she is indifferent to everything, even her own fate.

Salomé herself acts as a touchstone of character in a further, and crucial, respect. The ways people react to her typify the individual's response to experience in general, so that she becomes an embodiment of the desire for experience, or of that curiosity which produces such a desire. (The fact that Beardsley's first, uncommissioned, drawing for the play, "J'ai baisé ta bouche, Iokanaan", is a reinterpretation of Holman Hunt's 1859 engraving for "The Lady of Shalott" – published in Moxon's Tennyson – seems to confirm that he noticed this aspect of the play. See Plates 11 and 12) Wilde builds a long crescendo with repetitions of 'regarder' and 'voir' until finally we realise that the willingness to look at something and actually see it signifies the acceptance of new experience and the release from fear, habit, or ennui, while a refusal to do so results in neurosis, cynicism, or stultification. The Page, for instance, dare not look at anything – looking at things is dangerous. The Young Syrian can look at Salomé and see a poetic vision, but cannot bear to see that vision shattered. When Salomé tries to kiss Iokanaan, he kills himself in a hopeless attempt to divide them by his corpse. Herodias can countenance anything that does not detract from her self-esteem, but cannot bear Iokanaan's voice, nor the sight of Herod staring at Salomé: 'You look at her too much.' Herod, like the Page, anticipates personal threats in everything, and tries to preserve his equilibrium by specious arguments. Seeing red petals on the table cloth, he recalls all the blood that he has spilt. 'But that's nothing,' he decides. 'We mustn't find symbols in everything we see. That would make life impossible. It would be much better to say that bloodstains are as beautiful as rose petals.' Yet his capitulation is plain: 'Put out the torches. I do not want to look at things. I do not want things to look at me.[81] . . . Let us hide in our palace, Herodias. I am beginning to be afraid.' Most pathetic of all is the Page, lamenting over the Young Syrian's death: 'Ah, why didn't I hide him from the moon? If I had hidden him in a cavern, she would not have seen him.' In Herod's speech and the Page's, the act of beholding implies stronger verbs – face up to, judge, desire, attack, kill.

This visual strain climaxes in Salomé's attraction towards Iokanaan, which is expressed entirely in visual terms. His voice aroused her curiosity, but until he emerges from the cistern, pursuing his threats against Herodias, she shows no strong emotion; and once she has seen him, she refers only once to his voice: 'Your voice makes me reel' ('ta voix m'enivre'). Wilde makes double use of Iokanaan's dramatic entrance. Salomé 'recoils'; but the repetition of 'terrible' shows that her shock is aesthetic, not moral: 'But he is terrible, terrible. Above all, it is his eyes that are terrible. They are like black holes left by torches in a Tyrian tapestry, black caverns of Egypt where dragons find their shelter. They are like black lakes troubled by ghostly moons.' Iokanaan's words are merely the fuel with which Salomé feeds her fantasy, and in the rhythms of her speeches – most notably in the love speeches – she can almost be heard thinking her way into imagery, and thence into feeling.

In "The Critic as Artist", Wilde had developed an unusually extreme theory about the relationship between form and feeling:

> Yes; Form is everything. It is the secret of life. . . . Find expression for a joy and you intensify its ecstasy. Do you wish to love? Use Love's Litany, and the words will create the yearning from which the world fancies that they spring. Have you a grief that corrodes your heart? Steep yourself in the language of grief, learn its utterance from Prince Hamlet and Queen Constance, and you will find that Form, which is the birth of passion, is also the death of pain.[82]

Salomés love speeches vindicate this theory. The rise of her passion is matched by the increasing imaginative element and the quickening rhythms. In the first speech, the imagery is pure, cool, chaste, the rhythms leisurely and decorative:

> Iokanaan, I long for your body. Your body is white as the lily in the field where the reaper has never reaped. Your body is white as the snows what lie on the mountains, the snows that lie on the mountains of Judaea and come down to the valleys. The roses in the garden of the Queen of Arabia, the perfumed garden of the Queen of Arabia, the feet of the dawn as they dance on the leaves, the breast of the moon as she sleeps on the breast of the sea – nothing in the world is so white as your body. Let me touch your body.[83]

The second speech is more luxuriant and sensuous. Its languorous rhythms, dramatically personalised symbolism, and evocative synaesthesia push the speaker further into a dream world:

> It is your hair that I love, Iokanaan. Your hair is like clusters of grapes, like the clusters of black grapes that hang from the vines of Edom in the land of the Edomites. Your hair is like the cedars of Lebanon, like the great cedars of Lebanon that give shade to the lions, and to robbers who seek hiding during the day. The long black nights, nights when the moon does not show herself and the stars are afraid, are not so black. The silence that dwells in the forests is not so black. There is nothing in the world so black as your hair. Let me touch your hair.[84]

After a second rejection, Salomé picks up her earlier reference to 'vipers' and combines it with the crown of thorns, symbol of pain, defeat, and mockery, to create a haunting image which epitomises Iokanaan's role: a Christ-Medusa. Iokanaan's self-realisation lies in renunciation of the physical world through pain; but his effect on Salomé recalls the Perseus and Andromeda myth that I suggested was implicit in Wilde's lyrical dramas. The questing, heroic Salomé vanquishes convention, in Herod, only to come face to face with that severed head which, once perilously acquired, can still turn to stone all those who fail to use the precautionary mirror of art:

> Your hair is horrible! It is covered with mud and dust. It is like a crown of thorns planted on your forehead. Like a knot of black snakes that writhe round your neck.[85]

The third speech is almost pure stream-of-consciousness, the images becoming progressively less concrete and more subjective:

> It is your mouth that I long for, Iokanaan. Your mouth is a scarlet band on an ivory tower. It is a pomegranate cut by an ivory knife. The pomegranate flowers that bloom in the gardens of Tyre, and are redder than roses, are not so red. The red cries of trumpets that herald the coming of kings and bring fear to their enemies are not so red. Your mouth is redder than the feet of those who tread wine in the wine-press. Your mouth is redder than the feet of the doves who live in the temples and are fed by the priests. It is redder than the feet of one who returns from a forest where he has killed a lion and seen gilded tigers. Your mouth is like a branch of coral that fishers have found in the sea's twilight and are keeping for kings! Like the vermilion the Moabites find in the mines of Moab, and which the kings take from them. Your mouth is the bow of the king of the Persians, that is painted with vermilion and tipped with coral. There is nothing in the world so red as your mouth. Let me kiss your mouth.[86]

Passion, richness, rarity, perilous exploration, acquisition are the keynotes of this speech; yet all the images are visual. Even the trumpets speak colour. Salomé's attitude develops into a kind of all-enveloping visionary aestheticism, in which physical beauty, or an illusion of it, is the primary condition for love, and love so stimulated is the primary stimulus for behaviour. Here, if anywhere, lies her true heresy. Yet the heresy had early assumed the character of an unquestioning and all-absorbing faith which blinds her to everything except the visual. 'Do not come near me, daughter of Sodom,' cries Iokanaan, 'but cover your face with a veil, and put ashes on your head, and go into the wilderness to seek the Son of Man.' To Salomé, brought up in the barren palace, the wilderness promises little. 'Who is he — the Son of Man?' she asks. 'Is he as beautiful as you, Iokanaan?'

Wilde's use of visual metaphors to express acceptance or rejection of life is related to his discussion of Aristotle's *Poetics* in "The Critic as Artist":

> As a physiologist and psychologist, he knows that the health of a function resides in energy. To have a capacity for a passion and not to realise it, is to make oneself incomplete and limited. The mimic spectacle of life that Tragedy affords cleanses the bosom of much 'perilous stuff', and by presenting high and worthy objects for the exercise of the emotions purifies and spiritualises the man; nay, not merely does it spiritualise him, but it initiates him into noble feelings of which he might otherwise have known nothing. . . .[87]

By these terms, Salomé was realising a capacity for passion while Iokanaan allowed himself to remain incomplete and limited. This would suggest, contrary to Edouard Roditi's view,[88] that the play does not wholly lack *dianoai*, and does achieve some form of catharsis. These feelings 'of which [we] might otherwise have known nothing' may not be intrinsically 'noble', but the play may cleanse the spectator of perilous stuff, as it evidently cleansed Wilde — for 'That purification and spiritualising of the nature which [Aristotle] calls ηάθαρσις is, as Goethe saw, essentially aesthetic, and is not moral, as Lessing fancied.'[89]

To regard Salomé as some sort of tragic hero may seem absurd, yet there are dramatic grounds for it. Iokanaan's authority is in doubt. The court, Salomé, and the audience are all asked to calculate the likelihood of the preposterous Iokanaan being the harbinger of a new age. Herodias mocks. Herod prevaricates. Salomé eclipses Iokanaan's quasi-spiritual vision with a clear imaginative vision. Adding paradox to the already marked contrast between the visible and the invisible, she cries to Iokanaan's head, 'Over your eyes you placed the blindfold of a man who wishes to see his God.' In her preoccupation with surfaces Salomé is one with the court, but in her capacity to transform them into an ideal she is above it. For her fantasy has all the imaginative intensity of an ideal, and its metaphors are so real to her that she can say, 'I was a virgin and you deflowered me', when she had been ravished simply by the sight of Iokanaan.

In this, as in her death, she may characterise Wilde's modern artist. By a form of that aesthetic self-hypnosis already noted, anything that Salomé 'sees' becomes real to her. 'The poet', said Gide, 'is one who looks.' But

Wilde insisted on a distinction between looking and seeing; 'To look at a thing is very different from seeing a thing. One does not see anything until one sees its beauty. Then, and then only, does it come into existence.'[90] Salomé exemplifies this belief. First she taunts the head: 'Why don't you look at me, Iokanaan? Are you afraid of me, that you don't look at me?' Soon, however, she laments Iokanaan's blindness to beauty: 'Ah, why didn't you look at me, Iokanaan? You hid your face behind your hands, behind your blasphemies. Over your eyes you placed the blindfold of a man who wishes to see his God. Well, you have seen your God, Iokanaan, but me, me – you never saw me. If you had seen me, you would have loved me. I, I saw you, Iokanaan, and I loved you. Oh! how I loved you. I love you still.'[91] It is interesting to note that Heywood made his Salomé a Hebrew priestess converted to Christianity, and that Moreau, principal source for Beardsley's ritualistic vampire, also conceived of his Salomé as a hieratic, depersonalised figure. As Ian Fletcher has pointed out,[92] Moreau's many studies of the subject often show Salomé encrusted with decoration, almost a part of the architecture. Wilde's Salomé has none of these religious and ceremonial associations. The only dogma that she follows is the dogma of Romantic subjectivism.

Though it is highly unlikely that Wilde intended *Salomé* to be read as an anti-solipsistic parable, his other work leaves us in no doubt that Romantic imaginative reality can be guaranteed to sow the seeds of its own destruction. Her speech to Iokanaan's head, just quoted, is the last in a series of ecstatic but fatal moments. 'Our joy might grow / Tainted', Guido tells Bianca, 'as meat by flies; your beauty, even. / Pinnacled on this moment we are safe.'[93] We find the same idea in *Vera*. 'Sweet, you are safe,' the Czarevitch confirms, in a lull between revolutionary activities. 'Nothing can harm you here. O love, I knew you trusted me! You said you would have trust.' 'Yes, replies Vera, 'I have had trust. O love, the past seems but some dull, grey dream from which our souls have wakened. This is life at last.' 'Life at last,' comes the echo, and Vera's suicide follows a page later.

Salomé, at least, is no suicide. If we recall Wilde's suspicion that 'the artist's life is a long and lovely suicide'[94] – also the fates of painter and artist-in-life in *Dorian Gray* – her Romantic egotism may appear suicidal. Yet it is no more so than Iokanaan's repudiation of life – hardly as much, indeed. Salomé confronts life as hero, and when life, as Wilde so often feared, turns out to be a Medusa, she inevitably dies by the hands of those anti-heroic sceptics and cynics who survive in premature petrifaction. Iokanaan and Salomé may appear equally strong. History sides with the Baptist. But, whereas Salomé's attitude promises a transient victory, Iokanaan's negative puritanism brings only waste and defeat. As Wilde put it in "The Soul of Man under Socialism", gospel of the new Hellenism, 'though the cenobite realises his personality, it is often an impoverished personality that he so realises.'[95] From the standpoint of the Romantic egotist, there is little room for self-realisation in an unfulfilled passion for moral reform succeeded by a martyr's indifference to death.

Salomé reaches another sort of indifference once she has won her grotesque Pyrrhic victory. While waiting for the head to be brought up from the cistern, she had exclaimed, 'Why doesn't he cry out? Ah! If someone were trying to kill me, I would cry out, I would struggle, I wouldn't want to suffer.' Yet once she has got the head and kissed it, ideal and motive dissolve. Like the convict in *The Ballad of Reading Gaol*, she does not realise the value of the thing she loved until she has killed it, and yet she killed it because she loved it. Finally, she is convinced that 'the mystery of love is greater than the mystery of death: we should look only at love'.[96] Even if she hears Herod's order, she neither acknowledges nor resists her execution. 'Form, which is the birth of passion, is also the death of pain.' Petrifaction by the Medusa, life, and the dominance of imaginative form are alike complete.

Wilde's dramatic procedure is consistent both with his aim to express romantic individualism in an extreme and 'morbid' form, and with his anti-Naturalist aesthetic. One might add that Salomé falls victim to heredity, circumstances, and environment very much as the people in Zola's novels do, and that the play is consequently anti-Naturalist only in style. Salomé is the child of a palace of art and anarchy — Herod is usurper, Herodias a secular icon — and her behaviour reflects this double influence. She pursues with amoral egotism what she regards as the epitome of the visually beautiful. Yet, in a society where fear, superstition, lust, weakness, cynicism, and meaningless violence are the general rule, her strength, fearlessness, and faith in the world of imagination make a striking contrast.

What, as an audience, are we left with? We may feel unable to maintain critical disinterest beyond the duration of the play. We may decide that, if Salomé had any vision at all, it was a wrong one; that having chosen and risked does not in itself turn failure into success or 'crime' into 'culture'; that Wilde has done no more than to postulate a briefly convincing impossibility. We might conclude, on the other hand, that Salomé's success, such as it is, merely proves the world inescapably corrupt, and that she is therefore the symbol of a human nature 'entirely evil because uninhibited and unmodified by any restrictions'.[97] We might argue that Wilde sees the imagination as a pagan force which liberates, while traditional moral absolutes distort, constrict, and corrupt natural aspirations towards a personal ideal. This view, strikingly borne out by *Earnest*, raises the possibility of a further prototype of Marcuse's Orpheus.[98] Its logical extreme would be that *Salomé* is an art-for-art's-sake play in which the representative of art, or the concrete and visible, defeats the representative of ethics, or the intangible and invisible. If this were really so, then the reader sceptical of Wilde's serious commitment to art might find *Salomé* his aptest achievement: a play neither moral nor immoral, but depicting the overthrow of morality by a sterile and self-regarding art.

There are further critical possibilities. Richard Ellmann has suggested that Iokanaan and Salomé represent the forces of Ruskinism and Paterism as

Wilde understood them, and that Herod is significantly autobiographical. 'Wilde's tutelary voices from the university . . . seem to be in attendance, clamouring for domination.' Herod embodies both voices, fails to decide between them, and punishes both. 'In Herod, Wilde was suggesting that *tertium quid* which he felt to be his own nature, susceptible to contrary impulses, but not abandoned for long to either.'[99]

In fact, the opposing forces of self-expression and self-repression are present in all of Wilde's plays, though they reach their Romantic climax in *Salomé*. Herod may seem to be autobiographical in the sense that, although weak and vacillating, he is in nominal command of the forces in the play. Beardsley, as Professor Ellmann notes, gave Herod the face of the author ("The Eyes of Herod"). But he also gave Wilde's features to "The Woman in the Moon" and to the half-concealed moon in "A Platonic Lament". Whether this represents critical penetration on Beardsley's part, or merely indiscriminate satire, is unclear. He may be declaring the whole piece to be moonshine, and its author to be the man, or woman, in the moon. Alternatively, Beardsley may have perceived the autobiographical element in Salomé herself. For she is in actual control of those forces that Herod nominally commands. Her personality dominates the action, and it is surely she whom Wilde wishes – and fears – to be most autobiographical.

Such an interpretation would correspond with the balance of characters in *Dorian Gray* as Wilde described them: 'Basil Hallward is what I think I am: Lord Henry what the world thinks me: Dorian what I would like to be – in other ages, perhaps.'[100] Iokanaan duplicates Hallward's outspoken moral standpoint and the self-protectiveness of the artist and visionary. Lord Henry's worldliness, amorality, and distaste for positive action are mirrored in Herod. In Salomé we may see Dorian's ill-fated, Paterian, questing egotism, here stripped of its dandiacal disguise and the camouflage of a supernatural plot. Wilde's stated moral for the novel fits the play equally well: 'All excess, just as all renunciation, has its own punishment.'[101]

Finally, there is the possibility of taking Wilde's critical pronouncements at face value, and reading the play as an exercise in complete detachment, a chance to watch personalities fulfilling themselves and destroying themselves without our needing to develop any preferences or judgements. Dehumanised almost to the point of abstraction, *Salomé* would become in this case a kind of theorem, and 'neither art nor science knows anything of moral approval or disapproval'.

Wilde's detachment, however, is inevitably suspect to many critics, who have caught glimpses in *Salomé* of the author's domestic life. Edmund Bergler, for example, suggests that, once Wilde had convinced himself that women were monsters, he could move with a clear conscience to 'the less dangerous male'.[102] This view is weakened, surely, by Wilde's being married already to an apparently normal, if Victorian, woman who had borne him two children, and by Ross's claim that Wilde had begun his homosexual experiences five years earlier, in 1886. It even assumes a comic dimension, given that the 'less dangerous male' of 1891 would have been Alfred Douglas. If, in spite of this, the play is to be understood as a veiled statement of some kind of castration complex – a view brilliantly expressed by the poster for an all-male production in Paris in 1972 (see Plate 13) – then we might conclude that Wilde's puritanical 'male' super-ego was being castrated by his libidinous 'female' ego. We have his own assurance that 'the egoistic note is, of course, and always has been to me, the primal and ultimate note of modern art'.[103] We have the possibility of regarding Salomé as a representative modern artist, not moonstruck like the last Endymion or the Young Syrian, but almost the embodiment of the moon, and so of the art whose genius it is.[104] We have already seen that in the second "Mr W. H." Wilde drew a variant of the dark or fatal woman who is often identifiable with the artist's unconscious. If Salomé, too, is of this class, then she presumably represents those subliminal forces that the male writer distrusts or detests in himself – the artist 'as [he] thought [he was] not, and by such thinking came in strange manner, though but for a moment, really so to be.'[105]

Whatever we conclude, it is clear that Wilde went to unusual lengths to secure attention or admiration under an extreme, if not grotesque, disguise. (The gesture gains piquancy when we recall the engraving of a prehistoric monster with a predatory grin around its jaws, sent anonymously to him shortly before his arrest.[106]) The comedies made use of more elegant disguises. Yet even they suggest from time to time that the effects of Herod's court as projected by Wilde were not essentially different from the effects of late-Victorian society as the Decadents, and Wilde in particular, experienced them. From within the poised masquerade of modernity, Solomé will seem an hallucination or a nightmare, but a nightmare of frightening truth, Wilde's fullest statement of the impossibility of full self-statement.

After this, he committed himself to the ignominious art of compromise. The tetrarch's palace becomes a preposterous drawing-room; the lights go up; social comedy ousts lyrical tragedy.[107] Wilde's protagonist is now the dandy, who survives in society by playing the social game better than anyone else. As Baudelaire said, the dandy exemplifies the 'heroism of modern life' by being anti-heroic. He 'will shock without ever being shocked, and, if he ever feels pain at all, will smile like the Lacedemonian under the fox's bite'.[108] Wilde's dandyism, when devoted to anything more serious than casual conversation, will concentrate on undermining the puritan ethic, the doctrine of self-repression and the repression of others. Prince Paul, humanised, wages verbal war on the ghosts of Vera and Iokanaan.

Perhaps *Salomé*'s place in Wilde's development can best be fixed by reference to a further passage from "The Soul of Man":

Personality is a very mysterious thing. A man cannot always be estimated by what he does. He may keep the law and yet be worthless. He may break the law and yet be fine. He may be bad, without doing anything bad. He may commit a sin against society, and yet through that sin reach his true perfection.[109]

This is the voice of the enlightened anarchist, also of the passionate egotist. In one form or another, the conviction remained a constant in Wilde's personality. It is the key to his characterisation of Salomé, and it was to be reiterated as the keynote to his self-examination in *De Profundis*. Its straightforward statement in non-dramatic form seems to have heralded the death of Wilde's earliest objective mask, that of the woman hero – after Salomé she disappears. Still, the apparent distance between historicist drama and the modern comedy which succeeded it is, as Wilde no doubt appreciated, largely a trick of perspective. The comedies are built on the ethics and aesthetics of the dandy, attitudes hardly articulated before the proposals of "The Critic as Artist" and "The Soul of Man"; but they also hark back to the earlier phase in which, as we have seen, many of the critical attitudes were firmly rooted. Indeed, "The Soul of Man" itself is no more practical or practicable than the moral vacuum of Jacobethan pastiche, in which Guido had already anticipated the dandy-anarchist's liberal humanitarianism quoted above. 'Nay,' cries the lover, reconciled at last with the lover he had spurned,

> 'Twas but the passion-flower of your love
> That in one moment leapt to terrible life,
> And in one moment bare this gory fruit,
> Which I had plucked in thought a thousand times.
> My soul was murderous, but my hand refused;
> Your hand wrought murder, but your soul was pure.[110]

Prison robbed Wilde of his range of literary masks. They all depended on social acceptance, on his being looked at. But the anarchistic, or humanitarian, conviction persisted to the end of his creative career, and beyond. *Salomé*, seldom at present taken seriously, has good claim to be considered – together with its comic twin, *Earnest* – as the most intensely self-expressive of Wilde's plays.

5 The Comedy of Manners: Wit Restored

I. Barbey D'Aurevilly, Meredith, and the Intellectual Standard

Critical assessments of Wilde's comedies have traditionally been clouded by outside issues. The suspicion that the derider of the Protestant work ethic made quick money to cover his extra-marital extravagances leads inevitably to the belief that these plays were concessions to 'a fashion of the theatre that Wilde had too good a brain not to despise'[1] – 'comedy as self-degradation', in Roditi's phrase.[2] Recent academic criticism has turned to stylistic analysis, and there have been various attempts to interpret Wilde's dandyism.[3] But there is still a general feeling that the dandy, as Holbrook Jackson said of Wilde, was born 'too late' to have 'any purpose save play',[4] that he has no brief to be serious in any sense. The other much discussed matter is Wilde's chosen comic form – a 'photographic double exposure'[5] of the melodramatic problem-play and the 'banter and *marivaudage* of the comedy of manners'[6] which the dramatist brazenly[7] or ingenuously[8] adopted as a 'vehicle' for his epigrams.[9]

These assessments are inadequate partly because they ignore the relationship between Wilde's dramatic material and his ongoing preoccupations, partly because they misinterpret the significance of the dandy and of the relationship of Wilde's comic form to dramatic tradition. All four comedies attempt to rationalise in some way three of the dominant themes of his work: the conflict between intellect and emotion; the question of sex roles and their effect on the individual; and the individualist's position in a conformist, utilitarian, and hypocritical society. The attempt inevitably involved some criticism of contemporary conditions; and it has been a further source of complaint that Wilde offered this from within the patterns of established dramatic practice: 'In the age of Ibsen and Hauptmann, of Strindberg and Brieux, he was content to construct like Sardou and think like Dumas *fils*.'[10]

Interestingly enough, Hauptmann himself regarded Wilde as one of the two contemporary dramatists 'whose work shows fundamental brainwork or intellect',[11] and this, surely, is the right view. For Wilde the dramatist is demonstrably an extension of Wilde the critic. Letters, notebooks, and the comedies themselves all bear witness to this, while "The Critic as Artist" specifically cites drama as one of the 'objective forms' available to criticism.

Contemporary conditions go far towards explaining the ambiguity of Wilde's approach to comedy, if not the imperfections of his technique. The three issues I have mentioned are all traditional themes of the comedy of manners, and Wilde was clearly conscious of the opportunities offered by that genre. Moreover, the time was ripe for its resurgence. As Harry Quilter remarked:

> Not a single play of serious pretensions has been produced of late years which treated of English manners, and was entirely original work. . . . There is a positive outcry at the moment for a genuine English play, and such a one would enjoy a popularity of which ordinary successes give no conception.[12]

The serious drawback lay in the age itself – an age of sentiment, as Pinero said, rather than an age of manners.[13] Pinero believed that manners could be handled effectively only in farce, and Wilde eventually turned to it. But in the three 'serious' comedies dandies and puritans – manners and sentiment – exist side by side, hammering out the conflicts within the age, and within the author himself, and providing thereby a series of critical conclusions. If, for Arnold, sin was the snake in the modern garden which discredited the Hellenist's serenity, sentiment was for Wilde the modern condition which thwarted the attempts of the Hellenist critic to construct a comedy of manners based on an intellectual principle and devoted to the claims of wit and the classic goal of self-discovery. Wilde the critical dramatist, like Arnold the social critic, therefore temporised with prevailing conditions. Neither *saeva indignatio* nor laughing people out of their vices and follies was wholly feasible on the Victorian stage. Wildean comedy uses irony to comment on these conditions, and is redemptive rather than satirical: it chooses to pardon, preserve, and (where possible) educate its incompetent Establishment protagonists. This ironic manner governs a series of studied reversals. The *comédie à thèse*, developed to treat the problems of social sinners, is now devoted, by a reformed Romantic individualist and potential social sinner, to the problems brought upon the rule-setters by themselves. The character who expresses the standards of the critical dramatist is an exile from the manners tradition, the dandy – apparently a social parasite, a non-productive member of the ailing commonweal. In *The Happy Prince*, the child had educated its parents. In the comedies, the dandy educates the proper people.[14]

Wilde's rehabilitation of the dandy in a dramatic setting may have been encouraged by Boucicault's *London Assurance* (1841), a Regency pastiche of the manners tradition. This play was revived in London in November 1890, when *Lady Windermere's Fan* was beginning to take shape.[15] Wilde's delightful letter to the *Daily Telegraph* praising the costumes for the play expounds the dandy's philosophy of surfaces, and already strikes the note of

Lord Goring and Mrs Erlynne.[16] An exchange in *London Assurance* itself, however, indicates his more significant source. 'Oh!' cries Young Courtly, indignant against the London marriage market, 'that such a custom should have emanated from the healthy soil of an English heart!' 'No,' rejoins Grace Harkaway, prim country miss. 'It never did. Like most of our literary dandyisms and dandy literature, it was borrowed from the French.'[17]

Wilde clearly knew Baudelaire's sketch "Le Dandy" (1846), as well as the work which gave rise to it, Jules Barbey D'Aurevilly's *Du Dandysme* (1845), since he recut epigrams from both.[18] The significance of Barbey's essay, which is chiefly a study of Beau Brummel,[19] is that it places dandyism on an intellectual footing – describes it, in fact, as an ultra-sophisticated social philosophy for the superior misfit – and traces its origins to Louis XIV's court; thence, once in England, to the Restoration, when it entered stage comedy.

Dandyism, for Barbey, is a means by which the individual can negotiate the obstructionism of stagnant societies. 'In the social hurly-burly politely called society', destiny and abilities seldom coincide. Brummel, who possessed neither great wealth, rare talent, nor high birth (the three attributes stated by Disraeli[20] to be the indispensable passports into the highest society), fulfilled himself by 'elevating himself to the status of a thing': he 'became Dandyism itself'.[21] This could have been accomplished only in an ancient civilisation where 'comedy is at a premium and convention triumphs at the expense of boredom'.[22] England, 'society of the Bible and the law', epitomises that state; and if the conflict between comedy and convention were ever decided, dandyism would either emerge radically altered or would disappear altogether. For dandyism exists in an ambivalent relationship with convention, playing with the rules while apparently respecting them. This it can do because society supposes it to care only for externals. The dandy, however, 'suffers by the rules and revenges himself upon them by subduing them. When he eludes them, he calls upon them to bear him witness. He dominates and is dominated by turns: double and changeable character.'[23]

In the adverse conditions described by Barbey, dandyism therefore becomes 'a kind of self-respect'. Dandies, subordinating even their love of clothes, of food, and of attention to the principle which dictates that their exterior be symbolic of their interior value, remain impassively detached from their surroundings, and represent the philosophers of an advanced consumer society. (Wilde called his completest dandy, Lord Goring, 'the first well-dressed philosopher in the history of thought'.) Just as theoretical philosophers set up an obligation superior to that of the law, so the dandy, by virtue of his enlightened self-sufficiency, asserts a principle of conduct superior to the norm even of the most aristocratic and traditional circles: 'By his acidulous wit and his softening grace, he contrives the acceptance of this fluid principle which is ultimately no more than his own audacious personality.'[24]

If Barbey's essay suggested the character through which Wilde's critical values might be projected on stage, Meredith's *Essay on Comedy* (1877),[25] a survey of the high comic tradition, offered practical guidance and promised rewards commensurate with the expectations of Wilde's critical élite: 'A true perception of the Comic Spirit gives high fellowship. You become a citizen of a selecter world, the highest we know of in connection with our world, which is not supermundane. Look there for your unchallengeable upper class! You feel that you are one of a civilised community, that you cannot escape it, and would not if you could.'[26] Meredith's requirements for this critical comedy were 'a moderate degree of intellectual activity' and a prevailing sexual equality in the society for which it was written. Victorian England replaced these modest conditions by false propriety, sexual polarity with its notorious 'double standard', and the brainless 'Barbarism' and utilitarian or church-militant Philistinism anatomised by Arnold eight years earlier.[27] One result of this was the tyranny of the 'incubus' of boredom, that 'dread familiar' whom 'it is our present humiliation to be just alive enough to loathe, never quick enough to foil'. Critical comedy, Meredith asserts, would drive away this spirit, together with 'the vapours of unreason and sentimentalism', leaving 'a bright and positive, clear Hellenic perception of facts'.[28] Wilde's Mrs Erlynne, ironic to the last in her manipulation of conversational gambits, echoes this passage: 'The English climate doesn't suit me. . . . London is too full of fogs – and serious people, Lord Windermere. I don't know whether the fogs produce the serious people, or whether the serious people produce the fogs, but the whole thing rather gets on my nerves.' The only person in Wilde's first comedy who approaches 'a clear Hellenic perception of facts', and has unreason and sentimentalism under control, leaves England for 'the south'.

Though somewhat pessimistic about the chances for critical comedy in modern England, Meredith believed that the middle classes, the supporters of Molière, were the least forlorn hope. (Arnold had reluctantly come to a similar conclusion.) 'In all countries,' he argues, 'the middle class presents the public which, fighting the world, and with a good foot in the fight, knows the world best. It may be the most selfish, but that is a question leading into sophistries. Cultivated men and women who do not skim the cream of life, and are attached to duties, make acute and balanced observers.'[29] For Wilde, however, the selfishness was of paramount importance, the source of all utilitarian virtues – anti-intellectual. The middle classes might provide the best audience but could provide none of the best values.

Wilde had pointed out the intellectual inadequacy of the bourgeois dramatic tradition as early as 1883 in a letter commending *The Duchess of Padua* to the American actress Mary Anderson, who prudently refused it.[30] 'Audiences', says the fledgling dramatist, 'are well meaning but very stupid.' For this reason they need 'their vague emotions crystallised and expressed for them'. While the 'heart of art' consists in an 'emotional idea', the 'health of art' requires that an 'intellectual idea' take charge of the play. 'Emotion lives in terror of ridicule, and is never happy unless it has got hold of its big brother intellect by the hand.' Thus, an audience is always glad to emerge from the theatre having been given the rationalisation for their sympathy, 'the shield of intellect held over the new-born babe of pity'. The example of 'unhealthiness', or emotional one-sidedness, cited is *La Dame aux Camélias*.[31]

Wilde's conscious critical solution to the problem was precisely that fusion of disparate genres which has provoked much dissatisfaction, but which enabled him to demonstrate that the greatest problem facing the problem-play was its audience. 'Ladies and gentlemen,' he announced, summoned to the curtain on his London first night, 'the actors have given us a charming rendering of a delightful play, and your appreciation has been most intelligent. I congratulate you on the success of your performance, which persuades me that you think almost as highly of the play as I do.'[32] In the placid arena of stage comedy, the dandy transforms Juvenal's 'gladiator-ship of the intellect'[33] into an act of civilised condescension.

II. Libertine Patterns in Bourgeois Comedy

Though Wilde's writings contain no mention of Restoration comedy,[34] his characters and situations often resemble Restoration practice,[35] and the name of the footman in *An Ideal Husband* – Farquhar – may well summarise his attitude towards the senior *fin-de-siècle*. True, the name is never spoken, but that is perhaps the point.[36] In addition, Wilde's figure (just quoted) of the sibling relationship between intellect and emotion echoes an exchange in *The Provok'd Wife* (1697) where Vanbrugh had resolved with exemplary comic poise those issues which dominate *The Duchess of Padua* (as, indeed, all of Wilde's plays). Lady Fanciful objects that rational restraints – 'honour' – forbid her keeping an assignation with an unknown admirer in broad daylight. Her French maid replies that emotional release – 'pleasure' – counsels it, and that reason is insolent when she tries to admonish instinct, 'her elder sister'.[37] The echo might not signify were it not that Restoration comedy had afforded Wilde two precedents – a scheme of comic characterisation based on a hierarchy of 'wit', and a dramatic convention which was anti-dogmatic and anti-courtly by principle, and even contrived to subdue, for a time, a rival and contemporary stage tradition devoted to heroic sentiment and moralistic rhetoric.

Meredith, though willing to borrow Congreve's phrase 'the comic poet',[38] had condemned the bulk of Restoration comedy as morally penurious and, 'as to comic idea, vacuous as the mask without the face behind it'.[39] To a lapsed Romantic of Meredith's temperament, it must have seemed so. But, to a lapsed Romantic of Wilde's, Restoration comedy contained most of the rudiments of a late-nineteenth-century comic idea: frank élitism; hedonistic elevation of the pleasures of youth, health, and beauty over 'one's duty'; preference for town sophistication over country simplicity; pseudo-Epicurean rejection of involvement in public affairs; resolute, if sometimes crude, insistence on the individual's rights; a sceptical assumption that 'high' or 'respectable' society is hardly better than the 'condition of Warre' posited by Hobbes;[40] irreverence for bourgeois values; and a predominant tone of amorality which left ample scope for critical manoeuvre.

Barbey had also mentioned Restoration comedy, and with a reservation. The impassivity of his dandy resembled nothing more than 'the ravishing, impertinent, and very modern attitude of Girodet's Pyrrhus listening to Hermione's imprecations'.[41] (See Plate 4.) Therefore 'neither Etherege nor Cibber nor Congreve nor Vanbrugh could have introduced such a character into their comedies – for ridicule never touched him.'[42] Wilde follows Barbey's lead. Wildean dandies are never ridiculed, unless they depart in practice from their declared principles and thus prove themselves incomplete philosophers.

In another sense, however, the Wildean dandy is often much closer in spirit to the Restoration libertine than to Barbey's long-suffering cultural exile. Although animal spirits are now at a premium, his aim is more than painless survival. It is active pleasure. If he strikes the Stoic posture, it is generally second-best to a failed Epicureanism. 'Wit be my faculty and pleasure my occupation' is as apt a summary of the Wildean dandy's social code as it was of Bellmour's or Dorimant's intrigues. There are, of course, enormous discrepancies between Restoration and Victorian society – Lord Illingworth, for one, complains of them in a speech that Wilde's manager cut.[43] 'Pleasure' and 'wit' now mean very different things. But the Wildean dandy bears no less recognisable a relationship to moral norms than the Restoration libertine had done. The latter traduced Hobbes, debauched Epicurus, and damned religion for his own sensual ends. The former pursues the critical precepts of the new Hellenist, and, though necessarily diluting or trivialising them according to character and context, brings to the stage an example of 'the type the age has been looking for and is afraid that it has found'. Shadwell's libertine complained, 'Of Nature's freedom we're beguil'd / By laws that man imposes'.[44] Significantly, no one in Wilde accepts this proposition wholeheartedly, and lives to boast of it, until *The Importance of Being Earnest*.

Whether or not one accepts the view that 'the distinguishing feature of Restoration comedy down to Congreve is its attempt to rationalise sexual relationships',[45] the genre quite plainly presents the antagonism between the sexes and the conflict between intellect and emotion – 'wit' and 'passion' – which parallels it. In the relationship of Restoration comedy to heroic tragedy we may see, as Anne Righter has argued, a larger image of the divided age, since one form amounted to 'a photographic negative' of the other, tragic villains becoming comic heroes, and tragic heroines shrinking into comic dupes.[46] Similar reversals occur between Wilde's heroic and comic plays.[47] Indeed, Dr Righter's summary of the balance of factors affecting the Restoration period can be applied to Wilde's situation with only minimal adjustment:

> Faced with the real issues of the age, with the new Science and the doctrines of Hobbes, with the split between faith and reason, appearance and reality, [tragedy] retreated in confusion to a land of rhetorical make-believe. Comedy, as a result of this abdication, was left to fill the gap: to accept the warring impulses of the time, as Jacobean comedy had before it, and try to reconcile them in the momentary peace of a play.[48]

Substitute Darwin for Hobbes, and this could describe the 'warring impulses' of the Victorian era, in which tragedy – and, indeed, much 'serious' art – took refuge in medieval, Greek, or other forms of historical pastoral, or in eclectic pastiche. If Victorian apprehension often took the form of an appeal to 'history', Restoration anxieties surfaced most frequently in laughter,[49] that primitive form of self-defence, that 'baring of the fangs' propounded by Hobbes. The Victorians, proverbially, laughed too little; and when the radical intellectual comedy that they needed finally arrived (Gilbert and Pinero were not intellectual in this sense), it was almost inevitably misunderstood. Wilde himself, of course, compounded the misunderstanding. Never doubting the Romantics' establishment of art as self-crowned emperor, he assumed the position of a latter-day court wit who, like his Restoration predecessors, showed his self-division by laughing at his own and others' seriousness, thus making his comedy a portrait of the artist as well as a portrait of the age.

All of this emerges on stage in conversation. Intellectual comedy inevitably relies more on talk than on action. Etherege, said Rochester, 'writ two talking plays without one plot'.[50] Wilde, however, takes the principle to extremes. Conscious of his weaknesses when physical action was required (*Dorian Gray* was 'all conversation and no action. . . . My people sit in chairs and chatter'), he deliberately capitalised on them. 'I wrote the first act of *A Woman of No Importance* in answer to the critics who said that *Lady Windermere's Fan* lacked action. In the act in question there was no action at all. It was a perfect act.'[51] It is in this context that his claim to have subjectified 'the drama, the most objective form known to art', besides widening its range and enriching its characterisation,[52] should be understood. For the justification of these comic characters is precisely 'that the author is as he is' and not that other people 'are as they are'.[53] Wilde's dandies are the part of society he likes best – the part which hardly exists – just as his puritans are the part he likes least – the norm. But the two groups correspond, on a deeper level, to what the dramatist likes best and least in himself.

Basing three comedies on the attempt to enlighten morally arrested women has naturally laid Wilde open to charges of misogyny or paternalistic patronage. However, social realities, dramatic tradition (in the comedy of manners, at least), and Wilde's own suspicion that the poetic and romantic impulses were somehow intrinsically feminine, all dictated that the intellect-emotion conflict be expressed by the battle of the sexes. At its most vociferous in the 'strong scenes', the battle is audible throughout the dialogue at every level. 'Women are pictures. Men are problems.'[54] 'Woman is the intellectual helpmeet of man in public as in private life. Without her we would lose our true ideals.'[55] 'More marriages are ruined by the common sense of the husband than by anything else. How can a woman be expected to be happy with a man who insists on treating her as if she were a perfectly rational being?'[56] Obviously a strict adherence to this pattern would prejudice stage realism as it would Wilde's critical scheme, and it is modified by examples of domesticated men and of emancipated women. But in general the pattern serves, and it enables Wilde to approximate, entirely through speech, a hierarchy of wit analogous to the Restoration hierarchy of Truewits, Witwouds, and lackwits. At the top are the mediating dandies who influence dramatic action – notably Mrs Erlynne and Lord Goring – and who use the mask of triviality to protect and preserve their humane responses. Next come the dandies of the con-versational chorus, mostly verbal peacocks whose wit, though often telling, is largely for show – like Sir Fopling Flutter's amatory manoeuvres, or like Sparkish in The Country Wife: 'We wits rail and make love often but to show our parts: as we have no affections, so we have no malice.'[57] Next come the puritans, who have no intellectual authority, but are not comic dupes, because Wildean comedy is redemptive, not satirical. Last come the lackwits, mostly members of the older generation, who suffer from forgetfulness, malapropism (of language, or, more comically, of ideas), and other deficiencies. Though they are often comic butts, they, too, are kept from becoming comic dupes. Wilde's working principle resembles Lady Towneley's: 'We should love wit, but for variety be able to divert ourselves with the Extravagancies of those who want it.'[58]

According to this scheme, the false dandies are mere intellectual fops, as incapable of genuine feeling as the puritans are of genuine critical thought. But the true dandies, those given comic authority, are a 'healthy' blend of intellect and emotion, enlightened common sense and true sensitivity, Hellenism and Hebraism: in Barbey's phrase, 'double and changeable characters' who combine 'masculine' strength with 'feminine' grace, 'the androgynes of History as well as of Fable'[59] – in the critic's view, the best that society can hope for.

I have no space in which to give examples of Wilde's technique here, nor to show how he used social talk to determine the traditional comic issues of the treatment of excess and the administration of poetic justice. These points are touched upon in the discussions of individual plays. It should be pointed out, however, that while in criticism no limits are placed on conversation – for there no commitment is involved – in stage comedy epigram and the individual's use of conversational conventions become a test of personal integrity. The verbal fops can play with language harmlessly: they do not aspire to act. The characters who compromise dandyism by abusing social conventions or by indulging in intellectual dishonesty—activities which impinge on the action of the play—are dismissed. 'A simple-seeming word of this import', wrote Meredith, 'is the triumph of the spiritual, and where it passes for coin of value, the society has reached a high state of refinement: Arcadian by the aesthetic route.'[60] Typically, Wilde makes the moral errors of the aesthetic dandy look more like vulgarity than anything.

It is sometimes objected that the comedies offer self-indulgently happy endings: Wilde played the devil's advocate for his own marital position, it is said, and rigged a public absolution to follow a public confession.[61] But each of the serious comedies ends on a note of doubt. Though prospects are fair, we know so much about the characters' fragility that we can hardly be optimistic over their futures. The sceptical critic questions the authority of plot as the sceptical protagonists themselves had done in Restoration comedy. As Anne Righter says, 'Dorimant and Harriet, Millamant and Mirabell, describe marriage as the risk they take, not as the end of the story.'[62] Happy endings go with heroes and villains. 'The good ended happily and the bad unhappily. That is what Fiction means.'[63] It is the duffer's view. Plot is traditionally an image of social organisation, and, since the critical dramatist cannot accept society's standards, he will not respect the authority of plot. Significantly, *An Ideal Husband*, the best of the three serious comedies, follows the example of such plays as *The Changeling*, in which madness or the environment of madness in the sub-plot is used to criticise the 'sane' standards of the main plot. The dandies in Wilde's sub-plot are the consistently sane people. Thus, while outright satire proves unworkable, Wilde contrives to advance his artistic and his social challenge by analogous devices. Paradox, peripeteia, upending a trite plot until the tricks fall out of its pockets: all are natural means of expression for the outsider who chooses, or is obliged, to work with conventions that will not budge. Far from the creaking problem-play being a 'vehicle'[64] for Wilde's 'mob of courtier epigrams',[65] wit drives the tumbril and heads for the open road.

Admittedly, Wilde does not always evade the traps of an age of sentiment, but his comic form still approaches closely to the variety of 'mixed comedy', approved by Dryden, 'which is neither all wit, nor all humour, but the result of both . . . but I would have more of the *urbana, venusta, salsa, faceta*, and the rest which Quintilian reckons up as the ornaments of wit'.[66] Meredith noted the practical danger of intellectual comedy — that it threatened 'the fraternal agreement' between 'the dull people . . . that something is too clever for them'. Shaw, however, seems to have lighted on Wilde's method of dealing with this threat. 'The six worst epigrams' in *An Ideal Husband*, he wrote, 'are mere alms handed with a kind smile to the average suburban playgoer. The three best are secrets between Mr Wilde and a few choice spirits.'[67] Catering to the average playgoer by taking conventional forms and conventional situations, Wilde invites the few choice spirits under the 'shield of intellect' to partake in a critical comedy whose primary subject is the schooling of emotion.[68]

6 The Comedy of Manners: The Dandy's Progress

I. *Lady Windermere's Fan*: The Critic as Dramatist

Wilde's first comedy has two critical bases: the letter of 1883 in which he spoke of the importance of the 'intellectual idea' upon which 'the health of art' depended,[1] and Meredith's passage on the *aventurière*, 'Muse' of the problem-play. (Wilde may also have responded to Meredith's description of the fan as 'flag and symbol' of the English comedy of manners, although fans were high fashion in the 1890s, and Haddon Chambers' play *The Idler*, which Wilde saw and admired, was quickly cited by reviewers as a probable model for 'the business with the fan'.[2])

The *aventurière*, or social adventuress, wrote Meredith,

> is clever, and a certain division exists in the united scheme for confounding her. The object of this person is to reinstate herself in the decorous world; and either, having accomplished this purpose through deceit, she has a *nostalgie de la boue* that eventually casts her back into it, or she is exposed in her course of deception when she is about to gain her end. A very good, innocent young man is her victim, or a very astute goodish young man obstructs her path. This latter is enabled to be the champion of the decorous world by knowing the indecorous well. He has assisted in the progress of the *aventurières* downwards; he will not help them to ascend. The world is with him; and certainly it is not much of an ascension they aspire to; but what sort of a figure is he? The triumph of a candid realism is to show him no hero. You are to admire him (for it must be supposed that realism pretends to awaken some admiration) as a credibly living young man; no better, only a little firmer and shrewder, than the rest. If however, you think at all, after the curtain has fallen, you are likely to think that the *aventurières* have a case to plead against him. True, and the author has not said anything to the contrary; he has but painted from life, from the specimen he has presented in the bright and narrow circle of a spy-glass.[3]

Wilde makes the *aventurière* in his first comedy a dandy, a figure not merely capable of pleading her cause against convention, but whose life embodies a criticism of convention. He realises Meredith's hint in Act IV, 'to me the psychological act, the act that is newest, most true. For which reason, I suppose, the critics say "There is no necessity for Act IV". But the critics are of no importance.'[4] It is characteristic of Wilde, however, that the moral confrontations and adjustments all take place on a personal rather than a social level. Personality has a fateful quality – is more fateful, ultimately, than fate itself: 'misfortunes one can endutre – they come from the outside, they are accidents. But to suffer for one's own faults – ah! – there is the sting of life!' Windermere says this in Act I in defence of Mrs Erlynne, but it applies to all the main characters. The idea of self-responsibility permeates the play.

Wilde found progress at first very slow. Within a few days of his remarks to the *Daily Telegraph* about the costumes for *London Assurance*, he wrote to George Alexander, future producer of *Lady Windermere's Fan*, 'I am not satisfied with myself or with my work. I can't get a grip of the play yet: I can't get my people real.'[5] The revival of *London Assurance* may well have helped to crystallise Wilde's dramatic use of dandyism. Certainly, there is nothing in his later account of the play's genesis to suggest that the impenitent *aventurière* was to become the first comic woman-hero of modern life[6]:

> The psychological idea that suggested to me the play is this. A woman who has had a child, but never known the passion of maternity (there are such women), suddenly sees the child she has abandoned falling over a precipice. There wakes in her the maternal feeling – the most terrible of all emotions – a thing that weak animals and little birds possess. She rushes to rescue, sacrifices herself, does follies – and the next day she feels 'This passion is too terrible. It wrecks my life. I don't want to be a mother any more.' And so the fourth act is to me the psychological act, the act that is newest, most true.[7]

This is an entirely amoral framework based on purely instinctual egotism. There are no grounds for admiring Mrs Erlynne at all. In the completed play, however, the degree and nature of the admiration accorded her determine the quality of those who accord it.

The three stock situations mentioned by Morse Peckham[8] are the foundation of the dramatic machinery. The threat by the wife to insult the supposed mistress falls flat at the beginning of Act II; the scene of sexual jealousy between the same two characters is defused by Mrs Erlynne's remarkable maternal play-acting in Act III, which she discovers to be, for the moment, wholly true to her own life; and the recognition scene between parent and long-lost child (or rather, as Peckham observes, between child and long-lost parent) is forbidden in Act IV by the apparently selfish parent for wholly unselfish reasons. Wilde adds for good measure an adaptation of the screen scene from Sheridan's *The School for Scandal*. Instead of a lively young wife contemplating a mild flirtation to relieve the dullness of an aging husband, we find a puritan abandoning her husband and child on principle. Instead of Lady Teazle hearing from behind the screen her husband's kindly plans to settle a nice sum on her, and being shamed by it into future continence, Lady Windermere is obliged to listen to the cynical man-of-the-world chatter of Darlington's friends, which, even more perhaps than Mrs Erlynne's warnings, provoke her to exclaim, restored to safety, 'What a lesson!'

The pervasive ironies of the play begin with the first line: 'Is your ladyship at home this afternoon?' The puritan will receive a man capable of wooing her away from her husband, but fights to exclude the woman who turns out to be her own mother. The scene with Lord Darlington, and the introduction of the Duchess of Berwick, define the real nature of the standards that Lady Windermere supposes she ought to uphold, as well as the nature of the standard alternative.

Despite Darlington's partiality, his is the critical voice of the first half of the play. Lady Windermere feels that he is merely 'trivial', and insists that life is 'a sacrament. Its ideal is Love. Its purification is sacrifice.' Darlington's retort – 'Oh, anything is better than being sacrificed!' – is justified by later developments in action and dialogue: specifically, by Lady Windermere's willingness to sacrifice her child and its future; by Mrs Erlynne's socially suicidal sacrifice in Act III; and by Lady Windermere's fear, strange in the mouth of one who called sacrifice 'a purification', that her saviour may think twice about her good action once she calculates how much it has cost her. Ironically, while Darlington appears to be morally slipshod, it is actually the Duchess of Berwick, the Establishment mother, who exemplifies the prevailing *laissez-faire* morality. She tells Darlington that she will not let him know her daughter, because he is 'far too wicked', then promptly introduces him to her: 'Isn't he dreadful? Agatha, this is Lord Darlington. Mind you don't believe a word he says.' She admires Lady Windermere for making a stand about the 'dreadful people' who get asked everywhere, but openly admits their presence in her own house: 'The men get quite furious if one doesn't ask them.' San Juan has noted that Lady Agatha is used as a parody of Lady Winderemere's 'pure' and ingenuous standards;[9] but the whole pattern of the Duchess's relationship with her daughter is a comic reflection both on Lady Windermere's treatment of her infant and on Mrs Erlynne's treatment of the infant Lady Windermere years before. Skilled in the wiles of the marriage market, the Duchess remarks (ironically but ingenuously), 'A mother who doesn't part with a daughter every season has no real affection'. (The pair anticipate James's Duchess and her little Aggie in *The Awkward Age* (1899) – aptly enough, one might think, since Lady Windermere, though celebrating her coming-of-age, is still morally and psychologically at the awkward age.) The Duchess of Berwick's success with Lady Agatha completes the parody. The 'little chatterbox' is paired off with Mr Hopper, the rich Australian described by Cecil Graham as 'one of Nature's gentlemen – the worst sort of gentleman I know'; and this match achieves a symmetry of ingenuousness to which any liaison between Lady Windermere and Darlington could never approximate. Lady Agatha's thirteen yesses, with the last of which she secures her man, may have been suggested by a scene in *The London Cuckolds* (1681) by Edward Ravenscroft. Here a young wife, forbidden by her husband to reply anything but 'No' to strangers who might call, contrives to use the veto to secure the shrewd Towneley, whom she takes to bed. Whether Wilde knew of the parallel or not, his own scene is no less conscious of the rottenness of the respectable norm, whose watchword is 'Somebody should make a stand'.

The traditional opposition between country or pastoral values and town sophistication is also implied by Wilde's reuse of names from "Lord Arthur Savile's Crime": Lady Windermere, Mrs Erlynne ('a pushing nobody with red hair'), and Lord Arthur were all present. The hint of pastoral Selby at the end of the play recalls the ending of the earlier story, while the choice of so peculiarly Wordsworthian a name as Windermere (in this case, Wilde did not follow his frequent practice of choosing names from the district where he wrote the play) seems studied, especially when Lady Windermere's incompatibility with Darlington – an industrial, though not very urbane, centre near the opposite coast – is one of his most important points.

Having confronted Lady Windermere with the prevailing social values during the first half of Act I, Wilde puts her values to the test in the second half. When she confronts her husband with his supposed betrayal of their marriage, her 'virtuous' stand betrays itself by a persistent note of vulgarity, repeated in her later soliloquies. In pointed contrast to the discreet circumlocutions or colloquial trivialisations of Darlington and the Duchess, she talks of Windermere's 'mad infatuation' with an 'infamous woman'. She cries that she feels 'stained, utterly stained', and that 'every kiss that you have given me is tainted in my memory'. When Windermere tries to draw from her some objective concern for a woman who has suffered for her mistakes, his wife retorts merely, 'I am not interested in her – and – you should not mention this woman and me in the same breath. It is an error of taste.' Without waiting for any indication that Windermere's explanation might be genuine, she sweeps from the room: 'From this moment my life is separate from yours.'

In Act II the puritan's lack of self-control is contrasted with the dandy's perfect poise. It is, in fact, Mrs Erlynne's air of complete self-confidence, culminating in her conversation with Windermere about his settlement on her prior to her marriage with Lord Augustus, that pushes Lady Windermere off balance and convinces her to fly to the man who has offered her life 'to do with what you will'.

This action is the more perverse since Darlington has already betrayed his own precepts, offering friendship but planning conquest. It is only one of his 'little vanities' to pretend to be worse than other men, he says, adding that his 'modern affectation of weakness', as Lady Windermere calls it, is 'only an affectation'. Darlington thus plays the libertine playing the *honnête homme*, an amusing ultra-modern anachronism which counterbalances Lady Windermere's quasi-courtly puritanism. But in Act II Wilde springs a surprise by placing in the mouth of a dandy a speech urging self-fulfilment in outright contradiction of social restraints. The device implies that there is

more of the libertine – or the Romantic egotist – in Darlington than meets
the eye, and it establishes Wilde's standard of comic self-consistency. In Act I
Darlington had found Lady Windermere a 'fascinating puritan'. In Act II it is
the woman, not the abstraction, that charms: 'From the moment I met you, I
loved you, loved you blindly, adoringly, madly!' He challenges her to defy
society and 'be yourself!':

> I won't tell you that the world matters nothing, or the world's voice, or the
> voice of society. They matter a great deal. They matter far too much. But there
> are moments when one has to choose between living one's own life, fully,
> entirely, completely – or dragging out some false, shallow, degrading exis-
> tence that the world in its hypocrisy demands. You have that moment now.
> Choose! Oh, my love, choose.

When choice proves impossible for her, Darlington increases her confusion
by rhetorical sophistries designed to undermine her values: 'Who will blame
you? No one. If they did, what matter? Wrong? What is wrong? It's wrong
for a man to abandon his wife for a shameless woman. It is wrong for a wife
to remain with a man who so dishonours her. You said once that you would
make no compromise with things. Make none now.'

Darlington professes the amoral standards of the dandy, but in trying by
moral arguments to overbear someone committed to a strict moral standard,
he acts not in the interests of comic justice but in his own interests. In *A
Woman of No Importance*, Mrs Allonby chaffs Illingworth, 'What a bad man
you must be!' He asks, 'What do you call a bad man?' Her reply is, 'A man
who admires innocence.' This is what Darlington does. The point emerges
during the apparently pointless chatter of Act III, when a dandiacal discussion
of what women may reasonably expect from men shows Darlington in his
true colours – that anomalous creature, the romantic dandy, who cannot
make light of his feelings over cigars.

Darlington's role is to dominate the first half of the play, as Mrs Erlynne's
is to dominate the second half. Lady Windermere is first exposed to the
influence of a false dandy whom she trusts, then to the influence of a true
dandy whom she does not trust. Lady Windermere's flight to Darlington
appears the more absurd when we consider that in Restoration comedy he
could have played the perfect libertine, mouthing Rochester or one of his
imitators: 'Of Nature's freedom we're beguil'd / By laws which man
imposes'.[10] In the Victorian context, he sounds like an intruder from Wilde's
heroic mode, a disappointed idealist who has fallen back on the dandy's pose
without wholly relinquishing his grasp on the romantic's: 'We are all in the
gutter, but some of us are looking at the stars.' With such lines as this, he
could have made a legitimate hero in *The Duchess of Padua* or *A Florentine
Tragedy*. The discrepancy defeats him. 'Nowadays,' as he says, 'to be
intelligible is to be found out.' Mask and reality are too various. No unity
binds external form and inner substance. Darlington, once 'found out', is all

too intelligible. Lady Windermere – 'the only good woman I have ever met in my life' – is a paragon that the dandy ought to suspect, not to worship. His exclamation, 'What cynics you fellows are!', sets up his dismissal by Cecil Graham, the perfect type of the trivialised but active intellect. 'What is a cynic?' inquires Graham. Darlington's reply – 'A man who knows the price of everything and the value of nothing' – was to be confirmed in the wholly serious context of De Profundis:

> Delightful as cynicism is from its intellectual side, now that it has left the Tub for the Club, it can never be more than the perfect philosophy for a man who has no soul. It has its social value, and to an artist all modes of expression are interesting, but in itself it is a poor thing, for to the true cynic nothing is ever revealed.[11]

In comedy, however, Darlington's would-be Romanticism merits a riposte: 'And a sentimentalist, my dear Darlington, is a man who sees an absurd value in everything, and doesn't know the market price of any single thing.' The remainder of the passage from De Profundis places Darlington and Graham in their true relations: 'Remember that the sentimentalist is always a cynic at heart. . . . Sentimentality is merely the bank holiday of cynicism.' Darlington's cynicism about the badness of men by comparison with the goodness of women is only a refinement of sentimentality. Indeed, it is hardly less absurd than Lady Windermere's suspicion that all men are bad. In spite of his dandiacal facade, Darlington has too little self-security to qualify for Wilde's critical commonweal. To 'the average suburban playgoer' he may seem to disappear from the plot because of his attempt on the virtuous heroine. To the 'few choice spirits', he is dismissed by his fellow-dandies for having admired her at all.

In Act IV everyone reverts to type, most notably Windermere. Discarding his earlier tolerance, he now judges Mrs Erlynne entirely by appearances, like the rest of society. As soon as the audience has tangible evidence of Mrs Erlynne's true qualities, Windermere resorts to the platitudes of the *status quo*, and is doubly horrified when she assumes the dandy's mask to control her feelings:

> I have no ambition to play the part of a mother. Only once in my life have I known a mother's feelings. That was last night. They were terrible – they made me suffer – they made me suffer too much. For twenty years, as you say, I have lived childless – I want to live childless still. (*Hiding her feelings with a trivial laugh.*) Besides, my dear Windermere, how on earth could I pose as a mother with a grown-up daughter? Margaret is twenty-one, and I have never admitted to more than twenty-nine, or thirty at most. Twenty-nine when there are pink shades, thirty when there are not. So you see what difficulties it would involve. No, so far as I am concerned, let your wife cherish the memory of this dead, stainless mother. Why should I interfere with her illusions? I find it hard enough to keep my own. I lost one illusion last night. I thought I had no heart. I find I

have, and a heart doesn't suit me, Windermere. Somehow it doesn't go with modern dress. It makes one look old. (*Takes up hand mirror from the table and looks into it.*) And it spoils one's career at critical moments.

The subject of dress indicates that the dialogue has reverted to the philosophy of the superficial, 'the great dandiacal joke'[12] which exalts appearances over subjective truth. Mrs Erlynne knows well which role best suits her. She is determined to keep motive and manner in their proper balance – not to play the tragedy queen. Unlike Vera, Beatrice, or Salomé, she finds self-fulfilment through passionate action too horrifying. For her, 'hearts' belong in costume drama; 'modern dress' requires a different style. Windermere, unable to appreciate these complex reactions, feels outraged by what he thinks her callousness. Being a man of essentially 'natural' tastes, he fails to perceive that even the 'dark hair and innocent expression' of his wife's cherished miniature were 'the fashion' during Mrs Erlynne's youth when the likeness was taken. Like the audience for whom *La Dame aux Camélias* was written, he would have relished a reform. It would have flattered him by confirming the rightness of his values. At the end of *The Man of Mode*, Harriet, young and victorious, reminds Loveit, cast off and embittered and determined to 'lock myself up in my house and never see the world again', that a 'nunnery is the more fashionable place for such a retreat, and has been the fatal consequence of many a *belle passion'*. Mrs Erlynne, who seems almost to echo the speech, allows no one to upstage her – least of all Windermere, who is now firmly back in place as a caryatid of convention after his brief excursion into the world of flesh and blood:

> I suppose, Windermere, you would like me to retire into a convent, or become a hospital nurse, or something of that kind, as people do in silly modern novels. That is stupid of you, Arthur; in real life we don't do such things – not as long as we have any good looks left, at any rate. No – what consoles one nowadays is not repentance, but pleasure. Repentance is quite out of date. And besides, if a woman really repents, she has to go to a bad dressmaker, otherwise no one believes in her. And nothing in the world would induce me to do that. No; I am going to pass entirely out of your two lives. My coming into them has been a mistake – I discovered that last night.

By rejecting the moral for the aesthetic posture – society's narrowing alternatives – she may lose much that is valuable, but her position is at least rational, consistent, and free from self-deception or hypocrisy. To Windermere, she has made a 'fatal mistake': she can never 'get back'. Mrs Erlynne calls the error 'almost fatal': she alone knows how near to her daughter the real danger came. Windermere's change of heart emphasises her self-consistency. As San Juan points out, even her lapse into 'sentiment' in Act III corresponds with what Winderemere tells us about her past.[13] The past is laid again, however, and the audience allowed to emerge with the new-found 'shield of intellect' held over 'the new-born babe of pity'.

In a typewritten draft of the play,[14] Wilde made more of the miniature and of Windermere's rudeness, both of them presumably intended to increase Mrs Erlynne's humiliation or discomfiture by the conventional world. He also sketched out an exchange between the pair which would have intensified Windermere's disgust at her behaviour in Act III. Mrs Erlynne comes close to betraying her real motives for going to Darlington's rooms, and thus to revealing her daughter's 'mistake'. Windermere interprets her meaning more grossly, although his answers have, unknown to him, an ironic point. (Brackets indicate the part of the dialogue taken from the typescript.)

MRS ERLYNNE	(*shrugging her shoulders*): Don't use ugly words, Windermere. They are vulgar. I saw my chance, it is true, and took it.
WINDERMERE:	Yes: you took it – and spoiled it all last night by being found out.
MRS ERLYNNE	(*with a strange smile*): You are quite right, I spoiled it all last night.
[WINDERMERE:	I can't imagine what made you do it.
MRS ERLYNNE:	I wonder myself why I did it now. Suddenly there awoke in one's nature feelings that one thought were dead, or that one thought one never had at all. They wake in one's nature, and then they die.
WINDERMERE:	Are they dead?
MRS ERLYNNE:	I think so. I fear so.
WINDERMERE:	A good thing too.
MRS ERLYNNE:	Possibly.
	(*Pause.*)
WINDERMERE:	Mrs Erlynne, what are you plotting now? Don't imagine that you can get your reputation whitewashed again. I gave you your opportunity. You threw it away. Your going to Darlington's rooms was monstrous.
MRS ERLYNNE:	It *was* very foolish of me, wasn't it?
WINDERMERE:	It was stupid, utterly stupid.
MRS ERLYNNE:	Yes, I dare say it was.]
WINDERMERE:	As for your blunder in taking my wife's fan from here and then leaving it about in Darlington's rooms, it is unpardonable.

Mrs Erlynne is still given the chance to rebuke him for his bad grace – 'My dear Windermere, it is a social error to be uncivil, and a social crime to be candid. To be both uncivil and candid at the same time is quite unforgiveable!' – but the phrase that Wilde finally picked ('My dear Windermere, manners before morals!') says more in less, and gives us the motto of Wildean comedy.

The other significant change, made in rehearsal, concerned the secret of Mrs Erlynne's identity. Wilde had intended that the audience remain ignorant of the mother-daughter relationship until the last act.

Had I intended to let out the secret, which is the element of suspense and curiosity, a quality essentially dramatic, I would have written the play on entirely different lines. I would have made Mrs Erlynne a vulgar horrid woman and struck out the incident of the fan. The audience must not know until the last act that the woman Lady Windermere proposed to strike with her fan was her own mother. The note would be too harsh, too horrible. . . . If they knew Mrs Erlynne was the mother, there would be no surprise in her sacrifice – it would be expected. The cry with which Mrs Erlynne flies into the other room on hearing Lord Augustus's voice, the wild pathetic cry of self-preservation, 'Then it is I who am lost!', would be repulsive coming from the lips of one known to be the mother by the audience. It seems natural and dramatic coming from one who seems to be an adventuress, and who while anxious to save Lady Windermere thinks of her own safety when a crisis comes.[15]

The most remarkable aspect of this argument is its determined air of self-justification. Several of the points made do not relate directly to the play even in its draft form, and much of it is self-contradictory, in effect if not in word. George Alexander, who made the change during Wilde's temporary absence from rehearsals, seems to have realised, however, that Wilde's original scheme sacrificed motive and idea, which he had carefully worked out, to an idea of dramatic 'suspense' which was largely illusory. An adventuress who has hitherto shown no interest whatsoever in the fate of the wife whose husband she has been blackmailing is unlikely to spare a thought for that wife's social reputation at the expense of her own, particularly after all the hard work that she has put in to regain it. Wilde feared that the change would weaken the crucial last act: 'The chief merit of my last act is to me the fact that it does not contain, as most plays do, the explanation of what the audience knows already, but that it is the sudden revelation of what the audience desires to know, followed immediately by the revelation of a character as yet untouched by literature.'[16] The play as it stands preserves the element of revelation, but instead of revealing the mere fact of blood relationship, it reveals the psychological spring of Wilde's new character: the *aventurière* as dandy.

It must be admitted that the play does not run as smoothly as my summary suggests. Many smaller points were overlooked. Sometimes Lady Windermere fails to function properly even as a type, or times and other trivia of plot fail to fit. Wilde's main concern, however – a comic morality based on the idea of self-knowledge and self-consistency – emerges in spite of these imperfections and shapes our attitudes to all the main characters. Lady Windermere, titular recipient first of the audience's token admiration, then of their tolerant sympathy, is given her second chance with a well-meaning though dense husband. Darlington is dismissed by his own confusions, failing both as dandy and as Romantic lover, though temporarily successful as a wit. To Mrs Erlynne is left the task of assessing her own merits and deciding her own future. Her reversion to type is the most courageous act of the play. Windermere's grudging admiration of that capacity for explaining things which enables her to retain her hold on Lord Augustus – her only success in terms of her 'career' – gives Wilde two critical chances in the play's closing-lines. 'Well, you are certainly marrying a very clever woman', exclaims Windermere, still resonating with his personal experience of her cleverness. 'Ah,' rejoins Lady Windermere, 'you're marrying a very good woman.' (Wilde has in mind the last line of *Le Demi-Monde*:[17] 'You're marrying the honestest woman I know'.) Windermere's line is the reply of the conventional mind striving to be objective; his wife's is the reply of a woman eager to give away a flattering phrase that no longer suits her. Lady Windermere has learned that people cannot 'be divided into good and bad', but it is too much to expect that she will yet recognise the ineptness of bestowing on Mrs Erlynne the very title that Mrs Erlynne has shown to her to be worthless. This is Wilde's parting gesture to the double comic standard. For the conventionally minded playgoer, the 'good woman' of the sub-title (in early versions, the title was *A Good Woman*) starts as Lady Windermere but ends as Mrs Erlynne, and even so crude a 'critical' reversal has its value. To that part of the audience alive to the dandy's relative standards, the play contains no 'good woman' at all. Society, in the final analysis, is hardly as sophisticated as Mrs Gamp, and its 'good woman' is a Mrs Harris.

This lightness of touch, unexpected, perhaps, at the end of an action which somewhat narrowly avoids domestic (if not quite heroic) tragedy, is matched by Wilde's systematic use of the fan, 'flag and symbol of our so-called Comedy of Manners, or comedy of South-Sea islanders under city veneer'. As the fan passes from hand to hand and from room to room, it seems to define some progression in its owner's social maturity. It appears at first as Windermere's gift to his wife (an innocent 'child') on the occasion of her coming of age. Next, it is the instrument with which she threatens to insult Mrs Erlynne. At the reception she gives it to Lord Darlington to hold, and it becomes a physical sign of her need for 'a friend', or husband-substitute, 'tonight'. When the climax comes, she drops the fan on the floor. It next appears in Darlington's rooms, where she is almost betrayed by it. Mrs Erlynne steps in to interpret its presence, and returns it to its owner next day. By this time, the fan has assumed a definite symbolic significance: it is the attribute and weapon of the competent social adult. Mrs Erlynne's restoration of the fan to her daugher not only reunites owner and giver – husband and wife – but also presents Lady Windermere with a second chance at undergoing the ordeal by society: that second chance which Mrs Erlynne thereby gives up for herself. But the fan now bears a social stigma, and it changes hands once more, becoming a memento for the mother and virtually the staff of office of the adventuress. Finally entrusted to Lord Augustus, who is eager to abdicate from society into trouble-free disrepute, it becomes a symbol of his relationship with Mrs Erlynne: 'you would carry off anything gracefully, Lord Augustus.' Mrs Erlynne's parting pun is the biggest hyperbole in the play, and in being so, it defines her part in their joint future.

Below Wilde's poised estimate of social responsibilities, then, we can recognise the reservations of his earlier Romantic mode. The Windermeres retire to their country seat, but will doubtless return in due course. Darlington and Mrs Erlynne leave England, and on a much more permanent basis. Their departure is the more significant in that they are the only characters to whom we are inclined to accord any critical authority. Admittedly, they do not die, and this is one step closer to social integration than Vera, Guido, or Beatrice ever achieved. But there lingers the suggestion that the talented exception – especially the passionate talented exception – needs all his wits about him and a good deal of luck besides if he is to retain membership of the club. As Wilde argued in "The Soul of Man", 'what the world calls a sin against society' may simply be the fulfilment of a personality in some way of which society disapproves. Darlington, indeed, says as much to Lady Windermere. The offence itself, however, is finally of little account. The punishment is for that disregard of appearances which leads to discovery. In such conditions, private rather than public estimates of justice are the only humane ones. Wilde developed this conviction in *An Ideal Husband*, where the misdemeanour of an ingenuous wife was replaced by the misuse of privileged information by a public figure. By contrast with *Lady Windermere's Fan*, the play is optimistic: the comic libertine-Machiavel is dismissed, the erring hero reprieved, the sympathetic dandy-mediator integrated by marriage with the conventional part of society. After that, Wilde moved on, or back, to pastoral farce.

II.   *A Woman of No Importance*: A Neo-Restoration Conflict

Wilde's first comedy had been set entirely in town, and town values had dominated it. In his second, he turned to the country, and it is the only one which takes place wholly there. Already, in social fiction, he had associated the country with innocence, naïvety, or pastoral simplicity, and the American republican puritan *ingénue* had made her appearance as an instance of racial pastoral in contrast to the fallen state of an ancient and sophisticated aristocracy. Now these ideas were developed in the more demanding context of realistic comedy. *A Woman of No Importance* restates a number of the standard situations of Restoration comedy, and uses the stock antitheses of the genre – town and country, wit and sentiment, libertine and courtly attitudes, men and women, cits and aristos – as the basis of reference for a critical treatment of some of 'the real issues of the age'.

As I have suggested, Hester Worsley is essentially the country wife of the piece, culturally, morally, and in due course, when she takes Gerald to America, literally. Hester's only pun is made, suitably enough, on the word 'country':

LADY CAROLINE: Have you any country, what we should call country?

HESTER   (*smiling*): We have the largest country in the world, Lady Caroline.
They used to tell us at school that some of our states are as big as France
and England put together.

Illingworth is the play's closest approximation to Horner, although in
Wilde's comic scheme the relation between the rake and the country wife is
predictably reversed. Illingworth makes a half-hearted attempt to 'convert'
the Puritan by a kiss, but his wager with Mrs Allonby that he will do so is no
more than a somewhat irresponsible parlour-game – 'one of those utterly
tedious amusements,' as Mrs Cheveley says in *An Ideal Husband*, 'one finds
only in an English country house' – and it bears no comparison with the
seduction of Margery Pinchwife. If the libertine initiation of the *ingénue* fails
to materialise, so does its obverse, the taming of the rake. Hester shows none
of that interest in her pursuer which many of her more venturous but no less
literally virtuous predecessors had done – Harriet in *The Man of Mode*,
Angelica in *Love for Love*, or Dorinda in *The Beaux' Stratagem*, to name only
three. (Indeed, it remains for Cecily Cardew, in a wholly farcical treatment
of the themes here approached with honestly serious intention, to play the
capable virgin to Algernon's unicorn, domesticating the libertine-glutton
in earnest by offering him, among other things, a buttonhole and 'regular
and wholesome meals'.)

Mrs Arbuthnot is equally reluctant to dignify the rake with social
recognition, and takes social as well as personal revenge on him by refusing
his belated offer of marriage. Indeed, if anyone tames the rake, it is she – the
character who, like Loveit, has been wounded by excessive passion, and who
strikes a long-delayed blow for the comic dupe by snatching the laurels from
the man of mode's grasp and bestowing their stalks on the woman with a
past.

These attitudes, dramatically and morally critical of the libertine tradition,
confirm the significance of Wilde's description of this as 'a woman's play'.
The dandy's standards may carry the first two acts, but the puritans'
standards carry the last two and determine the outcome of the plot. In spite
of the varied and amusing social commentary of Act I and the dandy's
catechism in Act III, it is 'the woman question' which predominates. Even
Illingworth concedes to Gerald that women rule society. Even the female
dandy, Mrs Allonby, verbally glittering amongst the dowagers and coffee-
cups after dinner, builds a psychological maquette of the Ideal Man pinched
into changing shapes wholly at the whim of the female ego. Even Lady
Stutfield, who knows so few adverbs that she always uses them in pairs to
compensate, can perceive a woman's advantages as Mrs Allonby assesses
them: 'We have a much better time than they have. There are far more
things forbidden to us than are forbidden to them'. Even Hester, who first
declared that 'a woman who has sinned should never be forgiven', comes to
recognise Mrs Arbuthnot as a figure in whom 'all womanhood is martyred',
and sides with her against the common enemy.

The play resolves itself into a crude battle of sex between Hester and Mrs Allonby on the one hand and Lord Illingworth on the other, the booty being Gerald. Illingworth's parting vulgarism and Mrs Arbuthnot's retort to it define the antagonism succinctly. Rebuffed and chagrined, Illingworth assumes the manner of the professional rake: 'It's been an amusing experience to have met amongst people of one's own rank, and treated quite seriously too, one's mistress and one's –'; but he is cut short by a duellist's device: a glove (one of his own) slapped across his face. At the real moment of crisis, the woman meets the man of his own terms. The gesture, especially in the context of Illingworth's baldly emphatic upper-class egotism, recalls Meredith's description of Sir Willoughby reacting to one of Clara Middleton's unexpected thrusts:

> 'I remember hearing Mr Whitford say that cynicism is intellectual dandyism without the coxcomb's feathers; and it seems to me that cynics are only happy in making the world as barren to others as they have made it for themselves.'
> 'Old Vernon!' ejaculated Sir Willoughby, with a countenance rather uneasy, as if it had been flicked with a glove. 'He strings his phrases by the dozen.'[18]

It is also a deliberate echo of the exchange between Illingworth and Mrs Allonby in Act I, in which Mrs Allonby had suggested that, if Illingworth tried to kiss Hester, she would 'Either marry you, or strike you across the face with her glove. What would you do if she struck you across the face with her glove?' 'Fall in love with her, probably', replies Illingworth.

Although the women win the tug-of-war for Gerald, Wilde clearly has little sympathy with their position. To many of the audience, the vanquishing of the dandy or pseudo-libertine must have seemed like moral justice. To the dramatist it can only have seemed, depressingly, like more than usually accurate social realism. Illingworth admires the 'beautiful, passionate letter' written by Gerald to convince him to marry Mrs Arbuthnot at last, but adds, 'no son of mine should side with the Puritans: that is an error'. Indeed, Wilde went some way towards making the play explicitly anti-puritan after the best libertine tradition, but was obliged by Beerbohm Tree to cut his biggest libertine speech, presumably for fear of audience reaction.[19] Sufficient comment remained, even so, to make his intellectual position clear, for the puritan–dandy antagonism is expressed at every level. The orchid, 'as beautiful as the seven deadly sins', that Mrs Allonby goes to look for in the Hunstanton conservatory in Act I, is contrasted with Mrs Arbuthnot's sitting-room, visited by Lady Hunstanton and Mrs Allonby in Act IV, 'the room of a sweet saint' with 'fresh natural flowers' and 'books that don't shock one'. The female dandy's set piece on the Ideal Man is pointedly juxtaposed with Hester's jeremiad on English society, especially on Lord Weston, Lady Caroline's brother. Lady Hunstanton is 'afraid that some of this clever talk may have shocked' Hester, but Mrs Allonby replies, 'Ah, that will do her so much good!'.

In *Dorian Gray*, Lord Henry Wotton had offered a dandy's definition of civilisation which Illingworth, his immediate comic legatee, clearly accepted (and which Illingworth's female counterpart, Mrs Allonby, repeats almost verbatim):

> anybody can be good in the country. There are no temptations there. That is the reason why people who live out of town are so absolutely uncivilised. Civilisation is not by any means an easy thing to attain to. There are only two ways by which man can reach it. One is by being cultured, the other by being corrupt. Country people have no opportunity of being either, so they stagnate.[20]

This is Wilde's, and Illingworth's, view of Mrs Arbuthnot's condition; and, since Hester aligns herself with Mrs Arbuthnot, it becomes the typical condition of the Puritans. Obviously intellectual as well as moral stagnation is involved. Wilde hints as much in the following slight vignette set between larger conversations:

> MRS ALLONBY: You enjoy country life, Miss Worsley?
> HESTER: Very much, indeed.
> MRS ALLONBY: Don't you find yourself longing for a London dinner-party?
> HESTER: I dislike London dinner-parties.
> MRS ALLONBY: I adore them. The clever people never listen, and the stupid people never talk.
> HESTER: I think the stupid people talk a great deal.
> MRS ALLONBY: Ah! I never listen.

Hester's intellectual stagnation, however, is of little immediate account compared with the stagnation of Mrs Arbuthnot's whole outlook on life. Appalled at the prospect of losing her son to the man whose desertion of them has become the mark against which she habitually measures her maternal feeling, she accuses Illingworth of making Gerald discontented with his closed existence. 'Of course I made him so', Illingworth replies. 'Discontent is the first step in the progress of a man or a nation. But I did not leave him with a mere longing for things he could not get. No, I made him a charming offer. He jumped at it, I need hardly say. Any young man would.' To Mrs Arbuthnot this offer is a kind of treachery: 'Gerald', she insists, 'cannot separate his future from my past'. 'That is exactly what you should help him to do', retorts Illingworth. From his lips, this can hardly sound disinterested, yet it presents the situation in its simplest objective terms. 'What a typical woman you are', he adds. 'You talk sentimentally, and you are thoroughly selfish the whole time.' Again, this is far from being disinterested in context, although a perfectly accurate estimate of Mrs Arbuthnot's damaging if pathetic possessiveness.

The dialogue in this play intensifies, in fact, the running altercations between masculine and feminine, or intellectual and emotional principles.

Even Illingworth's mock courtship of Mrs Allonby is characterised as a mock fencing-match:

> ILLINGWORTH: Shall we go in to tea?
> MRS ALLONBY: Do you like such simple pleasures?
> ILLINGWORTH: I adore simple pleasures. They are the last refuge of the complex. But, if you wish, let us stay here. Yes, let us stay here. The Book of Life begins with a man and a woman in a garden. '
> MRS ALLONBY: It ends with Revelations.
> ILLINGWORTH: You fence divinely. But the button has come off your foil.
> MRS ALLONBY: I have still the mask.
> ILLINGWORTH: It makes your eyes lovelier.
> MRS ALLONBY: Thank you. Come.

For Illingworth, 'Nothing is serious except passion' and 'Nothing refines but the intellect'. Passion and intellect have an elemental purity. Emotion is a commodity merely, something which typifies an inferior attitude to life. Illingworth's elevation of passion and intellect has a firmly aristocratic basis. On the one hand, 'A really *grande passion*', as he tells Gerald, 'is the privilege of people who have nothing to do. That is the one use of the idle classes in a country.' On the other hand he is a firm believer in Wilde's cultural hierarchy in which 'the aristocracy of intellect' takes precedence over 'the democracy of suffering'.[21]

These issues are stated with exemplary conciseness in the dandy's catechism at the opening of Act III. The ostensible aim of this scene is to acquaint Gerald with the assumptions of his future life, although Illingworth's main purpose – more strongly expressed in the typescript – is to consolidate his advantage with Gerald over Mrs Arbuthnot. The cue speech is central to both. The draft version is between parentheses.

> ILLINGWORTH: A mother's love is very touching, of course, but it is often curiously selfish. I mean, there is a good deal of selfishness in it.
> GERALD: I suppose there is.
> ILLINGWORTH: Your mother is a thoroughly good woman. But good women have such limited views of life, their horizon is so small, their instincts are so petty, aren't they?
> GERALD: They are awfully interested, certainly, in things we don't much care about. . . .
> ILLINGWORTH: (The fact is, they are not modern, and to be modern is the only thing worth being. You want to be modern, don't you Gerald? You want to know life as it really is? Not to be put off with any old-fashioned theories about life [?] Well, what you have to do at present is simply to fit yourself for the best society. A man who can dominate a London dinner table can

GERALD: dominate the world. It is the exquisites who are going to rule — in spite of all that the Puritans may do or say.

GERALD: The Puritans, Lord Illingworth?

ILLINGWORTH: Yes, Gerald, the Puritans. My dear boy, the real enemy of modern life, of everything that makes life lovely and joyous and coloured for us, is Puritanism, and the Puritan spirit. *There* is the danger that lies ahead of the age, and most of all in England. Every now and then this England of ours finds that one of its sores shows through its rags and shrieks for the nonconformists. Caliban for nine months of the year, it is Tartuffe for the other three. Do you [not] despise a creed that starves the body and does not feed the soul? Why, I tell you, Gerald, that the profligate, the wildest profligate who spills his life in folly, has a better, saner, finer philosophy of life than the Puritan has. He, at any rate, knows that the aim of life is the pleasure of living, and does in some way realise himself, be himself. Puritanism is the hideous survival of the self-mutilation of the savage, man in his madness making *himself* the victim of his monstrous sacrifice. Profligate, Gerald, you will never be; you will choose your pleasures too carefully, too exquisitely for that. But Puritanism you will always reject. It is not a creed for a gentleman.[22] And, as a beginning, you will make it your ideal to be a dandy always.

GERALD: I should like to wear nice things awfully, but my mother says a man should never think about his clothes.

ILLINGWORTH: People are so absolutely superficial nowadays, that they don't understand the philosophy of the superficial. They can't realise that in the mere knotting of a necktie, or the colour of a scarf, or the cut of a waistcoat there is a whole creed of life. And as for women, I believe women rather like us to be badly dressed. They are a little afraid of the dandy. They want appearances always to be against us — appearances usually are. By the way, Gerald, you should learn to tie your tie better. . . .)[23]

There are echoes here of "Humanitad", *Dorian Gray*, and the letter about *London Assurance*. Even so, the speech comprises *mots de caractère*, not *mots d'auteur*. The 'profligate' might be thought of as a Wildean romantic egotist without the benefit of an intellectual aim or an aesthetic sense. The dandy, by contrast, has the mental qualities but has been de-animalised by a puritanical society. The Restoration libertine combined 'wit' with 'sense', intellectual framework with animal spirits. Illingworth is closer to the libertine than to 'the wildest profligate'; but his epigrams on the differences between men and women, wittily chauvinistic, also prove him to be closer to the libertine than to the Wildean true dandy, who is more interested in comprehension than in smart definition:

GERALD: It is very difficult to understand women, is it not?

ILLINGWORTH: You should never try to understand them. Women are
pictures. Men are problems. If you want to know what a
woman really means – which, by the way, is always a
dangerous thing to do – look at her, don't listen to her.

GERALD? But women are awfully clever, aren't they?

ILLINGWORTH: One should always tell them so. But, to the philosopher,
Gerald, women represent the triumph of matter over
mind – just as men represent the triumph of mind over
morals.

Two of Illingworth's observations, both of which bear directly on his
relationship with Mrs Arbuthnot, take us straight back to the Restoration.
The first is his Hobbesian conclusion to the catechism:

> And, now, Gerald, you are going into a perfectly new life with me, and I want
> you to know how to live. (*Mrs Arbuthnot appears on the terrace behind.*) For the
> world has been made by fools that wise men should live in it!

The second is made after the two men have been interrupted by other guests,
and implies what Illingworth's line of argument might have developed into:

> I was on the point of explaining to Gerald that the world has always laughed at
> its own tragedies, that being the only way in which it has been able to bear
> them. And that, consequently, whatever the world has treated seriously
> belongs to the comedy side of things.

Lady Hunstanton professes herself quite out of her depth, but Mrs Erlynne or
the wits of the Restoration theatre would have understood perfectly. It is a
mark against Mrs Arbuthnot that she is incapable of this comic balance.

LADY HUNSTANTON: . . . You and I, dear Mrs Arbuthnot, are behind the age.
We can't follow Lord Illingworth. Too much care was
taken with our education, I am afraid. To have been well
brought up is a great drawback nowadays. It shuts one out
from so much.

MRS ARBUTHNOT: I should be sorry to follow Lord Illingworth in any of his
opinions.

Lady Hunstanton's remarks have an ironic application to Gerald, who has
been brought up so carefully that he knows nothing of the world at all. Yet
even he, if only for a moment, shows a sense of the ludicrous pratfalls that
emotion may take. His mother, playing her last trump in an attempt to
dissuade him from widening his horizons and taking up a career with
Illingworth, tells him the anonymous narrative of her youthful error. The
effect is grotesque, a bedtime story with a wicked monster and a nightmare
ending, weighed down by self-conscious Biblical references. Gerald's
answer is a triumph of unconscious comedy – the instinctive response of the

ingenuous prig that Mrs Arbuthnot herself has made him: 'it all sounds very tragic, of course. But I dare say the girl was just as much to blame as Lord Illingworth was. – After all, would a really nice girl, a girl with any nice feelings at all, go away from her home with a man to whom she was not married, and live with him as his wife? No nice girl would.' In the typescript, Wilde added at the beginning of the speech, 'My dear mother, that is her story', but he evidently felt that it was emphatic enough as it stood. The 'democracy of suffering' clearly has its own case to plead; but, as clearly, this case is substantially incompatible with a form based on the assumptions of the 'aristocracy of the intellect'.

The sexual battle, then, expresses a conflict of temperament and personal ethics; but it tends also to reflect the conflict between aristocratic and middle-class standards. Obviously, the real class struggle is based largely on wealth and power, but Wilde's dramatic presentation of it reduces it to its cultural elements and expresses these through the sex war. The resulting dramatic tensions are analogous to that social tension for which Restoration comedy was in some measure a formalised or 'fantastic' solution. In the words of F. W. Bateson:

> To the Puritans, 'immorality' had virtually reduced itself to sexual irregularity, with drunkenness and blasphemy as poor seconds, a man's other sins being considered a private matter between him and God. (By the 1650 Act 'for suppressing the detestable sins of Incest, Adultery and Fornication' incest and adultery became capital crimes without benefit of clergy, as did fornication on the second offence, first offenders getting three months' imprisonment.) On the other hand, to the restored Royalists by a natural reaction sexual licence – and drunkenness and blasphemous oaths – almost became a political duty. 'Joy ruled the day and love the night', as Dryden summed up Charles II's reign in *The Secular Masque*. The two attitudes were the points of maximum social divergence between the two parties into which England remained divided. . . . If the political problem *par excellence* in the second half of the seventeenth century was to avoid the recurrence of a second Civil War, its social parallel, essentially, was to rationalise the sex instinct. Until such a rationalization had been achieved genuine communication between Whigs and Tories was hardly possible. Inter-marriage, the final solution, was unthinkable.[24]

The dandy-libertine, though self-sufficient and therefore a totally apolitical animal, obviously resembles the Tories, 'who spent their winter months in London applying to the pursuit of love the methods of the chase, which was their principal occupation on their country estates', more closely than the merchant Whigs, 'who treated their wives as pieces of property to be even more jealously guarded than their gold'[25] – the alternatives offered by dramatic tradition. But in *A Woman of No Importance*, the real inter-marriage at issue is cultural, not political. At a humorous level, it is racial: 'The English aristocracy . . . are sent over to us every summer, regularly, in the steamers, and propose to us the day after they land'; 'These American girls carry off all the good matches. Why can't they stay in their own country?' At a serious level, racial inter-marriage is obviously out of the question. Virginia Otis and the Duke of Devonshire make a pretty enough pair in artificial fiction, but in realistic comedy Hester and Lord Illingworth are totally at odds. Even a cultural inter-marriage within an English context is too much to expect. When Illingworth tells Mrs Arbuthnot that he is willing to marry her in order to repossess himself of a share in Gerald, adding with much candour but little grace that 'there are some ambitions I shall have to surrender: high ambitions, too, if any ambition is high', Mrs Arbuthnot predictably declines. The inevitable rebuke receives the inevitable response:

ILLINGWORTH: Do tell me your reasons. They would interest me en-
               ormously.
MRS ARBUTHNOT: I have already explained them to my son.
ILLINGWORTH: I suppose they were intensely sentimental, weren't they? You
               women live by your emotions and for them. You have no
               philosophy of life.
MRS ARBUTHNOT: You are right. We women live by our emotions and for
               them. By our passions and for them, if you will. I have two
               passions, Lord Illingworth; my love for him and my hatred
               of you. You cannot kill those. They feed each other.

The central scenes of the play, those between Illingworth and Gerald, and Illingworth and Mrs Arbuthnot, are studies in lack of communication. This dismissal is the first and only instance of 'genuine communication' between the rival parties. The well-intentioned scheme of the cultural orphan, Gerald, for uniting his disparate parents is intrinsically absurd, mere lip-service to the social conventions which, for differing reasons, they both despise. Instead, Gerald himself marries, rejecting the dandy's values and espousing those of the American puritan, who also happens to be literally an orphan, and to possess a large fortune. The two orphans and the natural mother retire to 'other countries over sea, better, wiser, and less unjust'. Mrs Arbuthnot exchanges a tainted pastoral – the 'little walled-in garden' of her love for Gerald – for the wide open spaces of the democracy where suffering is given its due. As in *Lady Windermere's Fan*, the puritans recoup their vital forces in the 'country'. As in *The Way of the World*, one might also remark, it is the passionate dupe, or her Wildean equivalents, whose last resort takes the form of pastoral retreat. 'Well, friend,' says the pathetic Lady Wishfort to the delinquent Marwoud, 'you are enough to reconcile me to the bad world, or else I would retire to desarts and solitudes; and feed harmless sheep by groves and purling streams. Dear Marwoud, let us leave the world, and retire by ourselves and be shepherdesses.'[26] The comic parallel is pertinent, for, from the dandy-libertine's viewpoint, the Arbuthnots' progression from Wrockley to America amounts to little more than exchanging a rabbit-hutch for a paddock. It may not be comic, but it ought to be laughable. As far as personal development is concerned, they might as well be dead. But in the interests of completer poetic justice, and complete comic peripeteia, Wilde lets Mrs Arbuthnot imply what we already suspect – that for her, Illingworth might equally as well be dead. It is implication rather than statement, for the last line of the play supports more weight, perhaps, than it is really built to bear. Is it the sign of Mrs Arbuthnot's long-awaited emancipation from her past, or is it merely dismissive revenge? Is she finally free of Illingworth's baneful tyranny over her imagination, or is she simply pleased to turn the tables on him, so reinforcing her self-destructive bitterness? Wilde leaves the epigram to its own devices, but the ending remains consistent with his ruling comic principle. Illingworth quits the scene, defeated and insulted, not as a result of anyone's moral denunciation but as a direct result of his own spontaneous vulgarity. 'Manners before morals' indeed. Those who exploit social gestures for their own ends must expect to be judged by them. Wilde's second pseudo-libertine, like his first, is dismissed from the critical commonweal not for interfering with the puritan's standards but for compromising his own.

III. *An Ideal Husband*: Public Law and Private Morality

An Ideal Husband was conceived and partly written at a cottage at Goring-on-Thames in 1893. Douglas, whose presence there soon became disruptive, was sharing the place with Wilde, who recorded the fact on the title-page of an early draft.[27] The same draft shows Lady Chiltern congratulating herself on a childless marriage. 'I am glad now,' she says, 'that it is only on me that your disgrace and dishonour will fall.'[28] Given Wilde's propensity for constructing situations with some sort of subjective basis, these details immediately suggest special pleading. Lord Goring's apparently misogynistic advice to Lady Chiltern seems to confirm that the bisexual dandy was conducting an overhaul of his embarrassing marital situation from the security of an all-male retreat.

Such considerations have diverted attention from the play's single most important feature, that refinement of Wilde's technique which prompted Shaw to call it 'in the purest integrity a play and nothing less'.[29] True, the 'modern note' which Shaw found struck by 'Sir Robert Chiltern's assertion of the individuality and courage of his wrongdoing as against the mechanical idealism of his stupidly good wife' is unlikely still to seem modern. Indeed, it may well constitute, now, that very 'thesis' which the socio-political Fabian eye could not detect.[30] *An Ideal Husband* remains, however, the one comedy, not excepting *Earnest*, in which Wilde's full contempt for the hypocrisy of social norms, and his fear of their power, are balanced by a detached presentation of a successful and socially acceptable alternative. If the puritans, as I have suggested, are in one sense Wilde as he wished not to be, then the Chilterns' plight can be understood as the plight of the Wildes of Tite Street. But if the dandies represent Wilde as he wished to be, then the Gorings (i.e. Lord Goring and Mabel Chiltern) become the ideal Wildes: the obverse of the Chilterns in every respect, an imaginative ideal, ideally unideal and unidealising. Superficially, the play presents a series of well-worn Wildean issues: the trivialisation of life by 'serious' people; the sterility into which excessive 'purity' leads; the relationship between motive and behaviour; the conflict between social restraints and self-realisation, and between emotion and intellect; but there is no sense of an obligatory and specific 'solution'. The punning in Shaw's astute review playfully suggests the real, implicit message of the piece: that the healthy social creature knows the value of play, and finds through that knowledge the most intelligent form of seriousness.

In a certain sense, Mr Wilde is to me our only thorough playwright. He plays with everything; with wit, with philosophy, with actors and audience, with the whole theatre. Such a feat scandalises the Englishman, who can no more play with wit and philosophy than he can with a football or a cricket bat. He works at both, and has the consolation, if he cannot make people laugh, of being the best cricketer and footballer in the world. Now it is the mark of the artist that he will not work. Just as people with social ambitions will practise the meanest economies in order to live expensively; so the artist will starve his way through incredible toil and discouragement sooner than go and earn a week's honest wages. Mr Wilde, an arch-artist, is so colossally lazy that he trifles even with the work by which an artist escapes work. He distils the very quintessence, and gets as product plays which are so unapproachably playful that they are the delight of any playgoer with twopenn'orth of brains.

Four characters in the main plot provide the dramatic conflicts: Lady Chiltern, who believes that 'Circumstances should never alter principles'; Mrs Cheveley, the libertine-Machiavel; Lord Goring, who hopes never to be taken seriously, but whose philosophy of surfaces does not prevent him from uttering the most serious lines of the play; and Sir Robert Chiltern, whose features suggest 'an almost complete separation of passion and intellect, as though thought and emotion were each isolated in its own sphere through some violence of will-power'.[31] This split in Chiltern's personality is expressed by his fighting the century opportunistically in public life 'with its own weapons', while proving in his domestic life hardly less idolatrous and sentimental than his wife. Wilde presents scenes which oppose the values of the two women, of the two political careerists, of the true and false dandy, of the puritan and the true dandy, of the responsible public figure and 'the idlest man in London'. To complete this microcosm of society, he adds two representatives of the older generation, Lady Markby, and Goring's father, Lord Caversham. To complete the playful sub-plot a new character is introduced: Mabel Chiltern, the dandy-*ingénue* who possesses 'the fascinating tyranny of youth and the astonishing courage of innocence'. Her alliance with Goring holds the optimistic 'serious' conclusion in balance by stating a comic alternative, and completes the integration of main plot with sub-plot, serious with comic, dandy with society.

Although *A Woman of No Importance* is the obvious example of Wilde's reworking Restoration motifs, *An Ideal Husband* bears various traces of the heroic mode and of Hobbesian ideas dressed as cynical utilitarian morality. Chiltern and Mrs Cheveley, the two characters with the widest practical experience, agree in their estimate of 'the age', if in nothing else: it is sordid and commercial; 'its god is wealth'; it is hypocritical in its attitudes, crudely selfish in its aims and values, crooked in its methods. Indeed, public life as presented here is very little different from Hobbes's 'condition of Warre', and it is not surprising to find that Baron Arnheim's philosophy, which influenced the young Chiltern so profoundly, can be traced back to Hobbes:

> One night after dinner at Lord Radley's the Baron began talking about success in modern life as something that one could reduce to an absolutely definite science. With that wonderfully fascinating quiet voice of his he expounded to us the most terrible of all philosophies, the philosophy of power, preached to us the most marvellous of all gospels, the gospel of gold. . . . and then he told me that luxury was nothing but a background, a painted scene in a play, and that power, power over other men, power over the world, was the one thing worth having, the one supreme pleasure worth knowing, the one joy one never tired of, and that in our century only the rich possessed it.

'Covetousness of great Riches, and ambition of great Honours, are Honourable; as signs of power to obtain them,' wrote Hobbes, and '*Joy*, arising from imagination of a man's power and ability, is that exultation of the mind which is called GLORYING'.[32] Chiltern does in fact 'glory' in his misdemeanour, and refuses Goring's judgment of Arnheim as a 'scoundrel' and of his philosophy as 'a thoroughly shallow creed'. '[H]e was a man of a most subtle and refined intellect', he says. 'A man of culture, charm, distinction. One of the most intellectual men I ever met.' Goring is surprised that 'you, of all men' should have yielded to the Baron's temptation. Chiltern repudiates the charge of weakness: 'To stake all one's life on a single moment, to risk everything on one throw, whether the stake be power or pleasure, I care not – there is no weakness in that. There is a horrible, a terrible courage.'

If Chiltern's manoeuvrings recall Hobbes, his relationship with his wife recalls the absolutes of Wilde's heroic mode. There are various recognisable verbal parallels with *The Duchess of Padua*, and the essentials of the main situation amount to a reversal of those of the earlier play. In *The Duchess*, it is the woman who inculpates herself in order to remove the one obstacle preventing self-fulfilment; it is the man who rejects her; there is a public trial, at which justice is perverted; the chief Machiavel is a man. In *An Ideal Husband*, the man has committed the crime; the woman rejects him; public law is avoided; the Machiavel is a woman. Two of the settings, used for symbolic effect, are also similar: the second act of *The Duchess*, requiring 'a state room hung with tapestries of *The Masque of Venus*'; and the first act of *An Ideal Husband*, requiring a stair-well lit by a chandelier and hung with a tapestry of 'the Triumph of Love, from a design by Boucher'. Like Guido, Chiltern regards his woman as 'white' and 'spotless', a redemptive enpedestaled figure, and the reversals in the plot structure that I have just mentioned result in various heated exchanges in which the Chilterns, belabouring one another with their sex roles, change place with Guido and Beatrice.[33]

Superficially, then, Chiltern is a practical man of action who fights the century with its own weapons in order to gain himself a position that he has used in the public interest. The parallels with *The Duchess of Padua* suggest that there is also something in him of the unclubbable anarchic impulse of Wilde's romantic dramas (his self-defence before his wife sounds not unlike the Duke of Padua explaining to his Duchess the ethics of political expediency[34]). Wilde, however, clearly regards Chiltern's act as justified though culpable, and Mrs Cheveley is introduced not merely to threaten his security but also to provide a standard of comparison. She too recalls the Duke of Padua – 'You have your price, I suppose. Everybody has nowadays. The drawback is that most people are so dreadfully expensive'[35] – and her status as schemer allows her to challenge Chiltern's behaviour, even if she is incapable of evaluating his motives. Her unscrupulous methods, her cynicism, vulgarity, and disregard of human feelings and relationships do not affect the dramatic propriety of her blackmailing the imperfect Chiltern, but they do ensure that her influence is totally at the level of plot. None of her value judgements ever becomes an issue, none of her epigrams rings true, while her exploitation of conversational gambits and social situations is often crude and distasteful. The vulgarest line in the play, 'I am afraid I am not fond of girl friends', is hers. (In earlier drafts Wilde made more of this characteristic,[36] and gave her a quip worthy of the true libertine-Machiavel: 'Leave conscience to console the failure – it is the only consolation they have'.[37])

Chiltern's real quality emerges in the scene in which he confesses his 'mistake' to Goring. The two men are presented as intellectual equals. Each has his individual stance, though they are of very different kinds: active commitment as opposed to sceptical non-commitment. The characteristic balance of Wildean comedy is struck when the inactive dandy, who knows 'nothing of practical life . . . by experience' but 'something by observation', is required to intercede on Chiltern's behalf, becoming not simply theoretical counsellor but effective rescuer. In the early scene, however, Goring's role is partly to provide a conventional foil for Chiltern's modern iconoclasm, partly to embody the voice of conscience (thus short-circuiting the disapproval of the audience), and partly to infiltrate among the moral norms a scale of relative comic values, one sign of which is his ready admission of his own failings: 'There is some flaw in each one of us. (*Strolls over to the fireplace and looks at himself in the glass.*) My father tells me that even I have faults. Perhaps I have. I don't know.'

Wilde's various sketches and drafts show how his attitude towards these moral questions developed. At first he is chiefly concerned about plot: how precisely to effect Chiltern's rescue by Goring. Mrs Cheveley was to have stolen an ornament from Lady Chiltern years before. Goring was to have broken off his engagement with Mrs Cheveley when he heard of it from Lady Chiltern, and Mrs Cheveley was to have written a confession, held by Goring, in exchange for withholding of charges. This scheme would have given Mrs Cheveley a specific grievance against Lady Chiltern besides her blackmail hold over Sir Robert. It would have involved Goring in a way which might seem to prejudice his role as non-moralising actor-commentator. It would also have introduced the precedent of an appeal to public law. A second scheme would have involved interference by the Berkshires (the family from whom the jewel was stolen in the published version) after they had seen Mrs Cheveley at the Chilterns' reception. In this case, the Berkshires own the confession, which is exchanged in Act III for Chiltern's incriminating letter. The final version involves no written confession, merely a sequence of vindictive and self-seeking manoeuvres by a woman whose only grievance against Lady Chiltern is her priggishness, while her only grievance against Goring is that he discovered her unreliability soon enough to break off their engagement, which lasted 'three days – nearly'. Thus, Goring's threat in Act III to call the police is merely the equivalent of Mrs Cheveley's threat in Act I to give Chiltern up to the newspapers. More importantly, however, Wilde adds a characteristic irony. In Act II Mrs Cheveley calls on Lady Chiltern to see whether the stolen brooch, lost at the reception, has been found. Goring knows nothing of this until she defends herself from his accusations (that she made the visit specifically to insult Lady Chiltern) by telling Goring her real motive. The systematic liar is condemned from her own mouth by the one instance of her speaking the bald truth. Her last hold over the Chilterns is broken when she bungles her attempt to make Chiltern misinterpret his wife's letter to Goring. After this she simply disappears from the play, and Wilde might therefore appear to have overlooked a loose end. The only alternative, however, would be pursuit, and individual pursuit would be pointless, legal pursuit dishonest.

Instead of giving over the last act to the processes of public law, Wilde devotes it to clarifying private morality. The act is cleverly constructed to extract maximum theatrical excitement from the various disclosures, but its basis is a series of three comic trials. Lord Goring undergoes one at Mabel's hands. Alarmed at the way his proposal of marriage is progressing, he is reduced to pleading 'Do be serious, please be serious'. Lady Chiltern undergoes another, first believing that her 'foolish' letter to Goring will not require an explanation, then realising that, unless she explains it, Goring's engagement to Mabel will seem inappropriate because of his apparent liaison with Mrs Cheveley. Chiltern undergoes a third when, fresh from his triumphant speech in the House, and delighted to learn that Goring has secured the incriminating letter, he is encouraged by his wife to resign from public life as a gesture of penitence. It is this decision which elicits from the dandy his one serious 'philosopher's' speech. Goring's advice takes account of character and situation as he knows them. Though offered as a statement of fact, and sounding, therefore, like male-chauvinist doctrine, it is a shrewd assessment of the balance of the Chilterns' marriage and of their personal capacities. It is also a candid summary of the values by which Lady Chiltern has chosen to live, and by which she must hold if she is to contribute to their joint future. As such, it is one more example of those truths from which the dandy dissociates himself – 'falsehoods', as he tells his valet in Act III, being merely 'the truths of other people'. As a result of this speech, Lady Chiltern tears up her husband's resignation letter, explaining her action by rote, like a child who has just learned but not completely assimilated a new lesson:

> A man's life is of more value than a woman's. It has larger issues, wider scope, greater ambitions. Our lives revolve in curves of emotions. It is upon the lines of intellect that a man's life progresses. I have just learned this, and much more, from Lord Goring. And I will not spoil your life for you, nor see you spoil it as a sacrifice to me, a useless sacrifice!

Act IV also focuses the contrasts between the dandies and the serious people. While Gertrude Chiltern attends meetings at the Women's Liberal Union, where such Fabian topics as 'Factory Acts, Female Inspectors, the Eight Hours' Bill and the Parliamentary Franchise' are discussed, and while she takes, even more ironically, a keen interest in 'Higher Education for Women', Mabel goes to stand on her head in tableaux to assist 'an excellent charity, in aid of the Undeserving. I am the secretary', Lord Goring the president. Goring's father constantly measures him against Chiltern's standard, calling him 'heartless', 'idle', and 'good-for-nothing', while Mabel defends him: 'How can you say such a thing? Why, he rides in the Row at ten o'clock in the morning, goes to the Opera three times a week, changes his clothes at least five times a day, and dines out every night of the season. You don't call that leading an idle life, do you?' Most importantly, while Chiltern tries to conceal his lapse from his wife, Mabel is obliged to concede her fiancé's comical candour:

MABEL: You are always telling me your bad qualities, Lord Goring.
GORING: I have only told you half of them as yet, Miss Mabel!
MABEL: Are the others very bad?
GORING: Quite dreadful! When I think of them at night I go to sleep at once.
MABEL: Well, I delight in your bad qualities. I wouldn't have you part with one of them.

The Gorings and the Chilterns are also contrasted as couples. The off-hand, zany courtship of the former compares very favourably with the marriage of the latter, threatened by their earnest pretensions. 'Oh! I wouldn't marry a man with a future before him for anything under the sun', Mabel tells her sister-in-law. 'You married a man with a future, didn't you! But then Robert was a genius, and you have a noble self-sacrificing character. You can stand geniuses. I have no character at all, and Robert is the only genius I could ever bear. As a rule, I think they are quite impossible. Geniuses talk so much, don't they? Such a bad habit. And they are always thinking about themselves, when I want them to be thinking about me.' Even the moment following her acceptance of Goring is filled by free admissions, a kind of postscript to the bargaining or 'proviso' scenes in Restoration comedy:

GORING: Do you know, I was awfully afraid of being refused!
MABEL   (*looking up at him*): But you never have been refused yet by anybody, have you, Arthur? I can't imagine anyone refusing you.
GORING   (*after kissing her again*): Of course, I'm not nearly good enough for you, Mabel.
MABEL   (*nestling close to him*): I'm so glad, darling. I was afraid you were.
GORING   (*after some hesitation*): And I'm – I'm a little over thirty.
MABEL: Dear, you look weeks younger than that.
GORING   (*enthusiastically*): How sweet of you to say so! – And it is only fair to tell you that I am fearfully extravagant.
MABEL: But so am I, Arthur, so we're sure to agree.

The name of the king of Camelot, Tennyson's ideal figurehead, has passed from the parody hero of "Lord Arthur Savile's Crime" to the unworthy conventional Windermere, and now remains with the ideally unheroic Goring. Wit shrinks the Chilterns', and all, heroic protestations to their proper size.

According to Wilde's elaborate stage-directions, which describe the characters in terms of works of art, Mrs Cheveley is pastiche, 'showing the influence of too many schools', while Mabel is 'to sane people' unreminiscent of any work of art. 'But', Wilde adds, 'she is really like a Tanagra statuette, and would be rather annoyed if she were told so'; and we learn also that she has 'the apple-blossom type of English beauty'. These details are interesting, but not vital to our appreciation of the contrast implied. Mrs Cheveley freely admits that she finds being natural 'such a difficult pose to keep up', while Mabel maintains without effort a disarming manner in which sophistication and spontaneity are perfectly harmonised. In her, art and nature converge, just as in the true dandy the individual converges with society. Unlike its predecessors, *An Ideal Husband* presents these as healthy working partnerships. Admittedly, society's norms as embodied in the persons of Lord Caversham and Lady Markby do not seem very threatening, but that is perhaps the real threat of all restrictive norms. Lady Markby's blissful ignorance is a state to which it would be inconceivable for society to regress:

> LADY MARKBY: I assure you that the amount of things I and my poor sister were
>   taught not to understand was quite extraordinary. But modern
>   women understand everything, I am told.
> MRS CHEVELEY: Except their husbands. That is the one thing the modern woman
>   never understands.
> LADY MARKBY: And a very good thing, too, dear, I dare say. It might break up
>   many a happy home if they did. Not yours, I need hardly say,
>   Gertrude. You have married a pattern husband. I wish I could
>   say the same for myself.

Lady Markby warns Mabel against being 'a little too modern'; but, while Lady Chiltern is modern by virtue of her political and social activities, Mabel and Goring belong to a younger generation of the intellect, a dandiacal invention beyond the grasp of most people but first mooted by Cecil Graham in *Lady Windermere's Fan*. 'My dear boy,' rumbles Lord Augustus, 'when I was your age – '. 'But you never were, Tuppy,' comes the retort, 'and you never will be.' It is, in fact, Lord Augustus' Conservative successor, Lord Caversham, who gives the cue for the critical line which caps the play:

> MABEL: You'll stop to luncheon, Lord Caversham, won't you?
> CAVERSHAM: With pleasure, and I'll drive you down to Downing Street
>   afterwards, Chiltern. You have a great future before you, a great
>   future. Wish I could say the same for you, sir. (*To* Lord Goring)
>   But your career will have to be entirely domestic.
> GORING: Yes, father, I prefer it domestic.
> CAVERSHAM: And if you don't make this young lady an ideal husband, I'll cut
>   you off without a shilling.
> MABEL: An ideal husband! Oh, I don't think I should like that. It sounds
>   like something in the next world.

Mabel's disclaimer echoes one of Goring's serious remarks in Act II,[38] also one of Wilde's apparently pointless exchanges in Act I, restoring that opening lightness of touch. Mrs Marchmont and Lady Basildon, 'the two ladies who are known to have the most admirable husbands in London', come to Lady Chiltern's receptions because they are bored stiff. 'My Reginald', says Mrs Marchmont, 'is quite hopelessly faultless. . . . There is not the smallest element of excitement in knowing him.' Lady Basildon agrees. 'We have married perfect husbands,' they conclude, 'and we are well punished for it.' The irony is increased by Lady Chiltern's having suggested they look for a serious purpose in life, and Lady Basildon's remarking, lorgnette at the ready, 'I don't see anybody here tonight whom one could call a serious purpose.' By comparison with these two bored women looking for social playmates, the Gorings know the virtues of constructive play.

They also realise that what both Chiltern and Mrs Cheveley call 'the game of life' extends into the domestic sphere. In the dandy's relative world, nothing is surer than play, nothing safer than gambling on a calculated risk. Absolutes result merely in schisms: worship and blame, purity and filth, a civil war within the personality such as that expressed in Chiltern's features, where thought and emotion, the masculine and feminine principles, are isolated in their separate spheres 'through some violence of will-power'. For if the Gorings' marriage implies the convergence of art and nature, it also embodies that androgynous blend of personality inherent in the dramatic character of the dandy. The individualist steps outside his stage and social gender. Mabel and Goring are the only people on stage who do not speak together of what 'men' and 'women' should expect or may expect from one another.

Wilde called *Vera* 'a play not of politics but of passion', and the description fits *An Ideal Husband* almost as well. George Woodcock objected to what he took to be Wilde's specious moral scheme:

> In a circle where all are guilty, Chiltern, who has gained most by his roguery, is able to escape without punishment, and the height of his career is reached in a hypocritical speech wherein he denounces 'the whole system of modern political finance' regardless of the fact that he is one of the worst examples of its use. His duplicity gains him universal praise for integrity, and so the political farce is drawn to its usual end.[39]

It ought to be said, however, that Chiltern makes the speech before he knows of Goring's success in retrieving the letter; also, that in an early draft Wilde had him offer to resign from public life while still uncertain of his future – a far less effective sacrifice than that offered in the published version. Finally, however, political ethics in themselves are of very minor interest. Chiltern is cast as a politician because politics offers the sharpest distinction between public life and private values. Modern society hurts itself by forcing the two apart and then refusing to acknowledge the distinction. To infer private virtue from public reputation, as Lady Chiltern tries to do, is therefore unreliable and unjust. To infer public probity from personal integrity and honourable motive, as Goring does when defending Chiltern's character against Mrs Cheveley; is both just and justified, the only way of measuring public virtue. The standards of society, as Wilde had already argued in criticism, are determined by the individual's standards. Society's judgements – public opinion – often amount to no more than corporate abrogation of the responsibility to form a critical judgement. The comic dramatist's solution to so uncivilised a situation it to rely not on a judicial but on a critical élite who set up, as Barbey said the dandy inevitably would, an obligation superior to that of the law.[40] *Faute de mieux*, the dandy is the unacknowledged legislator of the world.

I suggested earlier that none of Wilde's three serious comedies reaches a model happy ending, and this is, I think, true even of *An Ideal Husband*. Mabel tells Lord Caversham that Goring can be 'what he likes', but that she wants to be 'a real wife to him'. Caversham, too pragmatic to recognise much difference between a real and an ideal spouse, is always ready to recognise 'common sense', and tells Lady Chiltern that Mabel's remark contains 'a good deal' of it. Wilde intended having Goring add, finally, 'Ah, there is love, and that is everything, father'.[41] Instead, he decided on a brief critical coda between the Chilterns after the other characters have left the stage.

LADY CHILTERN	(*leaning over the back of the chair*): Aren't you coming in, Robert?
SIR ROBERT	(*taking her hand*): Gertrude, is it love that you feel for me, or is it pity merely?
LADY CHILTERN	(*kisses him*): It is love, Robert. Love and only love. For both of us a new life is beginning.

The Chilterns are still some way behind the Gorings in self-knowledge, and there is perhaps a hint of disunity in the phrase 'both of us'; but the fact that the question is raised at all holds out more hope for their future than did the pastoral retreats in the first two comedies. The echoes of Wilde's protesting Romantic heroes have all but died away. Goring need no longer profess even token doubts about whether it is 'tragic' or 'comic' that Lady Basildon (or Lady Chiltern) married a 'perfect' husband, or that she has been 'well punished for it'. Comedy emerges unequivocally victorious, and the victory belongs to the Truewits, those conscientious dandies whose benevolent despotism maintains 'the aristocracy of the intellect' and 'the democracy of suffering' in a profitable working partnership. As Wilde wrote in 1894, shortly before completing the play:

> To the world I seem, by intention on my part, a dilettante and dandy merely – it is not wise to show one's heart to the world – and as seriousness of manner is the disguise of the fool, folly in its exquisite modes of triviality and indifference and lack of care is the robe of the wise man. In so vulgar an age as this we all need masks.[42]

In Wilde's last play, Lord Goring's 'robe' is the uniform of the younger generation of the intellect, whose dominion over the norm becomes complete.

IV. *The Importance of Being Earnest*: The Providential Pun

> The hero of the future is he who shall bravely and gracefully subdue this Gorgon of fashion and convention ["Art and the Handicraftsman"][43]

I don't really know what a Gorgon is like, but I am quite sure that Lady Bracknell is one [Jack to Algernon, *Earnest*, Act 1]

Wilde's last play, 'a trivial comedy for serious people', is the dandy's holiday, a treat for 'the few choice spirits', an idyllic trip to the utopian land of 'doing as one likes' where only reason and external authority are denied entry. The text passed through various forms and was cut from four acts to three (robbing Wilde of his revenge on Du Maurier (see Plates 2, 3, 15))[44] but these vicissitudes strengthened it and it is rightly considered his tautest and most accomplished achievement. A summary and send-up of all his major themes, whether neo-Restoration, Romantic, or Victorian, and of practically all his critical or comic antitheses, it is the imaginative synthesis of its author's career and personality, and, paradoxically, the only work with which he succeeded completely in penetrating the fortress of established morality. For Mary McCarthy, indeed, it is the culmination of Wilde's usual propensity to make himself too much at home: 'Where the usual work of art invites the spectator into its world, already furnished and habitable, Wilde's plays do just the opposite: the author invites himself and his fast opinions into the world of the spectator.'[45] No doubt Wilde would retort that, if the artist did not invite himself into the usual world, he would never be invited anywhere by anyone. Even so, Miss McCarthy's complaint can hardly be justified by *Earnest*, a work which, whatever its debts to comic tradition or its feints towards social satire, creates and exhausts its own genre. Here, no one enters except by self-admission, for the play's burden is simply 'Be thyself'.[46] Since this proposition had proved impossible in all other genres, Wilde posits absurdity as the norm in order to keep at bay those 'other people' whose opinions are 'vulgar' and 'impossible'.

Although the play contains elements of comic autobiography and parody confessional, it is primarily a highly original fusion of Wilde's idiosyncratic redemptive comedy and his basically anarchic assumptions. Algernon, the confirmed Bunburyist, and Jack, the reluctant guardian, are finally confronted with their *alter ego*s only to see them dissolve hilariously into their actual selves. The author scours the realm of his 'infernal Arcadia'[47] like a benevolent maenad, dismembering his various literary aliases and tossing their limbs to anyone who can laugh. From this intoxicating, self-regenerating, self-fulfilling laughter only Lady Bracknell is excluded. Laughter in one who is 'a monster without being a myth' would clearly be out of place. Those to whom the proper aim of life is to 'gorgonise' the world with 'a stony British stare'[48] end up, Wilde says, by turning themselves into stone. For Lady Bracknell makes too many mistakes to be the bulky 'goddess' of Mary McCarthy's vision. Once, perhaps, she might have filled the role of goddess – possibly of all-knowing Athena, 'whose white and stainless bosom bears the sign Gorgonian',[49] mistress and arbiter of the steep heights of London society. But no one can believe in a divinity who is forced to pay for information, obliged to travel by a luggage train, and who seems as much at the mercy of the *deus ex machina* as the merest mortal. Equally clearly, she makes too few mistakes to be really human. Pretending not to be a person, earnestly saving face, she alone grows no wiser and gets no fun.

The element of self-parody in *Earnest* has long been realised, although its extent was not fully known until the publication of a limited edition of Wilde's drafts,[50] and, more recently, of the four-act version originally prepared for rehearsal.[51] For once, external rather than internal pressures edited Wilde's autobiographical touches out of the published work. George Alexander wanted to put on a curtain-raiser, and so Wilde cut two characters – a dispensable rustic gardener and a shady solicitor, the latter being his revenge on Du Maurier (see Plate 2). With the solicitor went the most specific references to Wilde's own debts: the writ from the Savoy Hotel (Wilde's unpaid bill there prevented all possibility of flight before the trial in 1895), the huge supper bill at Willis's (where Wilde often fed Douglas, 'Perrier-Jouet' being his favourite brand of champagne[52]), and the account at a Bond Street jeweller (Wilde reminded Douglas, in *De Profundis*, of the sleeve-links he had had made for him[53]). The 'private cigarette case' with its tell-tale inscription was multiplied at the trials,[54] while the gold-tipped cigarettes despised by Algernon, now that they have become cheap, were always beyond the means of the brainless Lord Alfred of *A Woman of No Importance* except when he was in debt.

The earlier drafts also contain more explicit literary self-parody. Cecily twice refers to the doctrine of "The Decay of Lying" to justify her indulging in what Wilde had there termed 'lying for some immediate personal advantage – lying with a moral purpose as it is usually called'.[55] She also quotes one of the "Phrases and Philosophies for the Use of the Young", given to the *Chameleon*, an Oxford undergraduate magazine, about the time that Wilde completed the play: 'Believe me, Miss Prism, it is only the superficial qualities that last. Man's deeper nature is soon found out.'[56] Prism's response – 'Cecily! I do not know where you get such ideas. They are certainly not to be found in any of the educational books that I have procured for you' – and Cecily's retort – 'Are there ever any ideas in educational books, dear [Miss] Prism? I fear not. I get my ideas in the garden' – quantify not only the tutorial relationship between the women but also the studied precociousness of the whole work. 'In examinations', Wilde had quipped, 'the foolish ask questions that the wise cannot answer,'[57] and in *Earnest* life itself becomes a burlesque exam. Prism's confusion of a book with a baby (fatal in a governess), the Canon's ineptitude with metaphor (crucial in a cleric), and Jack's ridiculous *viva voce* at the hands of Lady Bracknell, the 'really affectionate mother' who is actually his aunt, all tend to confirm that, if ever the older generation had the secret of life, they have long since lost it, and that it can only be regained by the 'experimental' approach, a prime example of which is Bunburying. Even Gwendolen, who was brought up 'to be short-sighted' and who attends the lectures of the

University Extension scheme, undermines the idea of Higher Education for Women – or of formal education for anybody – by never coming away 'without having been excessively admired'.

The three-act version preserves a number of such echoes, and their diverse origins testify to the flexibility, or restlessness, of Wilde's mirror-gazing. Algy, the experienced Bunburyist stammering his passion to Cecily, quotes from Darlington's declaration to Lady Windermere. The scene is even written to sound like an actor 'drying', while in Darlington's speech we can also detect the seed of Cecily's imaginary engagement: 'I love you – love you as I have never loved any living thing. From the moment I met you I loved you, loved you blindly, adoringly, madly! You did not know it then – you know it now.' What Algernon's speech does not owe to Darlington has been borrowed from the Basil of the first *Dorian Gray:* 'I quite admit that I adored you madly, extravagantly, absurdly,' he told Dorian; and the 1891 text continues, 'you became to me the visible incarnation of that unseen ideal whose memory haunts us artists like an exquisite dream.'[58] But the parody runs deeper than dialogue. Convinced, perhaps, that its impossible relationships could be resolved only in farce, Wilde overhauls *A Woman of No Importance* to create a dramatic structure in which the parallels with Restoration comedy are finally explicit,[59] and where the moral tolerance of redemptive comedy can be relaxed. The duties of the dandy-mediator are taken over by Providence,[60] and Providence, here, is only another name for personality. To perfect this unlikely equation, Wilde plumps up Lady Caroline Pontefract to make Lady Bracknell; demotes Archdeacon Daubeny into Canon Chasuble; turns Gerald, the aristocrat's bastard, into a Justice of the Peace, giving him a pastoral maiden as ward, a profligate *alter ego*, and comically murky origins; turns Illingworth, his libertine father, into Algernon, his 'wicked' younger brother; and shrinks Mrs Arbuthnot, his guilt-ridden mother, into Miss Prism, his ward's chaperone and tutor, the maiden lady whose youthful error with a baby is the crux of the plot. The false *dénouement* completes the dramatic prank: 'Miss Prism, more is restored to you than this hand-bag. I was the baby you placed in it. . . . Unmarried! I do not deny that is a serious blow. But after all, who has the right to cast a stone against one who has suffered? Cannot repentance wipe out an act of folly? Why should there be one law for men, and another for women? Mother, I forgive you.' Jan Gordon has argued that the search for historical, or family, origins is central to Victorian fiction, and has pointed out instances of the search in Wilde's tales.[61] The theory might be extended to *Earnest*, for the sense of psychological disunity or incompleteness which gave rise to such a search is resolved in Wilde's last play with an originality that fully justifies his claim to have subjectified the drama to an unprecedented degree.[62]

One further echo of *A Woman of No Importance* is relevant here. The dandy, Mrs Allonby, had married a pattern Victorian husband whose chin was 'quite, quite square', and, finding herself 'horribly deceived in Ernest', had projected a wholly different sort of Ideal Man. Wilde's last play reverses the situation. Both girls become engaged to an imaginary Earnest. 'We live in an age of ideals,' says Gwendolen, pompously, 'and my ideal has always been to love someone of the name of Ernest.' When Jack, whom she likes, discovers that he was christened Ernest after his soldierly father, she is satisfied. She lives and loves by appearances, and Jack, as Algernon says, is 'the most earnest-looking person I ever saw in my life'. For Jack, being 'earnest' means simply being who he is: Ernest. Cecily, on the other hand, has become engaged in her private fictional world to Jack's 'wicked younger brother', Ernest, so that her romance, too, parodies a Victorian fictional stereotype. When Algernon, wooing her as Ernest, is revealed to be Jack's real younger brother, even though not named Ernest, and shows, if not wickedness, at least a rampant propensity towards self-indulgence and a healthy disregard for all those virtues most often invoked by Miss Prism, Cecily also is satisfied. For her, the character of the 'wicked younger brother', the character which stirred her imagination, is more important than his name. In this way, all four bring their ideal into working relationship with reality. Algernon and Jack find that they have been living out the essential truth unwares. Cecily and Gwendolen come to relish the approximate embodiment of their airy ideals. Discipline, idealism, convention, or mere habit may impose themselves on us and hinder our development; but our fantasies and self-projections, Wilde suggests, are every bit as much in earnest as our public gestures, poses, or undertakings. Imagination is the real symptom of a healthy life: 'People never think of cultivating a young girl's imagination. It is the great defect of modern education.'[63]

Thus Cecily's references to "The Decay of Lying" were not without their thematic point. The 'telling of beautiful untrue things' determines the action of the play. The higher reality is reached here through falsehood, 'lying'. If the artist's labours can be seen as a 'gallant attempt to teach Nature her proper place', the creative individual is no less gallant in trying to teach Society hers. Perhaps that is why Shaw thought Earnest a step backwards — could not believe, in fact, that Wilde had not written it earlier and somehow kept it unsold.[64] For the play shows that while Society, like Nature, 'has good intentions', she can 'seldom carry them out'. Recognising in instincts her own murky past and in imagination her own embarrassing and voluble bastard, Society plays the role of 'a really affectionate mother' and tries to overlay them. But in farce, the latter-day Feast of Fools, they can spring free. Farce places fate in the artist's hand, and with this tool he shapes Dionysiac revel into Apollonian perfection of form. It may be a coincidence that the contemporary slang term used in Wilde's circle to refer to homosexual revels was 'wearing vine-leaves in the hair'. (Beardsley represented Wilde, in the frontispiece to John Davidson's Plays, as a placid Dionysus who seems to have his feet tied together; see Plate 8.) It is clear enough that here — 'at last!' — the individual's conscious and unconscious motives, idea and instinct, work in secret coalition to produce that ever-alluring combination of 'personality' and 'perfection': 'being earnest'. For the artist, Wilde had written earlier, 'there is no escape from the bondage of the earth: there is not even the desire of escape'.[65] The same might be said of the artist and the bondage of the self. Even for the non-artist, escape from the self may finally prove impossible, whether one tries to identify one's self with the authority of convention or with those anarchic spirits who strike out against it. 'Disobedience,' however, 'is the first step in the growth of a man or a nation', and disobedience, irresponsibility, and contradiction lead here to universal harmony and happiness. The only character who gains nothing is the one who thinks only of the rules – Lady Bracknell, Society herself.

Farce is thus the ultimate refinement of pastoral, the new idyll of self, the egotist's Nirvana. The 'child-philosopher' of Wilde's first set of fairy tales is replaced by its adult equivalent, the fearless *ingénue* with 'the fascinating tyranny of youth'. In that garden where romance buds and learning withers, and where she had first rejected fact for fiction, Cecily falls from art into life; tames the rake; unites town and country, 'science' and 'sentiment'; reconciles the demure spinster of Hebraism with the reluctant bachelor of Hellenism; 'explodes' vice and virtue as if they were no more than the dull people's Bunburys: 'I hope you have not been leading a double life, pretending to be wicked and being really good all the time; that would be hypocrisy.' She knows by instinct that, just as 'seriousness of manner is the disguise of the fool', so 'folly in its exquisite modes of triviality and indifference and lack of care is the robe of the wise'. She also senses, despite her distaste for German and Political Economy, that Lady Bracknell's reactionary notion of education – 'Ignorance is like a delicate, exotic fruit: touch it, and the bloom is gone' – is all wrong, not for social but for personal reasons. Fruits, even delicate exotic fruits, were not made just to be looked at, nor are young girls necessarily 'green'. Formal education may often amount to no more than gazing at the ignorance of others, but there is no more delicious prospect than biting into one's own ignorance. In this, Algernon is at one with her, both of them being as far ahead of Jack and Gwendolen as those two are ahead of the older generation. Lady Bracknell is alarmed to see Jack 'displaying signs of triviality' (he is kissing Gwendolen), but he knows at last 'the vital Importance of Being Earnest'. Chasuble is horrified at the 'disgraceful luxury of the age' as exemplified by Ernest's colossal supper bill: 'We are far from Wordsworth's plain living and high thinking', he sighs. But Algernon knows how far behind the times the Canon is in his estimate of the progress of sin. When he asks Cecily whether she will make it her 'mission' to 'reform' him, a suggestion to which she does not take kindly, she questions whether he ever was good. 'Oh,' he replies, 'everyone is good until they learn to talk.'[66] It is the social conversationalist's account of the fortunate fall. If we were not bad, we would never have the chance of talking to Cousin Cecily, and it is this chance which enables Algernon to talk himself into harmony with a newly completed family, newly completed feelings, and a new awareness of himself. Lastly, Lady Bracknell objects that 'in families of high social position strange coincidences are not supposed to occur', but Cecily, the orphan, wins hands down. Society discovers that she has a large sum in the Funds; but she also possesses 'those really solid qualities' that 'last and improve with time'. She knows that the basis of family, as of personal, life – always in its ideal manifestation – is knowing, showing, and living who you really are.

By coincidence, Brandon Thomas, in his non-intellectual romp, *Charley's Aunt* (1892), had already made explicit on stage an idea which remains implicit in Wilde's intellectual farce: namely, the undergraduate idyll. A letter written after his release from Reading gives the final gloss on the 'fortunate fall' into self-knowledge which is celebrated in *Earnest*. It is addressed to a Radley schoolboy, Louis Wilkinson: 'I envy you going to Oxford; it is the most flower-like time of one's life. One sees the shadows of things in silver mirrors. Later on, one sees the Gorgon's head, and one suffers, because it does not turn one to stone.[67]

Hindsight has generally considered *Earnest* prophetic of the downfall to come, but its status as a classic owes much to the removal of precisely those references capable of direct biographical interpretation. The first night, with the green carnation buttonholes, Queensberry's bouquet of vegetables, and the rumours circulating about Wilde and Douglas, already bore sufficient traces of an in-joke without explicit references on stage. Wilde must have realised this when preparing to publish the play in 1899. No one was now interested, if ever they had been, in the precise form of the indiscretions which put him into prison, and it was the three-act version that he printed.[68]

Two years earlier, in *De Profundis*, he had anatomised with vivid detail the unamusing character of his own Bunburys – or rather, Douglas', since Wilde seems always to have been cast as the unwilling host. 'How I used to toy with that tiger, Life,' he reflected; but, as the lion-cub in Aeschylus's *Agamemnon*, reared up by a lord in his own house, only turned on him and destroyed him,[69] so Wilde found the tiger breaking in on the elegant social game. It is usually assumed that this symbolically apt climax to his dramatic career is somehow the last word; that the antinomian, having run the gamut of irreverence, could progress no further. But, without the trials, he would have continued writing, either in the vein of *Earnest*, or in some other. For he had not relinquished all of his interest in more Romantic structures, and just at the time that *Earnest* was begun he was offering George Alexander a scenario in which, as he put it, '*I want the sheer passion of love to dominate everything. No morbid self-sacrifice. No renunciation. A sheer flame of love between a man and a woman.*'[70] Like the Romantic verse dramas of 1893 (also devoted to 'the sheer passion of love' between a man and a woman) which Douglas interrupted, this scheme may have more in it of wishful thinking than of committed artistic intent. But it is always dangerous to be too categorical about Wilde's motives. His work depended more on imagination than on daily experience – 'to most of us the real life is the life we do not lead'[71] – and utopian farce is no more literal or comprehensive a reflection of life than Romantic drama. Wilde encouraged posterity to regard his life as an art work, but the timeliness of its catastrophe tends to obscure the fact that the work continued beyond the point at which the audience ceased to watch. Writing to Robert Ross in 1896, after the refusal of his second bid for a remission of sentence, Wilde recognised this: 'I know that when plays last too long, spectators tire. My tragedy has lasted far too long: its climax is over: its end is mean; and I am quite conscious that when the end comes I shall return an unwelcome visitant to a world that does not want me.'[72] Before this happened, one further document of individualism emerged, to alter the author's relationship to all its predecessors.

7 Resolution

I. *De Profundis*[1]: The Messiah as Artist

> The axis of reality runs solely through the egotistic places – they are strung upon it like so many beads
>
> [William James].[2]

This remarkable letter brings Wilde's artistic career full circle. Although written in a 'subjective' form and ostensibly private, it is also something of an open letter. Its declamatory tone often seems to anticipate publication, and it would have been surprising if the individualist had not reserved the right to reconduct eventually his own trial.

Towards the end of the letter, Wilde recalls having sat in the dock 'on the occasion of . . . Lockwood's appalling denunciation of me. . . . Suddenly it occurred to me, "*How splendid it would be if I was saying all this about myself!*" '[3] As a result of this conviction, and of Douglas' eighteen-month silence, Wilde wrote with uncharacteristic passion. What he produced is a curious hybrid, part jeremiad, part Dunciad, and part formal confessions.

The central section on Christ is consciously poetic, but for the most part *De Profundis* is a critical work in both senses of that word. It takes pleasure in finding fault. But it also tries to perceive things in their true relations, to be 'a disinterested endeavour' to see 'the object as in itself it really is'; and, as in the rest of Wilde's criticism, the object under scrutiny is Wilde. 'It is the most important letter of my life,' he told More Adey, 'as it will deal ultimately with my future mental attitude towards life, with the way in which I desire to meet the world again, with the development of my character, with what I have lost, what I have learned, and what I hope to arrive at. At last I see a real goal towards which my soul can go simply, naturally, and rightly. . . . My whole life depends on it.'[4]

The only two topics that Wilde feels he could write on in the future are the topics considered in the letter: 'Christ, as the precursor of the Romantic movement in life', and 'the Artistic life considered in its relation to Conduct'. In fact, Wilde treats them as mutually dependent: the latter leads into the former and gives him the pattern for his own future.

Augustine's *Confessions* incorporated as metaphor the Prodigal Son's story.[5] Wilde's also chronicle a foolhardy desertion, not of God but of Art. After wasting his substance with Douglas, Wilde becomes literally and morally bankrupt and languishes in sorrow and disgrace. The experience grants him a reunion with his art, if only in vision; and it is a reunion of a totally unexpected kind. Prison becomes a formative educational experience: 'I want to get to the point when I shall be able to say, quite simply and without affectation, that the two great turning-points in my life were when my father sent me to Oxford, and when society sent me to prison.'[6] Prison's lesson is humility, but Wilde's conception of humility is idiosyncratic: it leads straight on to art. 'The artistic life is simple self-development. Humility in the artist is his frank acceptance of all experiences.'[7] Wilde now perceives the incompleteness of his former philosophy, the new Hellenism. Pain and sorrow, which it rejected, now seem truly self-expressive, and since 'Truth in Art is the unity of the thing with itself . . . the soul made incarnate', there is no truth comparable to sorrow.[8] The 'truth of masks' is social truth. 'What is interesting about people in good society . . . is the mask that each one of them wears, not the reality that lies behind the mask.'[9] For the social outcast there is no mask, thus 'subjective form' and subjective reality are all that remain.

The new truth absorbs Wilde so completely – 'I am now far more of an individualist than I ever was. Nothing seems to me of the smallest importance except what one gets out of oneself'– that he inadvertently reinterprets one of his own prose poems, "The Artist", giving it a meaning contrary to that originally intended. In 1894, it was the bronze image of '*The Sorrow that endureth for Ever*' that the artist had melted down in order to fashion instead '*The Pleasure that abideth for a Moment*'.[10] In 1897, quoting from memory, Wilde melts down passing pleasure to make lasting sorrow.[11]

This is only one of a series of reversals by which the artist returned to his earlier Romantic attitudes. When he entered prison, Wilde says, people told him to try to forget who he was, and then where he was. It was 'ruinous advice', because

> to deny one's experiences is to put a lie into the lips of one's own life. It is no less than a denial of the Soul. For just as the body absorbs things of all kinds . . . and converts them into swiftness and strength . . . so the Soul, in its turn, has its nutritive functions also, and can transform into noble moods of thought and passions of high import, what in itself is base, cruel, degrading: nay more, may find in these its most august modes of assertion, and can often reveal itself most perfectly through what was intended to desecrate or destroy.[12]

Between this passage and the utopian passage from "The Critic as Artist" which it echoes,[13] Wilde's personal experiences have turned him from an avowedly critical ideal to an avowedly emotional one: the 'democracy of suffering' has overrun the 'aristocracy of the intellect'.[14]

A similar *volte-face* is expressed by Wilde's contradictory self-estimates in the letter. 'I was a man who stood in symbolic relations to the art and culture of my age. I had realised this for myself at the very dawn of my manhood, and had forced my age to realise it afterwards. . . . Byron was a symbolic figure, but his relations were to the passion of his age and its weariness of passion. Mine were to something more noble, more permanent, of more vital issue, or larger scope.'[15] The cadence is familiar; and the 'something', as we might infer from Lord Goring's advice to Lady Chiltern,[16] is intellect. Again, however, prison effects a change, and Wilde quotes from himself to indicate its nature. 'I have said of myself that I was one who stood in symbolic relations to the art and culture of my age. There is not a single wretched man in this wretched place who does not stand in symbolic relations to the very secret of life. For the secret of life is suffering.'[17]

The key to these radical changes lies in Wilde's interpretation of Christ's personality. This, as he observes, was foreshadowed in his earlier work – notably in the fairy tales – and he recalls with pleasure having written in "The Soul of Man" that 'he who would lead a Christ-like life must be entirely and absolutely himself', also his remark to Gide that there was nothing that Christ had said 'that could not be transferred immediately into the sphere of Art, and find there its complete fulfilment'.[18] These two ideas form the basis for the new aesthetics of life.

De Profundis sees a return to the mode of the heroic anarchist martyr, the figure who sins through excess of passion, knows brief moments of ecstasy, and suffers the consequences. Wilde had always cast a woman in this demanding role. Now cast in it in his own person, with no literary mask and none of the right appurtenances, he tells Douglas bitterly, 'Everything about my tragedy has been hideous, mean, repellent, lacking in style.'[19] Yet there is one mitigating factor: the example of Christ. Having reached a true perception of Christ as one whose place is 'with the poets' – a true artist, an individualist, an antinomian, 'leader of all the lovers' – Wilde can come to terms with his own unshapely Passion. At last there is an artistic point of reference. For Christ, Wilde shows, had many of the Romantic artist's qualities. He held up children as 'the type of what people should try to become'. He thought life 'changeful, fluid, active, and that to allow it to be stereo-typed into any form was death'. He had no patience with 'the dull lifeless mechanical systems that treat people as if they were things, and so treat everyone alike. . . . For him there were no laws: there were exceptions merely.' Contrary to all the social pressures of the time, he 'preached the enormous importance of living for the moment', and 'those whom he saved from their sins are saved simply for beautiful moments in their lives', Mary Magdalen and the Prodigal Son, for instance: 'I feel quite certain about it.'[20] Most importantly, Christ, like the archetypal Romantic artist, set love and the imagination above everything. Indeed, his life equated the two, for 'he realised in the entire sphere of human relations that imaginative sympathy which in the sphere of Art is the sole secret of creation'.[21] This identification of love with imagination is so complete as to perform an artistic miracle:

To the artist, expression is the only mode under which he can conceive life at all.

To him what is dumb is dead. But to Christ it was not so. With a width and wonder of imagination that fills one almost with awe, he took the entire world of the inarticulate, the voiceless world of pain, and made of himself its eternal mouthpiece. . . . And feeling, with the artistic nature of one to whom Sorrow and Suffering were modes through which he could realise his conception of the Beautiful, that an idea is of no value till it becomes incarnate and is made an image, he makes of himself the image of the Man of Sorrows, and as such has fascinated and dominated Art as no Greek god ever succeeded in doing.[22]

In being tragic hero, he is also consummate tragic artist: life and art-work become one and the same. 'The strange figures of poetic drama and ballad are made by the imagination of others, but out of his own imagination did Jesus of Nazareth create himself.'[23]

As might be expected of the 'precursor of the Romantic movement in life', Christ possesses that combination of 'perfection and personality' which had formed the dominant note of the English Renaissance, 'our new Romantic movement', as of the movement's poetic precursor, Keats. To complete the chain of echoes, Wilde had already likened Keats to Christ as early as 1885 in his "Sonnet on the Sale of Keats's Love Letters".[24]

Wilde's new stand involves adjustments of earlier critical truths, even of those in the English Renaissance lecture. Surely, as Wilde said, 'medievalism' belongs 'not to time but to temperament', for the Greek in him is wholly overthrown. Now he regrets that 'Christ's own renaissance' was 'interrupted and spoiled by the dreary classical Renaissance'. Once, a Renaissance actor, Mr W. H., had seemed to prefigure Romanticism by his union of life with art in the artistic personality. Christ is more comprehensive. 'There is nothing in the entire cycle of Greek tragedy' to touch his life, that 'most wonderful of poems', for 'pity and terror';[25] while 'it is always a source of pleasure and awe to me' (Wilde completes the reversal by saying it) 'to remember that the ultimate survival of the Greek Chorus, lost elsewhere to art, is to be found in the servitor answering the priest at Mass'.[26]

The new Hellenism which overthrew Catholicism in *Poems* now yields to a reassertion of religious feeling, if not, yet, of orthodox faith. 'For, sweet, to feel is better than to know', wrote the Keatsian apprentice in 1881. To this ideal succeeded the ideal of the all-knowing critic. Now, by virtue of 'Sorrow' and 'Suffering', Wilde rejects the critic's ideal and reaches the fulfilment of the committed Romantic individualist. Christ's personality replaces Hegel's philosophic principle as the best expression of all-inclusiveness: 'Since his coming the history of each separate individual is, or can be made, the history of the world.'[27] If Wilde was aware of the importance of Christian metaphor to Romantic philosophy, particularly to the *peregrinatio* towards perfect knowledge, he never alludes to it. The message of *De Profundis* is wholly anti-rational: not *cogito ergo sum*, but *doleo ergo sum*.

II.   *The Ballad of Reading Gaol*: Art and Anonymity

Considering in *De Profundis* his literary future, Wilde concluded:

> Perhaps there may come into my art also, no less than into my life, a still deeper note, one of greater unity of passion, and directness of impulse. . . . I cannot put my sufferings into any form they took, I need hardly say. Art only begins where Imitation ends. But something must come into my work, of fuller harmony of words perhaps, of richer cadences, of more curious colour-effects, of simpler architectural-order, of some aesthetic quality at any rate.[28]

The hope was to remain unfulfilled. The true note of modern art is 'the cry of Marsyas'[29] and the *Ballad of Reading Gaol* re-echoes with it. Closer to 'Imitation' than anything else written by Wilde, the poem contains some striking and cogent stanzas, but is totally bereft of 'richer cadences' or 'more curious colour-effects'. Its architecture is not so much 'simpler' as non-existent, at least in the sense of a coherent and self-sufficient artistic plan. 'But surely you would admit', says Ernest in "The Critic as Artist", 'that the great poems of the early world, the primitive, anonymous collective poems, were the result of the imagination of races, rather than the imagination of individuals?' 'Not when they became poetry', Gilbert replies. 'Not when they received a beautiful form. For there is no art where there is no style, and no style where there is no unity, and unity is of the individual.'[30] There is a melancholy inevitability about the application of this to the *Ballad*. Wilde takes upon himself the burden which, in *De Profundis*, he had identified as Christ's peculiar triumph: the articulation of 'the voiceless world of pain'. He chooses as his subject the outcast among outcasts, the 'exception', the one prisoner who, because he has inexplicably killed 'the thing he loves', has 'got to swing'. But by a final instance of self-extension the poem argues that this exceptional individual is really only a symbol for that very type which thinks him most notoriously exceptional – namely, the majority, the virtuous or wicked unimprisoned: 'For each man kills the thing he loves'. The poem is less the apology of one who could not speak for himself than an elegy for universal innocence which incorporates both the poet's own acknowledge-ment of individual guilt and his belief in the complicity of society in all criminal acts.

It therefore suffers, as Wilde admitted, from a divided artistic purpose. In one sense, he is writing an 'anonymous collective poem' because he writes on behalf of all the nameless inmates of the Gaol. On the other hand, he writes as the outcast artist (when preparing the French translation, he explained the meaning of the word 'outcast' to his translator by mentioning Byron), and even such a detail as his frequent use of the pronoun 'one' is enough to compromise his anonymity. No doubt this mixture of faceless outcast and one-time individualist accurately reflects Wilde's status at Reading, most of all in his own eyes; but in literary terms it defeats its own ends. Literature keeps breaking in, and the imagery, stanza form, and subject of "The Rime of the Ancient Mariner" and Hood's "The Dream of Eugene Aram" bear witness to the artist's imperfect, if persistent, self-consciousness.[31]

Writing to Ross in October 1898, Wilde thought 'bits of the poem very good now. But I will never again out-Kipling Henley.' Whether this was a regret or a resolution is not clear, but shortly afterwards he resumed 'With much of your criticism I agree. The poem suffers under the difficulty of a divided aim in style. Some is realistic, some romantic: some poetry, some propaganda. I feel it keenly, but as a whole I think the production interesting: that it is interesting from more points of view than one is artistically to be regretted.'[32] The central problem may be summarised by reversing Gilbert's analysis: only individualism can accomplish artistic unity; only artistic unity can produce style; and without style there can be no art. In the first letter to Ross from which I quoted, Wilde developed an image from De Profundis which embodies the difficulties to be encountered in the unwritten and, as yet, probably unconceived poem. 'On the other side of the prison wall are some poor black soot-smirched trees that are just breaking out into buds of an almost shrill green. I know quite well what they are going through. They are finding expression.'[33] It is an uncharacteristic image, and it bodes ill for artistic work: 'One touch of Nature may make the whole world kin, but two touches of Nature will destroy any work of Art.'[34] Ten years before his own attempt at poetic realism, Wilde had noted of Henley's poems that such phrases as 'the green sky's minor thirds' provided 'a very refreshing bit of affectation in a volume where there is so much that is natural'.[35] In the Ballad also there are many artificial touches — echoes from Wilde's poem "The Harlot's House", from the fairy tales, from the smartly paced irony of book reviews and comic or critical dialogue — but they are ill at ease beside the imitation of Henley's realist manner in those very hospital poems of which Wilde had spoken in 1888, and this manner is in turn compromised by lofty literary imagery reminiscent of Wilfred Scawen Blunt's prison sonnets, In Vinculis.[36] Under these circumstances, the identification of the author on the title-page as 'C.3.3.' is an affectation, since most if not all of those likely to buy the book would realise who had written it. No doubt the pseudonym was practical — 'I see it is my name that terrifies', Wilde commented.[37] However, choosing the voiceless mask that society had clapped on him rather than resorting to complete anonymity suggests that individualism, far from flourishing more strongly than before, is faltering or fading away. Prison, like Baudelaire's opium, gave to the extraordinary mind extraordinary insights, while removing the capacity to make effective artistic use of them.

'The articulate utterances of men and things', Wilde wrote in De Profundis, had ceased to interest him. 'The Mystical in Art, the Mystical in Life, the Mystical in Nature — this is what I am looking for.'[38] But there is nothing mystical either about Wilde's post-prison life, as far as we know it, or about the *Ballad*. The nearest we get to mysticism is the assertion that the murderer's heart, rather than corrupting the earth in which it lies and tainting 'each simple seed they sow', would actually quicken them to greater beauty: 'the red rose would but blow more red / The white rose whiter blow. / Out of his mouth a red, red rose! / Out of his heart a white.' However, the irrelevant suggestion of Burns and the echoes of "The Fisherman and his Soul" and "The Nightingale and the Rose" are more Romantic than Symbolist; so is the reference to Tannhäuser, last of a series of fragmentary allusions throughout the tales: 'For who can say in what strange way, / Christ brings His will to light, / Since the barren staff the pilgrim bore / Bloomed in the great Pope's sight?'[39]

Ross evidently disliked the Romantic passages, but Wilde felt that they balanced the realistic ones – 'I can't always be "banging the tins"' he objected – and no doubt the poem would be uncharacteristic without them. For, like *De Profundis* in a critical context, the *Ballad* brings Wilde back to a point resembling that from which he started, and yet removed from it. The poetic fallacy of the roses springing from the sinner's corpse is not only a reminiscence of the posthumous blessing accorded to the young pagan Fisherman, but also the final echo of *Poems*. 'O we are born too late!' the last Endymion had cried. The figures of Greek legend know 'the far Lethaean spring / . . . Where one whose feet with tired wandering / Are faint and broken may take heart and go, / And from those dark depths cool and crystalline / Drink, and draw balm, and sleep for sleepless souls, and anodyne.'[40] But we who are born too late 'oppress our natures, God or Fate / Is our enemy, we starve and feed / On vain repentance. . . . / What balm for us in bruisèd poppy seed / Who crowd into one finite pulse of time / The joy of infinite love and the fierce pain of infinite crime?' Clearly, there is none. At the end of the poem, the ecstatic lover had envisioned a mystical reunion with nature: 'Methinks no leaf would ever bud in spring, / But for the lovers' lips that kiss, the poets' lips that sing'. This finds its hollow echo in the *Ballad* and *De Profundis*, where the lover has become one with the murderer and the poet's voice has faltered. If 'new splendour' is still to come to the grass and 'new glory to the flower', they will do so not through any Pantheist or mystical doctrine, but simply by the poet's leaving his cell for 'the visible world' where grass and flowers, which had to be imagined in prison, can be seen and touched: Wilde's last return to the 'concrete'.

> I tremble with pleasure when I think that on the very day of my leaving prison both the laburnums and the lilacs will be blooming in the gardens, and that I shall see the wind stir into restless beauty the swaying gold of the one, and make the other toss the pale purple of its plumes so that all the air shall be Arabia for me . . . There is not a single colour hidden away in the chalice of a flower, or the curve of a shell, to which, by some subtle sympathy with the very soul of things, my nature does not answer. Like Gautier, I have always been one *pour qui le monde visible existe*.[41]

There is more of Wilde's essence in these lines than in any of his early pantheism or his late determination to seek out 'the Mystical'.

Yet, if the Catholic-Hellenist tension first evident in *Poems* was never resolved in his work and was only concluded by supreme unction, the *Ballad* and *De Profundis* are unanimous on one point. Both present the protagonists of Wilde's early writing—pastoral hero, artist-martyr, passionate individualist—in their last apotheosis: the 'Phrygian Faun'[42] who does not, like the Apollonian 'great artist' of Wilde's Hellenist period, 'sing' with serene, willed utterance 'because he chooses', but cries out 'because he must'.

Pater argued that 'all art constantly aspires towards the condition of music',[43] and Wilde's work suggests a corollary to this proposition—that the artist aspires to it in his own person: 'If my heart must break / Dear love, for your sake, / It will break in music, I know, / Poets' hearts break so.'[44] In the context of *De Profundis*, the 'you' of this self-regarding lyric would no longer be Lily Langtry but Wilde's 'soul'. Truth in art may indeed be 'the unity of the thing with itself', so that sorrow is incomparably true. But pain and sorrow are not synonymous, however Wilde may have striven to equate them. One might equally argue that 'the unity of the thing itself' is as apt a definition of the state of nature as of truth in art; and it was to this 'condition' that the artist, flayed of his artistic and social aspirations, inevitably turned, progressing (or regressing) beyond 'the articulate utterances of men and things'[45]—beyond all utterance, in fact, except the most spontaneous. The 'purple pall' and 'mask of noble sorrow' which could have made tragedy bearable belonged on stage, as Wilde admitted. 'Life cheats us with shadows, like a puppet-master . . . We come across some noble grief that we think will lend the purple dignity of tragedy to our days, but it passes away from us, and things less noble take its place.'[46] The critic fulfilled his own prediction. Instead of tragic death, fit ending for a life allegedly brilliant in its approximation to a classic literary form, there ensued after Reading a shapeless, largely aimless existence, ignominiously dependent on friends. The possibility first implied in the fairy tales, later articulated in passing in "The Decay of Lying", and pushed to its conclusion in *De Profundis*—the possibility that 'the return to Nature would come to mean', for a receptive temperament, 'simply the advance to a great personality'[47]—is raised only to be laid again. When illness curtailed further pain and solitude some two years later, even Ross felt that it had been 'for the best'.[48]

'Life,' after all, 'is terribly deficient in form.'[49] 'It is said that all martyrdoms seemed mean to the lookers-on. The nineteenth century is no exception to the general rule.'[50] The lookers-on no doubt lacked imagination, that faculty which (Wilde told Douglas) 'enables one to see things and people in their real as in their ideal relations', and which at its finest—in Keats or in Christ—convinces even the sceptical critic that 'the two supreme and highest arts, life and the expression of life', can occasionally be reconciled in a fusion of 'personality' and 'perfection'. Wilde based his career on the idea of individualism transformed by imagination, eventually claiming to have 'stood in symbolic relations' to his age. Interpretations of the claim are notoriously various; but, if this in itself seems inadequate proof that 'when critics disagree the artist is in accord with himself', it is at least a tribute to Wilde's assessment of the mythopoeic element in literary criticism. Indeed, the fact that Wilde's life, his 'gallant attempt to teach Nature her proper place ', eventually took on so 'deficient' a form, may well be his aptest symbolic achievement. If it seems to justify the admonitions of the moralist, it also vindicates the transgressing artist's mythopoeic dream—'for to most of us, the real life is the life that we do not lead'. [52]

Notes

N.B. The *Letters of Oscar Wilde* (1962) and *Complete Works of Oscar Wilde* (1970) are referred to in these notes as *Letters* and *Works*, respectively (the 1908 collected edition is referred to as *Collected Works*). Unless otherwise indicated, references to published works are to pages. For fuller information on works cited, see the Bibliography.

Chapter 1

1. Bentley, *The Playwright as Thinker* (New York, 1955), 144.
2. "The Decay of Lying" (*Works*, 978).
3. "The Critic as Artist" (*Works*, 1034).
4. "The Soul of Man under Socialism" (*Works*, 1090).
5. *Letters*, 447.
6. "The Critic as Artist" (Works, *1045*).
7. "The Decay of Lying" (*Works*, 977).
8. See below, pp. 13–14.
9. MS Clark W6712L W6721 [188–?] (2314).
10. *Reviews* (1908), 482.
11. Preface to *The Picture of Dorian Gray* (*Works*, 17).
12. In an interview with the *Biograph and Review* in 1880, Wilde explained how, during his Oxford years, 'the Hellenic ideal imperceptibly took the place of the Catholic'. (He had already been awarded the Berkeley Gold Medal for Greek at Trinity College, Dublin, and gained First Class Honours in Literae Humaniores at Magdalen College, Oxford.) The article ends with the promise of 'a blank verse tragedy in four acts, some essays on Greek art, and a collection of poems'. The first appeared in 1883 as *The Duchess of Padua*; the third in 1881 as *Poems*. For the second, literary London had to wait until 1890, when "The Critic as Artist" appeared.
13. *Letters*, 185.
14. Ibid., 186.
15. "Hélas!" (*Works*, 709); see Ellmann, "Romantic Pantomime in Oscar Wilde", *Partisan Review* XXX (1963), 342–55.
16. MS Clark W 672 1M3 C734 [188–?] Boxed (2427), 37.
17. "The Critic as Artist" (*Works*, 1016).
18. Gide, *Oscar Wilde* (1913), 32.
19. *Letters*, 352.
20. "The Critic as Artist" (*Works*, 1045).
21. *A Woman of No Importance*, Act III (*Works*, 462).
22. See below, p. 132, note 55.

23. In fact, Mrs Humphrey Ward's translation of Amiel's journal appeared in 1885; Disraeli's Correspondence with his sister and Home Correspondence were published in 1886 and 1887 respectively.

24. See below, pp. 30–1.

25. MS Clark W672 1M3 A516 [1886?] (2417).

26. Ibid and Letters, 413.

27. "The English Renaissance of Art", Essays and Lectures (1909), 128.

Chapter 2

1. Letters, 110, note 3.

2. Punch, 1881, passim

3. So Wilde told the reporter of the San Francisco Examiner. See Lewis and Smith, Oscar Wilde Discovers America (1967).

4. Punch, 23 July 1881.

5. The Speaker, 4 July 1891; reprinted in Beckson (ed.), Oscar Wilde: The Critical Heritage (1970), 94–6.

6. Roditi, Oscar Wilde (1947).

7. San Juan, The Art of Oscar Wilde (1967).

8. Nassaar, Into the Demon Universe (1974).

9. The first two sub-section titles, "Eleutheria" and "Rosa Mystica", were present in the first edition (1881). Between the third and fifth editions (1882), four further sub-section titles were added (I have not been able to consult a copy of the fourth edition): "Wind Flowers", "Flowers of Gold", "Impressions de Théâtre", and the curiously named "The Fourth Movement". These were all reproduced in the first collected edition (1908).

10. Athenaeum, 23 July 1881; reprinted in Beckson, 33–6.

11. Max Beerbohm, "1880".

12. "The Garden of Eros", lines 224–8 (Works, 722).

13. 'We cannot but think good machinery is graceful, also, the line of strength and the line of beauty being one' ("Art and the Handicraftsman", Essays and Lectures (1909), 178). On his return to England, Wilde elaborated the idea for English audiences: 'There is no country in the world where machinery is as lovely as in America. I have always wished to believe that the line of strength and the line of beauty are one. That wish was realised when I contemplated American machinery. It was not until I had seen the water-works at Chicago that I realised the wonders of machinery; the rise and fall of the steel rods, the symmetrical motion of the great wheels is the most beautiful thing I have ever seen' (Mason, Oscar Wilde: Impressions of America (1906), 24). Wilde published some verses, later included in the collected Poems as "Impression: La Mer", in an American magazine on 15 February 1882. They include the lines: 'And in the throbbing engine room / Leap the long rods of polished steel.' (See Works, 821.)

14. Letters, 69.

15. Ibid., 21.

16. E. B. Browning, Aurora Leigh, (1856) ll. 146–173.

17. Lady Wilde, Poems by Speranza (1864).

18. I take this idea from Heilbrun, Towards Androgyny (1973). See below, pp. 130–47.

19. Wilde's Commonplace Book, MS. Clark (for details see note 4 to Chapter 1), p. 55.
20. T. W. Higginson, "Unmanly Manhood", reprinted from the *Woman's Journal* (Boston) in Beckson, 50–2. See also " In Earnest", *Punch*, 7 Jan 1882. The following passage from a provincial newspaper is quoted in Harris, "Oscar Wilde as Playwright", *Adelphi*, xxx, no. 3 (1954), 221: 'Mr Oscar Wilde seems to ignore the deeply-rooted prejudice that aestheticism, if not symbolic of weakness and effeminacy, is, at least, the antithesis of that moral and intellectual robustness which we, in this age, are accustomed to respect.'
21. See Chapter 1, note 15.
22. Cf. Pater's interpretation of Dionysos Eleutherios, "A Study of Dionysus", *Greek Studies* (1895), 11–13. (First published in the *Fortnightly Review*, Dec 1876.)
23. "Theoretikos, by Oscuro Wildegoose", *Punch*, 26 Nov 1881
24. Wilde's 'translation' of Helena Modjeska's Polish poem "San Artysty" was first published in 1880, but did not reappear until the publication, in 1908, of the first collected edition of Wilde's works. I have seen no manuscript of Wilde's version, nor a copy of the Polish original. As there is no evidence that Wilde knew Polish, and as the 'translation' contains images that he reused in non-poetic contexts in characteristic ways, I am treating "The Artist's Dream" as part of Wilde's own development.
25. D. G. Rossetti, "Hand and Soul", *The Germ* (1850); reprinted in Rossetti, *Poems and Translations* (1968).
26. *Letters*, 34–5.
27. *Aurora Leigh*, ll. 1018–19.
28. Ibid., 1020–2.
29. "Panthea", ll. 75–8 (*Works*, 781).
30. Cf. Roditi, 18.
31. Henry James, Preface to *The Portrait of a Lady*; see below, p. 135.
32. "Humanitad", ll. 144–50 (*Works*, 794).
33. Ibid., 369–72 (*Works*, 799).
34. Arnold, *Culture and Anarchy* (1869), chapter 4.
35. The image anticipates the dramatic climaxes in "The Young King" and *Dorian Gray*.
36. Roditi, 13.
37. "The English Renaissance of Art", *Essays and Lectures* (1909, reprinted 1977, Garland, New York), 129.
38. Roditi, 14–15.
39. Abrams, *Natural Supernaturalism* (1971), 224–5.
40. *Letters*, 146.
41. Ibid., 144.
42. Ibid., 147.
43. Published as preface to *Rose Leaf and Apple Leaf* (1882), a book of verse by Rennell Rodd. Wilde also designed the volume, linking title and contents by interleaving the buff pages with pastel green tissue.
44. "Mr Pater's Last Volume", *Speaker*, I: no. 12 (22 Mar 1890); reprinted in Ellmann (ed.), *The Artist as Critic* (1972), 229–34.
45. Delivered for the first time as a lecture in the Chickering Hall, New York, on 9 January 1882. I quote from Ross's 1908 collation of 'four copies of the lecture' in holograph and typescript (*Essays and Lectures*, 1909). Wilde never published

the piece, but clearly never intended wasting it.

46. *Essays and Lectures*, 117.
47. Ibid., 117.
48. Letters, 509.
49. *Essays and Lectures*, 128.
50. Ibid., 134.
51. Ibid., 148.
52. Ibid., 142.
53. First published in 1908 by Ross. The essay was entered for the Chancellor's English Essay Prize at Oxford in 1879, in which year the subject set was "Historical Criticism among the Ancients". The prize was not awarded. By the terms of the competition as they then stood, Wilde was clearly eligible: he had exceeded four years, but not more than seven, from the date of his matriculation. He seems to have spent most of 1879 in London, having taken his B.A. degree on 28 November 1878. However, as Magdalen College had renewed his demyship for a fifth year (*Letters*, 59) he was theoretically resident in Oxford. The origin of Wilde's work for the essay has not been uncovered, but there can be little doubt that he was trying to follow his 'double first' in Greats with another double: the Chancellor's English Essay Prize, and the Newdigate Prize for English poetry which he had won the previous year.
54. *Essays and Lectures*, 3.
55. Ibid., 5.
56. Ibid., 105–6.
57. Ibid., 106.
58. Ibid., 107–8.
59. Ibid., 108.
60. See below, p. 132, note 55.
61. All four were first published in 1887. "Lord Arthur Savile's Crime" was first published in the *Court and Society Review* (formerly *Orange-Blossoms*), on 11, 18 and 25 May; "The Canterville Ghost" in the same journal on 23 Feb and 2 Mar. "Lady Alroy" appeared in *The World* on 25 May, followed by "The Model Millionaire" on 22 June.
62. *Pall Mall Gazette*, XLI, no. 6230 (28 Feb 1885), 4; reprinted in Ellmann, *The Artist as Critic*, 17–20.
63. *Letters*, 121.
64. Isabel's imagined heroism in getting lost in the London streets: *The Portrait of a Lady*, chapter 31 (Penguin edition, 322).
65. Nassaar, 9–10.
66. Whistler, *The Gentle Art of Making Enemies* (Dover reprint, 144).
67. Cf. Nassaar, 72.
68. *Dorian Gray*, 1891 version, chapter 19 (*Works*, 157–8).
69. Beckson, 269.
70. MS. Mrs Mary Hyde.
71. Ellmann, "Romantic Pantomime in Oscar Wilde", *Partisan Review*, XXX (1963), 342–55.
72. *The Graphic*, 22 Aug 1891, 221; reprinted in Beckson, 107.
73. See below, pp. 70–8.
74. 'And the flying gold of the ruin'd woodland drove thro' the air' ("Maud", 12).
75. 'There is not wind enough to twirl / The one red leaf, the last of its clan, / That

dances as often as dance it can' ("Christabel", 48–50).

76. The significant exceptions are Roditi; and Nassaar, who sees in them the progression from an intrinsic to a higher innocence, achieved through contact with 'the demon universe'. See also Jan Gordon, " 'The Wilde Child': Structure and Origin in the *fin-de-siècle* Short Story", *English Literature in Transition*, xv, no. 4 (1972), 277–89.

77. Roditi, 72.

78. *Dorian Gray*, chapter 2 (*Works*, 36).

79. *Letters*, 218.

80. Ibid., 219.

81. Ibid., 237.

82. Ibid., 301–2.

83. Ellmann, "Romantic Pantomime".

84. *Letters*, 475–6.

85. Croft-Cooke, *The Unrecorded Life of Oscar Wilde* (1972). In fact, several of Wilde's unpublished early poems – "Choir Boy", for example – support this view, though they are hardly explicit.

86. Constance Wilde contributed an article on "Children's Dress in our Century" to the *Woman's World*, July 1888.

87. *Letters*, 484.

88. Empson, *Some Versions of Pastoral* (1966), chapter 7.

89. "Phrases and Philosophies for the Use of the Young", first published in the *Chameleon*, Dec 1894. (*Works*, 1205.)

90. "The Child-Philosopher", *Court and Society Review*, iv, no. 146 (20 Apr 1887); reprinted in Mason, *Bibliography of Oscar Wilde*, (1914), 28–31.

91. For example, Cyril Graham in *Lady Windermere's Fan*, Lord Goring in *An Ideal Husband*, Lord Henry Wotton in *Dorian Gray*, Gilbert in "The Critic as Artist".

92. The Swallow owes something, perhaps, to Swinburne's "Itylus", and to "Ce que disent les hirondelles" in Gautier's *Émaux et Camées*.

93. *Letters*, 475: ' . . . the passage [in "The Young King"] where the Bishop says to the kneeling boy, "Is not He who made misery wiser than thou art?", a phrase which when I wrote it seemed to me little more than a phrase.'

94. Swinburne, *Atalanta in Calydon* (1865), 69.

95. *Letters*, 218.

96. "The Princess", vii.

97. *Letters*, 509.

98. *Eros and Civilisation*, 162–70; quoted in Monroe K. Spears, *Dionysus and the City* (1970), 47.

99. For example, 'It is very much more difficult to talk about a thing than to do it'; 'nowadays so many conceited people go about Society pretending to be good, that I think it shows a rather sweet and modest disposition to pretend to be bad. Besides, there is this to be said. If you pretend to be good, the world takes you very seriously. If you pretend to be bad, it doesn't. Such is the astounding stupidity of optimism' (*Works*, 1023; 387).

100. Whistler, *The Gentle Art of Making Enemies* (Dover reprint, 99). The book was first published in 1890, but was retrospective.

101. *Letters*, 254.

102. "The New President [of the Royal Society of Artists]", (a book review of 1887), reprinted in Ellmann, *The Artist as Critic*, 127. Wilde also reviewed the

Nocturne in Black and Gold in "The Grosvenor Gallery", an article published in the *Dublin University Magazine* in July 1887, and reprinted in *Miscellanies (Collected Works)* 1908). It was, he quipped, 'worth looking at for about as long as one looks at a real rocket, that is, for something less than a quarter of a minute'.

103. The Rocket's notion of 'imagination', amounting to seeing things 'as they are not', is a further link with the "Ten O'Clock" lecture.

104. "The Butterfly's Boswell", reprinted in Ellmann, *The Artist as Critic*, 67.

105. "The Young King", first published in *The Lady's Pictorial* Christmas number, 1888 (with drawings by Bernard Partridge); "The Birthday of the Infanta", in *Paris Illustré*, Mar 1889; "The Fisherman and his Soul" and "The Star Child" previously unpublished.

106. *Letters*, 251–2.

107. "Mr Pater's Imaginary Portraits", *Pall Mall Gazette*, 11 June 1887, reprinted in Lucas (ed.), *A Critic in Pall Mall* (1919), 51 – 5.

108. "The Grosvenor Gallery", *Dublin University Magazine*, 1877; reprinted in *Miscellanies (Collected Works*, 1908), 5–23

109. Marcuse, *Eros and Civilisation*, 162; quoted in Spears, *Dionysus and the City* (1970), 47.

110. Lucas, 53.

111. *Letters*, 475.

112. Abrams, 181.

113. *Miscellanies, (Collected Works*, 1908), 11–12

114. *Letters*, 753n.

115. *Essays and Lectures*, 131.

116. Beckson, 113, 117.

117. *Letters*, 248.

118. Kermode, *Puzzles and Epiphanies* (1962), 27–8; quoted in Michael Hamburger, "Art as Second Nature", *Romantic Mythologies*, ed. Ian Fletcher (1967), 225–41.

119. For example, Bergler, "*Salomé*: Turning-Point in Oscar Wilde's Life", *Psychoanalytic Review*, XLIII (1956), 97–103; Mario Praz, *The Romantic Agony*, transl. Angus Davidson (1962), 232, 276–7, 290, 295, 332–7.

120. See above, note 106.

121. See Rothenstein, *Men and Memories* (1931), 184; quoted in Weintraub, *Beardsley* (1967), 57.

122. One reviewer thought that Wilde had lifted the idea of the soul as shadow from *Peter Schlemihl, the Shadowless Man*, by Adelbert von Chamisso, but there is little other resemblance between the two stories. (Beckson, 116.)

123. *Letters*, 233.

124. *Works*.

125. In a review of Mabel Wotton's *Word Portraits of Famous Writers*, Wilde commented on how unprepossessing many great literary men appeared to have been. However, he continued, 'We must console ourselves – if not with Mr. Hardy's statement that "ideal beauty is incompatible with mental development" – at least with the pictures of those who had some comeliness, and grace, and charm.' ("Some Literary Notes", *Woman's World*, Mar 1889, reprinted in *Reviews* (1908) 445 – 6.) Quote on p. 68 is Nassaar's (p. 76).

Chapter 3

1. Article on Richard Henry Wilde in the *Dictionary of American National Biography*
2. Cf. 'Tasso in the madman's cell' ("The Soul of Man under Socialism", *Works*, 1099).
3. *Letters*, 272.
4. Smalley (ed.), *Browning's Essay on Chatterton* (1948), 18–19.
5. Ibid., 133–4.
6. Ibid., 51–2.
7. Essay on Chatterton, MS. Clark, W 672, IM3, E78 [1886?] Bound (2440).
8. The subtitle was added in 1891.
9. *Dorian Gray*, chapter 1 (*Works*, 25).
10. After the battle of Hyderabad (1843), General Sir Charles Napier reputedly sent the Queen a telegram reading 'Peccavi' (i.e. 'I have sinned' (Sind)). The heroine of *Lady Audley's Secret* (1862), by Mary Elizabeth Braddon, adapted by the author and C. H. Hazlewood for the stage in 1863, was a bigamist. *Il Segreto di Susanna* (1909), is an operetta by Wolf-Ferrari. Susanna smoked.
11. 'See here – it's me you want: I'm the one who did it.' Virgil, *Aeneid*, ix, 427. Virgil's line is completed by the word 'ferrum'. Wainewright's omission of it implies that what Bonmot wants is less the honourable sword-thrust than dishonourable posthumous glamour.
12. *Letters*, 590.
13. MS. Clark, see note 7.
14. Cf. "The Portrait of Mr W. H." (*Works*, 1201), and below, p. 94. Cf. also Daniel Wilson, *Chatterton, A Biography* (1869), used by Wilde in his notes: 'Chatterton's masking began as an innocent dream of the child-poet, and appears to have been cherished by him to the last as an ideal reality.'
15. *Essays and Lectures*, 10.
16. "Mr Mahaffy's New Book", *Pall Mall Gazette*, XLI, no. 7066 (9 Nov 1887), 3; reprinted in Ellmann, *The Artist as Critic*, 80–4.
17. His review of *Intentions* for *The Speaker*, 4 July 1891; reprinted in Beckson, 94–6.
18. "The Critic as Artist" (*Works*, 1015–16).
19. *Mademoiselle de Maupin*, ed. Boschot (1966), 258. (First published 1835.) 'My tender dreams so softly caressed . . . were to be transformed into this perfidious sphinx with its dubious smile, its ambiguous voice, before which I stood with no courage to tackle the riddle.'
20. Ibid., 264. 'Through the veil of these borrowed expressions, under this theatrical mask, with these hermaphrodite words, he hinted at his real sex and at our common situation.'
21. Ibid., XIII. 'Her "ambiguous" contralto voice, her manly beauty and her truly womanly grace, created a sensation in the male-disguise role of Clorinda.'
22. "The Sphinx", lines 168–9 (*Works*, 842).
23. *Letters*, 247. Wilde told Ross that but for him the story would not have been written. It was originally offered to the *Fortnightly Review*, where it was declined; but the link with *Blackwood's* remains interesting.
24. "Women on Stage" and "The Actor's Personality" (*The Dramatic Review* 28

Mar and 12 Oct 1885); "The Woodland Gods" and "The Child-Players of the Elizabethan Stage" (*The Woman's World*, 1888).

25. *Letters*, 365–6.
26. Ibid., 233n.
27. Ibid., 715.
28. Ibid., 363.
29. Ibid., 281, 255n.
30. See also *Letters*, 397: 'Though my face be a mask of grief and my body worn out by solitude, you and you alone will recognise the soul which is more beautiful for having met yours, the soul of the artist who found his ideal in you, of the lover of beauty to whom you appeared as flawless and perfect.' Wilde later told Douglas that the series of Holloway letters was an attempt to 'keep love' in his heart; and while it seems idle as well as niggardly to try to gauge Wilde's 'sincerity' in them, it is at least clear that Douglas could serve as a projection for the artist's ideal, whether he ever fulfilled it or not.
31. *Letters*, 427.
32. Collection of Mrs Mary Hyde.
33. Hyde (ed.), *The Trials of Oscar Wilde* (1960), 112.
34. Ibid., 129.
35. *Letters*, 346–7, 427, 433, 434n.
36. Hyde, 235.
37. *Letters*, 446.
38. Ibid., 427, 432. (Note: in the original, the two sentences terminating this series of extracts immediately precede the first sentence quoted here.)
39. Tennyson, "Three Sonnets to a Coquette", ii (*Complete Poems*, ed. Ricks, 651).
40. Pater, "Love's Labour's Lost", *Appreciations*, (1927), 169. (First published 1878).
41. *Dorian Gray*, chapter 4 (*Works*, 56).
42. MS. Clark W672 1M3 E64 [189–?] (2439). Cf. *Dorian Gray* (*Works*, 161).
43. First published in *The Nineteenth Century*, Jan 1889; revised for inclusion in *Intentions* (May 1891). The revisions consist largely of added anecdotal material, and of the proposition that external nature imitates art. (This may have been Wilde's retort to Whistler's charges of plagiarism in the earlier version. See *Letters*, 253–4.)
44. See above, pp. 58–9.
45. See below, p. 105, note 76.
46. *Letters*, 236.
47. He asserted in "The Critic as Artist" that 'It is the Celt who leads in art' (*Works*, 1050), and described Shaw and himself as as comprising the 'great Celtic school' in drama (*Letters*, 339), but also spoke in *De Profundis* of his 'Celtic laziness', that inability to follow through and persevere which Arnold had contrasted with Germanic tenacity (*Letters*, 429). See also Grant Allen's essay, "The Celt in English Art", *Fortnightly*, (Feb 1891) and Wilde's response (*Letters*, 286–7); also Allen's "The Celtic Fringe", reprinted from the *Westminster Gazette* in *Table Talk* (1894).
48. In a review of *The Happy Prince*, Alexander Galt Ross faulted Wilde's 'natural history' in "The Nightingale and the Rose". See Beckson, 61. Wilde reprimanded him, anonymously, in Vivian's article in "The Decay of Lying" (*Works*, 981).

49. Conceivably, Wilde had come across a diminutive volume by Amelia Opie (the sleep-inducing novelist, Philomela Poppyseed, of Peacock's *Headlong Hall*) called *Illustrations of Lying in all its Branches* (1825). A convincing testament to the uselessness of morally preventative literature, it consists of a full list of lies (Active and Passive Lies of Vanity, Lies of Flattery, Lies of Fear, of Benevolence, of Convenience, of Interest, of First-Rate and Second-Rate Malignity, Lies of Wantonness or Practical Lies) supported by anecdotal demonstrations of their uses which confirm, ironically, that the author is as much of a liar as any of her protagonists.

50. Wilde's triple distancing is often overlooked. He is dissociated from Vivian's dogmatism first by placing the article, 'A Protest', inside a conversation; secondly, by calling the dialogue itself 'An Observation'; and thirdly by Vivian's declaring that 'Like Emerson, I write over the door of my library the word "Whim"'.

51. See Frierson, "The English Controversy over Realism in Fiction", *PMLA*, XLIII (1928), 533–50; also his "Realism in the 1890s", *French Quarterly* x (1928), 31–43; Clarence R. Decker, "The Aesthetic Revolt against Naturalism", *Publications of the Modern Language Association of America*, 53 (1938) 844–56; J. A. Symonds, "Realism and Idealism", *Fortnightly Review*, XLVIII (Sept 1887). See also Becker (ed.), *Documents of Modern Literary Realism* (1963), and Nochlin, *Realism* (1971).

52. Walter Pater, "A Novel by Mr Oscar Wilde", *Bookman*, Nov 1891, 59–60; reprinted in Beckson, 83–6.

53. *Queen*, LXXIV, no. 2189 (8 Dec 1888), 742–7; reprinted in Ellmann, *The Artist as Critic*, 101–8.

54. The title of the second chapter of *Culture and Anarchy*.

55. John Dryden, *Of Dramatick Poesie and other Critical Essays*, ed. Watson, 2 vols, 1962, I, ix.

56. The difference between Wilde's and Arnold's views of individual responsibility corresponds to that between the education of a Greek and a Roman boy, as noted in Wilde's Commonplace Book.

57. Goethe, *Conversations*, transl. Oxenford (1930); quoted in Stone, *Novelists in a Changing World: Meredith and James in the 1880s* (1972), 19.

58. "Wordsworth", *Appreciations*, 62.

59. "Mr Symonds' History of the Renaissance", *Pall Mall Gazette*, 10 Nov 1886; reprinted in Lucas, 39–44.

60. Quoted in Hamilton, *Manet and his Critics* (1969), 99.

61. *Imaginary Portraits* (1914), 114.

62. Ibid., 115.

63. "The Function of Criticism at the Present Time", *Matthew Arnold: Lectures and Essays in Criticism*, ed. Super (Ann Arbor, 1962), 285.

64. Commonplace Book, MS. Clark (for details see note 4 to Chapter 1), p. 74.

65. Abrams, 230–1.

66. Ibid., 188.

67. Ibid., 171.

68. Ibid., 181.

69. *A Woman of No Importance*, Act III (*Works*, 464).

70. *Appreciations* (1927), quoted in Stone, 18–19.

71. Commonplace Book, MS. Clark, p. 144.

72. Ibid., 145.
73. Roditi, 214.
74. Commonplace Book, MS. Clark, p. 100.
75. Carlyle, *On Heroes and Hero-Worship* (Everyman edition, 1973), 315.
76. Wilde misquotes from "Humanitad", lines 372–3 (*Works*, 800), making explicit the parallel with *Poems*: 'To make the Body and the Spirit one / With all right things'.
77. Principally on *Dorian Gray*. See *Letters*, 257–72; Beckson, 81–6; Mason, *Art and Morality* (1915).
78. *Works*, 25.
79. *Vera*, Act II (*Works*, 665).
80. *Novelists in a Changing World*. (cf. note 57).
81. Webb, "English Progress towards Social Democracy", *Fabian Tracts*, no. 15, (Dec 1890).
82. Clifford, *Essays and Lectures* (1879).
83. Delivered at the Royal Institution on 6 March 1868.
84. Commonplace Book, MS. Clark, p. 119. Clifford's "On the Scientific Basis of Morals" was published in *The Contemporary Review*, Sep 1875.
85. Commonplace Book, MS. Clark, pp. 2, 14.
86. Ibid., 69.
87. "Shakespeare", *Poems of Matthew Arnold*, ed. Allott (1965), 50. Wilde quoted the sonnet in his Chatterton lecture.
88. *Letters*, 473.

Chapter 4

1. Nassaar, 37–72.
2. Ellmann, "Overtures to *Salomé*", *Oscar Wilde: Twentieth Century Views*, (1969), 88–9.
3. Wilde was quoting from Poe's "William Wilson" when he commented to the Press that 'when Dorian Gray kills conscience he kills himself'. *Letters*, 264.
4. Andrew Lang curiously anticipated, or suggested, this debt in an article called "Literary Plagiarism", in which, after speaking of the inadvisability of reproducing, for example, Hawthorne's device (in *The Scarlet Letter*) of having a priest confess his sin unsuspected in a sermon, or of using the metre of *In Memoriam* (which Wilde was accused of having done in *The Sphinx*), Lang continued: 'Double personality is a theme open to all the world. Gautier and Poe and Eugène Sue all used it; but it is wiser to leave it alone while people have a vivid memory of Dr Jekyll and Mr Hyde. It is not inconceivable that the author might use the old notion as brilliantly and with as much freshness as Mr Stevenson has done; it is certain that if he tries he will be howled at by the moral mob' (*Contemporary Review*, June 1887, 838).
5. For a discussion of these and other possible debts, see Isobel Murray's edition of the novel (Oxford University Press, 1974); also her "Some Elements in the Composition of *The Picture of Dorian Gray*", *Durham University Journal*, LXIV (1972), 220–3. *Margery Merton's Girlhood*, a novel reviewed by Wilde in 1888, has not, I think, been cited yet, though its claims are as good as several others.

Wilde speaks of the book's place in ' "the art-literature" of our day', a genre
begun by Ruskin and Browning, and commends it as a 'little story' in which
'the creation of a picture forms the dominant motif'. The heroine wins a prize
for a painting of Joan of Arc, whom she depicts as a peasant 'standing in an
orchard, and listening in ignorant terror to the strange voices whispering in her
ear' ("Miss Alice Corkran's *Margery Merton's Girlhood*", *Essays and Reviews*
146–8).

6. *Letters*, 298n.
7. Ibid., 259.
8. Nickerson, "*Vivian Grey* and *Dorian Gray*", TLS, 14 Aug 1969, 909.
9. See *Letters*, 255n, 281 for Douglas; 312n for Gray; 249n for Ricketts and
   Shannon.
10. Ibid., 352.
11. See, however, Nethercot, "Oscar Wilde and the Devil's Advocate", and
    "Wilde on Subdividing Himself", *PMLA*, LIX (1944),
12. See Stuart Mason, *Art and Morality*, pp. 22 – 3.
13. *Lippincott's Monthly*, June 1890 (hereafter referred to as *Lippincott*), 60.
14. Chapter 3. (*Works*, 41).
15. See above, p. 91.
16. Chapter 1 (*Lippincott*, 11; *Works*, 26).
17. "Sonnet on the Sonnet" (1897), *Sonnets of Lord Alfred Douglas* (1947), 23.
18. *The Duchess of Padua*, Act v (*Works*, 645).
19. "The Critic As Artist" (*Works*, 1048).
20. *Letters*, 185.
21. Pierpont Morgan MA 883. Wilde knew slightly a French critic called Gabriel
    Sarrazin. See *Letters*, 241.
22. *Letters*, 313, 352.
23. "The Critic as Artist" (*Works*, 1040).
24. Ibid. (*Works*, 29).
25. *Gaston de Latour* (1917 edition), 71–2.
26. Ibid., 106.
27. *Lippincott*, 4; *Works*, 19.
28. The Pierpont holograph shows that Wilde originally conceived the first two
    chapters as one, which he decided to break at this point.
29. *Lippincott*, 17; *Works*, 31–2.
30. Wilde's retort, perhaps, to Higginson's review of *Poems*, in which he had been
    compared unfavourably with Sir Philip Sidney, who 'might, if he please, have
    set the fashion of a shoe-tie' but preferred 'to hold out a brave example of virtue
    and religion'. See Beckson, 52.
31. *Lippincott*, chapter 9, 66–7; *Works*, chapter 11, 104.
32. *Lippincott*, 65; *Works*, 102–3.
33. Commonplace Book, MS. Clark (for details see note 4 to Chapter 1), 183.
34. *Lippincott*, chapter 9, 75; *Works*, chapter 11, 112–13.
35. "The Soul of Man under Socialism" (*Works*, 1084).
36. *Letters*, 469.
37. Swinburne, "Notes on *Poems and Reviews*", *Swinburne Replies*, ed. Hyder
    (1965), 26.
38. *An Ideal Husband*, Act III (*Works*, 522).
39. Reade and Taylor, *Masks and Faces*, Act I (Oxford edition, 126).

40. *Lippincott*, chapter 3, 26–7; *Works*, chapter 4, 51–2.

41. *Lippincott*, chapter 5, 39–40; *Works*, chapter 6, 74–5.

42. *Lippincott*, chapter 6, 48–50; *Works*, chapter 8, 84, 86.

43. "The Critic as Artist" (*Works*, 1026).

44. Meredith, *The Egoist* (Penguin edition, 38). Willoughby's 'epitaph' dropped by Meredith in the Prelude.

45. The Preface was added to the 1891 version, having appeared in the *Fortnightly Review* in March, one month earlier.

46. "Mr Oscar Wilde's Novel", *The Christian Leader*, 3 July 1890, reprinted in Mason, *Art and Morality*, 135–57.

47. Any theory which equates the technique of Rossetti, Millais, and Hunt, and calls the style of the last 'photographic', can hardly be taken seriously on circumstantial evidence. The 'sweep and dash' of Basil's brush and his 'bold touch' bear no relation to the meticulous practice of the Pre-Raphaelite Brotherhood, none of whom had a penchant for youths posed in neo-Hellenic situations.

48. *Letters*, 266.

49. Nassaar, 69–70.

50. "The Critic as Artist" (*Works*, 1029).

51. This happened early in 1891. See *Letters*, 285–6.

52. Heilbrun, *Towards Androgyny*, esp. 49–112.

53. *Works*, 598.

54. "The Critic as Artist" (*Works*, 1045).

55. As far as I have been able to discover, there are five plays that Wilde left in a fragmentary state. After Douglas' return from Egypt in March 1894 (he had left the previous November) Wilde could not finish *A Florentine Tragedy*. He eventually succeeded, it seems, in completing *La Sainte Courtisane*, only to lose it in a Paris cab – 'a very proper place for it'. (*Letters*, 649). *A Florentine Tragedy* was completed by Thomas Sturge Moore for performance with *Salome* by the Literary Theatre Society in London in July 1906, under the general direction of Charles Ricketts. Like *La Sainte Courtisane*, it was first published in Ross's first collected edition in 1908. A blank verse tragedy called *Beatrice and Astone Manfredi*, a MS held by the Clark Library, appears to be identical with the so-called *Cardinal of Avignon*, a scenario for which appears in Mason's *Bibliography*. The extensive Clark fragment is similar in style to *The Duchess of Padua*, and may well date from Wilde's 1883 stay in Paris, when he had determined to finish two plays. An early date is suggested by the fact that the fragment is written at the back of a notebook largely devoted to a draft of *Vera*. Since the English production of *Vera* had been cancelled (see next note), Wilde would obviously be hoping to have the play produced in America, preferably during his tour, and negotiations began, at first through D'Oyly Carte, soon after his arrival. (See Mason, *Bibliography*, 255–70). It seems probable, then, that he would have taken his *Vera* notebooks with him, and that he would consequently have them to hand in Paris in the Spring of 1883. The scenario printed by Mason dates from April 1894. Unlike the MS draft, it contains clear signs of the 'strong scenes' and marked peripeteia of the comedies and *A Florentine Tragedy*. However, these qualities were also prominent in *Vera* and *The Duchess of Padua*. The Clark also possesses an all but undecipherable prose fragment entitled *A Wife's Tragedy*. It, too, bears the marks of a 'drawing-

NOTES

215

room' play, and presumably dates from the early or mid 1890s. The scenario sent to George Alexander in 1895 (*Letters*, 360–2) and eventually written up by Frank Harris as *Mr and Mrs Daventry* appears to have been Wilde's last dramatic sketch. (His having tried to sell it several times over seems to support this supposition.) Harris modified the characterisation and altered the balance of Wilde's plan. (See *Mr and Mrs Daventry*, ed. H. Montgomery Hyde, London, 1956; and T. H. Bell, "Oscar Wilde's Unwritten Play" – a personal reminiscence by Harris' secretary and cross-channel agent in the matter – *The Bookman*, April – May 1930, 144 – 9.) Of the Biblical plays reported by Gide, *Pharaon* and *Achab et Jésabel*, only the titles have survived (*Letters*, 649). For apocrypha and dubious "reconstructions", see the bibliographical essay by Ian Fletcher and John Stokes in *Anglo-Irish Literature: A Guide to Research*, Modern Language Association of America, 1976.

56. See *Letters*, 110, n. 3, and Mason, Bibliography, 254–73. All the arrangements were made for Mrs Bernard Beere (later to play Mrs Arbuthnot) to appear in the title role at the Adelphi Theatre, opening on 17 June 1881, but three weeks prior to this the production was cancelled, 'considering the present state of political feeling in England'. Czar Alexander II had been assassinated in March, and the new Czarina was the Prince of Wales's sister-in-law. Professor Simon Karlinsky has kindly pointed out a number of historical and geographical discrepancies in Wilde's Russian setting. In *Salomé* he rewrote history deliberately. In *Vera* he was evidently making palpable mistakes.

57. *Letters*, 148–9.

58. Ellmann, "Romantic Pantomime", 342–55.

59. *Salomé* was written in Paris during the winter of 1890–1, and published in its original French version, after corrections by Pierre Louÿs and Marcel Schwob, in 1893. The Alfred Douglas translation, with Beardsley's decorations, appeared in 1894.

60. *Works*, 1090.

61. Herod Antipas (Matt. xiv, 1), Herod the Great (Matt. ii, 1), and Herod Agrippa (Acts xii, 23). See Roberts Ross's Introduction to *Salomé* (London, 1909), xii – xiii.

62. The obvious French sources were noted by contemporary critics in some detail. See Beckson, esp. 135 – 42. Ellmann has noted the possible influence of J. C. Heywood's trilogy of *Herodias* (New York and Cambridge Mass., 1867; London, 1884), *Salome* (New York and Cambridge, Mass., 1867, London, 1887 and *Antonius* (New York and Cambridge, Mass 1867; London, 1885). Wilde reviewed *Salome* unfavourably in 1888 ("The Poets' Corner", *Pall Mall Gazette*, XLVII, no. 7128 (20 Jan), 3). Heywood's Salome has little in common with Wilde's: she is a Christian in love with a pantheist Roman general, converting him by her death. His *Herodias*, however, shows marked similarities to Wilde's *Salomé*, especially in Herodias's speech to the Baptist's head, where she appears as a gross prototype of Beardsley's Salomé. The moral scheme of Heywood's play, however, is wholly different. Salome, still a devout Christian, is blackmailed by Herodias into asking for John's head. Herodias goes mad and dashes away, as she thinks, into hellfire – 'I come! I come! world, for a space, goodnight. / Hail! Pluto, hail! Infernal horrors, hail!' – and the play ends with a moralistic chorus of Romans and Jews in Swinburnian metre. (Cf. Ellmann, "Overtures to *Salomé*", *Twentieth Century Views*, 73–91.)

63. Under the clause which forbade the representation of Biblical characters on stage. See *Letters*, 316–9, 332; also "The Censure and *Salomé*", reprinted in Glaezner (ed.) *Decorative Art in America* (1906), 137–43.

64. *The Times*, 23 Feb 1893; reprinted in Beckson, 133. The phrase 'an arrangement' was presumably an ironic reference to the titles of Whistler's paintings, with which *Salomé* would have been supposed to share Aesthetic characteristics. Compare also Wilde's own subtitles in *Lord Arthur Savile's Crime* (1891).

65. "The Soul of Man under Socialism" (*Works*, 1093).

66. 'I have one instrument that I know I can command, and that is the English language. There was another instrument to which I had listened all my life, and I wanted to touch this new instrument to see whether I could make any beautiful thing out of it.' ("The Censure and *Salome*", Glaezner, 141)

67. James's phrase for Isabel Archer in his Preface to *The Portrait of a Lady*.

68. Conclusion to *Studies in the History of the Renaissance* (1873).

69. For example,

SECOND SOLDIER: We must hide the body. The tetrarch mustn't see it.
FIRST SOLDIER: The tetrarch won't come this way. He never comes on to the terrace. He is too frightened of the prophet (*Enter Herod, Herodias, and the whole court.*)

70. *Dorian Gray*, chapter 19 (*Works*, 161).

71. Laforgue, "Salomé", *Moralités Légendaires* (1887).

72. Del Mar, *Richard Strauss* (1962), I, 249–50.

73. Ellmann, "Overtures to *Salomé*", *Twentieth Century Views*, 74.

74. Beckson, 137.

75. "The Decay of Lying" (*Works*, 975).

76. Wilde's dissatisfaction with Douglas' translation (which renders Wilde's contemporary French in the style of the King James Bible) is well-known. I quote from my own translation, giving the original text here in the notes.

LE JEUNE SYRIEN: Comme la princesse Salomé est belle ce soir!
LE PAGE D'HÉRODIAS: Regardez la lune. La lune a l'air très étrange. On dirait une femme qui sort d'un tombeau. Elle ressemble à une femme morte. On dirait qu'elle cherche des morts.
LE JEUNE SYRIEN Elle a l'air très étrange. Elle ressemble à une petite princesse qui porte un voile jaune, et a des pieds d'argent. Elle ressemble à une princesse qui a des pieds comme des petites colombes blanches. . . . On dirait qu'elle danse.
LE PAGE D'HÉRODIAS: Elle est comme une femme morte. Elle va très lentement. (*Bruit dans la salle de festin.*)
PREMIER SOLDAT: Quel vacarme! Qui sont ces bêtes fauves qui hurlent?
SECOND SOLDAT: Les Juifs. Ils sont toujours ainsi. C'est sur leur religion qu'ils discutent.
PREMIER SOLDAT: Pourquoi discutent-ils sur leur religion?
SECOND SOLDAT:: Je ne sais pas. Ils le font toujours. . . . Ainsi les Pharisiens affirment qu'il y a des anges, et les Sadducéens disent que les anges n'existent pas.
PREMIER SOLDAT: Je trouve que c'est ridicule de discuter sur de telles choses.

77. The stage directions require 'moonlight'. At the end of the play, Wilde suggests that 'a cloud' cover the moon. This can be regarded either as an inconsistency, or as an indication that the various changes attributed to the moon throughout the play are wholly imaginary, and were not intended to be reflected in the staging. None of the surviving plans or sketches for the set includes a moon.

78. Cf. *Salomé*, with an introduction by Holbrook Jackson (New York, 1938); Brasol, *Oscar Wilde*, (1938); and Joost and Sullivan, "*Salomé*, the Moon, and Oscar Wilde's Aesthetics", *Papers in Language and Literature*, VIII (supp. Fall 1972), 96–111.

79. 'Salomé, vous connaissez mes paons blancs, mes beaux paons blancs, qui se promènent dans le jardin entre les myrtes et les grands cyprès. Leurs becs sont dorés, et les grains qu'ils mangent sont dorés aussi, et leurs pieds sont teints de pourpre. La pluie vient quand ils crient, et quand ils se pavanent la lune se montre au ciel. . . . Eh bien! je vous donnerai cinquante de mes paons. Ils vous suivront partout, et au milieu d'eux vous serez comme la lune dans un grand nuage blanc. . . . J'ai un collier de perles à quatre rangs. On dirait des lunes enchaînées de rayons d'argent. On dirait cinquante lunes captives dans un filet d'or.'

80. Early in the play Salomé refuses Herod's fruit and wine. In the speech to the head, she echoes this scene, apparently involuntarily, in Herod's hearing: 'All other men fill me with disgust. But you, you were beautiful. . . . I love you still, Iokanaan. I love only you. . . . I am thirsty for your beauty. I am hungry for your body. And neither wine nor fruit can appease my desire.'

81. 'Eteignez les flambeaux. Cachez la lune! Cachez les étoiles! Cachons-nous dans notre palais, Hérodias. Je commence à avoir peur.'

82. "The Critic as Artist" (*Works*, 1052).

83. 'Iokanaan! Je suis amoureuse de ton corps. Ton corps est blanc comme le lis d'un pré que le faucheur n'a jamais fauché. Ton corps est blanc comme les neiges qui couchent sur les montagnes, comme les neiges qui couchent sur les montagnes de Judée, et descendent dans les vallées. Les roses du jardin de la reine d'Arabie ne sont pas aussi blanches que ton corps. Les roses du jardin de la reine d'Arabie, le jardin parfumé de la reine d'Arabie, ni les pieds de l'aurore qui trépignent sur les feuilles, ni le sein de la lune quand elle couche sur le sein de la mer – Il n'y a rien au monde d'aussi blanc que ton corps. Laisse-moi toucher ton corps!'

84. 'C'est de tes cheveux que je suis amoureuse, Iokanaan. Tes cheveux ressemblent à des grappes de raisins, à des grappes de raisins noirs qui pendent des vignes d'Edom dans le pays des Edomites. Tes cheveux sont comme les cèdres du Liban, comme les grands cèdres du Liban qui donnent de l'ombre aux lions et aux voleurs qui veulent se cacher pendant la journée. Les longues nuits noires, les nuits où la lune ne se montre pas, où les étoiles ont peur, ne sont pas aussi noires. Le silence qui demeure dans les forêts n'est pas aussi noir. Il n'y a rien au monde d'aussi noir que tes cheveux. Laisse-moi toucher tes cheveux.'

85. 'Tes cheveux sont horribles. Ils sont couverts de boue et de poussière. On dirait une couronne d'épines qu'on a placée sur ton front. On dirait un noeud de serpents noirs qui se tortillent autour de ton cou.'

86. 'C'est de ta bouche que je suis amoureuse, Iokanaan. Ta bouche est comme une bande d'écarlate sur une tour d'ivoire. Elle est comme une pomme de grenade coupée par un couteau d'ivoire. Les fleurs de grenade qui fleurissent dans les jardins de Tyr et sont plus rouges que les roses, ne sont pas aussi rouges. Les cris

rouges des trompettes qui annoncent l'arrivée des rois, et font peur à l'ennemi ne sont pas aussi rouges. Ta bouche est plus rouge que les pieds de ceux qui foulent le vin dans les pressoirs. Elle est plus rouge que les pieds des colombes qui demeurent dans les temples et sont nourries par les prêtres. Elle est plus rouge que les pieds de celui qui revient d'une forêt où il a tué un lion et vu des tigres dorés. Ta bouche est comme une branche de corail que des pêcheurs ont trouvée dans le crépuscule de la mer et qu'ils réservent pour les rois. Elle est comme le vermillon que les Moabites trouvent dans les mines de Moab et que les rois leur prennent. Elle est comme l'arc du roi des Perses qui est peinte avec du vermillon et qui a des cornes de corail. Il n'y a rien au monde d'aussi rogue que ta bouche. Laisse-moi baiser ta bouche.'

87. "The Critic as Artist" (*Works*, 1018).
88. Roditi, 45–50.
89. *Works*, 1018.
90. "The Decay of Lying" (*Works*, 986).
91. 'Ah! pourquoi ne m'as-tu regardée, Iokanaan? Derrière tes mains et tes blasphèmes tu as caché ton visage. Tu as mis sur tes yeux le bandeau de celui qui veut voir son Dieu. Eh bien, tu l'as vu, ton Dieu, Iokannan, mais moi, moi – tu ne m'as jamais vue. Si tu m'avais vue, tu m'aurais aimée. Moi, je t'ai vu, Iokanaan, et je t'ai aimé. Oh! comme je t'ai aimé. Je t'aime encore, Iokanaan.'
92. In a lecture on Beardsley's *Salomé* drawings, delivered at the Tate Gallery, London, in April 1976.
93. *A Florentine Tragedy*, MS. Clark W672 1M3 P567 [189 –] Bound (2474).
94. *Letters*, 185.
95. *Works*, 1102.
96. 'Le mystère de l'amour est plus grand que le mystère de la mort. Il ne faut regarder que l'amour.'
97. Nassaar, 92.
98. See below, pp. 190 – 2.
99. Ellmann, "Overtures to *Salomé*", *Twentieth Century Views*, 90.
100. *Letters*, 352.
101. Ibid., 259.
102. Bergler, "*Salomé*, Turning-Point in Oscar Wilde's Life".
103. *Letters*, 590.
104. Ibid., 509.
105. "The Critic as Artist" (*Works*, 1045).
106. Reproduced in Holland, *A Pictorial Biography of Oscar Wilde* (1966), 108.
107. *La Sainte Courtisane*, completed but left in a Paris cab, and *A Florentine Tragedy*, unfinished, both date from 1893. Wilde complained in *De Profundis* that Douglas had broken the mood which produced them. (*Letters*, 427; also 591, 638, 649.) For a reference to the unwritten Biblical plays described to Gide, see *Letters*, 649. For an account of Wilde's scenario, written up by Frank Harris as *Mr and Mrs Daventry*, see H. Montgomery Hyde's introduction to the play (1956), and Frank Harris's secretary's description of his dealings with Wilde on Harris's behalf: ' "Oscar Wilde's Unwritten Play", A Personal Reminiscence by T. H. Bell", *Bookman*, April – May 1930, 144–9.
108. "Le Dandy", *Le Peintre de la Vie Moderne*, ix (*Oeuvres Complètes*, 1178).
109. *Works*, 1086.
110. *The Duchess of Padua*, Act v (*Works*, 641).

Chapter 5

1. John Drinkwater on *The Importance of Being Earnest*, reprinted in Beckson, 403–5.
2. Roditi, 125–44.
3. Roditi; San Juan; Moers, *The Dandy* (1960); Ganz, "The Dandiacal Drama: A Study of the Plays of Oscar Wilde", *Dissertation Abstracts*, XVIII (Mar 1958).
4. *The Eighteen Nineties* (1927).
5. See also below, pp. 153–4.
6. Roditi, 134.
7. St John Hankin, "Collected Plays of Oscar Wilde", *Fortnightly Review*, May 1908, 791–802, reprinted in Beckson, 281–93; Ervine, *Oscar Wilde: A Present Time Appraisal* (1951); Rowell, *The Victorian Theatre* (1956).
8. Ganz, "The Divided Self in the Comedies of Oscar Wilde", *Modern Drama*, III (May 1960).
9. Beckson, 126.
10. Hankin, in Beckson, 293.
11. MS. diaries of Charles Ricketts, British Museum.
12. Harry Quilter, "The Decline of the Drama", *Contemporary Review*, Apr 1887, 549.
13. Arthur Wing Pinero, *The Cabinet Minister*, ed. M. Salaman (1892).
14. Cf. Wilde's review (1888) of David Ritchie's *Darwinism and Politics*: 'The cultivation of separate sorts of virtues and separate ideals of duty in men and women has led to the whole social fabric being weaker and unhealthier than it need be.' *Reviews* (1908), 488.
15. *London Assurance* opened at the Criterion Theatre on 27 November 1890.
16. *Letters*, 283–4.
17. Boucicault, *London Assurance* (*Laurel British Drama: The Nineteenth Century*, ed. R. Corrigan, 63).
18. For example, 'A really *grande passion* is the privilege of people who have nothing to do' (*A Woman of No Importance*, Act III; *Works*, 461); 'Vulgarity is the conduct of other people' (*An Ideal Husband*, Act III; *Works*, 522).
19. Gide reported that Wilde spoke – presumably during the 1890s – of writing a comedy about Brummel, but I have been unable to find the source for the remark.
20. Disraeli, *Vivian Grey*, chapter 8.
21. Barbey d'Aurevilly, "Du Dandysme", *Oeuvres Complètes* (Paris 1926–7), IX, 227–8.
22. Ibid., 229.
23. Ibid., 230.
24. Ibid., 240.
25. *An Essay on Comedy and the Uses of the Comic Spirit*. Originally delivered as a lecture on 1 Feb 1877 at the London Institution, it was published in the *New Quarterly Magazine*, Apr 1877. First published in volume form, 1897; ed. Cooper, 1972 (edition cited below).
26. Ibid., 143.
27. *Culture and Anarchy* (1869).

28. Meredith, *Essay on Comedy*, 125.
29. Ibid., 90.
30. Cf. *Letters*, 142n.
31. Ibid., 135–42.
32. Holland, *Pictorial Biography*, 89.
33. Juvenal, in his prefatory lines to the *Satires*; de Quincey's translation, in *Confessions of an English Opium-Eater*, 1821 (Everyman edition, 1964) 59.
34. Except for the half-humorous, half-irritable boast in *De Profundis* that his comedies 'beat Congreve for brilliancy and Dumas *fils* for philosophy, and I suppose everyone else for every other quality' (*Letters*, 500). Cf. also the following unpublished epigram, intended for *A Woman of No Importance*: 'People are so unfair. If a man says a moral thing in a book or a sermon or a public speech no one imagines that he really means it; if one gives a brilliant half-truth they imagine one a new Charles II and shriek for the Nonconformists.' MS. Clark W672 1M2 N911 [1894] Bound, Dulau 3 (2469).
35. The resemblances that have been pointed out tend to be incidental rather than crucial. See Foster, "Wilde as Parodist: A Second Look at *Earnest*", *College English*, XVIII (Oct 1956), 18–23; Ware, "Algernon's Appetite: Oscar Wilde's Hero as Restoration Dandy", *English Literature in Transition*, XIII no. 1 (1970), 17–26.
36. In fact, Farquhar, an alumnus (like Wilde) of Trinity College, Dublin, had been there a 'sizar', or undergraduate with certain menial domestic obligations. He ran away, without taking his degree, to become an actor. Stretching the point, perhaps, Mary Farquhar in *Earnest* might be seen as a *fin-de-siècle* comment on Farquhar's *Constant Couple* (1699). Algernon complains that 'she always flirts with her own husband across the dinner-table. That is not very pleasant. Indeed, it is not even decent – and that sort of thing is enormously on the increase' (*Works*, 327).
37. *The Provok'd Wife*, Act I, Scene i.
38. Congreve, "Concerning Humour in Comedy" (1695), reprinted in Spingarn (ed.), *Critical Essays of the Seventeenth Century* (1968), 242–52.
39. Meredith, *Essay on Comedy*, 83.
40. *Leviathan*, XIII.
41. "Du Dandysme" *Oeuvres Complètes*, IX, 239.
42. Ibid., 254.
43. See below, pp. 172–3.
44. Quoted in Underwood, *Etherege and the Seventeenth Century Comedy of Manners* (1957), 13–14.
45. Dobrée, *Restoration Comedy* (1924), 23.
46. Righter, "Heroic Tragedy", *Restoration Theatre*, Stratford-upon-Avon Studies no. 6 (1965), 135–57.
47. See below, pp. 179–80, 183, 186. Cf. also, e.g., Prince Paul (*Vera*, Act II; *Works*, 664–5) with Lord Darlington (*Lady Windermere's Fan*, Act I; *Works*, 386–7).
48. Righter, 137.
49. Cf. Righter, 136.
50. Quoted in Muir, *The Comedy of Manners* (1970), 29.
51. Holland, *Pictorial Biography*, 89.
52. *Letters*, 466.

53. "The Decay of Lying" (*Works*, 975).
54. *A Woman of No Importance*, Act III (*Works*, 460).
55. Ibid., Act I (*Works*, 439).
56. Ibid., Act II (*Works*, 446).
57. Wycherley, *The Country Wife*, Act II, Scene i.
58. Etherege, *The Man of Mode*, Act III, Scene ii.
59. "Du Dandysme" (*Oeuvres Complètes*, IX, 178).
60. Meredith, *The Egoist* (Penguin edition, 43).
61. See Ellmann, "Romantic Pantomime"; Ervine, *Oscar Wilde*, 259; Nethercot, "Oscar Wilde and the Devil's Advocate", *Publications of the Modern Language Association of America* (*PMLA*), LIX, 1944.
62. Righter, 153–4.
63. *The Importance of Being Earnest*, Act II (*Works*, 341).
64. See above, note 9.
65. Beckson, 81.
66. "Preface to *An Evening's Love*" (1671), reprinted in John Dryden, *Of Dramatick Poesie and other Critical Essays* ed. Watson (1962), 144–55. On p. 149 Watson provides the following note: '*Institutio oratoria* VI. iii. 17–20, where Quintilian distinguishes a number of words by which wit is described, the first four being *urbanitas* (of the language of cities and learning), *venustus* (graceful, charming), *salsus* (salty, piquant), and *facetus* (polished, elegant).
67. "An Ideal Husband", *Saturday Review* (12 January 1895), LXXIX 44–5; reprinted in Beckson, 176–8.
68. According to J. J. Blood, "The Play of the Future" (*Dramatic Review*, 21 March 1885), would be developed very much along the lines I have suggested. Gilbert, he says, is the single inventive mind at work in drama, and while his repetitions of 'situation and phraseology' show the limitations of his 'topsi-turvidom', he has still 'given the age an actual novelty in stage plays, something for which no precedent can be found'. In the future, perhaps, 'refined writers may be found who will combine more effectually the grace of the scholar with the robust, generous style always more or less necessary to affect an audience deeply.'

Chapter 6

1. See above. pp. 151–2.
2. Beckson, 122, 127–8. In fact, Chambers' device involved a bouquet, not a fan, and the resemblances would probably have passed unnoticed if *The Idler* (1902) had not been produced so recently at the same theatre, the St James's. Wilde later borrowed various bits and pieces from it for *An Ideal Husband*.
3. *Essay on Comedy*, 154.
4. *Letters*, 332.
5. Ibid., 282.
6. Baudelaire, "De L'Héroisme de la Vie Moderne" (*Oeuvres Complètes*, 949–52).
7. *Letters*, 331–2.
8. Peckham, "What did Lady Windermere Learn?", *College English*, XVIII (1956), 11–14.
9. San Juan, 148.

10. Shadwell, *The Libertine* (1676); quoted in Underwood, 14.
11. *Letters*, 501.
12. Ganz, "The Dandiacal Drama", 1429.
13. San Juan, 141–2.
14. MS. Clark, W672 M2 L157 [1892] Boxed (2448).
15. *Letters*, 308–9.
16. Ibid., 309.
17. Dumas *fils, Le Demi-Monde* (1855).
18. Meredith, *The Egoist* (Penguin edition, 100).
19. Pearson, *Beerbohm Tree* (1956), 69–70.
20. *Dorian Gray*, chapter 19 (*Works*, 157–8).
21. "Mr Symonds' History of the Renaissance", *Pall Mall Gazette*, 10 Nov 1886, reprinted in *A Critic in Pall Mall* (1919), 39–44.
22. Charles II once told Lauderdale that presbyterianism was not a religion for a gentleman. Sutherland, *English Literature of the Late Seventeenth Century* (Oxford, 1969), 6. C.f. also note 34 above, p. 152.
23. MS. Texas (Humanities Research Centre), reprinted in Pearson, *Beerbohm Tree*.
24. Bateson, "Second Thoughts: II. L. C. Knights and Restoration Comedy", *Essays in Criticism*, VII (1957), 56–67.
25. Ibid., 63.
26. Congreve, *The Way of the World*, Act V, Scene iv.
27. MS. Clark W672 1M2 I19 [1893] Bound, Part I, Dulau 2 (2454).
28. Ibid. [Act II].
29. Shaw, "An Ideal Husband", *Saturday Review*, LXXIX (12 Jan 1895), 44–5; reprinted in Beckson, 176–8.
30. Ibid., 177.
31. Wilde added these stage-directions in 1899 for publication.
32. Hobbes, *Leviathan*, I, x; I, iv.
33. I have no space to quote these instances, but the following speeches may be compared: Guido's 'You never loved me' etc. (*Works*, 614), Guido's 'I dare not look at you' etc. (*Works*, 616–7), and the Duchess's 'He lied to me' (*Works*, 603), with the crisis scene between the Chilterns, Act I (*Works*, 501–2), beginning, 'To the world, as to myself, you have been an ideal always', and Act II (*Works*, 520–1), beginning, 'Don't come near me, don't touch me.'
34. *Works*, 593.
35. *Works*, 583.
36. She calls Lord Goring 'Gertrude Chiltern's man' and rallies him, 'Lady Chiltern comes to see you in the evenings. How nice.' (MS. Clark; see above, note 25.)
37. MS. Clark (see above, note 25).
38. Goring, while giving wholly serious advice, contrives a mild satire on transcendental Romantic assumptions: 'No, Lady Chiltern, I am not a Pessimist. Indeed, I am not sure that I quite know what pessimism really means. All I do know is that life cannot be understood without much charity, cannot be lived without much charity. It is love, and not German philosophy, that is the true explanation of this world, whatever may be the explanation of the next.' *An Ideal Husband*, Act II (*Works*, 511).
39. Woodcock, *The Paradox of Oscar Wilde* (1950), 159.
40. "Du Dandysme" (*Oeuvres Complètes*, IX, 240). Any doubt that Wilde's attitude

differed from that of the majority might be corrected by comparing the conclusion of *An Ideal Husband* with that of an article by Edward Dicey published in June 1889: 'We are aware that if we are to hold our own, we must not believe everything that is told us. But we still act on the assumption, that when a man commits himself to a positive statement of fact on his own authority, he does not make that statement knowing it to be false and with intent to deceive. This assumption may be a mere convention: but it is a convention which regulates our public and private life. And one who offends against this convention is justly regarded as an offender against our social code, and anything which tends to upset the authority of this code is a public misfortune' ("The Ethics of Political Lying", *Nineteenth Century*, June 1889, 789–94).

41. MS. Clark, see note 1.
42. *Letters*, 353.
43. *Essays and Lectures*, 195.
44. Du Maurier may well have taken the idea for his character of Grigsby from the opening of *She Stoops to Conquer* with which Wilde was undoubtedly familiar. Du Maurier's Grigsby had appeared in Punch in the early 'eighties as a generic figure of Aesthetic pretence. Wilde's solicitor, Gribsby, is also an example of pretence. (The implication that this, also, is generic, gains obvious irony from the approaching trials.) Gribsby is both halves of Parker and Gribsby, a sort of Jekyll-and-Hyde firm of solicitors, answering to the former name on pleasant, to the latter on 'more serious', occasions. This detail, to be found in a MS version of Act II, does not appear in the four-act version printed in *Works*, while in the more widely published three-act version (*Collected Works*, 1908; etc.) the character of Gribsby, like that of Moulton, the gardener, has disappeared. See *The Importance of Being Earnest*, (2 vols.) ed. Sarah Augusta Dickson, New York Public Library, Arents Tobacco Collection Publication No. 6, 1956. This edition gives the contents of the MSS of Acts I and II (Arents Collection) and of Acts III and IV (British Museum), both in fascimile and in transcript.
45. Mary McCarthy, "The Unimportance of Being Oscar", from *Mary McCarthy's Theatre Chronicles* (New York, 1963); reprinted in *Oscar Wilde: Twentieth Century Views*, 107–10.
46. "The Soul of Man under Socialism" (*Works*, 1085).
47. Mary McCarthy, 109.
48. "Maud", ll. 464–5.
49. "Humanitad", ll. 149–50 (*Works*, 794).
50. See note 44.
51. As printed in *Works*, 1966 and thereafter. Previous editions of *Works* contained the three-act version, first published 1899.
52. *Letters*, 507.
53. Ibid., 507.
54. Hyde, *The Trials of Oscar Wilde*.
55. *Works*, 990.
56. Arents edition, vol. I, 96.
57. "Phrases and Philosophies for the Use of the Young" (*Works*, 1205).
58. *Dorian Gray*, chapter 9 (*Works*, 93).
59. Among various studies attempting to link Wilde's practice with Restoration models the following might be mentioned: Foster, "Wilde as Parodist"; Ware,

"Algernon's Appetite".

60. Reinert, "Satiric Strategy in *Earnest*", *College English*, xviii (Oct 1956), 14–18.
61. Gordon, "The Wilde Child: Structure and Origin in the *fin-de-siècle* Short Story".
62. *Letters*, 466.
63. Arents ed., vol. i, 89; *Works*, 354.
64. Shaw, *Saturday Review* (23 Feb 1895); reprinted in Beckson, 194–5.
65. *Essays and Lectures*, 117.
66. Arents ed., vol. i, 62.
67. *Letters*, 772.
68. There is, of course, some doubt that Wilde could have secured a copy of the earlier version, bearing in mind the piratical auction of his literary and other possessions at Tite Street following the declaration of his bankruptcy. The copy used for the published text was a typewritten one (see *Letters*, 738), presumably based on an authoritative prompt-copy.
69. *Letters*, 431.
70. Ibid., 360–2.
71. *Essays and Lectures*, 128.
72. *Letters*, 413.

Chapter 7

1. For full publication details, see *Letters*, 423–4. I use the text in *Letters*.
2. *Varieties of Religious Experience* (1902); quoted in Stone, *Novelists in a Changing World*, 20.
3. *Letters*, 502.
4. Ibid., 419.
5. Abrams, 166.
6. *Letters*, 469.
7. Ibid., 476.
8. Ibid., 473.
9. "The Decay of Lying" (*Works*, 975).
10. *Works*, 863. (The piece had first appeared in the *Fortnightly Review* for July 1894.)
11. *Letters*, 475–6.
12. Ibid., 469.
13. *Works*, 1058.
14. "Mr Symonds' History of the Renaissance", *Pall Mall Gazette*, 10 Nov 1886; reprinted in Lucas, 39–44.
15. *Letters*, 466.
16. See above, p. 182.
17. *Letters*, 473.
18. Ibid., 476.
19. Ibid., 490.
20. Ibid., 484–7.
21. Ibid., 476.
22. Ibid., 481.

23. Ibid., 482.
24. Ibid., 182–3.
25. Ibid., 477.
26. Ibid., 478.
27. Ibid., 480.
28. *Letters*, 490.
29. Ibid., 708.
30. *Works*, 1020.
31. These are the generally recognised models for Wilde's stanza form in the *Ballad*. Also, of course, both poems deal with murder and remorse. Hood's ballad tells the story of a murderer who is haunted by his deed, and the Gothic details are recounted for us, including the burial of the corpse. In Wilde's *Ballad* the real murder that is recounted is the execution, not the crime which led up to it. Wilde may also have known Bulwer's novel on the same subject, *Eugene Aram* (1833).
32. *Letters*, 654.
33. Ibid., 514.
34. "The Decay of Lying" (*Works*, 977).
35. "A Note on Some Modern Poets", *Woman's World*, II, no. 14 (Dec 1888), 108–12; reprinted in Ellmann, *The Artist as Critic*, 90–100.
36. These appeared in 1889. Blunt was imprisoned for two months in connection with an incident involving unrest among Lord Clanricarde's tenants at Woodford, Northern Ireland. Wilde reviewed the volume. See "Poetry and Prison", reprinted in Ellmann, *The Artist as Critic*, 116–20. Some of Wilde's assessments of the value of prison experiences for 'the modern soul, lapped as it is in physical sloth and self-indulgence' anticipate passages in *De Profundis*.
37. *Letters*, 698.
38. Ibid., 509.
39. *Ballad*, IV, 77–80 (*Works*, 855).
40. "Panthea", lines 75–8 (*Works*, 781).
41. *Letters*, 509.
42. Ibid., 490.
43. "The School of Giorgione", *The Renaissance*.
44. "To L. L." (*Works*, 811).
45. *Letters*, 509.
46. "The Critic as Artist" (*Works*, 1035).
47. "The Decay of Lying" (*Works*, 978).
48. *Letters*, 861.
49. "The Critic as Artist" (*Works*, 1034).
50. *Letters*, 490.
51. Preface to *Dorian Gray*.
52. "The Decay of Lying" (*Works*, 970).
53. *Essays and Lectures*, 128.

Bibliography

(Full critical listings, together with Wilde apocrypha, will be found in Ian Fletcher and John Stokes, "Oscar Wilde"., *Anglo-Irish Literature: A Guide to Research* (Modern Language Association of America, 1976). This bibliography simply represents the more significant works consulted by the author.)

Abrams, M. H., *Natural Supernaturalism* (Norton, 1971).

Agate, James, "Oscar Wilde and the Theatre", *Masque*, III (1947).

Aslin, E., *The Aesthetic Movement* (1969).

Amiel, Henri-Frédéric, *Journal*, transl. Mrs Humphrey Ward (1885).

Arnold, Matthew, *Complete Prose Works* (Ann Arbor: University of Michigan Press, 1960–).
  The Poems, ed. K. Allott (1965).

Barbey d' Aurevilly, Jules, "Du Dandysme", *Oeuvres Complètes* (1926–7), IX.

Barnfield, Richard, *Poems*, ed. A. B. Grosart (1876).

Bateson, F. W., "Second Thoughts II: L. C. Knights and Restoration Comedy", *Essays in Criticism*, VII (1957).

Baudelaire, Charles, "De L'Héroisme de la Vie Moderne", *Salon de 1846*; and "Le Dandy", *Le Peintre de la Vie Moderne*, IX. Both contained in *Oeuvres Complètes* (Pléiade, 1961).

Becker, George (ed.), *Documents of Modern Literary Realism* (Princeton, 1963).

Beckson, Karl (ed.), *Oscar Wilde: The Critical Heritage* (1970).

Bentley, Eric, *The Playwright as Thinker* (New York, 1955).

Bendz, E., *The Influence of Walter Pater and Matthew Arnold on Oscar Wilde's Prose* (Gothenberg / London, 1914).

Beer, Gillian, *Meredith: A Change of Masks* (1970).

Beerbohm, Max, "1880", *Works* (1896).

Bergler, Edmund, "*Salomé*: Turning Point in Oscar Wilde's Life", *Psychoanalytic Review*, XLIII (1956), 97–103.

Billy, André, *L'Époque 1900* (Paris, 1951).

Biograph and Review 1880.

Blunt, Wilfrid Scawen, *The Love-Sonnets of Proteus* (1881).
  In Vinculis (1889).

Booth, Michael, *English Plays of the Nineteenth Century* (1969).

Boucicault, Dion, *London Assurance* in *Laurel British Drama: The Nineteenth Century*, ed. R. Corrigan (1966).

Brasol, Boris, *Oscar Wilde: The Man, the Artist, The Martyr* (1938).

Browning, Elizabeth Barrett, *Aurora Leigh* (1856).

Carlyle, Thomas, *On Heroes and Hero-Worship, and the Heroic in History* (1841; ed. W. H. Hudson, Everyman, 1908).

Cazamian, L., *A History of English Literature* (1927).

Chambers, E. K., *The Elizabethan Stage* (1923).

Chamisso, Adelbert von, *Peter Schlemihl, the Shadowless Man*, transl. Sir John Bowring (1910).

Charbonnier, S., "L'Intellectualisme d'Oscar Wilde", *Revue Anglo-Américaine*, XII, no. 6 (Aug 1935), 508 – 19.

Charlesworth, B., *Dark Passages* (University of Wisconsin, 1965).

Chatterton, Thomas, *Poetical Works, with Notices of his Life*, ed. C. B. Willcox (1842).

Clifford, William Kingdom, *Essays and Lectures* (1879).

Congreve, William, *Complete Plays*, ed. H. Davis (Chicago, 1967).

Corkran, Alice B., *Margery Merton's Girlhood* (1888).

Croft-Cooke, R., *The Unrecorded Life of Oscar Wilde* (W. H. Allen, 1972).

Decker, C., "The Aesthetic Revolt against Naturalism in Victorian Criticism", *PMLA*, LIII (1938).

De la Mare, Walter (ed.), *The Eighteen Eighties* (1930).

Del Mar, Norman, *Richard Strauss* (1962).

De Quincey, Thomas, "Murder Considered as One of the Fine Arts", *Blackwood's Magazine*, 1824.

    Confessions of An English Opium-Eater (1821; Everyman edn 1964).

Dicey, Edward, "The Ethics of Political Lying", *the Nineteenth Century*, June 1889, 789–94.

Disraeli, Benjamin, *Vivian Grey* (1826).

                           Correspondence (1886–7).

Dobrée, Bonamy, *Restoration Comedy* (1924).

Douglas, Lord Alfred, *Sonnets* (1947).

Dramatic Review, 1885–6.

Dryden, John, *Critical Essays*, ed. George Watson (1962).

    Complete Plays, ed. Montague Summers (1931–2).

Dumas *fils*, Alexándre, *Théâtre Complet*, 10 vols (1868 – 92).

Dyson, A. E., *The Crazy Fabric* (1965).

Egan, Rose F., "The Genesis of the Theory of 'Art for Art's Sake' in Germany and England", *Smith College Studies in Modern Languages*, July 1921 and Apr 1924.

Ellehauge, M., "The Development of the English Problem-Play", *Englische Studien*, LXVI (1931–2).

Ellmann, Richard, "Romantic Pantomime in Oscar Wilde", *Partisan Review* XXX (1963), 342–55.

    (ed.) *Oscar Wilde: Twentieth Century Views* (Prentice-Hall, 1969).

    (ed.) *The Artist as Critic: Critical Writings of Oscar Wilde* (New York, 1969; London, 1972)

Empson, W., *Some Versions of Pastoral* (1966).

Ervine, St John, *Oscar Wilde: A Present Time Appraisal* (1951).

Etherege, Sir George, *Works*, ed. H. B. Brett-Smith (1927).

Farmer, A. J., *Le Mouvement Esthétique et Décadent en Angleterre, 1873–1900* (Paris, 1931).

Farquhar, George, *Complete Works*, ed. C. Stonehill (1930).

Flaubert, Gustave, *Trois Contes* (1877).

    Salammbô (1862).

    La Tentation de Sainte Antoine (1874).

Fleming, George, *Mirage* (1877).

    The Head of Medusa (1880).

Fletcher, Ian (ed.), *Romantic Mythologies* (1967).

Foster, Richard, "Wilde as Parodist: A Second Look at *Earnest*", *College English*, XVIII (Oct 1956), 18–23.

Frierson, W. C., "The English Controversy over Realism in Fiction", *PMLA*, XLIII (1928), 533–50.

"Realism in the 1890s", *French Quarterly*, X (1928), 31–4.

Fujimura, T., *The Restoration Comedy of Wit* (New York, 1952).

Fussell, B. H., "The Masks of Oscar Wilde", *Sewanee Review*, LXXX, No. 1 (winter 1972) 124–39.

Ganz, Arthur, "The Dandiacal Drama: A Study of the Plays of Oscar Wilde", *Dissertation Abstracts*, XVIII (Mar 1958).

"The Divided Self in the Comedies of Oscar Wilde", *Modern Drama*, III (May 1960).

"The Meaning of *Earnest*", *Modern Drama*, VI (May 1963).

Gaunt, W., *The Aesthetic Adventure* (1957).

Gautier Théophile, *Emaux et Camées* (1852).

Mademoiselle de Maupin (1835; ed. A. Boschot, 1966).

The Germ, 1850.

Gide, André, *Oscar Wilde: In Memoriam* (1913).

Journals: 1889–1949, transl. Justin O'Brien (Penguin: 1967).

Glaezner, R., *Decorative Art in America* (1906).

Goethe, Johann Wolfgang von, *Conversations with Goethe*, transl. John Oxenford (1930).

Gordon, Jan, B. "The Wilde Child: Structure and Origin in the *fin-de-siècle* Short Story", *English Literature in Transition*, XV, no. 4. (1972), 277–89.

"The Imaginary Portrait", *Windsor Review*, VI (Autumn 1970).

Gourmont, Rémy de, *Decadence and other Essays*, transl. W. A. Bradley (1922).

Grundy, Sidney, *The Dean's Daughter* (1891).

Halls, W. D., *Maurice Maeterlinck* (1960).

Hamilton, G. Heard, *Manet and his Critics* (Norton, 1969).

Hamilton, Walter, *The Aesthetic Movement in England*, (1882).

Harris, Allan, "Oscar Wilde as Playwright: A Centenary Review", *Adelphi*, XXX, no. 3 (1954).

Harris, Frank, *Mr and Mrs Daventry*, introduced by H. Montgomery Hyde (1956).

Hart, Jerome K., *Sardou and the Sardou Plays* (1913).

Hegel, G. F. W., *The Phenomenology of Mind*, transl. Baillie (1967).

Heilbrun, Carolyn, *Towards Androgyny* (1973).

Heywood, J. C., *Herodias* (New York, 1867; London, 1884).

Salome (New York, 1867).

Antonius (New York, 1867; London 1885).

Himmelfarb, G., *Darwin and the Darwinian Revolution* (1959).

Holland, N., *The First Modern Comedies* (Harvard, 1959).

Holland, Vyvyan, *Oscar Wilde: a Pictorial Biography* (1966).

Hough, Graham, *The Last Romantics*, 1949.

Huysmans, J.-K., *Certains* (1889).

A Rebours (1919).

Hyde, H. Montgomery (ed.) *The Trials of Oscar Wilde* (1960).

Jackson, Holbrook, *The Eighteen Nineties* (1927).

James, Henry, *The Portrait of a Lady* (1881; Penguin edition, 1974).

James, Norman, "Oscar Wilde's Dramaturgy", *Dissertation Abstracts*, XX (1960).

James, William, *Varieties of Religious Experience* (1902).
Jones, Henry Arthur, *Saints and Sinners* (1891).
   Renascence of the English Drama (1895).
Joost, N., and Sullivan, A., "*Salomé*, the Moon, and Oscar Wilde's Aesthetics", *Papers in Language and Literature*, VIII (supp. Fall 1972), 96–111.
Kermode, Frank, *Romantic Image* (1961).
   Puzzles and Epiphanies (1962).
Laforgue, Jules, *Poésies Complètes* (1970).
   Moralités Légendaires (1887).
Lang, A., "Literary Plagiarism", *Contemporary Review*, June 1887.
Lawler, Donald L., "Oscar Wilde's first MS. of *Dorian Gray*", *Studies in Bibliography*, XXV (1972), 125–35.
Lehmann, A. G., *The Symbolist Aesthetic in France, 1885–95* (1950).
Lemaître, Jules, *Revoltée* (1901).
Lethève, Jacques, *Impressionistes et Symbolistes devant la Presse* (1959).
Lewis, L., and Smith, H. J., *Oscar Wilde Discovers America* (1967).
Lucas, E. V. (ed.), *see under* Wilde.
Lytton, the Earl of, "Mary Anderson's Juliet", *Nineteenth Century*, Dec 1884.
Maeterlinck, Maurice, *Théâtre Complet* (1922–25).
Mahaffy, J. P., *Three Epochs in the Social Development of the Ancient Greeks* (1869).
   Social Life in Greece (1874).
Marcuse, H., *Eros and Civilisation* (1961).
Martino, *Parnasse et Symbolisme* (1930).
Mason, Stuart, *Oscar Wilde: Impressions of America* (1906).
   A Bibliography of Oscar Wilde (1916; reissued 1967).
   Oscar Wilde: Art and Morality (1915).
   Oscar Wilde and the Aesthetic Movement (1920).
McCarthy, D., "Artificial Comedy", *New Statesman and Nation*, XVIII, no. 444 (26 Aug 1939, 305–7).
McCarthy, Mary, "The Unimportance of Being Oscar", *Mary McCarthy's Theatre Chronicles* (New York, 1963); reprinted in R. Ellmann, (ed.), *Oscar Wilde: Twentieth Century Views* (1969).
Meinhold, W., *Sidonia the Sorceress*, transl. Lady Wilde (1847).
Meredith, George, *An Essay on Comedy and the Uses of the Comic Spirit*, ed. Lane Cooper (Kennikat Press, 1972):
   The Egoist (1879; Penguin edition, 1968).
Middleton, Thomas, *The Changeling*, ed. N. C. Bawcutt (1961).
Mill, John Stuart, *On Liberty* (1859).
   Principles of Political Economy (1848).
Miner, Earl (ed.), *Restoration Dramatists: Twentieth Century Views* (Prentice-Hall, 1966).
Moers, Ellen, *The Dandy*: Brummell to Beerbohm (1960).
Moore, George, *Confessions of a Young Man* (1886) ed Susan Dick (McGill, 1972).
Muir, Kenneth, *The Comedy of Manners* (1970).
Murray, Isobel, "Some Elements in the Composition of *Dorian Gray*", *Durham University Journal*, LXIV (1972), 220–3.
   (ed.) *The Picture of Dorian Gray* (Oxford English Novels, 1974).
Nassaar, Christopher, *Into the Demon Universe: A Literary Exploration of Oscar Wilde* (Yale, 1974).

Nethercot, Arthur, "Oscar Wilde and the Devil's Advocate", *PMLA*, LIX (1944).
"Oscar Wilde on Subdividing Himself', ibid.
Nickerson, Charles,"*Vivian Grey* and *Dorian Gray*", *TLS*, 14 Aug 1969.
Nochlin, Linda, *Realism* (1971).
Opie, Amelia, *Illustrations of Lying in all its Branches* (1825).
Ormond, Leonée, *George du Maurier* (1969).
O'Sullivan, Vincent, *Aspects of Wilde* (1936).
Opinions (1959).
Otway, Thomas, *Works*, ed. J. C. Ghosh (1932).
Partridge, E., "The Importance of Not Being Earnest", *Bucknell Review*, IX, no. 2 (May 1960), 143–58.
Pater, Walter, *Collected Works*, 1910.
Appreciations (1927).
Imaginary Portraits (1914).
Gaston de Latour (1889, 1917).
Studies in the History of the Renaissance (1873).
Pearson, Hesketh, *Modern Men and Mummers* (1921).
Beerbohm Tree (1956).
Peckham, Morse, "What did Lady Windermere Learn?", *College English*, XVIII (1956), 11–14.
Perry, H. T. E., *Masters of Dramatic Comedy and their Social Themes* (Harvard, 1937).
Pick, J., "Divergent Disciples of Walter Pater", *Thought*, XXIII (Mar 1948), 114–28.
Pinero, A. W., *The Cabinet Minister*, ed. A. Salaman (1892).
The Second Mrs Tanqueray (1895).
Poe, Edgar Allan *Tales of Mystery and Imagination* (Everyman, 1966).
Praz, Mario, *The Romantic Agony*, transl. A. Davidson (1954).
"Christopher Marlowe", *English Studies*, XIII, no. 6 (Dec 1931).
"Restoration Drama", *English Studies*, XV, no. 1 (Feb 1933).
Punch, 1880–90.
Queensberry, the Marquess of, and Colson, Percy, *Oscar Wilde and the Black Douglas* (1949).
Quilter, H., "The Decline of the Drama", *Contemporary Review*, Apr 1887.
Racine, Jean, *Théâtre*, illustrated by Girodet (1813).
Raynaud, E., *Baudelaire et la Religion du Dandysme*, (1918).
Reade, Brian, *Beardsley* (1967).
Reade, Charles, and Taylor, Tom, *Masks and Faces*, in *Nineteenth Century Plays*, ed. G. Rowell (Oxford University Press, 1960).
Reinert, Otto, "Satiric Strategy in *Earnest*", *College English*, XVIII (1956).
Ricketts, Charles, MS. Diaries, British Museum.
Righter, Anne, "Heroic Tragedy", *Restoration Theatre*, Stratford-upon-Avon Studies no. 6, (1965), 135–57.
Robinson, J. K., "The English Parnassians – A Neglected Phase in the Aesthetic Movement", *PMLA*, LXVIII (1953).
Robertson, W. Graham, *Time Was* (1931).
Rodd, Rennell, *Rose-Leaf and Apple-Leaf* (Philadelphia, 1882).
Roditi, Edouard, *Oscar Wilde* (Norfolk, Conn., 1947).
Ross, Margery (ed.), *Robert Ross: Friend of Friends* (1952).
Rossetti, Dante Gabriel, *Poems and Translations* (Oxford University Press, 1968).
Rothenstein, William, *Men and Memories* (1931).

Rowell, George, *The Victorian Theatre* (1956).
 Victorian Dramatic Criticism (1971).
Ryals, Claude de L., "Oscar Wilde's *Salomé*", *Notes and Queries*, VI, no. 2 (Feb 1959), 56–7.
San Juan Jnr., Epifanio, *The Art of Oscar Wilde* (Princeton, 1967).
Sardou, V., *Théâtre Complet* (1934–8).
Scribe, E., *Théâtre Choisi* (1932).
Schiff, H., "A Critical Study of Oscar Wilde's *Intentions*", M.A. Thesis, University of London.
Shadwell, Thomas, *Works*, ed. M. Summers (1927).
Shakespeare, William, *Sonnets*, ed. Ingram and Redpath (1967).
Shaw, George Bernard, *Anarchism and State Socialism* (1889).
Sherard, R., *The Life of Oscar Wilde* (1906).
Singer, I., "The Aesthetics of 'Art for Art's Sake'", *JAAC*, XII, no. 3 (Mar 1954).
Smalley, Donald (ed.), *Browning's Essay on Chatterton* (Harvard, 1948).
Spears, Monroe K., *Dionysus and the City* (Oxford University Press, 1970).
Spingarn, J. E. (ed.), *Critical Essays of the Seventeenth Century* (Clarendon Press/Indiana, 1968).
The Spirit Lamp, 1893–4.
Starkie, Enid, *From Gautier to Eliot* (1960).
Stone, Donald D., *Novelists in a Changing World: Meredith and James in the 1880s*, (Harvard, 1972).
Sutherland, James, *English Literature of the late Seventeenth Century* (Clarendon Press, 1969).
Sutton, Denys, *Whistler* (1966).
Swinburne, A. C., *Complete Works*, ed. E. Gosse and T. Wise (1925–7).
 Swinburne Replies, ed. Clyde K. Hyder (Syracuse, N.Y., 1965).
Symonds, J. A., "Realism and Idealism", *Fortnightly Review*, XLVIII (Sep 1887).
Symons, Arthur, "The Decadent Movement in Literature", *Harper's Monthly Magazine*, LXXXVII, no. 522 (Nov 1893).
 A Study of Oscar Wilde, 1930.
Taylor, F. A., *The Theatre of Alexandre Dumas fils* (1937).
Tennyson, Alfred Lord, *Poems*, ed. Ricks (1969).
Tillotson, G., *Criticism and the Nineteenth Century* (1951).
Toliver, H., "Wilde and the Importance of Sincere and Studied Triviality", *Modern Drama*, V (Feb 1963).
Underwood, Dale, *Etherege and the Seventeenth Century Comedy of Manners* (Archon, 1957).
Vanbrugh, Sir John, *Complete Works*, ed. B. Dobrée and G. Webb (1927–8).
Vigny, Alfred de, *Chatterton* (1835).
Wainewright, Thomas G., *Essays and Criticisms*, ed. W. Carey Hazlitt (1880).
 'Some Passages' in the Life of Egomet Bonmot, Esq., edited by Mr. Mwaughmaim and now first published by ME. (1825).
Ware, James M., "Algernon's Appetite: Oscar Wilde's Hero as Restoration Dandy", *English Literature in Transition*, XIII no. 1, (1970), 17–26.
Webb, Sidney, "English Progress Towards Social Democracy", *Fabian Tracts*, no. 15 (Dec 1890).
Weintraub, Stanley, *Beardsley* (1967).
 Whistler (1974).

Whistler, J. A. McNeill, *The Gentle Art of Making Enemies* (1890; Dover reprint, 1967).

Wilcox, J., "The Beginnings of '*L'Art pour l'Art*'", *JAAC*, xi no. 4 (June 1953).

Wilde, Lady Jane, *Poems by Speranza* (Dublin and London, 1864).

Wilde, Oscar, *Collected Works of Oscar Wilde* (1908), 14 vols.

    Complete Works of Oscar Wilde (Collins, 1966).

    Salomé (Paris, 1893).

    Salomé, transl. Lord Alfred Douglas, illus. Beardsley (London, 1894).

    Salomé, ed. Ross (1909).

    Salomé, introduced by Holbrook Jackson (New York, 1938).

    Salomé, transl. R. A. Walker, with an introduction to Beardsley's complete designs (1957).

    Letters of Oscar Wilde, ed. Sir Rupert Hart-Davis (1962).

    Reviews (vol. 13 of the *Collected Works*, 1908).

    Miscellanies (vol. 14 of the *Collected Works*, 1908).

    Essays and Reviews (1901).

    Essays and Lectures (1909; reprinted 1977, Garland, New York).

    A Critic in Pall Mall, E. V. Lucas (1919).

    The Importance of Being Earnest, ed. Sarah Augusta Dickson, New York Public Library, Arents Tobacco Collection, publication no. 6, (1956).

    (ed.) *The Woman's World*, 1887–9.

Woodcock, George, *The Paradox of Oscar Wilde* (1950).

Wotton, Sir Henry, *Letters to Sir Edmund Bacon* (1661).

Wycherley, William, *Complete Plays*, ed. G Weales (New York, 1967).

Yeats, W. B., *Autobiographies* (1926).

NOTE: Important material, particularly on Renan's influence upon Wilde, is to be found in: Hartley, Kelver, *Oscar Wilde: L'Influence Française dans son Oeuvre* (Paris, 1935), which I discovered too late to make use of.

Index

2 Questions - MT. ⎤
Read The Bear ⎦ Wed.

Study til 12 — ⎦
get up at 6am ⎤
Do paper til 6pm ⎦ Study

Finished at Columbia.